This is the only career book that gets you to *all* the places where jobs and internships in education and with non-profit organizations are advertised, not just on the Internet but also in print and on job hotlines that *all* job seekers can use.

It's the only book you can keep up-to-date with free *Update Sheets* available by mail and on the Internet.

Featured in **Cosmopolitan's** *Life After College* and in *Executive Female*

A perfect 10

"Nobody in this business seems to put quite as much into career books as Daniel Lauber. His contain thousands of useful facts, leads to employment resources, references to additional information and far more. Now he has focused on jobs with non-profit agencies and produced another book that can be **rated a 10**. The fact that the well-known Joyce Lain Kennedy agreed to write the forward is the final bit of evidence of its merit."
— *Career Opportunities News*

"**Excellent resource for employment opportunities.**"
— *Community Jobs*

"**Great resource!** The book gave me lots of ideas and pushed me to be more productive."
— *Sheryl Kaplan, successful user of this book*

"Thanks for a great nationwide resource for job leads."
— *P. Klein, successful user of this book*

"Not your typical job hunter's resource ... inexpensive ... humorous. What's **special** about this book is that it steers you to periodicals, journals, job-matching services, computerized job listings, job hotlines, etc. **where you can actually find the job openings you're looking for** — the ones that aren't necessarily in the classifieds. **This book can help you get a job.**"
— *Job Training and Placement Report*

The Job Finders Series

Get the Job Finder that's right for you!

The *Job Finder Series* includes four books that get you to all the best job sources for whatever type of job search you want to conduct. Just like the *Non-Profits and Education Job Finder,* each book gives you full details on everything you need to find a job. All four highly-praised *Job Finders* are available at bookstores and directly from Planning/Communications. See the Job Search Resources Catalog at the end of this book for ordering information. Each title is also available in a hard cover edition.

Non-Profits and Education Job Finder, which you are reading now, details over 2,222 job-search tools to find vacancies in education and the rest of the non-profit sector. Includes over $225 in discounts on key job search resources. 340 pages, 1997–2000 edition, $16.95 paperback, ISBN: 1–884587–06–2. Hard cover: $32.95, ISBN: 1–884587–09–7.

Government Job Finder, 3rd edition, reports on over 2,002 sources of job openings in local, state, and federal government. It's the *only* book that helps you get a job in local and state government where 75 percent of all government jobs are located. Includes over $150 in discounts on key job search resources. 336 pages, 1997–2000 edition, $16.95 paperback, ISBN: 1–884587–05–4. Hard cover: $32.95, ISBN: 1–884587–08–9.

Professional's Job Finder reports on over 3,003 job-finding tools to locate job openings in the largest segment of the economy, the world of business, namely the private sector. Includes over $200 in discounts on key job search resources. 518 pages, 1997–2000 edition, $18.95 paperback, ISBN: 1–884587–04–6. Hard cover: $36.95, ISBN: 1–884587–07–0.

International Job Finder: Where the Jobs are Worldwide gives you the scoop on 1,001 sources for jobs in international careers, mostly located outside the U.S. Includes over $50 in discounts on key job search resources. 192 pages, 1997–2000 edition, $16.95 paperback, ISBN: 1–884587–10–0. Hard cover: $32.95, ISBN: 1–884587–11–9. Available beginning October 1997.

Non-Profits and Education Job Finder

1997–2000

DANIEL LAUBER

PLANNING/COMMUNICATIONS
River Forest, Illinois

Copyright 1997 by Daniel Lauber. All rights reserved.

Published in the United States of America. No part of this book may be reproduced or utilized in any form or by any means, electronic or mechanical, including photocopying, recording, or by any information storage or retrieval system, without express written permission from Daniel Lauber, except for brief quotations used in reviews written specifically for inclusion in a periodical or online computer service.

For quantity discounts and permissions, contact the publisher:
Planning/Communications
7215 Oak Avenue, River Forest, Illinois 60305; phone: 708/366-5200
Internet URL: http://jobfindersonline.com

Distributed to bookstores by:
National Book Network
4720-A Boston Way, Lanham, MD 20706; phone: 800/462-6420

Front cover design by Salvatore Concialdi

Graphics used by permission from *Megatoons* by Phil Frank, *Task Force Clip Art*, *Corel Draw*, and *MapArt Stock Image Series USA* by Cartesia.

Disclaimer of All Warranties and Liabilities

The author and publisher make no warranties, either expressed or implied, with respect to the information contained herein. The information about job sources reported in this book is based on facts conveyed by their publishers and operators either in writing or by telephone interview. The author and publisher shall not be liable for any incidental or consequential damages in connection with, or arising out of, the use of materials in this book.

Library of Congress Cataloging-in-Publication Data

Lauber, Daniel.
 Non-Profits and Education Job Finder / Daniel Lauber
 p. cm.
 Includes bibliographical references and index.
 ISBN: 1-884587-09-7 (hard cover): $32.95 — 1-884587-06-2 (paperback): $16.95

 1. Job hunting —United States—Information services —Handbooks, manuals, etc. 2. Nonprofit organizations —United States – Information services —handbooks, manuals, etc. 3. Occupations –United States – handbooks, manuals, etc. 4. Job hunting —United States — Bibliography. I. Title.

 HF5382.75.U6L328   1997

   331.12'8'0973—dc20   96-92661
                                                                      CIP

Table of contents

Foreword by Joyce Lain Kennedy v
Preface vii
1   **Job hunt tools for your successful job search** **1**
     Tools for your savvy job quest. 3
     Seven steps to job hunt success 15
2   **The online job search explosion** **17**
     The players in the online job search 18
     Email 19
     The World Wide Web 21
     Gopher servers 25
     Usenet newsgroups. 26
     Mailing lists. 27
     FTP file transfers 27
     Bulletin board services 28
     Online growing pains 29
     Offline resources for your online job search. 30
     Launching pads your online job search. 32
3   **General job sources** **38**
4   **Advocacy and organizing** **54**
5   **Agriculture** **57**
6   **Animals** **60**
7   **Arts and entertainment** **64**
     Arts and entertainment in general 64
     Music and dance. 70
     Theater 73
     Visual arts and film 77
8   **Association management.** **78**

9 Computers ... 83
10 Education ... 85
Education in general ... 85
Administrators ... 90
Elementary and secondary education ... 95
Higher education ... 99
Trades and vocational education ... 115
11 Emergency management ... 118
12 Environment ... 119
13 Finance and accounting ... 127
14 Forestry and horticulture ... 130
15 Foundations and grants ... 133
16 Health care ... 144
Health care in general ... 144
Dentists ... 154
Doctors ... 155
Nurses ... 161
Pharmaceuticals ... 163
Research ... 164
Therapy–mental ... 165
Therapy–physical ... 168
17 Housing, planning, and development ... 171
18 Legal services ... 179
19 Media ... 183
Media ... 183
Marketing ... 189
20 Museums and libraries ... 190
Museums ... 190
Libraries ... 192
21 Parks and recreation ... 198
Parks and recreation ... 198
Camps and camping ... 200
Coaching and sports ... 201
22 Philanthropy ... 204
23 Records management and archives ... 206
24 Religion ... 208
25 Research ... 213
26 Safety ... 216
27 Science ... 218
Science in general ... 218

Table of contents

  Biological sciences 221
  Chemistry 226
  Engineers 227
  Mathematics 234
  Physics 235
  Utilities 237
28 Social sciences 238
29 Social services 242
30 Savvy job and grant sources for each state 254
  City and state job–finding tools 255
  Job and grant sources by state 261
  Alabama 261
  Alaska 262
  Arizona 263
  Arkansas 264
  California 264
  Colorado 268
  Connecticut 269
  Delaware 270
  District of Columbia 271
  Florida 273
  Georgia 274
  Hawaii 275
  Idaho 276
  Illinois 277
  Indiana 279
  Iowa 280
  Kansas 280
  Kentucky 281
  Louisiana 282
  Maine 282
  Maryland 283
  Massachusetts 285
  Michigan 286
  Minnesota 287
  Mississippi 288
  Missouri 289
  Montana 290
  Nebraska 291
  Nevada 292
  New Hampshire 292
  New Jersey 293

New Mexico 295
New York 295
North Carolina 298
North Dakota 299
Ohio 300
Oklahoma 301
Oregon 301
Pennsylvania 303
Rhode Island 304
South Carolina 304
South Dakota 305
Tennessee 305
Texas 306
Utah 308
Vermont 308
Virginia 310
Washington 312
West Virginia 314
Wisconsin 315
Wyoming 316

Index **317**
Budget–stretching discount coupons **328**
Job search resources catalog **332**
Reader feedback form **339**
About the author **340**

Foreword

Are you a motivated, concerned person? Do you have a sense of mission for a higher purpose? Do you feel your job should be as important as the chief executive's job? If so, I've got good news for you.

A non-profit organization or teaching may offer exactly the outlet for the self-actualization for which you've been searching. The **Non-Profits and Education Job Finder** will make your job search much more efficient than possible in past years because this book provides instant access to a veritable mega-mall of 2,222 online and offline job-finding resources for virtually every type of job hunt.

There's more good news. The non-profit world is no longer an ivory tower for idealists who don't mind living on pennies to serve a cause. As the millennium approaches, you need not be poor to do good. But you do need strong business skills (financial planning, marketing, management) or pragmatic operational abilities to earn higher salaries and to keep your NPO (non-profit organization) afloat. A good heart and wishing alone won't make it so.

My comments stem from personal experience. Before I became a careers columnist, I spent several years working for two NPOs — a United Way and a Girl Scout Council, both in St. Louis, Missouri. Those were some of the happiest days of my life. The interaction with people of good cheer was delightful.

NPOs typically attract volunteers, and when people are interacting on a volunteer basis, they often are at their very best which makes them a joy to be around. Further, it was clear that the job I was doing in providing staff support and guidance to a large team of volunteers mattered a great deal to the lives and well-being of legions of beneficiaries.

It's always been a real challenge to find jobs and internships in the non-profit world since so many have been filled by word of mouth. Today non-profits have joined the business community and government in using a wide variety of means to attract applicants for jobs and internships. In addition to networking, they're advertising their openings in specialty and trade periodicals, on job hotlines, and on the Internet. More NPOs are using job banks and job-matching services to find qualified candidates. Nobody really knew how extensively non-profits are using these new vehicles for spreading the word about their job vacancies...until now!

Eight years ago I discovered Daniel Lauber's outstanding research effort, now titled the **Government Job Finder**. This remarkable book helps readers go beyond the usual guidance in finding government employment by leading them to over 2,002 sources of information on openings in local, state, and the federal government. In my column, I called the book *"the most comprehensive compendium of resources for government job hunters I've ever seen"* — and I meant it. I added, *"If you have a fair idea of the type of government job you want, this is a **dynamite job hunting tool**."* His 1989 edition of that book was among the first to include electronic job sources such as job databases available on bulletin board services.

Now Lauber and his research team have done it again, spending untold hours and dollars in completing another magnificent research project. With his new **Non-Profits and Education Job Finder,** he has uncovered and identified over 2,222 sources of job leads and job-search resources in the non-profit sector: jobs that focus on bettering prospects for education, housing, food, health, justice, safety, and peace. Jobs that make a difference. Jobs that make the world a better place to live. And he has added a slew of new electronic job sources that focus on non-profits: job databases, resume banks, and directories of non-profits and schools available on the Internet and on bulletin board services.

I didn't meet Daniel Lauber until last year, but I developed an enormous respect for his uncommon willingness to turn over every rock and look in every crevice to find a source on the topic he is researching. The man is obsessive about collecting job-finding resources. I like that. I think you will too after reading this book.

You deserve an easier time finding work. After all, you're dedicating yourself to helping society cope with the multitude of serious unmet needs it faces. With the **Non-Profits and Education Job Finder** in hand, I wish you Job Speed.

Joyce Lain Kennedy
Nationally-syndicated careers columnist
and author of *Job Interviews for Dummies,*
and other leading career books

Preface

As with the other sectors of the economy, the non-profit and education world has gone far beyond the classifieds of the local newspaper to fill its job openings. Now 2,222 of the most helpful tools you can use for every type of job search are gathered together in the *Non-Profits and Education Job Finder*. And employers in the education and non-profit sector can learn what the best places are to advertise their job vacancies and generate applications from the most qualified candidates.

While most job resource books today focus solely on using the Internet in your job search, all the books in the *Job Finders Series* recognize that most Americans, so far, do not have access to the Internet and must rely on what I call "offline" job sources. As I've been doing since the first *Job Finder* was published in 1989, I've fully integrated the online job sources into each chapter so those of you who do have Internet access can learn about them as well as the offline resources that every job seeker can use.

The *Job Finder Series* is unique because it offers you free updates to each book on our Web site at URL: **http://jobfindersonline.com** and by mail. See page 8 for details on how to keep this book current. We rely on you, in large part, to help us keep it up-to-date. Please use the *Reader Feedback Form* on page 339 to let us know about any changes you discover in the job sources you find in this book.

Acknowledgments

Producing a book of this scope and detail is not a task for just one person. It required months of expensive, detailed research to discover the 2,222 job sources described here and to verify exactly what each one offers.

This book could not have been produced without the incredible work of Senior Research Associate Robert Pruter. He joined Planning/Communications after 27 years at *New Standard Encyclopedia* where he researched and wrote thousands of articles for that tome. It didn't take long for him to realize that the research for this book and the others in the *Job Finders*

Series was more demanding than researching any encyclopedia. Author of two highly-regarded books himself — *Chicago Soul* and *Doowop: The Chicago Scene*—as well as liner notes to scores of compact disks and record albums, Bob displayed a doggedness, devotion to accuracy, and resourcefulness that has made a major contribution to all four *Job Finders,* but especially to this book. I thank him from the bottom of my heart and am honored for the opportunity to have worked with him.

Other researchers who merit recognition for their contributions to this book are Chris Wienke, Maureen Flagg, and Brian Dichter. Their efforts in the early stages of conducting research for this book were most valuable.

The very kind cooperation of the people who publish and operate the job sources described in these pages was crucial. I thank them for providing the information needed to determine if the job-quest tools they produce and operate would really help people seeking work in education and the rest of the non-profit sector.

Joyce Lain Kennedy's support and very kind *Foreword* she wrote for this book are very much appreciated. All career writers value her efforts to keep her readers informed of new, effective career books from small publishers. It was a real pleasure to finally meet her last year. Thanks also go to career authors Ronald Krannich, Richard Bolles, Martin Yate, Dennis Damp, and Brian Krueger for their words of wisdom and encouragement along the way. They've all helped set a standard for writing substantive career books that really do help job seekers find their way.

Most of all, I thank my wife Diana, for not only putting up with my eccentricities while researching and writing this book (during which I did a very accurate impression of an obsessed workaholic), but for also offering valuable advice on the manuscript as well as moral support when the going got tough. I doubt if I could have written this book, much less three books at once, without her love and understanding.

The discrimination disease

I had originally written a fairly extensive *Afterword* for each book in the *Job Finder Series* to address how racial discrimination in hiring and promotions is so costly to America. With 25 years experience as an urban planner and several research projects on racial discrimination under my belt, I hope I'm reasonably qualified to write on this subject.

When I asked several other career writers if I should include this *Afterword* in any of the *Job Finders,* I got three different answers: "Yes," "No," and "Why bother? Nobody really seems to care anymore."

The bottom line turned out to be that these are books about *finding jobs.* The best way to use these books to help overcome discriminatory employment practices is to include information on job sources that were created to combat discrimination. These job periodicals feature job ads from employers who want potential employees to know that their hiring policies are inclusionary, and they do not discriminate in hiring or promotions. They want potential employees to know that they offer a level playing field where hiring and promotions are based on merit.

Rather than segregate these job sources into a special section of their own, they are fully integrated throughout each *Job Finder* to encourage readers to use the full range of job-search resources available. I am not implying that the employers who advertise vacancies only in the other job sources engage in illegal racial discrimination. I am simply suggesting that some employers want members of minority groups to know that they do *not* discriminate.

Each potential employee should be evaluated on her own merits and nothing else. Race, gender, religion, physical limitations not related to job performance, and other factors unrelated to carrying out the job are not legitimate reasons to reject a job applicant. It's an open secret that illegal discrimination, largely based on race, continues to be widespread, particularly throughout the business world. Who can forget the disparaging remarks a group of top Texaco executives made about African American employees, statements that revealed how ingrained and vicious this discrimination can be? But as Texaco's own president and chief executive officer Peter Bijur reported on national television, the attitudes shown by Texaco's executives were just the "tip of the iceberg" in corporate America.

There is simply no rational justification for discrimination in hiring or promotions. To systematically exclude anybody from equal access to quality jobs due to the color of their skin only results in damaged lives and wasted "human capital," to put it in terms the business community might understand. It only creates costly problems that drain the economy and national budget. It is completely unAmerican. I only pray that our elected officials and business leaders begin a real war to eradicate the disease of racial discrimination as soon as possible. Racial discrimination in the workplace is so ingrained that it will take a massive inoculation to cure this debilitating affliction.

Now that I've had my say, I do want to thank you for purchasing the *Non-Profits and Education Job Finder*. If you follow the suggestions in chapters 1 and 2, this book will help you find the education or non-profit job you want, where you wish to live.

Daniel Lauber

Daniel Lauber
Author

Non-Profits and Education Job Finder

Chapter 1

Job hunt tools for your successful job search

Despite the "me–first" attitude that seems to define our nation these days, *you* still care enough to be part of the relatively small portion of the populace that works in education and the non–profit sector. As the 1990s end, quality educators are a hot commodity once again — as well they should be! No nation can prosper without superior teachers preparing its children for adulthood. And there seems to be a growing interest in "doing good," to actually contribute to bettering society. Interest in careers in the non–profit sector has rarely been higher than it is today, even among upper echelon management in the business world.

In the not–so–distant past many a person interested in working for non–profits has been discouraged by how hard it is to find job vacancies with non–profit organizations. While only about 20 percent of all jobs are ever advertised in local newspapers, the proportion of non–profit jobs advertised there has been even lower. You pretty much had to rely on word–of–mouth to find job openings in the non–profit sector…until now!

That's all changing today. As you'll quickly discover reading this book, there's been an explosion of resources for finding job openings in education and the rest of the non–profit sector, much of it online on the Internet, but most of it "offline" where everybody can access the job vacancies. The

Non-Profits and Education Job Finder shows you exactly where to look for the jobs that aren't advertised in the local classifieds so you can turn your job quest into a successful journey with the proverbial happy ending: the education or non-profit job you want, in the place you wish to live.

Do you plan to network your way to a new job? Do you intend to strategically pick a few non-profit organizations for which you want to work and steadfastly pursue them until one hires you? Use the print and online Internet directories described in this book to identify individuals in your profession with whom you should network and ascertain how to contact them. Discover how to reach hiring executives by email who would ordinarily decline to accept a stranger's phone call. Use other directories in this book to learn a great deal about the non-profit agencies and schools that hire people in your discipline and decide which ones you want to approach for a job even before a job vacancy is made public.

Want to find ads for job openings? Use the specialty and trade newsletters and magazines detailed in this book to find thousands of vacancies. Follow the instructions in Chapter 2 and use some of the online Internet job databases presented throughout this book to find job vacancies in your profession and for the state in which you'd like to work.

Prefer to find jobs from the comfort of your easy chair? Just call some of the job hotlines referenced in this book where you'll find an abundance of job vacancies just a phone call away.

Want to have somebody else do the work for you and match you to job vacancies? Want to have lists of new job vacancies regularly pop up in your electronic mailbox? Sign up for some of the job-matching services and online mailing lists recommended in the chapters that follow.

All the practical tools you need to conduct every type of job search are now in your hands. This book gives you enough information about each job-quest resource so you can decide which ones you want to use without having to spend time and money making long distance phone calls or writing for additional information. After you read this chapter and Chapter 2 to get a thorough overview of how to use this book and its many resources, it's up to you to decide which job-search strategies you'll utilize and which of the myriad job resources in this book you'll use. Employ all the techniques that work best for your occupation.

In his career classic *What Color is Your Parachute?* Richard Bolles strongly warns readers not to rely on just one strategy to find jobs. He snatched the words right out of my mouth. The most successful job seekers are those who are astute enough to employ three or four different strategies to find employment. This savvy job hunt should be the foundation of every job seeker's efforts. The *Non-Profits and Education Job Finder* delivers to you all the resources you need to conduct all the job-search strategies you choose to use.

Read this chapter first

Tools for your savvy job quest

No single job-search strategy is so much better than all the others that you should use it exclusively. The remainder of this chapter examines the major job-hunt strategies and explains how to use the 2,222 job-quest tools presented in the *Non-Profits and Education Job Finder* to find job openings and get hired. I cannot stress enough that the smart job seeker uses three or four of these strategies to greatly enhance the chances of landing the job you want where you want to live.

Tools for finding job vacancies

Many years ago the local newspaper was *the* place to look for job openings. Experts now estimate that only seven to 20 percent of job vacancies make it into the local newspaper. During the 1990s non-profit employers and schools began to realize that their ads in the local classifieds were generating far too many responses from unqualified applicants. Since somebody on the payroll had to spend time looking at all these applications, employers sought venues to advertise their vacancies that would attract a more qualified body of applicants. The result has been a blossoming world of sources for job ads both in print and in cyberspace on the Internet.

Specialty and trade periodicals offer employers a more focused audience, often members of a professional association who are much more likely to be qualified for a job than many of the people who respond to an ad in the local classifieds. Employers also found that job listing periodicals offered an even more focused, bigger-bang-for-their-advertising buck. In more recent years, the Internet has become a source of job vacancies with job databases, newsgroups, mailing lists, and home pages of non-profit agencies and educational institutions that sometimes include listings of job vacancies. Chapter 2 offers a detailed explanation of how these online Internet-based sources of job ads work and how they are presented in this book.

From the job seeker's perspective, print publications still have a big advantage over online services. As explained in Chapter 2, there is no way to know where the job ads offered on an Internet site or bulletin board service come from. Many of these services lift job ads from other sources which means that many of the ads are for jobs that have already been filled. Periodicals, however, charge employers to advertise their positions. You can be pretty confident that a non-profit employer or school will not spend money to advertise a position that is filled.

Specialty and trade periodicals. Many specialty and trade periodicals include a good number of job ads for the profession the publication serves. Chapter 3 introduces you to specialty and trade peri-

See page 8 for how to keep this book current

odicals that feature ads for jobs in all aspects of the non-profit sector, including education. Chapters 4 through 29 each cover a broad occupational area. Chapter 30 reports on periodicals for each individual state that have job ads for all types of education and non-profit positions in that state. You should also consult the Index to locate the job sources that are listed in places you would not intuitively expect them to be found.

The vast majority of specialty and trade magazines are available to the general public. If a professional association is the publisher, members usually receive the periodical as part of the dues package or at a substantial discount. Some are available only to organization members. As will be noted several times in this book, you'd be wise to join your professional organization even if its job resources are available to the general public as well as members. Most people in an organization who make hiring decisions believe that membership in a professional association reflects a greater commitment and dedication to one's profession — which can only enhance your prospects for getting hired.

Job listing periodicals. One of the best sources of jobs for an occupation is the periodical devoted entirely to job ads or announcements. The number of job ads in a typical issue ranges from about a dozen to several hundred. As with specialty periodicals, a job listing periodical may be available only to members of the organization that publishes it. Most, however, are available to nonmembers as well, although members often receive the job magazine as part of their membership package or for a reduced subscription fee.

Since so many professional organizations publish job ads in their periodicals, Chapter 3 also tells you about several directories of associations so you can track down associations that escaped our attention.

State chapters of professional associations. Many of the associations that publish periodicals with ads for non-profit positions have state or regional chapters that also announce job openings in their chapter newsletters. Some also operate job services. Unfortunately, few of these national federations could tell us which of their chapters publish job ads or operate any job services. You will have to contact an organization's national office to obtain the current addresses and phone numbers to reach the chapter president or chapter newsletter editor who can tell you if their newsletter features job openings. Throughout this book, the address and phone number given for a publication or job service an association operates is almost always that of the association's headquarters. In some instances the address or phone number will be strictly for subscriptions. In those instances, ask for the organization's direct number.

As noted earlier, you would be very wise to join the national professional association for your occupation. Not only will this give you access to the association's job services and periodicals which may be available only to association members, but simply belonging to the association demon-

Read this chapter first

strates a tangible commitment to your profession that most employers like to see. In addition, most professional associations include in their membership package publications at no extra cost that offer a great way to continue your professional education. And don't forget, professional associations are often great places at which to work — they are non-profits.

Positions wanted. In addition to listing jobs which are available, many of the periodicals included in this book let job seekers advertise themselves under a category like "Positions Wanted." We'll tell you which ones offer this option. Before placing a "Positions Sought" ad, you'd be smart to first examine the periodical. Try to get a sample copy or inspect one in a library. After you've identified the periodicals in which you want to advertise yourself, contact them directly to learn if they place any restrictions that limit such self-advertising to members only, how much it costs to advertise yourself, and whether you can publish a "blind" ad without your name in it. In a blind ad, a box number at the publication is given for responses. The periodical regularly mails the responses to you. This way you can remain anonymous and avoid tipping off your current employer that you are in the job market. You can find many of these periodicals at your local public library or a university library. The libraries of professional associations are also likely to carry relevant periodicals. It's usually worth it to subscribe to a periodical rather than rely on seeing it at your library because subscribers invariably receive their periodicals at least a few days to weeks before they are available at any library.

Internships. Throughout the chapters that follow, you'll come upon some directories of internships as well as some periodicals and job services that carry internship announcements. These directories function more like the periodicals described above since they provide job descriptions for the internships they list. Be sure to consult the Index under "Internships" to find job sources scattered throughout this book you can use to find internship opportunities.

Local newspapers. Even with all these new job sources, do not ignore the local classifieds. The classifieds are still the primary place to advertise jobs that do not require an advanced education, like blue collar and clerical positions, or that are very localized in nature. In some locales the Sunday edition of the local newspaper may be the most accessible source for job openings, even for positions that require advanced training and education. In some states, a major newspaper is the best source for job ads for locations throughout the state, and in areas like New England, throughout the region. The *Non-Profits and Education Job Finder* identifies these newspapers in Chapter 30. If you wish to see classifieds from newspapers in other parts of the country, Chapter 3 includes a periodical and online computer services that compile want ads from many newspapers throughout the country.

See page 8 for how to keep this book current

About half the nation's daily newspapers have placed their classified sections on the Internet thus giving you immediate access to them even when you are thousands of miles away. Chapter 2 gives you a number of key sites on the Internet that will get you to these online job classifieds.

What descriptions of periodicals with job ads include. *The Non-Profits and Education Job Finder* tells you everything you need to know about each periodical or online classifieds section so you can make an informed decision whether or not to subscribe without having to call or write the publisher for more information. Sources of job ads are listed under the heading "Job ads."

Each entry includes information on subscription rates for members and nonmembers, frequency of publication, where the job ads appear in the periodical, how many jobs are advertised in a typical issue, and the publisher's phone number and address for ordering a subscription or sample issue, if available.

There's a lot of confusion about what bimonthly and semimonthly mean. The prefix "bi" means every other and "semi" means twice within the time period. So when a periodical comes out "bimonthly," you receive an issue every other month. A "semimonthly" publication will be delivered to you twice a month. "Biennial," for example, means every two years.

Job databases. There's been a wild growth in online job databases and job banks which anybody can access with a computer and modem. Most job databases are located on the Internet for which you'll also need special software to access. Other job banks are located on bulletin board services (BBSs) which do not require special software. See Chapter 2 for details on all the elements of the online job search.

Some universities and colleges participate in online job databases for use strictly by their graduates. Since you can simply ask your school's placement office for details on any such services in which it participates, there is no need to include them in the *Non-Profits and Education Job Finder*.

What descriptions of job databases include. In this book, Internet sites and BBSs that feature only a job database are listed under "Job ads." Each entry for a job database includes its name and Internet address, the "URL" that is explained in Chapter 2; the typical number of job openings listed; the identity of the operator, when available; how to contact the operator by phone or regular mail, if available; costs, if any; any membership requirements; any registration requirements; and, in the case of a bulletin board service, how to set your modem and the phone number to dial to connect to the BBS.

Job hotlines. Many professional and trade associations that serve the non-profit sector operate job hotlines which usually offer a prerecorded announcement of job openings. These hotlines have become much more sophisticated thanks to the wonders of the "automated attendant" device.

Read this chapter first

Tools for your savvy job quest   7

You will almost certainly need a touch-tone phone to call them because the recorded voice at the other end will give you instructions that can be implemented only with a touch-tone phone. The most sophisticated job hotlines allow you to specify the geographic area(s) in which you are interested and the types of jobs about which you want to hear.

Getting started

It is crucial that you read this chapter and Chapter 2 before you delve into the meat of this book. If you skip either of these chapters, you will be unable to find all the job sources you need for your job search.

Some of the low-tech hotlines simply give you a recording that lists jobs. You have no control over what you hear. Often you will first hear a list of all the job titles available. If you want to hear a detailed description and how to apply for a particular position that was just listed, keep listening because that information is often conveyed next.

Pay attention to the area code of the job hotline you are about to call. If the area code is 900, the call not only isn't free, but you will be charged an additional fee directly on your phone bill. When a 900 number is given, the charges are usually specified.

The *Non-Profits and Education Job Finder* tells you about job hotlines that cover different types of territory. You'll find a number of job hotlines that include jobs for all occupations throughout the country. Other hotlines consist of jobs for a specific occupation. Still others are for specific schools or non-profits. Listing all of the job hotlines that exist could fill a book of its own. Fortunately, Chapter 3 will tell you all about two such books.

What descriptions of job hotlines include. In the *Non-Profits and Education Job Finder* job hotlines appear under the heading "Job services." If a job hotline is free, the *Non-Profits and Education Job Finder* gives you the phone number to call. If there is a telephone device for the deaf phone number, that number is also given with the acronym **TDD** in boldface type. The entry for most job hotlines also includes the names of the job hotline and of the entity that operates it; the operator's address and regular phone number, if available; operating hours and days; how many job vacancies are typically offered; how often job listings are changed; and whether or not membership in an organization is required to use the job hotline. If association membership or a prepaid fee is required to use the job hotline, the actual hotline number is not given here. You'll get the hotline number after you join the organization or pay your fee. The job hotlines will tell you how to apply for the vacant positions they list. Be sure to visit our home page on the Internet at URL: **http://jobfindersonline.com** to learn about any new directories of job hotlines for positions with specific non-profits and educational institutions.

See page 8 for how to keep this book current

User newsgroups. These online sites include listings of job vacancies and allow users to reach one another via electronic mail (email) which also makes them quite useful for networking. Chapter 2 explains how to use newsgroups in your job quest.

Mailing lists. These online services will send you lists of job openings when you subscribe to them. Subscriptions are nearly always free. Job openings are sent by email. Chapter 2 presents a detailed discussion of using mailing lists in your job search.

School and agency job pages on the Internet. A growing number of non-profit organizations and schools ranging from elementary through graduate institutions maintain home pages on the Internet where they announce job openings. See Chapter 2 to learn how the Internet works. Chapter 2 also gives you information about a number of prime Internet sites that connect you to these job pages on the Internet. Other online sites that include directories of home pages for non-profits and educational institutions are noted throughout this book.

Tools for helping non-profits recruit you

Throughout this book you will find descriptions of resume banks or databases and job-matching services listed under the "Job services" appellation. These are the tools that enable employers to find you. A resume

Keep current
with the latest *Update Sheet*

Many of the job sources in this book undergo frequent change. The secret to keeping current is to get our latest *Update Sheet* that reports these changes by:

▣ Visiting our home page on the Internet for our most recent *Update Sheet*. We're located at URL: **http://jobfindersonline.com**.

▤ Sending a photocopy of this page with a self-addressed, stamped (one ounce postage) #10 business envelope to: Planning/Communications, NPJF97 Update, 7215 Oak Ave., River Forest, IL 60305 — *after* September 1, 1997.

Read this chapter first

bank is a repository for the resumes of job seekers. Employers are able to access the resume database themselves and search for candidates who match their hiring criteria. You can submit your resume by real mail, fax, or email. The major drawback of any resume bank occurs if your current employer uses it to identify potential hires. If your current employer comes upon your resume in a resume database, your goose is literally cooked and you'll probably need a new job sooner than you had expected.

A growing number of resume banks allow you to substitute a code number for your name. When an employer wants to contact the job seeker with this kind of confidential resume, the operator of the resume database contacts you for your approval to send your complete resume, including your name, to the employer. Unfortunately, this approach does not really keep your identity confidential because your employer could recognize you from your resume's description of your current job.

A much more secure derivative of the resume bank is the job-matching service. You submit your resume just like you do for a resume database. Instead of employers searching the resume database themselves, they pay the job-matching service to conduct a search for candidates that meet the employer's hiring criteria. When a match is made, many of these services contact you first to see if it is okay to give your resume to the employer. Alternatively, some job-matching services allow you to specify in advance which employers can never see your resume. Such job-matching services clearly offer much better protection than resume banks to assure that your current employer does not discover you are looking for a new job. Generally speaking, job-matching services and resume databases make their money by charging employers to use them.

A growing number of universities and colleges participate in computerized job-matching services strictly for their graduates. Because you can ask your school's placement office for details on which of these services it participates in, there is no need to include them in this book.

Some of these job services work really well and generate interviews pretty quickly for the better qualified people who use them. Attractive as these services sound, many can be frustratingly slow in getting you a job interview. Despite all the hype that surrounds them, most are relatively new services without proven track records. If you are the sort of person who is likely to find a job quickly by using other methods, you may also be matched to a job fairly rapidly when using one of these services. But if you've been having trouble getting interviewed when using more proven job-search methods, you probably should not expect instant results using a job-matching service or resume bank.

Follow the instructions the service gives for submitting your resume. A few of these services will want one or more copies of your conventional print resume which they send to an employer after a match is made. But the vast majority require an "electronic resume" that differs greatly in format from a print resume. These services need to put your resume into

See page 8 for how to keep this book current

a database. This database is then searched, often looking for specific words in your resume that match criteria the employer is looking for in a new employee. Consequently, electronic resumes emphasize keyword nouns rather than verbs and appearance. You will have to submit your resume either by email or in a print format that allows it to be scanned into the resume database. Chapter 2 tells you about several excellent guides that explain how to transform your resume into an electronic resume and one that is suitable for scanning and inclusion in a resume bank or job-matching service. Some of the "gateway" online services noted in that chapter also get you to Internet World Wide Web sites that also provide this guidance for resume makeovers into an electronic form.

What descriptions of resume banks and job-matching services include. Since online services generally allow you to send an email message to the operator, there's no reason to include their email addresses in this book. Each entry for a resume database or job-matching service includes the names of the service and operator of the service; the operator's real world address and phone number when available; the kind of resume to submit (printed, scannable, electronic); any cost to you to use the service; whether job-matching is done by computer or real live people; whether employers can search the resume database themselves or searches are conducted by the service's operator; confidentiality options; who contacts whom when a match is made; and the length of time your resume is kept on file.

Tools for networking

Job hunting lore is replete with stories of job seekers discovering vacancies by asking somebody they know or get to know. This technique is networking, a job-search tool that can get you to job vacancies before they are advertised and to job vacancies that are never advertised. Networking has long been the primary means for finding jobs in the non-profit sector.

Networking is an essential part of the job search for those professions where jobs aren't widely advertised. You'll find some disciplines in this book where the number of entries under "Job ads" and "Job services" is mighty sparse. For those specializations, networking is particularly valuable.

Networking, of course, starts with contacting your relatives and friends to see if they know of jobs anywhere, or perhaps, know of somebody working for an agency or school who might know of job openings with that employer. A further step is "networking by association." As I suggest time and again, join your professional association. Most will give you a membership directory (and others will sell it to nonmembers). Go through that directory and pick a few people to call to ask whom you should contact to learn about seeking a job in the geographic area where that person works or lives. The local chapters of professional associations often offer

Read this chapter first

events that are great for building contacts. While you will undoubtedly make some contacts without preparing for a chapter event, you'd be smart to identify who it would be worth meeting prior to the event. Use your organization's directory to learn something about the people you want to meet so you have something at least halfway engaging to discuss with them.

You may also want to examine directories of non–profits or educational institutions and pick an appropriate person to call for advice on finding jobs in your area and with his agency or school. Visit the home page of non–profits and schools on the Internet where you will often find a directory of key management employees. See Chapter 2 to learn how to use "search engines" to comb the Internet for these sites. Many will give you an email address for each of their key employees. While many top managers are unlikely to take your phone call, you'd be amazed at how many will respond favorably to an email message from a complete stranger who is seeking career advice.

For details on how the networking game works, see books like *Dynamite Networking for Dynamite Jobs* by Ron and Caryl Krannich (for your convenience, it's available from the Job Search Resources Catalog at the end of this book).

A growing number of professional associations now offer their membership directories on the Internet where you can search for people by location as well as by name. You will find print and online directories throughout the *Non–Profits and Education Job Finder* under the heading "Directories."

What descriptions of directories include. The entry for each directory will give you its title; publisher with contact information when available; whether the directory is printed, available on floppy disk or CD–ROM, or on the Internet; price to members and nonmembers if a professional

Job sources are presented under these four labels:

Job ads
Job services
Directories
Salary surveys

Within each classification, the first sources listed are those with the broadest coverage and the most job openings. They're followed by sources with a more specialized focus and/or fewer job openings. Sources that cover the same specialties are usually grouped together.

See page 8 for how to keep this book current

association publishes it; number of pages; publication date; what's included in the directory; how it's indexed if it's a print directory; and how you can search it if it's an electronic directory (floppy disk, CD-ROM, or Internet).

Please note that some print directories are available free to qualified "professionals." To obtain a free subscription, you usually must complete a detailed application form that appears in the magazine or is available from the publisher upon request.

Tools for researching schools and non-profits

The really savvy job seeker will conduct some research to learn more about an employer at several stages in her job hunt. When responding to a job ad, you'll want to know more about the employer so you can tailor your cover letter to that employer and greatly increase the chances that your resume will be read and your application seriously considered.

At the other end of the job search, you would be most prudent to know a lot about the organization before you enter the job interview. You will score points with the interviewer if you are reasonably familiar with what the organization does. You should have enough of an idea of what the agency does so you can explain how you can contribute to its success. Having some knowledge of the community and agency will also help you frame pertinent questions to ask at the interview. The questions you ask at the interview are often more important than the answers you give to the interviewer's questions.

At least try to learn enough so your potential employer won't feel you are too much of an outsider to learn the vagaries of the organization. Use membership directories to see if you can learn anything about the person or persons who will interview you and who make the hiring decision so you can present the side of you that will appeal the most to their sensibilities. It is possible that other people you know in your profession — perhaps a contact you made while networking — may be able to tell you something about your interviewer and the agency or school for which she works.

If you are conducting the sort of job search where you knock on the door of employers that interest you, whether or not they have any known vacancies, you would be smart to know a lot about an employer before you contact it. Armed with a thorough knowledge of the educational institution or non-profit agency, you will be able to open many more doors than if you walk in clueless about it, its history, and its "corporate" philosophy. Many of the print and online directories listed in the *Non-Profits and Education Job Finder* give you a wealth of information about thousands of non-profits and schools that will help you decide which ones to approach. The directories included in the state-by-state chapter focus on a single state or metropolitan area.

Read this chapter first

Resources for careers with non-profits

Jobs and Careers with Nonprofit Organizations by Ronald Krannich ($15.95, 244 pages, 1996) helps you determine your aptitude for working in the non-profit world. Revealing the myths, realities, and current trends, Krannich helps you select the type of work in which you can really thrive.

100 Jobs in Social Change by Harley Jebens ($14.95, 216 pages, 1996) offers details on 100 entry-levels jobs in social services, advocacy, organizing, education, media, politics, and non-profits in general. It includes insightful profiles of actual workers and lots of real world information.

Making a Living While Making a Difference by Melissa Everett ($10.95, 343 pages, 1995) offers a ten-step program for identifying your personal ethics, job interests, and strengths to help you select your non-profit job.

All are available from the Job Search Resource Catalog at the end of this book. As we discover other useful resources, we'll post them on our Web site at URL: **http://jobfindersoline.com**.

See the earlier section on "Tools for networking" for details on what the entries of these directories include.

You can also use these directories to identify the right person to contact about job opportunities. Speaking directly to the right individual can give you a genuine competitive edge. It tells the hiring person that you've done your homework. Also, you can learn a lot more about the nature of vacant jobs and the character of the hiring agency by talking to someone in the know than just by reading job ads.

Many of the directories enumerated in this book include the name of an agency's director of personnel or human resources. Most do not. You can, however, use these to contact a potential employer and ask to whom to send a job inquiry or application.

Some of the directories listed in the *Non-Profits and Education Job Finder* are rather lengthy tomes that cost the proverbial arm and a leg. No rational individual would spend the hundreds, or even thousands, of dollars some of these cost. Fortunately, most of them are available at well-stocked public libraries and can be found through interlibrary loan systems. Reference libraries and libraries at colleges and universities are even more likely to carry many of the directories described in this book. The libraries of professional associations are also good places to find relevant directories.

Tools for the creative approach

In *What Color is Your Parachute?* author Richard Bolles reports that one of the most successful job-search techniques is the "creative approach to job hunting or career change." He spends over 120 pages guiding you through this technique. It boils down to conducting a thorough assessment of yourself to identify your skills and interests and the kinds of fields in

See page 8 for how to keep this book current

which you want to ply those skills. It involves networking with people in those kinds of jobs and learning if they like their jobs and how they found their jobs. Next it requires identifying the non-profits or schools where you would like to work, whether or not you know they have vacancies, and then researching them thoroughly before your approach them. Finally, you should identify the person who actually has the authority to hire you and get to see him so you can show him how you can help his agency or school do its job more effectively.

This approach is not mystical. It's good common sense and is actually a logical combination of many of the techniques discussed earlier in this chapter. If you are interested in pursuing it, particularly the self-assessment part, you should get the latest edition of *What Color is Your Parachute?* (Ten Speed Press, $16.95, 531 pages, published each November; available from Planning/Communications' catalog at the end of this book).

With its abundance of organization and membership directories, the *Non-Profits and Education Job Finder* helps you quickly and easily find many of the tools you need to implement Bolles' "creative approach." As always, be sure to use at least three or four of the different job-search techniques to vastly increase your chances of finding a job and getting hired.

Tools for using search firms and recruiters

Some search firms specialize in non-profits or education. Three of the directories described in Chapter 3 tell you about them. I've included these directories of recruiters for two reasons. First, if you want to use an executive recruiter, these are the most affordable resources for identifying the recruiter that is right for your needs. Second, you can use them to identify recruiting firms that focus on non-profits or education for which you may wish to work.

Tools for negotiating salary

Negotiating salary is one of the most sensitive steps in the job hunt. The bottom line is that you do not want to discuss salary until the employer has definitely said she wants to hire you. Once you've reached that stage, there's a big payoff if you have a real good idea of what the going rate is for your experience and education in the state or region the job is located. The more you know about the wage and benefit scales for a particular position in the locale or region, the better you can negotiate salary and meet the employer's expectations in the job interview. In addition, knowing differences in salary between states and regions can help you decide where to look for a job.

Read this chapter first

For timeless advice on how to successfully negotiate salary, see *Dynamite Salary Negotiations* (Impact Publications, $13.95, 164 pages, 1994) by Caryl and Ron Krannich and *The Smart Woman's Guide to Interviewing and Salary Negotiation* (Career Press, $12.99, 224 pages, 1995) by Julie Adder King. Hard to find in bookstores, both books are available from the Job Search Resources Catalog at the end of this book.

What descriptions of salary surveys include. Most salary surveys are published as stand-alone reports. Some, though, appear in magazines and newsletters, or even on the Internet on sites of professional associations, educational institutions, and non-profit organizations. The vast majority of salary and benefit studies appear in this book under the moniker "Salary surveys." But be sure to also check the "Job ads" and "Directories" sections of a chapter for other places where salary surveys appear when they are included as part of a periodical or directory. The descriptions of salary surveys include their title and publisher; how and where to obtain a copy; the price, if any; publication date; type of salary and benefit information reported; and geographic scope of the study.

Seven steps to job hunt success

To get the full picture of the job resources available for all the different job-quest techniques recounted in this chapter, read Chapter 2 next. The job resources available on the Internet expand all the different job-search techniques by offering faster, less expensive, and more accessible information. Chapter 2 will explain how to access the Internet even if you do not own a computer and modem. It reports on all the different Internet tools that enhance your job-search capabilities and how to use them. It also offers great resources that go into considerable depth about the online job search, preparing resumes for resume banks and job-matching services, and expansive sites on the Internet that connect you to more job resources than anybody could gather into a single book.

After reading this chapter and Chapter 2 you are ready to begin to use the rest of the *Non-Profits and Education Job Finder* to discover the specific tools that will make your job search end with offers for the kind of job you want from the employer you prefer that is in the location you crave. Since there are over 2,222 resources in the rest of this book, follow these seven steps to learn how to navigate through this book most effectively and succeed in your job hunt.

1 Start by reading the first two chapters. Heck, you're already halfway there. They explain how to most effectively use the resources in this book for the different job-search strategies you decide to use.

See page 8 for how to keep this book current

2 Read Chapter 3 to learn about general, broad-based job sources that cover all occupations within the broad non-profit and education sector of the economy.

3 Turn to the Table of Contents to identify the other chapters that focus on the profession or professions that interests you. Use those chapters. Be sure to pay attention to any cross references offered to other chapters or sections within a chapter.

4 Look up your specialty in the Index where you will find references to job sources that are not located where you would intuitively expect to find them. To keep the size of this book more or less under control, we've included index references to many job sources that serve several specialties rather than repeating the job source in several different places. Many obscure disciplines are also included in the Index. If you are having trouble finding an index listing for a profession, try some variations and you will probably connect. When you do find an index reference, turn to the designated page or pages. The profession will be mentioned by name in an entry on that page. Be sure to also look in the other job resources in the same part of the section. For example, if the index reference takes you to the "Job ads," you will probably find additional job resources for your profession under "Job services," "Directories," and "Salary surveys."

5 If you want to target a particular state, go to Chapter 30 where you will find sources of job ads, directories of schools and non-profits, salary surveys, and other valuable resources for finding jobs in each of the 50 states and the District of Columbia. This chapter also explains how to reach and use the services offered by local Job Service Offices and local and state chapters of professional associations. In addition, these offices participate in a national job database you can access through the Internet.

6 If you are looking for an Internship, be sure to look in the Index under "Internships."

7 Check out the *Budget-stretching discount coupons* near the end of this book where you'll find $225 in discounts on some of the most effective resources recommended in the *Non-Profits and Education Job Finder*.

There's a whole lot of valuable information out there to make your job search successful, no matter what the state of the economy may be. If you follow these guidelines and conduct a savvy job search, you will find the job resources that will help you get your new job or internship more quickly and easily than ever before.

Read this chapter first

Chapter 2

The online job search explosion

The online job search has exploded onto the scene to become the most heavily hyped way to find jobs today. Amid all the hubbub people tend to forget that the online job hunt is only a few years old; it's still just an infant trying to find its walking legs. But some of the hype is rightly justified — the Internet in particular offers an astounding array of job resources that enable job seekers to quickly and inexpensively find current job vacancies where they live as well as thousands of miles from home. My mind boggles at the scope of these online job sources and how they add a new dimension to today's job search.

But the cyberspace job search is still very much in its infancy. In 1994 it barely existed. By the beginning of 1996, fewer than 35 percent of all U.S. households had a computer and less than a third of them were actually connected to the Internet. Still, that's nearly 9 million U.S. households using the Internet, a figure expected to double or triple by the year 2000.

As of this writing, many Internet job resources are really more ballyhoo than substance. Some job databases simply lift job ads from other venues, such as newspapers, specialty and trade periodicals, and other Web sites. Many others fail to remove job ads, or "postings," after a vacancy is filled. The result is that online job seekers are looking at job ads and applying for positions that have been filled, but are still being advertised. Despite all their value, Internet job–search tools do have their weak spots and need to mature before they are ready for prime time.

But as the end of the twentieth century arrives, electronic job-seeking tools have become an important new supplement to the more concrete job resources of specialty and trade periodicals, job hotlines, job-matching services, directories, and networking. A job seeker who relies *exclusively* on the Internet to find a job is as foolish as one who relies solely on networking or on job hotlines. Maybe by the time the Chicago Cubs get into a World Series — well, maybe sooner, like in your lifetime — the electronic job search will mature sufficiently, and become accessible enough to replace the traditional tools used in today's job quest. Until then, the Internet offers another vehicle, albeit an exciting and promising one, for finding jobs. The successful job seeker will use the Internet alongside the other job-search tools reported upon in the *Non-Profits and Education Job Finder.*

This chapter introduces you to the players in this electronic job-search revolution and gives you enough information to enable even "techno-bozos" to effectively use these online resources to find job vacancies and get hired. For readers who want to know even more about the online job search, this chapter also presents some excellent resources that go into far more depth about using computers, modems, and the different online job-search tools. The chapter ends with detailed descriptions of amazing Internet sites that are good places to start your online job search; sites that contain links to many job and resume databases and/or directories and other job-related sites. These sites are great places to discover new job resources on the Internet as they become available.

The players in the online job search

It seems, at times, that everybody is talking about the Internet. Actually, as of late 1996, only ten percent of U.S. households were connected to the Internet, although many more people use it at work or at school. By the end of the century, this figure should double or even triple.

The Internet is simply a massive network of computers connected to each other via modems and wires such as telephone lines. Originally created way back in the 1960s as a communications network for the federal government, it was used mainly by government, universities, and research institutions until the middle of the 1980s when some wag dubbed it the "Internet."

But you can't just turn on your computer and modem and hop on the Internet. To actually get on the Internet, you must subscribe to an Internet Service Provider (ISP) or an online service like CompuServe, America Online (AOL), Prodigy, or the Microsoft Network (MSN). ISPs connect you only to the Internet. In addition to connecting you to the Internet, online services offer their own area in cyberspace where it is real easy to access the benefits

If you skipped it, go back and read Chapter 1 now

the online service offers. Both types of services give you software that is called a Web browser. This browser is the electronic tool that enables you to connect to the Internet and use its different elements.

None of this comes free. Some services charge a flat rate like $20 per month and allow use of their service for as many hours as you wish. Others charge a fee that entitles you to five hours of free time plus another $2.95 for each additional hour you use the service.

There are actually several components to the Internet, which is the main vehicle for the online job–search explosion. Explaining each of them will help you grasp the possibilities of how these online tools can enhance your job search, no matter which job–seeking techniques you choose to use.

Email

Email is the one element of the Internet that touches all its other components. Email is shorthand for electronic mail. It enables you to send messages, letters, and documents to anybody with an email address, including potential employers, anywhere on the Internet. A good number of the online job services described throughout this book allow you to submit your resume to employers via email. Some let you actually place your resume in a resume database via email.

To send somebody email, you must, of course, know their email address. My email address is *lauber@jobfindersonline.com*. The first part before the "at" sign, @, is my user name. The part that comes after the @ sign is the domain name. A domain is simply a location somewhere on the sprawling Internet. The address letters "jobfindersonline" is the first part of the domain name where I receive email. The extension letters, "com," indicate that this is a company or corporate domain. If an Internet address does not include the @ symbol, it is not an email address.

If you use an online service such as CompuServe, America Online, Prodigy, or the Microsoft Network, your email address will consist of your user name on the service and the online service's domain name. If there are any commas in your user name, you must change them to periods to send email on the Internet. If your CompuServe user name is *10000,1041* (not a real user name), then your email address would be *10000.1041@compuserve.com*.

There are several ways to find the email address for, say, a potential employer you wish to contact. You can, of course, call the non–profit organization or educational institution and ask that person or her secretary for that person's email address. The receptionist may even have it. An increasing number of people now include their email address on their business cards and letterhead. When you make contact with a potential employer through a newsgroup, discussed later in this chapter, you will see that person's email address. Write it down and keep it for future reference. You can also visit some of the online directories of email addresses or

See page 8 for how to keep current

directories of non-profits or schools. If you know that the agency or school is connected to an online service like CompuServe, you can probably find her email address by accessing CompuServe's member directory.

Save yourself some connect time charges and help keep traffic on the Internet down by typing your email message before you actually turn on your Internet connection. Simply type your message using the email software that is part of your online service or Web browser, or use your word processor to compose your letter and "cut and paste" it into your email software. By the time you read this, most email software may allow you to format your text. American Online already enables members to use boldface and italics and do some elementary formatting of the email they send. Once you've written your letter, connect to the Internet.

You can also use email as an electronic networking tool. Other users will see your name on the postings you place and possibly contact you by email. You, of course, can contact other users by email as well and do some of your networking online. You'd be surprised at how many high ranking officials who would not give you the time of day in person or on the phone will answer email messages from complete strangers.

You should be aware that email is not flawless. A small percentage of email messages, like real world mail, is lost every day. On very rare occasions, your Internet service provider or online service may break down and lose your email. Email has also been used to send computer viruses that can destroy your computer. So be cautious. One thing to keep in mind is that the actual email message sits on a computer far away from you until

Blindness is no barrier to using the Web anymore

People who are blind or whose vision is severely impaired can use the Internet to find job vacancies thanks to a new software program called *pwWebSpeak*. This nifty application reads aloud the text displaced on your computer screen. It can also display Web sites in very large type. *pwWebSpeak* works with most computer hardware and does not require an expensive speech synthesizer. It can work with the relatively inexpensive speech synthesizer called *SoftVoice*. You can download a sample copy of *pwWebSpeak* at Internet URL: **http://www.prodworks.com** or get more information by calling the manufacturer, The Productivity Works, at 609/984-8044 in Trenton, NJ. Individuals with vision impairments can obtain *pwWebSpeak* for free, with a $50 charge for technical support. Others must pay for the software.

If you skipped it, go back and read Chapter 1 now

you click the icon that opens each email message. If you're suspicious, do not open a suspect email message; simply click "delete" and it is erased on that distant computer and never gets onto yours.

The World Wide Web

The best known segment of the Internet is the World Wide Web, where the bulk of the job-search action is located. You must dial up the Internet from a computer with a modem. You also need to subscribe to an Internet Service Provider (ISP) to gain access to the Internet and its Web. For a monthly fee, the ISP enables you to access the Internet via your ordinary phone lines, your computer, and your computer's modem. Most online services such as CompuServe and America Online also serve as ISPs to give you access to the Internet.

However, in order to make the electronic connection to the Internet and its World Wide Web, you need to install software that is called a Web browser. While there are at least 20 browsers on the market, the two giants are Netscape Navigator and Microsoft's Internet Explorer. Their current versions enable you to view Web sites complete with graphics, sound, tables, and frames that make for a more pleasant graphical presentation of information. They allow you to print the contents of the page you are viewing and to download files that you can then view on your computer after you've exited from the Internet. As you use the Internet, you'll notice that a lot of sites tell you they are best viewed with Netscape or Internet Explorer. You'll often find a link that will take you to a site from which you can download the Web browser for free.

No matter how much I tell you about how to use the Internet, and no matter how much you read about it in other books, including those recommended here, the only way you'll really learn how to use the Internet in your job search is to simply use it. If your online service or browser offers a tutorial or tour on using the Internet, take it. Expect to stumble a bit, well maybe a lot, when you first connect to the Internet. Accept that most adults will need to spend a few hours using the Internet before they become even slightly comfortable with it. Don't let any initial foul-ups and tie-ups discourage you. You will become accustomed to using the Internet with just a few hours of practice — and there is nothing you can do on the Internet to break your computer. Once I connected to the 'Net, it took me about ten hours using the Internet to get comfortable with it.

Throughout the entries for Internet sites described in the *Non-Profits and Education Job Finder* you'll see the acronym "URL" followed by some terms that usually make little sense to the untrained eye. URL stands for Uniform Resource Locator. The URL is the cyberspace "address" of a site on the Internet. It essentially tells your computer and the ones to which you are connected on the Internet, the coordinates of where you want to go on the Internet. For example, the URL for Planning/Communications'

See page 8 for how to keep current

Web site is **http://jobfindersonline.com**. Note that some URLs are case sensitive. If there are capitalized letters in a URL, you *must* type them as capitals when you enter the URL into your browser. Where do you type the URL? You should find a long, narrow box near the top of your Web browser's window where you type in URLs. In Netscape, this box is labeled "Location." Microsoft's Internet Explorer dubs this box "Address."

Throughout this book, URLs are printed in boldface type to help you find online job sources more easily.

It may help to understand what the different segments of a URL mean. The information that goes before the two slashes and colon (//:) tell your software how to connect to the Internet; "http" in the example above. The information that follows the two slashes and colon is the address of the site to which you want to connect; "jobfindersonline.com" in the above example. As you'll quickly discover, many Internet addresses have additional information to guide your browser to a specific directory or file. These segments of the address are separated by slash marks as in **http://www.jobweb.org/catapult/catapult.htm**, an excellent job resource site described later in this chapter.

These URLs can get pretty long and cumbersome. If you run into difficulty connecting to a site, try eliminating some of the URL starting with whatever comes after the last slash. It's possible that the directory or file

How to access Internet job resources even if you don't own a computer

Even if you don't have a computer at home or work, there's a good chance you can still access the Internet's job resources and use email to get hired.

First check with your local public library. A growing number of public libraries offer their patrons free Internet access. You may have a friend or relative who will let you use her computer. You may be able to rent time on a computer while chugging caffeine at one of the "cybercafes" that are springing up all over the country. And you may be allowed to use the computer and Internet connection at your college alumni relations office.

Whatever way you get on the Internet, you will want to establish an email account where you can receive responses to your inquiries, job applications, and networking efforts.

You can set up a **free email account** by going to either of these Web sites at URLs: **http://www.hotmail.com** or **http://www.juno.com**. You'll be able to choose a password that will prevent other people from seeing your email.

If you skipped it, go back and read Chapter 1 now

The World Wide Web

you are seeking has been moved or its name changed. Backing up one level at a time will usually enable you to connect to the site you want and find the relocated or renamed directory or file. For example, you could just type in **http://www.jobweb.org/** and once there, navigate to the "catapult" directory.

You should also know what the extension in the first part of a URL means. It signifies the domain name, or genre, of the site. "Edu" stands for educational institution. "Org" shows that a non–profit organization operates the site. "Com" means that the site is owned by a business. "Gov" signifies the U.S. government. "Mil" stands for military. "Net" refers to an administrative organization for a network. Other countries have their own domain names such as ".ch" for Switzerland or ".jp" for Japan. Additional extensions proposed at the time of this writing include "store" for businesses offering goods, "info" for information services, "firm" for businesses or firms, "web" for entities that emphasize activities related to the World Wide Web, "rec" for recreational groups or entertainment activities, and "nom" for the personal web sites of individuals.

Remembering most URLs is not easy, and retyping them correctly can be a hassle. Web browsers let you keep your own address book of URLs, commonly called bookmarks. When you come upon a Web site you think you'll want to revisit, you can record its URL in your address book by clicking on the "Bookmarks" button on your browser's menu bar and selecting "Add a bookmark." When you want to revisit the site, you click on the "Bookmarks" button and select the site you recorded from the list of bookmarks that drops down from the menu bar.

The first screen you see when you go to a Web site is known as its "home page." To get to another screen, or "page" that is part of a Web site, you click on what's called a "link." This link is shown as a graphical image, or a highlighted or underlined word or phrase. Usually your pointer will change to a different shape when it's placed over a link, and the URL of the linked site will appear at the bottom of your Web browser's screen. These links help make Web sites so useful and, frankly, fun. Clicking on a link to another Web site can transport you far away to another Web site anywhere in the world.

Most of the online job sources mentioned in this book are easily accessible on the World Wide Web. You should know, however, that you can quickly find information on the Web by conducting what's called a "search" by using a "search engine." A search engine is a piece of online software that will look all over the Internet to find the Internet sites that contain what you tell it to find. At this point in time, these searches are free.

These amazing tools search the Internet for sites you want to see. To reach a search engine's Web site, type its URL on your Web browser. You'll be transported to the search engine's Web site and a search dialogue box will appear. Next you type into that box a "keyword" or "keywords" such

See page 8 for how to keep current

as a topic, URL, or Web page name. Most search engines will let you type in a combination of words such as "nurse AND jobs." Each search engine's site includes helpful instructions on how to conduct complex searches. After you enter your "keywords" and press the button usually marked "Submit," you'll soon see a list of links to other Web pages and Internet sources related to the keyword(s) you typed. These lists almost always give you a slight description of each site your search uncovers. It is best to make your search as narrow as possible; otherwise you could get thousands of sites included in the result of your search. Simply click on the link to a site found in your search and you're transported there.

The number of search engines continues to grow. In its December 3, 1996 issue, *PC Magazine* reviewed some of the best search engines. Your local library may still have a copy on file. See the section of the magazine entitled "The Netsearcher's Ultimate Cheat Sheet" for "the tips, tools, tricks, and know–how you need to search the Web, Usenet, White Pages services, and MetaSearch sites." The search engines reviewed include:

- *AltaVista Search* at URL: **http://www.altavista.digital.com** which can search for Web and Usenet content.
- *Excite* at URL: **http://www.excite.com** where you can search for Web content, Usenet news, Usenet classifieds, and Excite's reviews of other sites.
- *HotBot* at URL: **http://www.hotbot.com** which searches for Web and Usenet content.
- *Yahoo!* at URL: **http://www.yahoo.com** which searches Web content through a directory of prescreened sites, Usenet content, and email.

While it's pretty easy to find the job database, resume database, directory, or salary survey you seek on most Web sites cited in the *Non–Profits and Education Job Finder*, some sites make you play detective and bury job resources pretty deep. So, even though many sites often change their structure, I decided to include instructions on how to reach the job resources at most sites.

Keep in mind, though, that a site's structure may have changed by the time you visit it and the instructions given here may have become obsolete. Even when that happens, the instructions presented here should still give you some sense of how to navigate the site and find the job resources you want.

If you skipped it, go back and read Chapter 1 now

Gopher servers

- *infoseek®* at URL: **http://www.infoseek.com** which searches for Web content, Usenet content, company directory listings, infoseek select sites, email addresses, timely news, and Web FAQs.
- *Lycos* at URL: **http://www.lycos.com** which searches for general Web content, pictures, sounds.
- *WebCrawler* at URL: **http://www.webcrawler.com** where you can search for Web content.
- *Magellan Internet Guide* at URL: **http://www.mckinley.com** which searches for Web pages and sites rated and reviewed by Magellan.
- *Open Text Index* at URL: **http://index.opentext.net** where you can search for Web content, newsgroups, and email.
- *World Wide Web Worm* at URL: **http://wwww.cs.colorado.edu/wwww** which searches for Web content (no relation to Dennis "Worm" Rodman).

Another excellent resource to find Internet addresses is the **Web Site Sourcebook** (Omnigraphics, Inc., 2500 Penobscot Bldg., Detroit, MI 48226; phones: 800/234–1340, 313/961–1340) $65 plus shipping, 550 pages, published each January. It includes URLs and full real world contact information for over 11,000 government agencies, major U.S. businesses, non–profit organizations, and educational institutions. It's organized by the name of the sponsoring entity and by subject.

The number of job databases on the Internet is growing almost exponentially. You can get a handle on them by reading the **Cyberhound's Guide to Internet Databases** (Gale Research, Inc.; available from Planning/Communications' Job Search Resources Catalog at the end of this book) $99.00, 800 pages, published every March. It describes over 4,000 Internet databases and how to access and retrieve them. It also provides information on searching elements and routines, main file names, and more. It includes several comprehensive indices.

Gopher servers

Occasionally you'll come upon a URL that begins with the word "gopher." This is not a reference to the Iowa Congressman who once played that role on the *Love Boat* television series. Gophers are text–based Internet sites that just aren't as visually appealing as the graphical Web pages discussed above. Instead, gopher sites eschew graphics to provide valuable information in a straightforward manner. A good number of university or government Internet sites are served up to us as gophers.

See page 8 for how to keep current

Usenet newsgroups

Many of the 10,000 or so "newsgroups" in the Usenet portion of the Internet are valuable tools for job seekers, especially for networking. Some wags describe newsgroups as being a bit like a bulletin board at your local grocery or laundromat where you can put up a notice and people who are interested in your notice can write their own responses to your message. A newsgroup is an Internet site where you can read messages other people have "posted" there and also submit your own comments to the site in response to the posted message. Alternatively, you can send your comments directly to a specific person by email rather than posting your remarks where all users of the newsgroup can read them. In a sense, you can engage in electronic conversation with another person or persons interested in the same topic as you.

Employers place announcements of job vacancies on a good number of newsgroups that focus on a specific city and/or particular profession. Placing a notice in a newsgroup is also called "posting" a message. There are a number of newsgroups such as **news:misc.jobs.resumes** where job seekers post their resumes. Many recruiters and employers have started to treat the resumes at this newsgroup as a resume bank of prospective employees. Unfortunately, few newsgroups serve the non-profit sector.

One of the beauties of newsgroups is that information can be added by anybody at any time. So they are constantly changing and constitute one of the most dynamic portions of the Internet. Fortunately, virtually all Web browsers include a built-in "news reader" that enables you to easily reach newsgroups. To access a newsgroup, such as **news:biz.jobs.offered**, a site with job vacancies in business that are nontechnical, you simply type: **news:biz.jobs.offered** in the same place in your Web browser as you type URLs.

You should be careful with newsgroups. Each one has its own sense of Emily Post — much like a company's corporate culture. While newsgroup etiquette is largely a matter of common sense and courtesy, you would be prudent to learn the newsgroup's implied rules before you open your electronic mouth. Read the frequently asked questions (FAQ) section that most newsgroups offer for new participants. There's also a Web site that keeps track of these newsgroups' FAQs. Go to URL: **http://www.cis.ohio-state.edu/** and click your pointer on "Internet Services." Then select "Usenet FAQs." You can browse alphabetically or search to find the newsgroups that interest you so you can learn their rules of etiquette.

New newsgroups are arising all the time. Listing all the current job-related newsgroups in this or any other book would be an exercise in futility. You can view and print out updated annotated lists of job search newsgroups from several of the Internet sites described later in this chapter.

If you skipped it, go back and read Chapter 1 now

Mailing lists

How would you like to have notices of new job vacancies regularly arrive in your email box without having to lift a finger? That's what Internet mailing lists essentially do. They are a lot like newsgroups, except that instead of sending email to individuals, any email you send goes to *all* users of the site. Sometimes jobs are posted via mailing lists well before they are advertised elsewhere. To receive a mailing list, you "subscribe" to it by sending an email message to list's sponsor which will then send you the mailing list's information on a regular basis.

You can also use mailing lists as an electronic networking tool. Other users will see your name on the postings you place and possibly contact you by email. You, of course, can contact other users by email as well and do your networking online.

While a few mailing lists are described throughout the *Non-Profits and Education Job Finder,* you should visit one or more of these Web sites to get current information on active mailing lists. For each mailing list you'll be told where to send an email to subscribe and what message your email should contain. Once you've emailed your subscription be sure to check your email regularly for information the mailing list sends to you.

The following Internet sites are excellent places to start searching for mailing lists:

- *Publicly-Accessible Mailing Lists* at URL:
  http://www.neosoft.com/internet/paml/ where you'll find a set of mailing lists accessible to the general public that you can search by category (try the jobs, employment, and career categories).
- *Liszt Directory of E-Mail Discussion Groups* at URL:
  http://www.liszt.com/ where you can search for mailing lists by entering any word or phrase. There are over 67,500 listserv, listproc, majordomo, and independently managed lists at 2,124 sites noted here. This directory is updated weekly.
- *List of Lists* at URL:
  ftp://sri.com/netinfo/ where you should select "interest-group.text" to access the directory of mailing lists.

FTP file transfers

Don't go into a panic when you come upon an Internet address that starts with the letters "ftp." They merely stand for "file transfer protocol," which is just a set of rules, albeit important, that dictate how files are sent and received over the Internet. Just type in the address as you would any other URL.

See page 8 for how to keep current

Bulletin board services

Long before the Internet became a popular source for job hunting in 1995, hundreds of dial-up bulletin board services (BBSs) offered free job and resume databases online. They are not as easy to use as Web sites, but they are free and only require that you have a modem on your computer. You do not use an online service or Internet provider to reach bulletin boards. Instead, you have your modem dial a bulletin board and follow the instructions on the BBS to access any job databases it hosts or submit your vita to any resume banks it runs.

Generally speaking, it is more difficult to contact a BBS and obtain job information from it than it is to reach job sources on the Web. Job database files on many a BBS must be downloaded onto your computer and then expanded before they can be read. Since many of the files you will download have been compressed to reduce their size (and therefore download much more quickly), learn how to "unzip" files and download files via your modem. Try to use the z-modem protocol if possible since it is the fastest, most reliable, and easiest to use. To learn how to operate your modem, do something nobody ever wants to do — read the instructions and practice using it.

A fair number of BBSs appear in the *Non-Profits and Education Job Finder*. Each BBS entry, which always appears under "Job services" or "Job ads," includes the phone number for your modem to dial, the baud rate and other settings for your modem, and the maximum modem speed for connections. We've included how many job vacancies are listed at the BBS whenever we could determine this figure. It would be folly to try to include a complete list of BBSs in a book since they are probably the most volatile group of online career services; many open and close at a rapid rate.

To help you find bulletin board services with job listings on them, take a peek at **Dial Up! Gale's Bulletin Board Locator** (Gale Research, Inc.; available from Planning/Communications' Job Search Resources Catalog at the end of this book) $49, 1,081 pages, published in even-numbered years. For over 10,000 U.S. bulletin board services, you'll get all the information you need to decide which will help you and how to connect: maximum modem speed and settings, special BBS software (if required), contact information (phone, fax, email), membership requirements (if any), target audience, subscription fees (if any), sign-on limits, and a detailed description. Also included is a listing of bulletin boards available through such online services as CompuServe, America Online, Prodigy, DELPHI, and Genie. Listings are arranged by state and alphabetically within area codes. The topic index is divided into 28 categories.

Several of the other resources presented later in this chapter include directories of job-related BBSs that you might wish to consult.

If you skipped it, go back and read Chapter 1 now

Online growing pains

Dave reprinted by permission of Tribune Media Services. Copyright 1996. All rights reserved.

Online growing pains

The Internet can be mighty sluggish! As you use the Internet, you'll come upon many sites that seem to take forever to download onto your computer screen. Far too many Internet sites are built by webmeisters who prefer style over substance. They fill their sites with excessive and complex graphics that make downloading a Web page mighty sluggish. As the Internet matures, site designers will do a better job of balancing snazzy graphics and content so their Web pages will download much more quickly. Until then, be prepared to often hurry up and wait, and wait, and wait some more for all too many Web pages to appear on your computer screen.

Factor in "Internet overload" and you understand the other cause of slow download times. Simply put, too many people are using the Internet during peak times resulting in busy signals when dialing up the Internet or your online service, slow download times, and frequent disconnections. It has been particularly bad with some online services that advertised aggressively for new users, but lacked the capacity to handle all the calls. Some industry insiders believe the Internet will collapse from its mounting traffic. For both sides of the story, see the October 1996 issue of the magazine *PC World*, pages 145 to 156.

Exciting as all these new Internet job sources are, they come with some pitfalls and growing pains. For example, not all occupations are treated equally on the net. According to Steve Osserman, co–author of *The Guide to Internet Job Searching*, in 1996 sixty percent of the job vacancies posted on the Internet were for technical jobs (computer, engineering, science, high technology). These 1996 figures reflect a massive shift from 1994 when 90 percent of the advertised jobs were for technical positions. As time goes by and the technophobia of many professions eases, the number and proportion of nontechnical positions available via the Internet will continue to grow.

Unlike jobs advertised in the print media or on job hotlines, many of the jobs posted on Web sites and with newsgroups are already filled by the time you see them. When an employer has to pay to advertise its vacancies, you can be pretty sure that it will pull its job ad when the position is filled.

See page 8 for how to keep current

But when an employer can simply place a job ad online for free, or when an Internet job site operator lifts job ads from other media and other career sites, job ads often appear long after somebody has been hired. I'm not making this up. At least one operator of a major job database on the Web has told me that his staff rewrites job ads that appeared in newspapers — and he's not alone. This practice will continue until the Internet matures and develops into the site for commerce that so many pundits anticipate will happen.

Many Internet job sources are not going to remain free to job seekers. As we near the next millennium, the great legend of the Internet is that it gives away information for free. If the Internet continues to turn into a commercial medium, that generosity will cease. Businesses are not flocking to the Internet out of the goodness of their hearts. They intend to make a profit from their sites. So far, the most lucrative use of Web sites has been to sell advertising on the sites. That's why so many of the job locations you will visit include ads, often for products completely unrelated to the job hunt. A small, but growing number of job and resume databases on the Web already charge job seekers a fee. If they can make a profit, this practice will spread. Much as we may love the freeness (pun intended) of the Internet, that will not last forever once the lords of commerce put on the squeeze.

Offline resources for your online job search

To make room for the 2,222 job resources described in the *Non-Profits and Education Job Finder*, I had to make this chapter only a crash course on how to use the Internet. If you want to learn more about using the Internet in your job search, here some resources that do a great job of teaching newcomers how to use the Internet and all its components in their job quest. Because these books are often hard to find in bookstores, they are included in Planning/Communications' catalog at the end of this book.

How to Get Your Dream Job Using the Web (Coriolis Group Books; available from the Job Search Resources Catalog at the end of this book) $34.99, 400 pages, 1997. This book is the perfect supplement to the *Non-Profits and Education Job Finder* for anyone who wants to conduct a full-fledged online job search. Probably the single best book that focuses strictly on the electronic job search, this new edition offers a great introduction to using the Internet that is actually understandable to people who have a life. It even helps you intelligently choose an Internet provider (included is an extensive directory of providers). In addition to offering an abundance of Internet job resources, it also presents details on job bulletin board services and how to use them. The authors Shannon Bounds Karl and Arthur Karl show the computer illiterate how to create an effective electronic resume, successfully network on the Internet, and create your own home page to market yourself to employers. The free CD-ROM that

If you skipped it, go back and read Chapter 1 now

comes with the book overflows with incredible resources including direct links to Internet sites, job hunting software, shareware and free programs you can use to create your own home page, and software for handling email.

The Guide to Internet Job Searching (VGM Career Horizons; available from Planning/Communications' catalog at the end of this book) $12.95, 213 pages, 1996. This is the widely–hailed basic guide written by Steve Osserman, Margaret Riley, and Frances Roehm. It includes a good explanation of how to connect to the Internet and instructions for posting a resume electronically, as well as extensive listings of Internet sites with job ads and resume databases. It also offers a thorough directory of bulletin board services that offer job listings and a useful chapter on online career development sites. It includes an entire chapter on non–profits.

Net Jobs: Use the Internet to Land Your Dream Job (Michael Wolf & Company Publishing; available from Planning/Communications' catalog at the end of this book) $20.00, 284 pages, 2nd edition, 1997. This handy book offers descriptions of a ton of Internet sites where you can find job listings, resume databases, and directories of non–profit organizations and schools of all types. It also includes information about Internet sites that help you with assessing your career goals, planning your career, career counseling services, preparing an electronic resume, preparing for interviews, and researching non–profits and schools. There's a lot of substance here in a compact book.

Electronic Job Search Revolution (John Wiley & Sons; available from Planning/Communications' catalog at the end of this book) $12.95, 183 pages, 1995. Joyce Lain Kennedy and Thomas Morrow provide the "intellectual" framework for online job market and application process. This book is particularly useful for learning the underpinnings of online resume and job databases plus online interviewing. It differs from all the others by really explaining how employers use these online tools to make hiring decisions. It includes a good glossary of terms used in the electronic job search world. Although it introduces you to relatively few online resources, it does a great job of explaining how to effectively use the different online job–search resources.

Hook Up, Get Hired! (John Wiley & Sons; available from Planning/Communications' catalog at the end of this book) $12.95, 250 pages, 1995. Joyce Lain Kennedy moves beyond her *Electronic Job Search Revolution* book to offer more hands on, practical advice for using the Internet in your job search. Filled with information on specific Web sites, newsgroups, and bulletin board services, this book covers the online job search gamut and is right on target for job seekers who don't want to read a 400–page book.

Electronic online resumes. The electronic resume you submit online or mail in for scanning should be quite different than your printed resume. You suddenly have to switch from using certain verbs to nouns to

See page 8 for how to keep current

convey your qualifications — "keywords" are what count. You no longer use bold face and snazzy designs to attract attention — only the words matter when your resume turns electronic. Two books offer valuable advice and practical examples of how to make this transition to the electronic resume.

Electronic Resumes (McGraw Hill; available from Planning/Communications' catalog at the end of this book) $19.95, 255 pages plus 3.5-inch Windows™ disk, 1996. Going beyond any other book about online resumes, authors James and Wayne Gonyea walk you through the steps of converting your print resume to electronic format, how to distribute it to resume banks, and how to submit directly to employers who are advertising vacancies online. In addition, they explain in considerable detail how to use the free software that comes with the book to create an online multimedia resume complete with graphics and sound. Over 100 pages of sample electronic resumes and cover letters are included.

Electronic Resume Revolution (John Wiley & Sons; available from Planning/Communications' catalog at the end of this book) $12.95, 228 pages, 1995. Kennedy and Morrow team up again to present everything you need to know about preparing an electronic resume and how to use it effectively. It includes 30 sample resumes transformed into electronic vitae.

Launching pads for your online job search

When you take your job hunt online, you'll quickly discover that you could easily spend forever in cyberspace discovering new job sites through the links that many job sites offer to other sites. If you follow these links over a few weeks, you'll also realize that the number of Internet job sites is growing rather rapidly and these sites frequently change their content and appearance. There's simply no way that any book can keep current with all the changes in Internet job resources.

Planning/Communications maintains a free *Update Sheet* for the *Non-Profits and Education Job Finder* to apprise you of changes we discover in the online and offline job sources described in this book. As explained on page eight, you can always obtain this *Update Sheet* by sending a stamped, self-addressed envelope to Planning/Communications. You can also view these updates sheets online on our Web site at URL: **http://jobfinders online.com**. Be sure to select the *Update Sheet* for the *Non-Profits and Education Job Finder,* 1997–2000.

Gateway sites and meta-lists. There are, however, a number of other resources you can use to keep abreast of the latest changes in online job resources: gateway sites and meta-lists. These extraordinary Web locations include links to an incredible array of the same kinds of online job resources featured in this book. Many of them serve as "gateways" that open the door to other Internet sites through the extensive set

If you skipped it, go back and read Chapter 1 now

Launching pads for your online job search 33

of links they offer. To keep this book affordable, we had to make some tough choices of what to include. So some favorite sites of experienced web surfers probably did not make it into this book. However, the gateway sites and meta-lists offered in this chapter will connect you to virtually every site we could not include here. Use them prudently. It is very easy to spend hours wandering through the links these sites offer.

You should also use these gateway sites and meta-lists to identify online job sites that have appeared since the *Non-Profits and Education Job Finder* went to press, as well as Internet sites that added education positions and jobs with non-profits to their coverage after this book was printed.

Like most Internet job sites, the sites described in this chapter focus primarily on the private sector. However, the ones cited here also include non-profit organizations or educational institutions at all levels. Also note that many of these sites also feature their own job or resume banks and/or directories of non-profits or schools. Several key gateway sites that focus solely on non-profits or education are featured in the next chapter; in Chapter 10, "Education;" and in Chapter 30, the state-by-state chapter.

There is no separate chapter in this book devoted solely to the online job resources. Instead they are mixed with the offline sources throughout this book to encourage you *not* to rely solely on the Internet. As explained in Chapter 1, your chances of getting hired are greatly increased when you conduct a savvy, full-fledged job search that utilizes at least three or four of the different types of job sources, not just the Internet.

Since the quality of online job resources varies so widely, the first resource offered below helps you narrow your online job search by evaluating these online job sites.

Internet Jobs Kit (DataTech Software; available from Planning/Communications' catalog at the end of this book for $38.95) $49.95/retail, CD-ROM for Windows™ 3.1 or higher. This remarkable CD-ROM is filled with reviews of over 1,500 Internet job sites of all types. You can easily and quickly identify Internet sites that have job ads for your discipline and geographic area. Each site is rated for usefulness. Since this software works with any Internet browser, you can go directly to a site you want to see. You are entitled to 60 days of free updates that you can download from DataTech's own Web site. This CD-ROM will essentially help save you time (and money) by enabling you to quickly identify Internet job sites that focus on your profession. By rating the sites, it will also help steer you to those that are most helpful.

Jobs in Higher Education is an Internet site that goes far beyond education. Go to URL: **http://volvo.gslis.utexas.edu/~acadres/jobs/index.html** where you are linked to the home pages of over 30 professional associations with job listings, Web sites of periodicals with job openings in education, sites of academic job banks, and home pages with job listings for individual colleges and universities. The site also links you to sources of jobs in student affairs, Web sites for several publications that feature ads

See page 8 for how to keep current

from employers who seek to be inclusive in their hiring practices, and several major Internet sources of job openings in the non–profit sector. This is a great gateway site for academics as well as those who wish to work for professional associations.

Nonprofit Resources Catalog (Phillip A. Walker) free. This Interent site offers links to over 2,570 other Web sites related to non–profits. Go to URL: **http://www.clark.net/pub/pwalker/** where you can choose from a dozen or so broad categories. To find links to over 20 Web sites related to jobs with non–profits, pick "General Nonprofit Resources" and then select "Jobs." From the home page click on "Fundraising and Giving" to reach links to scores of foundations plus several online directories of foundations.

Meta–Index for Nonprofit Organizations (Philanthropy Journal; email: sbailey@nando.net) free. Go to Internet URL: **http://www.philanthropy–journal.org** and select "Meta–Index of Nonprofits." Here you will find links to other general lists of non–profit organizations; links to Web sources of information about non–profit organizations and activists; links to sites dealing with human rights, civil liberties and politics, health and human services, and environmental issues and animal rights.

JobHunt located at URL: **http://www.job–hunt.org** continues to blow me away with its extraordinarily comprehensive collection of links to hundreds upon hundreds of job sites of all types on the Internet. It would take several pages to really describe everything that is here. Visit this site today to get a good idea of all that the Internet offers job seekers.

The Riley Guide situated at URL: **http://www.jobtrak.com/jobguide** offers an extensive set of links to other job sites on the Internet including perhaps the very best set of links to online job sites for individual states.

Where to find the different Internet job sources in the chapters that follow

If an online site includes only a job database, it is listed under "Job ads." If the site includes a job database plus a resume bank, directory, and/or salary survey, it is located under "Job services." An Internet site with a resume bank plus any other services will be found under "Job services." A site that includes only a directory, appears under "Directories." A site with just a salary survey is found under "Salary surveys."

What's not included in this book. Online career sites that only offer advice on the job search or on choosing or advancing in your career are *not* included in the *Non–Profits and Education Job Finder*. To be included in this book, an online site must offer at least a job or resume database, a directory of governments, a salary survey, or links to other sites that offer these features.

If you skipped it, go back and read Chapter 1 now

Launching pads for your online job search

Internet Job Surfer located at URL: **http://www.eng.rpi.edu/dept/cdc/jobsurfer/joba.html** is a straightforward alphabetical listing of links to job databases, resume databases, and other services for human resources. It includes links to a plethora of job services. It's an excellent place to quickly find links to new and obscure job sources on the Internet.

Career Resource Center (CRC, Suite 147, 2508 Fifth Ave., Seattle, WA 98121; phone: 206/233–8672) free. Go to Internet URL: **http://www.careers.org** where you can choose between "Jobs Available," "Employer Sites," "Regional Pages," "Career Reference," and a few other categories. This may be the motherload of all Internet job search resources with over 10,000 links with Internet newsgroups, online job and resume databases, online job-matching services, employer job listing pages and home pages, state employment services, directories of companies, and much much more. Online sources of internships are also included. We would need several pages to list all the types of job-search resources listed at this site, so just go here and use this site as a springboard for your Internet job search.

Elsewhere in this book we note that many colleges and universities offer very useful career services to their alumni. Use the *Career Resource Center's* extensive links to college alumni associations to find your school's alumni office and its services you can use.

America's Employers (Career ReloCorp, 630 Third Ave., New York, NY 10017; phone: 212/681–6800) free. This Internet site offers extensive links to a multitude of job sites on the Internet. Go to URL: **http://americasemployers.com** and select from a list of "rooms" to access the type of job sources you want. "Professional Academic Openings" gets you the sites where positions at colleges and universities are advertised. There are also choices for "Medical and Legal Positions," "Jobs for Engineers and Scientists," "Job Postings by Government Agencies," and "International Assignments," as well as "Advertised Positions" which gets you to links to job and resume databases including ones posted by individual companies. You can also find links to newsgroups where many jobs are listed.

Back in the "rooms," you can also find links to "Recruiters" to access employment agencies and executive recruiting firms; "Company Databases" you can search by industry, location, and name (updated weekly); "Entrepreneurial Options" where you'll find links to business and franchise offerings; "Networking;" and "Resume Bank." All in all, this is quite an extraordinary place with which to start or expand an electronic job search.

Career Mosaic (Bernard Hodes Advertising) is an incredibly extensive site at which to enrich your online job search. Go to Internet URL: **http://www.careermosaic.com/cm/** and choose "J.O.B.S. Database" or "CareerMosaic J.O.B.S." to search through thousands of job ads. You can search by job title, city, state, and/or zip code. To place your electronic resume online here for free, choose "Resume/CM."

See page 8 for how to keep current

This ever-expanding site is a great place to find links to newsgroups where 57,000 jobs are claimed to be posted daily. CareerMosaic's index of these newsgroups is updated daily. To get to the newsgroup index, select "USENET jobs.offered" or simply go directly to URL: **http://www.career mosaic.com/cm/usenet.html**. You can search by keyword and/or location. Follow the instructions presented at the site. These newsgroups are for specific metropolitan areas or for states, for specific occupations within a metropolitan area, for specific occupations throughout the U.S., and for foreign countries. They are a rich source of job postings, albeit little is known about how many people actually get jobs via these listings.

To find links to the home pages of hundreds of major employers where jobs may be advertised, select "Employer Profiles." For job listings specifically in the health care industry, select "The Health Care Connection."

JobWeb™ and the *Catapult on JobWeb*™ (National Association of Colleges and Employers, 62 Highland Ave., Bethlehem, PA 18017; phones: 800/544–5272, 610/868–1421) free. Go to Internet URL: **http://www.job web.org** where you will find a rich variety of offerings. To access the job database, click on "Jobs." Next choose "Job Postings." You can limit your search to "internships or co-op opportunities." You search by keyword and state, national, or international. You can alternatively select "Employer Directory" to search an extensive listing of employers by keyword, state(s), nationally, or internationally.

There's much more here. To access an abundance of links to job resources on the Internet, go to URL: **http://www.jobweb.org/catapult/catapult.htm** where you'll find the "Table of Contents," which is filled with great links to Internet employment centers and a wealth of Internet job resources. One of the most valuable links appears, oddly enough, under "Business Sites on the Web." There you will find "JobWeb's Database of U.S. School Districts," which is a searchable database of 16,588 elementary and secondary school districts throughout the U.S.

American Society for Agricultural Engineers Home Page offers links to over 175 job sites on the Internet including job and resume databases as well as specific non-profit agencies and schools with job sites. These linked sites are great resources for all job seekers, not just agricultural engineers. Go to URL: **http://asae.org/** and select "Employment" and then browse through "Other Sources of Employment."

Quintessential Career and Job–Hunting Resources Guide links you to a veritable ton of other Internet job sites. Go to URL: **http://www.stetson .edu/~hansen/career.html** and select "Lots of Career Links" which does exactly what its name implies. You'll find links to Web sites, each of which connects you to other job sites.

If you skipped it, go back and read Chapter 1 now

Launching pads for your online job search

Emory Colossal List of Career Links is an Internet site that offers a surfeit of links to Internet job sites. Go to Internet URL: **http://www.emory.edu/CAREER/Links.html** where you'll find commentary on favorite sites and links to many more career sites. This is another great place to start an Internet job search and to keep your Internet job search sites current.

Advancing Women located at URL: **http://www.advancingwomen.com** features a job database. Pick "Women and Workplace Strategies," then choose "Career Resources and Job Search," and then select "Employment, Jobs and Careers" to access the job database plus links to other job sites and networking contacts.

What Color is Your Parachute: Job Hunting Online is an Internet site offered by the *Washington Post* at URL: **http://washingtonpost.com/parachute** where *Parachute* author Richard Bolles offers extensive lists of links to job-search sites on the Internet. His listings include sites like those mentioned in this chapter that are gateway sites, sites that will refer you to lots of other job-search Internet locations. He also includes a lengthy list of vacancy or job-listing sites. Also included is a list of links to resume banks and sites that help you write your electronic resume. He also includes sites for networking purposes and sites where you can obtain information about potential employers. Career counseling sites are also listed.

College Grad Job Hunter offers online job-search advice geared toward college students and recent graduates. Located at URL: **http://www.collegegrad.com.** It includes a job database with over 100 positions that you can browse or search by keyword or job title. Select "Job Postings" and then enter your keyword to search or pick "View All Employment Ads." Includes links to lots of job-related Internet sites. This site is closely related to Brian Krueger's incredibly thorough guide to the job search, *College Grad Job Hunter*, ($14.95, 340 pages, 1997, available from Planning/Communications' catalog at the end of this book).

Kaplan Career Center is a strong resource center for job seekers located at URL: **http://www.kaplan.com/career**. The resume database can be accessed by selecting "Resumes and Cover Letters" and then picking "Career/NET: Multimedia Resources." Choosing "Classifieds" gets you to links to many sites of job databases as well as links to advice on interviewing, preparing resumes, and other job search sites.

Portland State University Career Center offers links to numerous sites where internships are posted. Go to Internet URL: **http://www-adm.pdx.edu/user/carc/** and click on "Internship Information." You'll also find links to other sites where job vacancies are posted.

See page 8 for how to keep current

Chapter 3

General job sources

    This chapter reports on the job–hunting tools with a national scope that cover more than a single occupation in education and the rest of the non–profit sector. For job sources that focus on individual disciplines such as the arts, association management, education, health care, housing, museums, religion, social services, and dozens of other specialties — and their related technical, trades, labor, and office support positions — see chapters 4 through 29. Because so many of these specialities overlap, cross references are made to related fields and to specific job sources described elsewhere in the *Non–Profits and Education Job Finder*. For the fields that do not have helpful job aids focusing on them alone, job openings can be found in the general periodicals and other job resources listed in this chapter. Also, be sure to consult the Index for references to the specialties that interest you. Chapter 30 gives you job resources for each state.
    Sorry to keep hounding you, but please do not proceed any further if you have not read chapters 1 and 2 to learn how to use this book most effectively. You will find only a small fraction of the job sources for your occupation if you do not pay careful attention to the first two chapters of this book. For example, you'll be lost trying to find online job services without first reading the explanation in those chapters of which types of Internet services are listed under which headings. There really is a rational method to the madness. In addition, Chapter 2 is filled with details on great "gateway" Internet sites from which to begin an online job search as well as sites where you can keep updated on new online job services made

General job sources

available after this book was written. Reading those chapters before you go any further is so important that the footers throughout this book will remind to you read them first.

For some fields, the best job sources that include jobs with non-profits and educational institutions are those that focus on private sector jobs or government positions. In those instances, you will be referred to one or both of the companion books to this volume, the *Professional's Job Finder,* which covers the private sector, or the *Government Job Finder.* For your convenience, they are available from the Job Search Resources Catalog at the end of this book. The job sources described in these two companion books include some education, research, and non-profit positions in addition to private sector or government positions.

General job sources

How to proceed. The job-finding resources described in this chapter are broad in scope. Each one covers either the whole gamut of the non-profit sector or a wide variety of non-profit or education disciplines. As noted in chapters 1 and 2, you should examine these first to see which of them would help your job search. Some of these sources include openings for office support jobs, labor, trades, and technical positions.

Under the "Directories" heading you will find a number of directories of professional associations. Since the vast majority of these organizations are non-profit in nature, you may want to also use these directories to identify specific associations as potential employers.

After examining the job sources in this chapter, you should see the more narrowly-focused sources in the chapters that follow. Also be sure to look in the Index at the end of this book to find job sources in an occupation that are not listed where you would intuitively expect to find them.

Job ads

Community Jobs (ACCESS: Networking in the Public Interest, Suite 838, 1001 Connecticut Ave., NW, Washington, DC 20036; phone: 202/785-4233) monthly, individuals: $25/three-month subscription, $39/six-months, $69/annual, $6/single issue; also available at bookstores. Each issue lists about 100 to 250 job vacancies and internships in the non-profit world. A regional biweekly edition for New York and New Jersey, and one for the District of Columbia are each available for additional $5 for every three months; see the entries for the appropriate states in Chapter 30. It is possible that this valuable periodical will have changed its name by the time you read this. We'll announce any name change in the *Update Sheet* to this book. See page 8 for details on how to keep current.

Jump start your job quest by reading chapters 1 and 2 first

The Chronicle of Philanthropy (P.O. Box 1989, Marion, OH 43305; phones; 800/347–6969, 202/466–1032) 24 issues/year, $67.50/annual subscription, $36/six–month subscription. The "Professional Opportunities" section advertises 60 to 90 job openings in all aspects of the non–profit and education worlds, from grant writers to CEOs. Also included is a section filled with new grants listed by foundation (includes address and phone) which you can use to identify foundations at which you may wish to work or from which you may wish to seek a grant. You can also use this list to identify non–profit organizations receiving these grants for which you may wish to work. Each issue also includes an extensive "Directory of Services" filled with ads from companies for which you may wish to work.

The NonProfit Times (Suite 318, 240 Cedar Knolls Rd., Cedar Knolls, NJ 07927; phone: 201/734–1700) monthly, $59/annual subscription (U.S.), $89/Canada, $129/elsewhere, free/qualified full–time non–profit executives, write for qualification form. "The National NonProfit Employment Marketplace" carries 20 to 30 ads for all sorts of positions with non–profits, particularly administrative. Go to the Web site at URL: **http://www.nptimes.com/** for a host of valuable links to other non–profits.

Nonprofit Jobs will offer a database of jobs with non–profit organizations once it's operational. It may be running by the time you read this. Go to URL: **http://www.nonprofitjobs.com/** to check it out.

Good Works offers a job database on the Internet. Go to URL: **http://www.essential.org** and click on "Good Works Job Search" which will allow you to see job vacancies by state. The number of jobs advertised varies widely by state. On the day you connect, some states may have no jobs listed.

Human Services & Liberal Arts Careers (KB Enterprise/NHSE, 13137 Penndale Ln., Fairfax, VA 22033; phone: 703/378–0439) weekly, $42/six consecutive issues, $45/six issues every other week, $60/12 consecutive issues, $65/12 issues every other week; contact for rates for longer periods of time. From 250 to 330 short descriptions of job openings appear in every issue. The jobs listed are paid ads from employers, come from the Sunday edition of leading newspapers across the country, and Internet postings. While more than 80 percent of the job vacancies are in social services, there is a sprinkling of teaching, media, health care, administrative, and other positions for which a liberal arts background is appropriate. A good number of the jobs are in the non–profit sector.

The Employment Review (Recourse Communications, Suite 1600, 1655 Palm Beach Lakes Blvd., West Palm Beach, FL 33401; phone: 407/686–6800) monthly, $13.95/six–issue subscription, $24.95/annual subscription, $3.50/single issue. Hundreds of jobs are advertised under the categories: professional, health care, general, and engineering. The most ads are in engineering and health care. A moderate number of these positions are in the non–profit sector. You can see these job ads on Recourse Communications' job database on the Internet at URL: **http://www.bestjobsusa.com**.

No photocopying please

General job sources

National Business Employment Weekly (84 Second Ave., Chicopee, MA, 01020; phones: 800/562–4868, 413/592–7761) weekly, $35/eight–week subscription, $52/12–weeks, $112/26 weeks, $199/annual subscription, $3.95/single issue; available at newspaper stands and bookstores. Forty or so ads for middle to senior level positions in the non–profit sector appear in a special section in the first and third issue each month. Hundreds more positions for professionals and managers in the private sector also appear in each issue.

The Black Collegian (Black Collegiate Services, 140 Carondelet St., New Orleans, LA 70130; phone: 504/821–5694) semiannual, $8/annual subscription (U.S.), $14/Canada, $16/elsewhere. The annual jobs issue published in February includes advertisements for 50 to 150 professional positions under "JASS" and in display ads throughout the magazine.

To find job sources that have moved...

With a little sleuthing you can usually track down any job source that has moved or changed its phone number. First, be sure to visit our Web site at URL: **http://jobfindersonline.com** to check our latest *Update Sheet* to see if we've posted any changes. If we don't have the change posted there, here's how to track down changes yourself.

If you wrote to the job source, call it just in case it kept the same phone number when it moved. If that number has been disconnected and no forwarding number is given, see if your local library has a phone directory for the city in which the job source was last located, or call directory assistance for that city (area code + 555–1212). Another possibility is that the area code has changed. Check with the operator for any new area codes or visit Internet URL: **http://www.555–1212.com** where they keep track of area code changes.

If that doesn't work, see your library's directories of periodicals, online services, and/or associations which give addresses and phone numbers. Several of these directories are described in this chapter under "Directories."

If you still can't find the new address or phone number, you can use the ***Reader Feedback Form*** to let us know. Write to us or send us an email at our Web site. We will find out what happened to the job source, and send you the new information.

One request: When you do find a new address or phone number, please use the *Reader Feedback Form* or use our Web site to let us know about the change so we can put it in the next *Update Sheet* (see Chapter 1) and post it on our Web site to help your fellow job seekers.

Jump start your job quest by reading chapters 1 and 2 first

Job Recorded Bulletin (Job Opportunities for the Blind, 1800 Johnston St., Baltimore, MD 21230; phones: 410/659–9314, 800/638–7518) six issues/year, free to U.S. residents who are legally blind. Designed for people who are blind and persons who assist them, this service will not only send you a voice recorded job bulletin on a 90–minute cassette tape that describes a moderate number of jobs with non–profit organizations each issue (whatever they can fit into 15 or more minutes of time), it will also teach job hunting skills, make you aware of other jobs blind persons are performing, help you network with blind people who are presently working, and help to make direct matches through its office.

Careers and the disABLED (Equal Opportunity Publications, Suite 200, 1160 Jericho Turnpike, Huntington, NY 11743; phone: 516/421–9421) quarterly, $8/annual prepaid subscription. Over 40 display ads throughout this magazine feature positions for college graduates from employers who certify they are equal opportunity employers who will hire people who have disabilities.

Employment Resources for People with Disabilities is an Internet site filled with links to other Web sites that have jobs advertised from employers who do not discriminate against individuals who have disabilities. Go to URL: **http://wwww.disserv.stu.umn.edu/TC/Grants/COL/listing/disem/** where you will find these links. You'll also uncover direct links to companies that hire people with disabilities.

Equal Opportunity (Equal Opportunity Publications, Suite 200, 1160 Jericho Turnpike, Huntington, NY 11743; phone: 516/421–9421) three issues/year, $13/annual subscription, free to minority college graduates and professionals. Over 25 display ads throughout this magazine feature positions in all areas.

The Nation (P.O. Box 37072, Boone, IA 50037; phone: 800/333–8536) weekly, $52/annual subscription (U.S.), $70/foreign. Ads for jobs with left–leaning non–profits dominate the half dozen or so job ads under "Classified–Positions Available."

Roll Call (Roll Call Inc., 900 Second St., NE, Washington, DC 20002; phone: 202/289–4900) twice weekly, $225/annual subscription. Among the 30 to 40 job ads under "Roll Call Classifieds—Employment," are positions with non–profit organizations, political organizations, and private industry that require a knowledge of politics and Capitol Hill: lobbyists, government affairs/relations directors, legislative assistants, administrative assistants/executive secretaries, press directors, etc.

Job services

Non–Profit Organization Search (ACCESS: Networking in the Public Interest, Suite 838, 1001 Connecticut Ave., NW, Washington, DC 20036; phone: 202/785–4233) $30. You specify up to four regions, states, or cities you

No photocopying please

General job sources

prefer and which of 23 job categories interest you. ACCESS searches its extensive database of non-profit organizations to find up to 100 that meet your criteria. The report you get gives the name, address and phone number for each organization along with a description of it. While this service doesn't direct you to organizations that necessarily have current job openings, it does enable you to identify organizations for which you may wish to work so you can set up informational interviews and contact them to learn about future openings.

Here's everything you need to know to use this service. Send ACCESS your check and the following information: your name, address, and phone number; and the geographic areas you want searched: up to four cities, regions, and/or states. Then specify which of the following organizational focus categories you want included in your search (give them the code letter for each one): A–Arts, culture, humanities; B–Education; C–Environmental; D–Animal related; E–Health (general and rehabilitative); F–Health (mental health, crisis); G–Health (diseases, disorders, medical discipline and support organizations); H–Health (diseases, disorders, medical disciplines–research); I–Crime and delinquency prevention; J–Employment/jobs; K–Food, nutrition, agriculture; L–Housing/shelter; M–Public Safety, emergency relief; N–Recreation; O–Youth development; P–Human services; Q–International/Foreign; R–Civil rights, social action, advocacy; S–Community improvements and building; T–Philanthropy and volunteerism; U–Research, science, planning, technology; V–Social sciences; W–Public policy, government agencies, consumer protection; X–Religion and spiritual development; Y–Mutual/membership benefit organizations.

Public Allies Program (Public Allies, Suite 330, 1511 K St., NW, Washington, DC 20005; phone: 202/638–3300) free. The idea behind this service is to make it financially feasible for young adults, particularly from non-wealthy households, to pursue a career in the non-profit sector. Applications are available each year beginning in February and are due by May 1. The program has over 130 participants, called "Allies," ages 18 to 30. Stipends average $13,000 to $15,000 plus benefits for ten months of service. Allies are placed in ten-month paid apprenticeships, beginning each September, at non-profits and government agencies that work on everything from school reform to gang prevention to economic development. One day each week, Allies receive intensive skills and leadership training. During the second half of the apprenticeship, teams of Allies tackle specific local issues.

Community Career Center (Enterprise Inc., Suite L345, 2160 W. Charleston, Las Vegas, NV 89102; phone: 702/259–9580) is an Internet site at URL: **http://www.nonprofitjobs.org** where you can select "Search New Job Openings" to access a database of 30+ jobs at all levels with non-profits of all types. You can search by job title, location, keyword, employer, and/or minimum salary. You can place your resume online via email for $25 for six months by selecting "Post New Candidate Profile."

Jump start your job quest by reading chapters 1 and 2 first

Jobs & Careers Online! (1480 Oddstad Dr., Redwood City, CA 94063) free. About ten percent of the jobs advertised at this Internet site are in the non-profit sector. Go to URL: **http://www.servonet.com/temp_jc/JOBS _CAREERS_HOME.html** and click on the "Jobs & Careers Online" button. Then choose between broad occupational groups such as technical, part time, administrative (secretarial, clerical, bookkeeping, office support), medical, financial, sales, management, and general. Once you are in the specialty, you are given an opportunity to email or fax your resume to the operators of this site where it will be kept on file for three months. You will presumably be notified when jobs come in that match your skills.

***E-Span JobSearch*®** (E-Span Employment Advertising Network, Suite 170, 8440 Woodfield Crossing, Indianapolis, IN 46240; phones: 800/682-2901, 317/469-4535) free. Go to Internet URL: **http://www.espan.com/** where you can select "Job Search" to access *E-Span's* extensive job database. You can perform a keyword search of job listings on *E-Span* as well as popular Internet newsgroups. You can place your resume in *E-Span's* resume bank as well as the resume banks of other popular Internet sites — choose "Job Search" and then "Resumes." Click "Jobs by Email" to participate in the free "E-Span Career Mail" service where you'll be sent via email announcements for jobs that fit the criteria you submit. Unlike the vast majority of Internet job services that have sprung up in the past two years, this site is operated by a highly-respected company that has been offering electronic job services for years. It's one of the true pioneers of its genre.

Saludos Web: Careers, Employment & Culture is an Internet site that includes a job database and resume database for employers who openly do not discriminate against people of Hispanic heritage. Go to URL: **http://www.hooked.net/saludos.index.html** and pick "Job Listings" where you can browse through hundreds of job ads (with lots of technical positions) or search by occupation. About ten percent of the positions are in education. You can place your resume in the resume bank for two months by picking 'Resume Pool" and then "Submit Your Resume."

HispanData (Hispanic Business, Suite 300-C, 360 S. Hope Ave., Santa Barbara, CA 93105; phone: 805/682-5843) $25; resume kept on file indefinitely, an update form will be sent to you every six months. Send your check and one copy of your resume to *HispanData*. When a job match is made, you'll be contacted to prescreen the job fit and verify your availability and interest in the position. Jobs filled are generally mid-level professional and managerial positions that require three to five years experience as well as entry level positions. New college graduates must have a B or better grade point average to participate in *HispanData*. Employers include non-profits, government, and private sector companies.

Almanac of Joblines (JOBS by Phone™, Suite 1200, 301 E. Ocean Blvd., Long Beach, CA 90802; phone: 310/434-5627) bimonthly, $24.95/single issue, $69.95/six-month subscription, $119.95/annual subscription. Each issue of this 96-page magazine features detailed information on job

General job sources

hotlines for specific educational and research institutions, medical centers, and major non-profit organizations, although most of the hotlines are for private sector businesses. Unlike other directories of individual job hotlines, this one includes the full address, the name of the person job applicants contact, regular voice and fax numbers, **TDD** number if available, when the job hotline is updated, and the primary standard industrial classification code for the entry. Also included is a state-by-state list of **TDD** relay phone numbers.

The National Job Hotline Directory (McGraw Hill; available from the Job Search Resources Catalog at the end of this book) $14.95, 310 pages, annual. This directory gives you the phone numbers you can call to hear job listings any time for over 6,000 free job hotlines, many of which are job hotlines at major non-profit organizations and educational and research institutions. Hotlines are listed by state and then by type of business or organization. The vast majority of hotlines in this book, however, are for private sector businesses and local governments.

Saluki Job Hotline (Southern Illinois University, Career Services, Woody Hall, Carbondale, IL 62901; phone: 618/453-4571) $16/six-month registration; $26/six-month registration with *Resume Referral Service* described immediately below. Call with your credit card handy to receive your hotline access number so you can listen to this service's 24-hour recording of job openings throughout the country. You can select up to three career codes which give you access to more than 300 jobs in all areas. Updated two or three times per week.

Resume Referral Service (Southern Illinois University, Career Services, Woody Hall, Carbondale, IL 62901; phone: 618/453-2391) $16/six-month registration; $26/six-month registration with *Saluki Hotline* described immediately above. Write for the registration form and submit it with one copy of your resume. Your resume is given to employers for which you meet job requirements. The employer is responsible for contacting you. Most matches are done by computer. You are not able to exclude specific employers from receiving your resume.

4-Sights Network (Upshaw Institute for the Blind, 16625 Grand River, Detroit, MI 48227; phone: 313/272-3900, modem: 313/272-7111) free. This bulletin board service provides information about people who are blind and the careers they pursue so you can identify potential career options. There is a very limited set of job listings for jobs with organizations and educational facilities that serve people with visual impairments. The BBS is oriented toward people who are blind or visually-impaired and to their families and professionals who work with them. It also offers information about advances in computer technology that benefit people with visual impairments.

Jump start your job quest by reading chapters 1 and 2 first

Directories

Good Works: A Guide to Careers in Social Change (Barricade Books; available from the Job Search Resources Catalog at the end of this book) $24, 700 pages, 1994. Describes over 1,000 non–profits that facilitate social change. Each entry tells you to whom to apply for a job, the phone number and address, the staff size and composition, how many job openings are typical each year, salary range, internships, and where it advertises job openings. There's also a directory of "networks:" clearinghouses, action–research projects, and training schools. If you are looking for an employer that offers jobs that will let you help make the world a better place to live, this book is an essential resource.

National Directory of Nonprofit Organizations (Taft Group, 835 Penobscot Bldg., 645 Griswold St., Detroit, MI 48226–4094; phones: 800/877–8238, 313/961–2242) $470, two volumes, 5,876 pages, published each summer. Details are presented on over 256,000 private, non–profit organizations. Each entry includes the name and address, annual income, and activities. Volume one ($305) lists 172,000 organizations with over $100,000 annual income. The second volume ($190) lists 84,000 non–profits with $25,000 to $99,999 annual revenues.

Nonprofit Employer Directory (ACCESS: Networking in the Public Interest, Suite 838, 1001 Connecticut Ave., NW, Washington, DC 20036; phone: 202/785–4233) $42.90, published each April. Lists organizations alphabetically. Each entry includes address, phone, staff size, mission, year funded, executive director, and coded fields.

Internet Nonprofit Center, located at Internet URL: **http://www.non profit.org/** offers a "Nonprofit Locator" that enables you to search its database of over one million (so it claims) tax–exempt organizations in the U.S.A. You can search by keyword and/or state. Once you find an organization that interests you, you'll be given its address and information about its assets and income. Phone numbers are not given. Click on "Organizations" for an alphabetical list of non–profits in this rather extensive online database.

YAHOO! Business and Economy Organizations is a part of the *Yahoo!* search engine site that offers extensive links to the sites of non–profit organizations and to professional associations. Go to Internet URL: **http://www.yahoo.com/Economy/Organizations/**.

YAHOO: Charity is a part of the *Yahoo!* search engine site that offers extensive links to the sites operated by charities. Go to Internet URL: **http://www.yahoo.com/Society_and_culture/Charity/**.

Volunteerism: Organizations, Training, Programs, and Publications (R.R. Bowker; available through Reed Elsevier, P.O. Box 31, New Providence, NJ 07974; phone: 800/521–8110) $119 plus 7 percent shipping, 1,164 pages, 1991. Provides details on over 5,300 volunteer organizations in over 80

No photocopying please

General job sources

The secret route to jobs with non-profits: Volunteering

Ready to work for a non-profit, but not sure what type of non-profit to work for? Try volunteering first. As a volunteer you can get a pretty good idea of what an organization is like, working conditions, and the sort of work you'd perform as an employee. You also get to meet the right people with whom to network. Volunteering also lets you demonstrate your skills and value to the organization so it would have a pretty good idea of how well you would work out as an employee. And as a volunteer, there's a good chance you will learn of a job vacancy before it is made public.

Volunteer opportunities are mentioned in some of the job sources described throughout the *Non-Profits and Education Job Finder*. However, the following resources, one online and one offline, are particularly helpful. You can use them to find volunteer opportunities as well as to identify non-profit organizations for which you may wish to work.

Impact Online (Impact Online, Suite 4, 715 Colorado Ave., Palo Alto, CA 94303; phone: 415/327–1389; email: respond@impactonline.org) free. Go to Internet URL: **http://www.impactonline.org** where you'll find more than just advice about volunteering. If you select "Volunteer America" you will have the opportunity to type in your zip code and select when you'd like to begin your volunteer work (this week, next week, in two weeks, etc.). After clicking on the "Submit" button, you will quickly be given a list of links to organizations with volunteer opportunities that are located within five miles of your zip code. This function originally served only the San Francisco area. As of this writing, it is available for about five metropolitan areas across the U.S.A. By the time you read this, it should cover a lot more areas throughout the country.

All job seekers, however, will want to use the growing directory of non-profit organizations on this site. Select "Listings" which gets you to a directory linking you to over 1,000 non-profits across the country. You can search by name or browse by type of non-profit either geographically or alphabetically. This directory is expected to grow to include over 10,000 non-profits by 1998.

Volunteer America (Ferguson Publishing; available from the Job Search Resources Catalog at the end of this book) $89.95, 600 pages, 1997. This authoritative and comprehensive tome provides information for over 1,450 non-profit organizations that offer volunteer opportunities to adults as well as high school and college students. Each entry includes the organization's purpose, sponsors, contact person and information, and detailed description. Also included is contact information for nearly 500 local volunteer centers across the U.S. where you learn of volunteer opportunities in that geographic area. A list of 12 national organizations with volunteering information also appears. Also featured is a list of the Governor's office in each state that offers support to local volunteer centers and other volunteer groups — offices that can put you in contact with local volunteering opportunities. Geographical and alphabetical indexes.

Jump start your job quest by reading chapters 1 and 2 first

areas, including substance abuse, AIDS, teenage pregnancy, homelessness, environment, literacy, people with disabilities, senior citizens, and physical and mental health. Although this directory's title suggests volunteerism, the organizations it describes generally do have some paid staff to coordinate all the volunteers.

Job Hunter's Sourcebook (Gale Research, Inc., 835 Penobscot Bldg., Detroit, MI 48226–4094; phone: 800/877–4253) $70, 1,100 pages, 1996. This tome lists specialty periodicals that often include help wanted ads; placement and job referral services; employer directories; handbooks and manuals about each profession; employment agencies and search firms; electronic resources; and other leads, primarily associations that don't offer any job services, but that can provide general information about a profession.

This is a good source for identifying job recruiters and executive search firms for the 155 careers into which the book is divided. It also identifies extremely useful books and manuals that will help you learn about a specific field. Unfortunately, when it lists periodicals, it doesn't tell you anything about them except the address and phone number. Many of the periodicals mentioned in this directory do not, and have never, carried job ads.

Directory of Executive Recruiters (Kennedy Publications; available from the Job Search Resources Catalog at the end of this book) $44.95, 688 pages, published every December. Although the vast bulk of the recruiters described in this extensive directory serve the private sector, you'll find close to 200 firms that specialize in recruiting for non–profit, academic, and research positions. Overall this new edition of the most thorough affordable directory of executive recruiters provides full details on over 8,300 recruiters at 3,467 firms throughout the U.S.: full contact information, individual recruiter specialties, description of firm, specific functional areas and industries served, branch offices and contact information, international offices, affiliated firms, lowest salary for positions handled by the firm, and membership in networks of independent recruiting firms. Indexed by 406 recruiter specialties, 61 management functions, 63 industries, location, and key principals. You'll find recruiters that serve non–profits and research and educational institutions under such categories as associations; non–profits; research; fund raisers and other non–profit services; higher education; museums, galleries, music/arts, libraries and information services, membership, and other non–profits; retirement housing; and public affairs. Includes a free PC disk on strategies for working with recruiters. This a good, affordable directory for identifying recruiters that may help your job search.

Directory of Executive Recruiters, Corporate Edition (Kennedy Publications; available from the Job Search Resources Catalog at the end of this book) $149, 1,200 pages, published every January. This expanded version of the *Directory of Executive Recruiters* described immediately above offers

No photocopying please

General job sources   49

much longer descriptions of each recruiting firm. It is available as a Windows™ or DOS database entitled *SearchSelect™* ($195.00, annual) that includes every entry in the printed directory plus 228 executive temporary placement firms. This is a really good directory for identifying recruiting firms that may help your job search.

1997 Guide to Executive Recruiters (John Wiley & Sons; available from the Job Search Resources Catalog at the end of this book) $24.95, 848 pages, 1997. Among the 6,500 executive recruiters are about 30 that specialize in placing professionals with non-profit organizations. Each entry includes contact information, minimum salary of placements, level placed, and recruiting specialty. Includes only recruiters whose fees are paid by the hiring company.

Associations Yellow Book (Leadership Directories, 104 Fifth Ave., 2nd Floor, New York, NY 10011; phone: 212/627-4140) semiannual, 900 pages, $190/annual subscription. Being published twice a year may make this volume the most accurate (and affordable) directory of professional associations with which you could seek a job in the non-profit sector. Includes over 1,175 associations with names of over 45,000 officers, number of employees, publications, and annual budget. Eight indexes.

Encyclopedia of Associations (Gale Research, Inc., 835 Penobscot Bldg., Detroit, MI 48226; phone: 800/877-4253) 4,000 pages in three volumes, published each December, often available at public libraries. Volume 1: *National Organizations of the U.S.*, $460/set of three parts, includes information on 23,000 associations. Each entry includes contact information, the name of the executive director, and information about the association such as the periodicals and directories it publishes. Volume 2: *Geographic and Executive Indexes*, $355, enables you to locate organizations in a particular city and state. Volume 3: *Supplement*, $370, published every August provides full entries on new associations not listed in Volume 1. If your occupation is so obscure that you can't find job sources for it in the *Non-Profits and Education Job Finder,* you should consult the *Encyclopedia of Associations* to see if there are any professional organizations in your field that might offer job services of some sort.

The CD-ROM version is called *Associations Unlimited.* It's a Windows™ program that sells for $1,595 and is updated each May. Included are an *Encyclopedia of Associations Module; Regional, State, and Local Organizations Module; International Organizations Module; Government Nonprofit Module;* and an *Associations Materials Module* that includes full-text reproductions of 2,000 association membership applications.

The *Encyclopedia of Associations* is also available on GaleNet at URL: **http://www.gale.com/gale.html** for a subscription fee. For pricing information, contact Tim Brandner at 800/877-4253, extension 1882.

Asian-Americans Information Directory 1994-95 (Gale Research, Inc., 835 Penobscot Bldg., Detroit, MI 48226-4094; phone: 800/877-4253) $75, 577 pages, 1994. Describes nearly 6,000 national, regional, state, and local

Jump start your job quest by reading chapters 1 and 2 first

organizations, agencies, institutions, programs, and publications concerned with the life and culture of Americans with an Asian heritage. Each entry includes contact person, address, phone, fax, and, usually, a description. This is a good, almost affordable source for identifying non-profit organizations with this specialty for which you may wish to work.

Black Americans Information Directory 1994–95 (Gale Research, Inc., 835 Penobscot Bldg., Detroit, MI 48226–4094; phone: 800/877–4253) $85, 556 pages, 1993. Describes over 5,200 national, regional, state, and local organizations, agencies, institutions, programs, and publications concerned with black or African–American life and culture. Each entry includes contact person, address, phone, fax, and, usually, a description. This is a good, almost affordable source for identifying non–profit organizations with this specialty for which you may wish to work.

Hispanic Americans Information Directory 1994–95 (Gale Research, Inc., 835 Penobscot Bldg., Detroit, MI 48226–4094; phone: 800/877–4253) $85, 515 pages, 1994. Describes over 5,394 national, regional, state, and local organizations, agencies, institutions, programs, and publications concerned with the life and culture of Americans with an Hispanic heritage. Each entry includes contact person, address, phone, fax, and, usually, a description. This is a good, almost affordable source for identifying non–profit organizations with this specialty for which you may wish to work.

Native Americans Information Directory (Gale Research, Inc., 835 Penobscot Bldg., Detroit, MI 48226–4094; phone: 800/877–4253) $85, 371 pages, 1993. Describes nearly 4,500 national, regional, state, and local organizations, agencies, institutions, programs, and publications concerned with Native American life and culture. Each entry includes contact person, address, phone, fax, and, usually, a description. This is a good, almost affordable source for identifying non–profit organizations with this specialty for which you may wish to work.

Women's Information Directory (Gale Research, Inc., 835 Penobscot Bldg., Detroit, MI 48226–4094; phone: 800/877–4253) $75, 763 pages, 1993. Describes nearly 6,000 national, regional, state, and local organizations, agencies, institutions, programs, and publications concerned with women in the United States. Each entry includes contact person, address, phone, fax, and, usually, a description. This is a good, almost affordable source for identifying non–profit organizations with this specialty for which you may wish to work.

Directories in Print (Gale Research, Inc., 835 Penobscot Bldg., Detroit, MI 48226–4094; phone: 800/877–4253) $345, annual, 2,320 pages in two volumes plus the *Supplement,* $235, 122 pages, annual, 650 new entries. Details on 14,900 directories in the U.S. and worldwide. In addition to traditional print directories, this volume tells you about directories published on CD–ROMs, as online databases, diskettes, microfiche, and mailing labels. It's a pretty good source for directories of non–profit organizations.

No photocopying please

General job sources

National Trade and Professional Associations of the United States (Columbia Books, Suite 330, 1212 New York Ave., NW, Washington, DC 20005; phone: 202/898–0662) $80. With information on over 7,250 trade and professional associations, this annual volume enables you to identify any professional associations beyond those included in the *Non–Profits and Education Job Finder.*

State and Regional Associations (Columbia Books, Suite 330, 1212 New York Ave., NW, Washington, DC 20005; phone: 202/898–0662) $65, annual. Gives details on over 7,300 professional associations that operate on the state and regional level.

Washington Information Directory (Congressional Quarterly, Inc., 1414 22nd St., NW, Washington, DC 20037; phones: 800/638–1710, 202/822–1475) $105, 963 pages, June 1996–97 edition. Provides information on many non–profit organizations with national headquarters in the nation's capitol in addition to information about federal government agencies.

Big Book of Opportunities for Women: The Directory of Women's Organizations (Ferguson Publishing; available from the Job Search Resources Catalog at the end of this book) $39.95, 455 pages, 1997. Over 4,000 programs that offer educational and career assistance to women are described in this huge book. Also included are organizations targeted toward members of "minority" groups, women who have disabilities, displaced homemakers, and athletes. There's an extensive directory of national professional, trade, and other organizations, commissions on women, women's colleges, and research organizations as well as directories and periodicals of interest to women. There's a good chance you may find a potential employer among all these listings.

Big Book of Minority Opportunities (Ferguson Publishing, Suite 300, 200 W. Madison, Chicago, IL 60606; phone: 800/306–994) $39.95, 630 pages, 1995. Reports on over 6,000 programs that offer educational and career assistance to people labeled as "minorities." Covers pretty much the same ground as the *Big Book of Opportunities for Women* described immediately above.

The Internship Bible (Princeton Review; available from the Job Search Resources Catalog at the end of this book) $25, 469 pages, published every September. Features half–page descriptions of over 100,000 internship opportunities in virtually every profession, including a good many with non–profit organizations. Each entry includes location, duration, compensation, selectivity, application deadline, perks, and a description of the work.

Internships 1997: The Hot List for Job Hunters (ARCO; available from Job Search Resources Catalog at the end of this book) $19.95, 418 pages, 1997. Author Sara Dulaney Gilbert profiles more than 25,000 internship opportunities. Entire chapters are devoted to internships in the arts, culture and education, environment, health care, public affairs and nonpartisan poli-

Jump start your job quest by reading chapters 1 and 2 first

tics, science and research, social services, and associations. For each internship employer, she offers the number of internships, functions and duties, stipend or pay, academic credits, eligibility requirements, application procedures, full contact information, and more. Also includes internships for people who are members of groups that often face discrimination such as women, minorities, and people with disabilities. Each chapter includes additional sources of internships. Thoroughly indexed.

Internships (Peterson's Guides; available from Job Search Resources Catalog at the end of this book) $24.95, published every October. This 422-page book provides detailed descriptions and application instructions for paid and unpaid internships with over 1,700 organizations and companies, including a good number of non-profits. It includes geographic and alphabetical indexes, and details on regional and national internship clearinghouses.

America's Top Internships (Princeton Review; available from Job Search Resources Catalog at the end of this book) $20, 408 pages, published every November. Furnishes in-depth details on thousands of internship opportunities in non-profits and elsewhere. Each entry includes candid descriptions of the work from past interns, responsibilities, application procedures and deadlines, how many apply and how many are accepted, prerequisites, location, quality of life, and how much busy work you're handed.

The National Directory of Internships (National Society for Experiential Education, Suite 207, 3509 Haworth Dr., Raleigh, NC 27609-7229; phone: 919/787-3263) published in November of odd-numbered years, $29/nonmembers, $23/members, $75/annual membership dues. Lists 28,000 internship opportunities in 75 different fields with chapters on the arts, business, clearinghouses, communications, consumer affairs, education, environment, health, human services, international affairs, museums and history, public interest, sciences, women's issues, and resources for international internships.

The New Careers Directory: Internships in Technology and Social Change (Student Pugwash USA, Suite 814, 815 15th St., NW, Washington, DC 20005; phone: 202/393-6555) $18, $10/students (add $3 shipping). Offers full details on where and how to apply for internships and entry-level jobs with non-profits and government agencies in the environment and energy, development, communications, peace/security, health, law, and general science.

Summer Jobs for Students (Peterson's Guides; available from Job Search Resources Catalog at the end of this book) $16.95, 344 pages, published each November for the following year. Describes over 20,000 summer job openings in the United States and Canada with environmental programs, resorts, camps, amusement parks, expeditions, theaters, national parks, and government. Each detailed employer description includes salary and benefits, employer background, profile of employees, and whom to contact to apply. Includes category, employer, and job title indexes.

No photocopying please

General job sources

Salary surveys

Compensation in Nonprofit Organizations (Abbott, Langer & Associates, 548 First St., Crete, IL 60417; phone: 708/672–4200) Part 1: Professional Societies and Trade Associations, $135; Part 2: Other Types of Nonprofit Organizations: $150; both combined: $225, 1,355 pages, annual. Based on information from 2,099 non–profits for over 45,000 positions in 95 different job categories, this study reports on salaries by type of non–profit organization (association, chamber of commerce, social service, etc.), location, number of employees, annual budget, and more. Eight separate state and regional editions are available ranging from $110 to $150.

Compensation of CEOs in Nonprofit Organizations (Abbott, Langer & Associates, 548 First St., Crete, IL 60417; phone: 708/672–4200) $25, annual. This is a subset of this firm's more extensive report *Compensation in Nonprofit Organizations*.

Nonprofit World Salary Survey (The Society of Nonprofit Organizations, Suite 1, 6314 Odana Road, Madison, WI 53711; phone: 800/424–7367) appears in *Nonprofit World* magazine, usually the May/June issue, $15/single copy. This is a four–page summary of the Abbott, Langer & Associates survey described immediately above.

Innovative Compensation Practices in Nonprofits (Applied Research & Development Institute, Suite 633, 2121 S. Oneida St., Denver, CO 80224; phone: 303/691–6076) $29.95 plus $3.50 shipping, 1995. Provides a detailed study of benefits practices of non–profits, such as bonuses, merit pay, noncash awards, flexible benefit plans, and spending accounts.

The American Almanac of Jobs and Salaries 1997–1998 (Avon Books, available from the Job Search Resources Catalog at the end of this book) $20, 688 pages, published in October of even–numbered years. This is a good general source on salaries. It covers a broad spectrum of careers, including non–profits and education, and salaries for very general categories of non–profit jobs. It is not nearly as detailed as the salary studies conducted by trade and professional organizations.

American Salaries and Wages Survey (Gale Research, Inc., 835 Penobscot Bldg., Detroit, MI 48226–4094; phone: 800/877–4253) $105, 800 pages, published in May of odd–numbered years. Covers more than 4,500 occupational classifications with salary ranges, entry level, highest paid. Figures are derived from more than 300 publications issued by federal, state, and local governments, and professional organizations.

Available Pay Survey Reports: An Annotated Bibliography (Abbott, Langer & Associates, 548 First St., Crete, IL 60417; phone: 708/672–4200) Part 1: U.S. surveys, $450; Part 2: Non–U.S. surveys, $160. Covers over 1,200 individual pay survey reports. Heavily indexed to help you find the specialities that interest you.

Jump start your job quest by reading chapters 1 and 2 first

Chapter 4

Advocacy and organizing

Advocacy and organizing

Also see the entries in the "Housing, planning, development" chapter.

Job ads

Community Jobs (ACCESS: Networking in the Public Interest, Suite 838, 1001 Connecticut Ave., NW, Washington, DC 20036; phone: 202/785–4233) monthly, individuals: $25/three–month subscription, $39/six–month subscription, $69/annual subscription (U.S.). Also available at bookstores. Each issue lists about 100 to 250 positions in the non–profit world, including a good number of organizing jobs. This is probably the single best source of job vacancies for organizers. Regional biweekly editions for New York, New Jersey, and the District of Columbia are available free upon request with subscriptions to *Community Jobs*; see the individual states in Chapter 30.

In These Times (2040 N. Milwaukee Ave., Chicago, IL 60647; phone: 312/772–0100) 26 issues/year, annual subscription: $36.95/individuals (U.S.), $59/institutions, $61.95/Canada, $75.95/elsewhere, $2.50/single issue. Jobs listed under "Classifieds." Publishes ads for five to ten organizing jobs per

Advocacy and organizing

issue. These jobs also appear on the Internet at URL: **http://www.inthesetimes.com**. This site is under construction; it may be operational by now. Check it out.

The Ark (National Organizers Alliance, 715 G St., SE, Washington, DC 20003, phone: 202/543–6603) quarterly, contact for price. Each issue contains about 20 to 25 ads for organizing positions that pay, plus executive positions. These ads are culled from a job list book maintained by the headquarters and which is available for anyone to consult.

Poverty & Race (Poverty & Race Research Action Council, Suite 207, 1711 Connecticut Ave., NW, Washington, DC 20009; phone: 202/387–9887) bimonthly, $25/annual subscription. In the typical issue, a dozen or more organizing and advocacy jobs, including management–level positions, appear under "Job Ops/Fellowships/Grants."

The Nation (P.O. Box 37072, Boone, IA 50037; phone: 800/333–8536) weekly, $52/annual subscription (U.S.), $70/foreign. Ads for jobs with left–leaning non–profits dominate the four or five job ads under "Classified–Positions Available."

The Village Voice (VV Publishing, 36 Cooper Sq., New York, NY 10003; phone: 800/857–2997) weekly on Wednesday, $53/annual subscription (U.S.), $87/foreign; $2.25/single issue at bookstores and newsstands. The "Classifieds" section includes ads for organizing positions from across the country, not just New York.

Non–Violent Activist (War Resisters League, 339 Lafayette St., New York, NY 10012; phone: 212/228–0450) six issues/year, $15/annual subscription, $30/foreign. "Activist News–Job Openings" has just one or two vacancies an issue, sometimes none. Includes lobbyist positions.

Job service

Union Jobs Bank (Union Job Bank, P.O. Box 511, Dayton, NJ 08810) free. This is a resume service that acts as a jobs clearinghouse for persons who are looking for work in union organizing. Send your resume and a cover letter to UJB, and it will make it available to unions upon request that are looking for organizers. The union will contact you directly.

Directories

Charities USA is a gateway Internet site where you will find many advocacy and organizing groups among the 400 links to charitable organizations here. Go to URL: **http://www.charitiesusa.com/**, and select among the following: Animal, Children, Christian Services, Conservation & Preservation, Education, Health, Human & Civil Rights, Human Service, Medical Research, Military & Veterans, Women, and World Service.

We advocate reading chapters 1 and 2 first

Alternative Press Index (Alternative Press Center, P.O. Box 33109, Baltimore, MD 21218; phone: 410/243–2471) annual subscription: $50/individuals and movement groups, $225/institutions. Many of the "alternative" or "progressive" periodicals identified in this index carry ads or announcements for organizing positions. Contact for details.

Directory of U.S. Labor Organizations (Bureau of National Affairs, BNA Books, P.O. Box 7814, Edison, NJ 08818; phone: 800/960–1220) $55 plus $6/shipping, 118 pages, annual. Includes the name, address, phone, and fax number for officers and key staffers of the nation's labor unions and labor publications. Includes state federations and local offices.

American Directory of Organized Labor (Gale Research, Inc., 835 Penobscot Bldg., Detroit. MI 48226–4094; phone: 800/877–4253) $275, 1,638 pages, 1992. Details over 225 national unions as well as almost 40,000 independent, regional, state, and local unions, including the growing sector of government and education unions. Great source to identify potential employers and learn more about them.

HungerWeb is an Internet directory of advocacy and organizing groups who work to relieve hunger and aid the poor. Go to URL: **http://www.hunger.brown.edu/hungerweb/**, and select from two directories: "Advocacy and Policy" will give you the home pages of the foremost advocacy groups on hunger–related issues, and "Field Work" will give you the home pages for nongovernmental organizations (NGOs) that work to relieve hunger among the needy. NGOs are listed geographically into North American, International, and Third World categories.

Directory of Partners (Alliance for National Renewal Partners, Suite 300, 1445 Market St., Denver, CO 80202–1728; phone: 303/571–4343) is an Internet directory and collection of links of non–profit organizations dedicated to renewal of the community. There's a wide range of groups here, many of them involved in advocacy and organization, for such areas as government improvement, prevention of drug abuse, education, economic development, combating racial injustice, and developing affordable housing. Go to URL: **http://www.ncl.org/anr/**, and select "Directory of Partners" for an alphabetical list of members, which you access by clicking on the letters of the alphabet graphic. The directory supplies street and email addresses, phone and fax numbers, and key contact names, and if an entry is underlined, it is linked to its home page.

Left Links (Democratic Socialists of America, 180 Varick St., New York, NY 10014; phone: 212/727–8610) is an Internet site with links that, despite its name, covers a wide spectrum of advocacy and organizing groups. Go to URL: **http://www.dsausa.org/**, and select "Left Links," which will give you an array of other link categories: "Left Meta–Sites," "Meta–Political Sites," "Labor Movement," "The Right," "Democratic Party," among others. Skip the really far–out fringe sites and you can find a lot of useful contacts here.

Please, no photocopying

Chapter 5

Agriculture

Agriculture

*Also see entries in the "Environment" and "Forestry and horticulture" chapters. For many more job sources for private sector and government positions, see the **Professional's Job Finder** and **Government Job Finder** respectively.*

Job ads

Agronomy News (American Society of Agronomy, 677 S. Segoe Rd., Madison, WI 53711; phone: 608/273–8080) monthly, $12/annual subscription (U.S.), $16/foreign, free/members. About 25 openings for agronomists and crop and soil scientists are described under "Personnel."

APSnet (American Phytopathological Society, free. Go to Internet URL: **http://www.scisoc.org** and select "Career" and then "APS Placement Service Listings" to browse through the 60 jobs listed for everything in plant pathology including teaching and research positions. By selecting "Directories," you can choose between the "APS Member Directory," "Directory of Suppliers to the Plant Health Industry," and "Directory of Other Internet Information Resources" where you'll find links to related sites for professional organizations, laboratories, and companies.

Phytopathological News (American Phytopathological Society, 3340 Pilot Knob Rd., St. Paul, MN 55121; phone: 612/454–7250) monthly, free to members only. About ten positions in plant pathology, genetics, or pesticides with the Department of Agriculture and extension services appear under "Classified."

Resource: Engineering & Technology for a Sustainable World (American Society of Agricultural Engineers, 2950 Niles Rd., St. Joseph, MI 49085; phone: 616/429–0300) monthly, $49.50/nonmember annual subscription (U.S.), $73.50/foreign, free/members. Under "Personnel Service," you'll find over a dozen ads for agricultural, irrigation, watering systems, chemical, and biosystems engineers, mostly faculty and research positions. Job ads may also be viewed on the Internet for free at URL: **http://asae.org/** and selecting "Employment" and then choosing "ASAE Personnel Service" where you'll find about 20 postings for jobs in the agriculture/biological industry.

Within ASAE (American Society of Agricultural Engineers, 2950 Niles Rd., St. Joseph, MI 49085; phone: 616/429–0300) bimonthly, free/members only. Eight to ten ads for agricultural engineers appear under "Personnel Services." "Position Wanted" ads are also printed.

Alternative Agriculture News (Henry A. Wallace Institute for Alternative Agriculture, Suite 117, 9200 Edmonston Rd., Greenbelt, MD 20770; phone: 301/441–8777) monthly, $16/annual subscription (U.S.), $21/Canada and Mexico, $22/elsewhere, free/members. Two to three ads in the typical issue.

American Journal of Alternative Agriculture (Henry A. Wallace Institute for Alternative Agriculture, Suite 117, 9200 Edmonston Rd., Greenbelt, MD 20770; phone: 301/441–8777) quarterly, $24/annual subscription (U.S.), $27/Canada and Mexico, $28/elsewhere. Two or three jobs ads appear in alternative agriculture.

Job services

Career Development and Placement Service (American Society of Agronomy, 677 S. Segoe Rd., Madison, WI 53711; phone: 608/273–8080) $15/annual fee, free to members, resume on file 12 months, $7.50 fee to update resume during that year. The job seeker submits a copy of her resume. When a match is made, the resume is forwarded to the interested employer who is responsible for contacting the job seeker for an interview.

APSnet: Plant Pathology On-Line (American Phytopathological Society, 3340 Pilot Knob Rd., St. Paul, MN 55121; phone: 612/454–7250)free. Go to URL: **http://www.scisoc.org** and select "Careers" and then "Job Place-

Agriculture

ment" to access 50 to 60 job openings for faculty and researchers, agriculture research assistants, plant pathologists, weed scientists, and agronomists, about 80 percent of which are in the education and research. Jobs are updated weekly; they are left on for three months unless pulled by the employer. You can browse or search by key word. Also includes APS candidate profiles that employers can access and a list of plant pathology schools.

APS Placement Service (American Phytopathological Society, 3340 Pilot Knob Rd., St. Paul, MN 55121; phone: 612/454–7250) free/members only. Every four to six weeks, this service sends job announcements to participating members who then contact employers. At the APS annual meeting, current resumes are available to employers to examine. Positions are generally in plant pathology, genetics, or pesticides.

Directory

American Phytopathological Society Membership Directory (APS, 3340 Pilot Knob Rd., St. Paul, MN 55121; phone: 612/454–7250) free/members only, 120 pages, published every summer. Gives name, address, and phone for over 5,000 plant pathologists. Also available to members only on the Internet at URL: **http://www.scisoc.org/linksinfo.htm**.

You'll blossom if you read chapters 1 and 2 first

Chapter 6

Animals

Animals

Job ads

The Animals' Agenda (Animal Rights Network, 3201 Elliot St., Baltimore, MD 21224; phone: 410/675–4566) bimonthly, $24/annual subscription, $30/Canada and Mexico, $37/elsewhere. Fewer than five jobs and internships with animal shelters appear under "Classifieds."

Animal Keepers Forum (American Association of Zoo Keepers, 635 S.W. Gage Blvd., Topeka, KS 66606–2066; phones: 800/242–4519, 913/273–1980) members only, annual subscription rates: $30/full–time zoo keeper (professional members), $25/affiliates and associates. Six to 11 vacancies for animal keepers, veterinary technicians, and education specialists appear under "Opportunity Knocks."

Shoptalk (American Humane Association, 63 Inverness Dr. East, Englewood, CO 80112; phone: 303/792–9900) quarterly, $10/year annual subscription (U.S.), $25/elsewhere. As many as six jobs for animal care and control professionals (including administrative) appear in a typical issue under "Employment."

Communiqué Magazine (American Zoo and Aquarium Association, Oglebay Park, Route 88, Wheeling, WV 26003–1698; phone: 304/242–2160) monthly, free/members only. About 12 to 16 jobs are listed under "Position Directory."

Animals

Journal of the American Veterinary Medical Association (American Veterinary Medical Association, Suite 100, 1931 N. Meacham Rd., Schaumburg, IL 60173; phone: 847/925–8070) semimonthly, $120/annual nonmember subscription (U.S.), $140/foreign, free/members. Among the 200 to 300 "Classifieds" are many positions for veterinarians and veterinary technicians.

Veterinary and Human Toxicology (c/o Comparative Toxicology Laboratories, Kansas State University, Manhattan, KS 66506–5606; phone: 913/532–4334) semimonthly, $60/annual subscription (U.S.), $60/Canada, $80/elsewhere (airmail). Forty to 50 openings, including positions for veterinarians, toxicologists, biologists, and health professionals appear under "Job Opportunities." A membership directory of related organizations is published once a year in this journal.

Journal of Animal Science (American Society of Animal Science, 1111 N. Dunlap Ave., Savoy, IL 61874; phone: 217/356–3182) monthly, $200/annual nonmember subscription (print version only), free/members (electronic Internet version only). The typical issue includes ads under "Placement" for about five to ten professor positions in animal science, agronomy, agriculture, and veterinary science.

Job services

Zoos and Aquariums of AZA (American Zoo and Aquarium Association) offers a directory and job listings on the Internet. Go to URL: **http://www.aza.org** and select "Monthly Communiqué Highlights" and then pick "Position Listings" where you can browse through ads for 25 or so jobs of all types with zoos and aquariums. You will also find a directory of zoos and aquariums that AZA accredits as well as link to the home pages of AZA member institutions, a directory of AZA related organization members, and a directory of AZA commercial members ranging from animal food suppliers to tour operators.

AVMA Job Placement Service (American Veterinary Medical Association, Suite 100, 1931 N. Meacham Rd., Schaumburg, IL 60173; phone: 847/925–8070) free/AVMA members and veterinary technicians. Complete an application form and this service will match you with vacancies in higher education, government, clinical practice, or private industry.

Photocopying strictly prohibited

Directories

Directory of Animal Care and Control Agencies
(American Humane Association, 63 Inverness Dr. East, Englewood, CO 80112; phone: 303/792–9900) $50 (or $2 per state listing) for non–profit agencies, $500 (or $10 per state listing) for individuals and profit–making organizations, 250 pages. Lists more than 6,000 animal care and control agencies in the U.S. and is maintained on computer and published in a binder. Agencies are listed alphabetically by state and city. This directory is also available as cheshire or pressure sensitive labels.

ZooNet offers several useful directories online. Go to Internet URL: **http://www.mindspring.com/~zoonet/** where you will find a "U.S.A. Zoo Index" and "World Zoo Index" as well as links to home pages of zoos and links to other zoo–related sites on the Internet.

Zoo Profiles of 102 Zoos, Aquariums, and Wildlife Parks in the United States (Random House, available in bookstores) $12, 1994. Essentially a guidebook to these 102 facilities committed to conservation, this book helps you in your job search by providing comprehensive information on each facility so you can be better prepared for a job interview or send a better "blind" job application letter. Currently out of print, you might be able to find it at a library.

Zoological Parks and Aquariums in the Americas (American Zoo and Aquarium Association, Oglebay Park, Route 88, Wheeling, WV 26003–1698; phone: 304/242–2160) $85/nonmembers, $40/members, 441 pages, published in the summer of even–numbered years. Lists 175 zoos and aquariums nationwide, plus addresses, key personnel names, and phone numbers.

ACVS Directory of Diplomates (American College of Veterinary Surgeons, Suite 401, 4340 East West Hwy., Bethesda, MD 20814; phone: 301/718–6504) $15, published in late summer of even–numbered years. Includes nearly 700 board–certified veterinary surgeons: name, address, phone, specialty, and education.

Grants for Environmental Protection & Animal Welfare
(The Foundation Center, 79 Fifth Ave., New York, NY 10003–3076; phones: 800/424–9836, within New York State call 212/620–4230) $75 plus $4.50/shipping, 250 pages, published in October of odd–numbered years. Describes recent foundation grants of at least $10,000 given for animal protection and welfare, wildlife preser-

Animals

vation, zoos, botanical gardens, and aquariums. This directory is useful for identifying foundations and grant recipients for which you may wish to work

National Guide to Funding for the Environment and Animal Welfare (The Foundation Center, 79 Fifth Ave., New York, NY 10003-3076; phones: 800/424-9836, within New York State call 212/620-4230) $95 plus $4.50/shipping, 527 pages, May 1996. Describes more than 1,700 foundations and corporate direct giving programs for projects involved in animal protection and welfare, wildlife preservation, conservation, ecological research, waste reduction, and advocacy.

California Museum Directory: A Guide to Museums, Zoos, Botanic Gardens, and Historic Buildings Open to the Public (California Institute of Public Affairs, P.O. Box 189040, Sacramento, CA 95818; phone: 916/442-2472) $25, 192 pages, 1992. Each entry includes name, location, mailing address, telephone, hours open, tours available, whether admission is charged, publications issued, and descriptions of collections of 1,200 institutions. Listings are by location, with indexes of names, subjects, and counties.

Chapter 7

Arts and entertainment

Arts and entertainment in general

*The job sources here include positions in the non-profit sector. You'll find a much greater number of job sources for the art and entertainment world in the **Professional's Job Finder**.*

Job ads

CAA Careers (College Art Association, 275 Seventh Ave., New York, NY 10001; phone: 212/691–1051) bimonthly, $30/annual nonmember subscription (U.S.), $37/foreign, free/members. From 200 to 300 positions for all aspects of art are in a typical issue (the largest issue is January). Jobs include studio artists, graphic artists, printmakers, painters, photographers, sculptors, art and drawing instructors, art historians, internships, art education, conservators, administrative positions with museums and galleries, and many more.

WESTAF's Artjob (Western States Arts Federation, 236 Montezuma Ave., Santa Fe, NM 87501; phone: 505/471–4148) biweekly September through May, monthly June through August, $75/annual subscription ($85/foreign), $40/six-month subscription ($60/foreign). Each issue contains over 100 vacancies in theater, dance, and music: arts administration, performance,

Arts and entertainment in general 65

production, technical, and academia as well as information on grants, residencies, internships, and competitions. Jobs are also posted for two weeks at Internet URL: **http://www.westaf.org/artjob/** where you must first choose "Subscribe Now." The subscription rate is the same as for the print version.

The Art DEADLINES List (Resources, Box 381067, Cambridge, MA 02238; email: adl@rtuh.com) monthly, $12/six–month subscription, $24/annual; specify whether you want your subscription sent to your email address or sent on paper via real mail. Each issue includes notices of 200 job vacancies, internships, and fellowships as well as art competitions, contests, calls for papers/entries, grants, and scholarships in the arts and related areas (painting, drawing, animation, poetry, writing, music, multimedia, reporting and journalism, cartooning, dance, photography, video, film, sculpture, etc.). You can see the *Readers Digest* version of the newsletter for free at Internet URL: **http://rtuh.com/adl**.

Entertainment Employment Journal (Suite 320, 5632 Van Nuys Blvd., Van Nuys, CA 91401; phone: 818/901–6330) semiweekly, $95/annual subscription (U.S.), $110/annual subscription (Canada), $60/six–month subscription (U.S.), $35/three–month subscription (U.S.). From 50 to 75 jobs in all aspects of the entertainment industry fill these pages.

The Actor's Trunk is located at Internet URL: **http://www.xmission.com/~wintrnx/vh/trunknfo.htm**. To access the extensive database of auditions and casting calls, select "Auditions and Casting Calls." You can respond directly to openings by email from this site.

CastingOnline is located on the Internet at URL: **http://www.aloha.net/~wrap/**. Over 25 jobs in the performing arts including acting, dancing, and singing can be found by selecting "To Search." You can search for vacancies by job titles or browse through them.

NAEA News (National Art Education Association, 1916 Association Drive, Reston, VA 22091–1590; phone: 703/860–8000) bimonthly, $50/annual subscription (includes *Art Education Journal,* a bimonthly that alternates with the *NEA News;* you cannot subscribe to just one of them), free/members. "Professional Opportunities" in both periodicals lists five to 20 teaching and administrative positions in art education in the U.S. and elsewhere.

New Art Examiner (Chicago New Art Association, 314 Institute Pl., Chicago IL 60610; phone: 312/649–9900) 10 issues/year, $35/annual subscription. About four "Employment Opportunities" for administrators of art centers and galleries are advertised in the usual issue as are around 20 "Exhibition Opportunities."

Jobline News (Graphic Artists Guild of New York, 11 W. 20th St., New York, NY 10011; phone: 212/463–7794) weekly, $75/six–month nonmember subscription, $100/annual nonmember, $50/six–month member sub-

Not artsy, but valuable: Read chapters 1 and 2 first

scription, $75/annual member, $35/six-month student subscription, $50/annual student. Ten to 15 job ads for graphic designers, illustrators, surface and textile designers, and computer artists.

Audition News (Chicago Entertainment Company, 6272 W. North Ave., Chicago, IL 60639; phone: 312/637-4695) monthly, $24.95/annual subscription, $14.95/six-month subscription. Dozens of job openings appear throughout. Positions are mostly in acting, singing, and dancing, as well as in production. Covers the Midwest.

Daily Variety (P.O. Box 7550, Torrance, CA 90504; phone: 800/552-3632) daily, $187/annual subscription. As many as 50 openings in all aspects of entertainment appear under "Job Opportunities."

Variety (P.O. Box 6400, Torrance, CA 90504; phone: 800/323-4345) weekly edition, $189/annual subscription, $195/Canada, $315/Europe. Six jobs of all sorts in the entertainment industry, plus business opportunities are listed under "Audition Talent."

Performing Arts Forum (International Association of Performing Arts Administrators, Suite 205, 2920 Fuller Ave., NE, Grand Rapids, MI 49505; phone: 616/364-3000) eight issues/year, free/members only. Several positions for arts administrators (CEO of performing arts center, senior arts positions, director of marketing) are under "Position Openings." Two internships a year are offered to postgraduates and students currently enrolled in graduate arts management, public administration, law, or business programs. Application deadline early April.

Employment Opportunities (National Guild of Community Schools of the Arts, P.O. Box 8018, Englewood, NJ 07631; phone: 201/871-3337) monthly, free/members only. About four job vacancies for administrators in art schools (music, dance, and visual arts education) are announced in the typical issue.

Community Arts News (Alliance of Ohio Community Arts Agencies, 2nd Floor, 77 South High St., Columbus, OH 43215; phone: 614/241-5327) quarterly, free. At the end of this newsletter, you'll find two or three announcement of job vacancies in community and multi-media arts, performing arts, classes, exhibitions, and administration.

The Washington International Arts Letter (P.O. Box 12010, Des Moines, IA 50312; phone: 319/358-6777) quarterly, $124/annual subscription. "Deadlines" features details on 30 to 50 grants, awards, and residency programs in administration, architecture, design, film/TV/radio, music, performing arts, photography, research and training, visual arts, and writing.

Arts & Cultural Funding Report (Education Funding Research Council, Suite 875, 4301 N. Fairfax Dr., Arlington, VA 22203; phone: 703/528-1000) monthly, $138/annual subscription. Reports on available federal and foundation grants. The "Grants Alert" section announced specific grant deadlines.

Photocopying strictly prohibited

Arts and entertainment in general

Sculpture (International Sculpture Center, Suite 250, 1050 17th St., NW, Washington, DC 20036; phone: 202/785–1144) ten issues/year, $45/annual nonmember subscription (U.S. Canada, and Mexico), $105/elsewhere, $65/members. "Opportunities" section, available only with member subscription, lists four pages of classified ads for sculptors and artists as well as dozens of competitions, grants and fellowships, residencies, calls for artists, and studio exchanges. Also lists "Wanted/Apprenticeships."

Job services

Artjob (Western States Arts Federation, 236 Montezuma Ave., Santa Fe, NM 87501; phone: 505/471–4148) free. On the Internet go to URL: **gopher://gopher.tmn.com/ll/Artswire/artjob** to find this extensive job database filled with performance jobs, production, academic positions, administrative jobs with arts centers and agencies.

ArtsNet Career Services Center is located at Internet URL: **http://www.artsnet.heinz.cmu.edu/career/career.html**. To access the free and extensive job database, pick "The ArtsNet Career Services Center" and then "Search for Job Openings." You can search by keyword. To place your resume in the resume database by choosing "Resume Posting." Resumes are kept on file for one month. This site also offers links to other career services on the Internet.

Ray Osborne's Home Page includes a job database for positions in the arts and engineering as well as a resume database. At Internet URL: **http://www.jobs.index.com/**, you choose "The Grapevine" and then "Talent Bank" to access both services.

Sculpture Source (International Sculpture Center, 1050 17th St., NW, Suite 250, Washington, DC 20036; phone: 202/785–1144) contact for price. Registrants complete this service's forms and also submit slides of their work. The computerized database is used to match sculptors with potential art sponsors. At this writing, the ISC was shifting this service to the Internet. Check our free *Update Sheet* for more timely details.

Directories

World Wide Art Resources is the motherlode of Internet art directories that has to be seen to be believed when you go to URL: **http://www.wwar.com/**. Choose "Art Museums" and you'll get a links to more than 970 of them. Choose "Art Galleries" and you'll get thousands (that's what they claim!) of links to galleries and exhibitions. Choose "ARTS LOCATOR" and you can select by state and locate detailed descriptions of art museums, galleries, and other institutions in more than 930 cities of the U.S. The country menu gives you scores more links worldwide.

Not artsy, but valuable: Read chapters 1 and 2 first

American Art Directory (Reed Elsevier, P.O. Box 31, New Providence, NJ 07974; phone: 800/521-8110) $186 plus 7 percent shipping and handling, 820 pages, published in February of odd-numbered years. Offers details on more than 7,000 art organizations, museums, libraries, schools, and galleries throughout the U.S. and Canada.

Who's Who in American Art (Reed Elsevier, P.O. Box 31, New Providence, NJ 07974; phone: 800/521-8110) $199.95 plus 7 percent shipping and handling, 1,473 pages, published in April of odd-numbered years. Lists over 11,800 artists, critics, curators, administrators, librarians, historians, collectors, and dealers in the U.S., Mexico, and Canada.

Who's Who in Entertainment (Marquis Who's Who; available from Reed Elsevier, P.O. Box 31, New Providence, NJ 07974; phone: 800/521-8110) $235 plus seven percent shipping and handling, 702 pages. Last edition 1992-93; next edition, 1997-98. Provides complete and accurate biographical information on more than 18,000 individuals in the entertainment business from actors, directors, and technicians to educators, agents, and executives.

International Directory of the Arts (R.R. Bowker, available from Reed Elsevier, P.O. Box 31, New Providence, NJ 07974; phone: 800/521-8110) $275 plus 7 percent/shipping, 1,450 pages, published in even-numbered years. Offers more than 130,000 names and addresses of museums and public galleries, auctioneers, restorers, antique trade and numismatics, art publishers and journals, associations, universities, and academies, and galleries throughout the world.

National Association of Artists' Organizations Directory (National Association of Artists' Organizations, 918 F St., NW, Washington, DC 20004; phone: 202/347-6350) $25/nonmembers, free/members, published in spring of even-numbered years.

Art & Auction International Directory (P.O. Box 11344, Des Moines, IA 50340; phones: 800/777-8718, 212/582-5633) 11 issues/year, $42/annual subscription (U.S.), $54/Canada, $90/Europe; single issue available for $15 in book stores. Essentially a directory of over 7,000 antique dealers and shows, auction houses, art galleries, art services, and art fairs.

Sunshine Artists (Sun Country Enterprises, 2600 Temple Dr., Winter Park, FL 32789; phone: 407/539-1399) monthly, $29.95/annual subscription (U.S.), $41.50/Canada and Mexico. Features a calendar directory of art fairs and craft shows in the U.S. and Canada.

Where It's At: A Guide to Arts and Crafts Shows (7204 Buckmell Dr., Austin, TX 78723; phone: 512/926-7954) ten issues/year, $25.95/annual subscription, $12.95/three-month subscription, $5/single issue. This is essentially a monthly directory of arts and crafts shows in these "southwestern" states: Alabama, Arizona, Arkansas, Colorado, Georgia, Kansas, Louisiana,

Photocopying strictly prohibited

Arts and entertainment in general

Mississippi, Missouri, New Mexico, Oklahoma, Tennessee, and Texas. This directory lists up to 5,000 shows per year and each issue is updated monthly with 300 to 600 shows.

Directory of North American Fairs, Festivals & Expositions (BPI Communications, 1515 Broadway, New York, NY 10036; phone: 800/247–2160) $55 plus shipping, published every January. Includes information on over 4,000 fairs, festivals, and expositions in the U.S. and Canada.

Art in America (Brant Art Publications, 575 Broadway, New York, NY 10012; phones: 800/925–0859, 212/941–2800) monthly, single issue: $7.50 plus $3/shipping (U.S.), $5/shipping (foreign); August issue costs $15 plus $3/shipping (U.S.), $17/Canada plus $5/shipping ; $39.95/annual subscription (U.S.), $64.15/Canada, $69.95/elsewhere. This directory contains an alphabetical list by city and state of museums, galleries, non-profit exhibition spaces, corporate consultants, private dealers, and print dealers. It provides basic information plus a short description of the type of art shown and artists presented. The August issue is an enlarged annual guide edition. This is often available at bookstores or newsstands.

National Directory of Grants & Aid to Individuals in the Arts, International (Washington International Arts Letter, P.O. Box 12010, Des Moines, IA 50312; phone: 319/358–6777) $30/nonmembers, $22/members, 260 pages, spring 1997. Grant information from foundations, government sources, individuals, and donors that support the arts.

National Guide to Funding in Arts and Culture (The Foundation Center, 79 Fifth Ave., New York, NY 10003–3076; phones: 800/424–9836, 212/620–4230) $145, 1,138 pages, June, 1996. Describes over 4,200 foundations and corporate direct giving programs including 10,000 of the grants they've made to theaters, museums, archaeology projects, orchestras, dance groups, and others.

Grants for Arts, Culture & the Humanities (The Foundation Center, 79 Fifth Ave., New York, NY 10003–3076; phones: 800/424–9836, within New York State call 212/620–4230) $75 plus $4.50/shipping, 452 pages, published odd-numbered years each October. Describes recent foundation grants of at least $10,000 given to arts and cultural organizations, historical societies and historic preservation, media, visual arts, performing arts, music, and museums. This directory is useful for identifying foundations and grant recipients for which you may wish to work.

Handel's National Directory for the Performing Arts (R.R. Bowker; available from Reed Elsevier, P.O. Box 31, New Providence, NJ 07974; phone: 800/521–8110) $250 plus 7 percent shipping and handling, two-volume set, 2,289 pages, 1992. This directory provides virtually every professional dance, music, and theater organization in the U.S. as well as educational institutions that offer training and degrees in the performing arts. *Volume One: Performing Arts Organizations and Facilities* alphabetically lists organizations and facilities by state, city within state, and arts

Not artsy, but valuable: Read chapters 1 and 2 first

area. Listings contain the names of artistic and administrative management, board, paid staff, budget and attendance statistics, type of facility and stage, building costs, architect, resident group, facility rental information, and more. *Volume Two: Performing Arts Educational Institutions* lists alphabetically universities, colleges, schools, and institutions offering degrees and courses in dance, music, and theater. These two volumes must be purchased together.

International Association of Performing Arts Administrators Membership Directory (IAPAA, Suite 205, 2920 Fuller Ave., NE, Grand Rapids, MI 49505–1010; phone: 616/364–3000) free/members only, 250 pages, published each January. Offers a mini–resume of each of the 350 members including their education, expertise, and current responsibilities. This directory is available on the IAPAA's Internet site at URL: **http://www.ispa–online.org**.

Peterson's Professional Degree Programs in the Visual and Performing Arts (Peterson's, P.O. 2123, Princeton, NJ 08543–2123; phone: 800/338–3282) $24.95 plus $6.75/shipping, 624 pages, annual. Covers all 400+ accredited U.S. and Canadian colleges and universities that offer undergraduate and graduate degrees in dance, music, theater, and the visual arts, including film and photography.

Music and dance

Job ads

Music Faculty Vacancy List (College Music Society, 202 W. Spruce St., Missoula, MT 59807; phones: 800/729–0235, 406/721–9616) monthly, free/annual subscription members only. Lists 40 to 80 of positions of all types in college music teaching, administration, research, and orchestra performing. Nonmembers as well as members can purchase mailing labels for $85 per 1,000 address labels of institutions, faculty members, and departments.

Job Bulletin (New England Conservatory of Music, Career Service Center, 290 Huntington Ave,. Boston, MA 02115) monthly, $28/annual subscription. Lists jobs in university and public school music education, performance, and arts administration.

New York Opera Newsletter (P.O. Box 278, Maplewood, NJ 07040; phone: 201/378–9549) 11 issues/year, $48/annual subscription. From 30 to 50 positions (primarily for singers, some musicians) with opera companies and choruses with symphony orchestras appear under "Auditions." Despite the periodical's title, these jobs are located through the U.S.A.

Photocopying strictly prohibited

Music and dance

OPERA America Newsline (Opera America, Suite 810, 1156 15th St., NW, Washington, DC 20005; phone: 202/293–4466) ten issues/year, free/members only, $40/annual dues, $25/students. Three to ten positions in opera management are listed under "Positions Available."

Conducting Service Announcements (American Symphony Orchestra League, Suite 800, 1156 15th St., NW, Washington, DC 20005; phone: 202/776–0212) monthly, free/members only, $85/annual dues. About five to ten job openings for conductors are in the typical issue.

Update (American Alliance for Health, Physical Education, Recreation and Dance, 1900 Association Dr., Reston, VA 22091; phone: 703/476–3400) bimonthly, $45/annual nonmember institution subscription (individual subscriptions not available), free/members. "Job Exchange" features 30 or more jobs for coaches, athletic directors, and health and physical education teachers. Jobs can also be found on the Internet at URL: **http://www.aahperd.org/**, where you can select links to other national organizations listing jobs in physical fitness, recreation, sports, and dance.

Journal PERD (American Alliance for Health, Physical Education, Recreation and Dance, 1900 Association Dr., Reston, VA 22091; phone: 703/476–3400) nine issues/year, $100/annual nonmember institution subscription (individual subscriptions not available). The "Classifieds" feature about five positions, including dance instructors, usually with camps and universities. Jobs can also be found on the Internet at URL: **http://www.aahperd.org/**, where you can select links to other national organizations listing jobs in physical fitness, recreation, sports, and dance.

Dance/USA Journal (Dance/USA Suite 820, 1156 St., NW, Washington, DC 20005–1704; phone: 202/833–1717) quarterly, $40/annual nonmember subscription (U.S.), $50/Canada, $70/elsewhere, free/members. From seven to ten positions for dancers, administrators, trainers, etc., appear under "Positions Available."

Member Bulletin (Dance/USA Suite 820, 1156 St., NW, Washington, DC 20005–1704; phone: 202/833–1717) eleven issues/year, $11/annual nonmember subscription, free/members. Includes "Positions Available" and "Opportunities" announcements. You can have this one–page newsletter either mailed or faxed to you.

Job Express Registry (American Dance Guild, 31 W. 21st St., Third Floor, New York, NY 10010; phone: 212/627–3790) monthly, $33/three–month nonmember subscription, $18/members. Fifteen to 20 job ads for positions in dance administration and education fill this newsletter. As of late 1996 this publication was temporarily on hiatus. Check with ADG for its current status.

Not artsy, but valuable: Read chapters 1 and 2 first

Job service

Resume Clearinghouse (American Symphony Orchestra League, Suite 800, 1156 15th St., NW, Washington, DC 20005; phone: 202/776–0212) free, available only to members, $85/annual dues. You complete their registration form and submit it with ten copies of your resume. When matched to a job opening, your resume is sent to the employer who is responsible for contacting you directly. Fields covered include: conductors, arts administration and management (primarily orchestras, but also some other arts organizations): development, marketing, operations, education, and public relations.

Directories

Stern's Performing Arts Directory (33 W. 60th Street, 10th Floor, New York, NY 10023; phones: 212/248–8937, 800/458–2845) $65, issued each September. Lists ballet companies, modern dance and tap, choreographers nationwide, college and summer study programs, singers, duos, chamber music, opera companies, managers, consultants, designers, service organizations, festivals, and resources.

Concerts, Sponsors, and Promoters Directory (James Lloyd, P.O. Box 3, Ashland, OR 97520; phone: 541/899–8888) $34.95 plus $2.75/shipping, prepaid only. Lists information on over 5,000 promoters, sponsors, and concerts with a Christian slant.

The Register (Opera America, Suite 810, 1156 15th St., NW, Washington, DC 20005; phone: 202/347–9262) $9, 112 pages, published every July. Includes contact information on 143 professional opera companies, 300 affiliated organizations, and over 1,000 individuals in the opera business.

Musical America International Directory of the Performing Arts (Musical America, K–III Directory Corp., 10 Lake Dr., Hightstown, NJ 08520; phones: 800/221–5488, 609/371–7700) $95, 832 pages, published each December. Lists orchestras, performing arts series, performers, managers, festivals, concert sites, and schools — only for classical music. Geographical listings with alphabetical and category indexes. Includes U.S., Canada, and rest of the world.

Member Profiles (Dance/USA Suite 820, 1156 St., NW, Washington, DC 20005–1704; phone: 202/833–1717) $40/nonmembers, free/members, published in October of odd–numbered years. Lists all the members of Dance/USA. The Internet also has a directory of members at URL: **http://www.artswire.org/Artswire/danceusa/home.html**, and clicking on "List of Dance/USA members."

Photocopying strictly prohibited

Dance Links is an Internet directory of worldwide dance resources, including links to dance companies, performance listings, and organizations. Go to URL: **http://www.physics.purdue.edu/~jswhite/dance_links.html**, and select the directory category you want.

World Wide Arts Resources: Dance Companies is an Internet directory that provides a worldwide listing of dance companies. Go to URL: **http://wwar.com/dance/company.html**, and browse or search by keyword.

Theater

Job ads

ArtSEARCH (Theatre Communications Group, 355 Lexington Ave., New York, NY 10017; phone: 212/697–5230) 23 issues/year, $54/nonmember annual subscription, $45.90/members; $75/institutions (U.S. and Canada), $125/elsewhere. Features from 200 to 400 positions in theater for administrators, actors, dancers, musicians, designers, technicians, production, marketing, interns, and faculty. In addition to receiving the print version, for an additional $10/year you can have the job ads for the categories you select (administration, artistic, production, career development, education) sent to you by email about a week before each issue is mailed.

THEater JOBLIST: The National Employment Service Billboard for Theater Arts (THEater Service, P.O. Box 15282, Evansville, IN 47716–0282) phone: 812/474–0549) monthly, $45/annual nonmember subscription, $30/members of Association for Theater in Higher Education; $36/members of Alliance for Theater and Education or United States Institute for Theater Technology. From 10 to 90 positions appear throughout for technicians, designers, and mostly for college teaching positions.

Theatre Central Online is a fabulous gateway site that provides innumerable links to professional and non–profit theater companies, many which provide audition opportunities. Go to URL: **http://www.theatre-central.com/**, and select "Resources." Then for non–profit theaters you can choose "Non–Professional Theatre Companies" or "Specialty Professional Theatre Companies." Also check out the links to various casting services by clicking on "Contact Services."

Callboard (Theater Bay Area, Suite 402, 657 Mission, San Francisco, CA 94105; phone: 415/957–1557) monthly, $37/annual subscription (includes membership in TBA), single copy available at Bay Area bookstores. Over 20 technical, production, acting, and administrative positions appear under "Job Bank." "Auditions" features about 35 opportunities. These openings are located almost entirely in the San Francisco Bay Area.

Not artsy, but valuable: Read chapters 1 and 2 first

Newsletter (International Ticketing Association, 333 E 46th St., New York, NY 10017; phone: 212/949-7350) eight issues/year, free/members only. Ten to 12 positions in box office management appear under "ITA/Search."

Teaching Theater (International Thespian Society, 3368 Central Parkway, Cincinnati, OH 45225; phone: 513/559-1996) quarterly, free/members only. Features three or four positions for directors and drama teachers under "Positions Available."

Short Subjects (Greater Philadelphia Cultural Alliance, Suite 500, 320 Walnut St., Philadelphia, PA 19106; phone: 215/440-8100) 11 issues/year, $20/annual subscription, $2.50/per issue. Under "Job Bank" you'll find around 20 ads in the Philadelphia area for administrative positions, entry level to executive directors, and occasionally volunteer/intern/fellowship opportunities.

Job services

CenterStage@Buzz is located on the Internet at URL: **http://www.buz znyc.com/**. Select "Casting Notice" to access the database of 150 jobs for staff and technical personnel for stage, television, and film productions. Choose "The Buzz" and then "Resume Online" to place your resume in the "Talent Directory" resume database for one year for $59.95. You will also submit a printed copy of your resume.

Theatre Jobs Online is an Internet service that lists 250 to 300 positions in professional and non-profit theater, for all kinds of jobs: performers, directors, set designers, stage crew, teachers, and administrators. Go to URL: **http://www.theatrejobs.com/**, and select "Preview All Ads Online." Then pick keywords in "General Category," "Job Category," and "State," and click on "Submit Search," where you will get a generous list of jobs fitting your search criteria. You can also post a resume by clicking on "Post Your Resume."

The Casting Connection appears on the Internet at URL: **http://mem bers.aol.com/rlshelly/rlshelly.htm**. To access the job database with over 50 openings for actors, models, agents, and talents, select "The Casting Office." You can place your resume in this resume bank by selecting "Guidelines."

The Talent Network is located on the Internet at URL: **http://www.talent net.com/**. Over 20 jobs for professional performers appear in the job database which you reach by first selecting "Access the Talent Network" and then picking "Notice Board and Forum." You next select a region of the country where you'd like to perform. You can browse or search for

Photocopying strictly prohibited

Theater

positions by job title. To place your resume in the resume database, first pick "Access the Talent Network" and then "Professional Performers and Models."

International TalentMart, located on the Internet at URL: **http://www.edn.net/~talentmart/**, offers a resume database with 15 or so positions for artists, actors, models, and photographers. Access the database by clicking on "Jobs." You can enter your resume in their resume database by selecting "Information."

Internet Stage & Screen Resources offers both a job and resume database for actors on the Internet at URL: **http://www.stagenet.com/**. Enter the job database by picking "Employment Opportunities." You can place your resume in their resume database for a minimum of three months for $32 by selecting "Information" or "Registration."

ActorNet is located on the Internet at URL: **http://www.infohouse.com/actornet/**. See the small database of jobs for actors and other performers by selecting "Casting Notices." You can also place your resume into their resume database at this site for free.

Job Bank (Greater Philadelphia Cultural Alliance, Suite 500, 320 Walnut St., Philadelphia, PA 19106; phone: 215/440-8100) free. You may send your resume, which is kept on file for one to two years. Employers may look through these resumes for employees in administration, marketing, production, development, teaching and other support positions in the cultural arts field. The service will give a copy of your resume to the potential employer who is then responsible for contacting you.

Arts-Online.com – Theater sits on the Internet at URL: **http://www.arts-online.com/theatre.htm**. Select "Welcome" and then follow the instructions for sending an email message to get your resume into the resume database. The resume database is for actors, comedians, and other entertainers. Pick "Theaters" to access a directory of theaters in the Boston area. Select "Organizations" to access a directory of theater organizations in the Boston area.

Directory of Theatre Professionals on the Net is an Internet service provided by Theatre Central that serves as a resume bank. It consists of an alphabetical listing of performers, directors, playwrights, set designers and other people involved in professional and non-profit theater, with contact information and their specialty. For a free listing go to URL: **http://www.theatre-central.com/dir/pro/**, and select "Post Your Resume" to complete the form online. You *must* have an email address.

Directories

American Association of Community Theater Membership Directory and Handbook (AACT, 4712 Enchanted Oaks, College Station, TX 77845; phone: 409/774-0611) free/members only, 170 pages, published each

Not artsy, but valuable: Read chapters 1 and 2 first

October. Lists individuals and community theaters by state, and for each theater provides contact names, size of budget, number of performers, and kind of programming.

Theatre Directory (Theatre Communications Group, 355 Lexington Ave., New York, NY 10017; phone: 212/697–5230) $5.95 plus $3/shipping, 96 pages, published each September. Furnishes complete contact information for over 350 not–for–profit professional theaters and related arts organizations throughout the United States Each entry includes business, box office, and fax numbers; email address; Internet site; performance seasons; and Actors' Equity Association contract information.

Theatre Profiles 12: The Illustrated Guide to America's Nonprofit Professional Theatre (Theatre Communications Group, 355 Lexington Ave., New York, NY 10017; phone: 212/697–5230) $22.95 plus $3/shipping, 240 pages, biennial. Provides comprehensive information on 250 nonprofit professional theaters including a statement of purpose from each theater's artistic director as well as production histories from the 1993–94 and 1994–95 seasons. Full contact information, types of stages, performing seasons, operating expenses, and union contracts are also included

Regional Theater Directory (American Theater Works, Inc., P.O. Box 519, Dorset, VT 05251; phone: 802/867–2223) $16.95 plus $2.75/shipping, published each spring. Lists details on 430 equity and non–equity regional and dinner theaters.

Summer Theater Directory (American Theater Works, Inc., P.O. Box 519, Dorset, VT 05251; phone: 802/867–2223) $15.95 plus $2.75/shipping, published each winter. Covers the May to September theater season with opportunities at over 450 summer theaters, theme parks, cruise lines, and summer training programs, both equity and non–equity.

Directory of Theater Training Programs (American Theater Works, Inc., P.O. Box 519, Dorset, VT 05251; phone: 802/867–2223) $24.95 plus $2.75/shipping, 5th edition. Present detailed profiles of 420 undergraduate and graduate theater training programs at colleges, universities, and conservatories.

Theater Directory of the Bay Area (Theater Bay Area, Suite 402, 657 Mission, San Francisco, CA 94105; phone: 415/957–1557) contact for latest prices, published autumn 1996. Provides details on the theater companies in the nine–county San Francisco area.

Theater Directory (Theatrical Communications Group, 355 Lexington Ave., New York, NY 10036; phone: 212/697–5230) $5.95, issued each September. Lists names, addresses, phones, and faxes of theaters and artistic directors.

GPCA Membership Directory and Resource Guide (Greater Philadelphia Cultural Alliance, Suite 500, 320 Walnut St., Philadelphia, PA 19106; phone: 215/440–8100) $23, issued annually. Lists GPCA members, non–

profit art and cultural organizations in the Philadelphia area, a guide to government officials in the area, media sources and non–profit resource organizations, and consultants from the Philadelphia area.

Visual arts and film

Job ads

Afterimage (Visual Studies Workshop, 31 Prince St., Rochester, NY 14607; phone: 716/442–8676) bimonthly, $30/annual subscription (U.S.), $35/foreign. Under "Notices–Etc." are listed 15 to 20 jobs in media arts and photography, curators, administrative, and visual arts museums. In addition, there are about ten grants, five internships and residencies, plus 30 notices to submit to exhibitions.

Documentary Editing (Association for Documentary Editing, c/o Department of History, University of South Carolina, Columbia, SC 29208; phone: 803/777–6526) quarterly, free/members only. Four or five jobs for documentary editors appear under "Positions Available."

The Independent (Foundation for Independent Video and Film, 304 Hudson St., 6th Floor, New York, NY 10013; phone: 212/807–1400) ten issues/year, individual issues available at newsstands for $3.75, subscriptions are free/members only. The "Notices–Opportunities–Gigs" section lists five positions for video/television directors, curators, media artists, and in marketing — anything to do with film and video.

SCREENsite: Employment Office Opportunities is an Internet site for film and television positions, largely faculty and academic positions in film and TV studios. Go to URL: **http://www.sa.ua.edu/TCF/teach/employ/index.htm**, and select "Film/TV Positions" for a list of about 15 to 20 job vacancies.

Directories

Money for Film & Video Artists (available from American Council for the Arts, 1 E. 53rd St., New York, NY 10022; phones: 800/321–4510, 212/223–2787 ext. 241) $15.95 plus $5/shipping, 304 pages, 1993. Comprehensive resource to grants, fellowships, awards, low–cost facilities, and more with full contact information for each entry. Indexed by media and format.

Money for Visual Artists (available from American Council for the Arts, 1 E. 53rd St., New York, NY 10022; phones: 800/321–4510, 212/223–2787 ext. 241) $14.95 plus $5/shipping, 244 pages, 1993. Comprehensive resource to grants, fellowships, awards, artist colonies, and more with full contact information for each entry. Indexed by media and format.

Not artsy, but valuable: Read chapters 1 and 2 first

Chapter 8

Association management

Association management

Be sure to also see the job sources described in Chapter 3, especially the directories of associations.

Job ads

ASAE Career Opportunities (American Society of Association Executives, Suite 1190, 1575 I St., NW, Washington, DC 20005; phone: 202/408-7900) biweekly, nonmembers: $57/five-issue subscription, $117/12 issues, $197/24 issues; members of the ASAE: $57/six-issue subscription, $117/14 issues, $197/28 issues. Each issue contains ads for more than 200 jobs with non-profit associations that have annual salaries ranging from $30,000 to $50,000. About half the jobs are located in the Washington, D.C. area and the rest are scattered throughout the country.

CEO Job Opportunities Update (American Society of Association Executives, Suite 1190, 1575 I St., NW, Washington, DC 20005; phone: 202/408-7900) biweekly, $90/seven-issue subscription, $160/13-issue subscription, $300/annual. Each issue features about 100 to 150 vacancy announcements for chief

Association management

operating officers or executive directors for all sorts of non-profit associations plus around 50 to 75 vacancies for senior staff. These ads are for jobs above the $50,000 compensation level.

ASAE Career Starters (American Society of Association Executives, Suite 1190, 1575 I St., NW, Washington, DC 20005; phone: 202/408-7900) weekly, free. This is an Internet service updated every Tuesday that lists 30 to 60 entry-level jobs in the non-profit sector. Salaries are up to $30,000 per annum. About half the jobs are located in the Washington, D.C. area and the rest are scattered throughout the country. Go to URL: **http://www.asaenet.org/**, and select "ASAE Executive Employment Services," then "Professionals Seeking Employment," and finally "Career Starters." Be sure to check out the links to other similar organizations by clicking on "Gateway to Associations."

Association Trends (Martineau Corporation, Suite 1150, 7910 Woodmont Ave., Bethesda, MD 20814; phone: 301/652-8666) weekly, $95/annual subscription (U.S.), $165/foreign. Ads for 15 or more job vacancies for secretaries to executive directors are in these "Classifieds." The magazine also publishes job seeker ads under "Free Resumes." For a $63 fee, your 30-word resume appears in three consecutive issues of *Association Trends*. As part of this service, you also submit ten copies of your resume. When an interested employer contacts the newspaper, they send out your resume. You also receive a copy of each issue of the newspaper in which your ad appears.

NSFRE Employment Opportunities (National Society of Fund Raising Executives, Suite 700, 1101 King St., Alexandria, VA 22314; phone: 703/684-0410) monthly, $25/nonmember annual subscription, free/members. About 45 vacancies for development professionals, fundraisers, and other association personnel appear under "ESS Employment Opportunities." Also available to members only on the Internet at URL: **http://www.nsfre.org**, and selecting "Employment Opportunities." You need to enter a user ID and password to gain access to the job listings under the following categories: arts/cultural/humanities, consulting/sales, education, health, human services, public/society benefit, religious, software company, telecommunications, and telemarketing. To submit a resume click on "How to Submit Resumes."

The NonProfit Times (Suite 318, 240 Cedar Knolls Rd., Cedar Knolls, NJ 07927; phone: 201/734-1700) monthly, $59/annual subscription (U.S.), $89/Canada, $129/elsewhere, free/qualified full-time non-profit executives, write for qualification form. "The National NonProfit Employment Marketplace" carries 20 to 30 ads, particularly for non-profit administrators. Go to the Web site at URL: **http://www.nptimes.com/** for a host of valuable links to other non-profits.

Meeting & Hospitality Opportunities Report (American Society of Association Executives, Suite 1190, 1575 I St., NW, Washington, DC 20005; phone: 202/408-7902) biweekly, $90/six-issue subscription, $165/12-issue subscrip-

Associate with chapters 1 and 2 first

tion, $300/annual; members of American Society of Association Executives: $80/six issues, $145/12 issues, $270/annual. Each issue features 50 to 75 job ads for meeting planners and managers, convention visitor bureau staff, and convention services as well as private sector positions in food and beverage catering services, exhibition services and management, sales and marketing, destination management, and hotel management. The advertised jobs pay over $50,000 a year.

Association Management (American Society of Association Executives, Suite 1190, 1575 I St., NW, Washington, DC 20005; phone: 202/626–2723) monthly, $30/annual nonmember subscription (U.S.), $35/Canada, $40/elsewhere, $24/members. The "Executive Search" section includes about three or four executive director positions with trade or professional associations. Includes "Positions Wanted."

ACA News (American Compensation Association, 14040 N. Northsight Blvd., Scottsdale, AZ 85260; phone: 602/951–9191) monthly, $50/nonmember annual subscription, free/members. The "Marketplace–Career Network" has ads for 20 to 40 compensation professionals in government, private sector (mostly), and non–profits. Includes a "Position Wanted" section and search firms.

Job services

Jobseeker Service (Martineau Corp., Suite 1150, 7910 Woodmont Ave., Bethesda, MD 20814; phone: 301/652–8666) $63. Send ten copies of your resume (up to three pages long) and a 30–word classified ad. Your ad, with a box number, will run in three consecutive issues of *Association Trends*, described above under "Job ads." Unless otherwise requested, your resume will be sent to all employers who ask for it. The employer is responsible for contacting you for an interview. A typical issue sports about a dozen of these ads under "Free Resumes."

NEA Vacancy Telephone (National Education Association, Human Resources Office, 1201 16th St., NW, Washington, DC 20036; phone: 202/822–4000) free. Call 202/822–7642 24–hours a day to hear a recording that describes five to ten job vacancies at NEA's headquarters in the nation's capitol. Usually five to ten positions are available. Job vacancies are also available free on the Internet at URL: **http://www.nea.org/jobs**, and selecting "NEA Vacancy List." You can also download an application form from the site.

Association management

Directories

Directory of Association Meeting Planners & Conference/Convention Directors (The Salesman's Guide; available from Reed Elsevier, P.O. Box 31, New Providence, NJ 07974; phone: 800/521–8110) $237 plus 7 percent shipping and handling, 1,056 pages, 1995. Includes more than 8,700 national associations that hold more than 29,000 conventions, seminars, and meetings with 14,000 meeting planners by city and state.

National and Trade and Professional Associations of the U.S. (Columbia Books, Suite 330, 1212 New York Ave., NW, Washington, DC 20005; phone: 202/898–0662; $80) which provides details on over 7,500 national trade and professional associations, and over 400 full–service association management companies for which you may wish to work.

ASAE Membership Directory (American Society of Association Executives, Suite 1190, 1575 I St., NW, Washington, DC 20005; phone: 202/408–7900) is an Internet listing available to members only. Go to URL: **http://www.asaenet.org/**, and select "ASAE's Membership Directory," then log–in your name and membership ID number. Nonmembers can click on "Directory of Allied Associations" for headquarters contacts on each of the 68 regional allied associations; and click on "Directory of Association Management Companies" for headquarters contact information on related organizations. Be sure to check out the links to many other similar organizations by selecting "Gateway to Associations."

NSFRE Membership Directory (National Society of Fund Raising Executives, Suite 700, 1101 King St., Alexandria, VA 22314; phone: 703/684–0410) free/members only, 521 pages, published each January. Lists more than 16,000 members, with phone numbers, real addresses, and email addresses. Includes "Annual Consultants Directory."

Government Affairs Yellow Book (Leadership Directories, 104 Fifth Ave., 2nd Floor, New York, NY 10011; phone: 212/627–4140) semiannual, 1,000 pages, $181/annual subscription. Being published twice a year may make this volume the most accurate directory of 17,000 government affairs professionals who lobby at the state and federal levels on behalf of business, government agencies, and professional associations. Includes a directory of leading lobbying firms. Each entry includes coverage of each organization's in–house government affairs operations as well as its outside lobbyists. Indexed by organizations, subject, current legislative issues, location, and individual name.

Associate with chapters 1 and 2 first

Salary surveys

NSFRE Membership Profile and Salary Survey (National Society of Fund Raising Executives, Suite 700, 1101 King St., Alexandria, VA 22314; phone: 703/684–0410) $20/nonmembers, free/members, printed every three years, last published December 1992. A list of association members cross–referenced by salary, education level, type of organization, and geographic location.

Cordom's Salary Survey of Nonprofit Organizations (Martineau Corp., Suite 1150, 7910 Woodmont Ave., Bethesda, MD 20814–3015; phone: 301/652–8666) $103, published each autumn. Covers over 110 Washington, D.C. area non–profit organizations.

Salary Survey (Martineau Corp., Suite 1150, 7910 Woodmont Ave., Bethesda, MD 20814; phone: 301/652–8666) $130, 80 pages, published annually. Prepared by the Greater Washington Society of Association Executives' Association, this covers District of Columbia area non–profit groups.

Compensation and Benefits Survey (Chicago Society of Association Executives, Suite 3000, 20 N. Wacker Dr., Chicago, IL 60606; phone: 312/236–2288) $175, published each October. This survey reports on salaries and benefits at 178 Chicago area non–profits.

Salary Budget Survey Report (American Compensation Association, 14040 N. Northsight Blvd., Scottsdale, AZ 85260; phone: 602/951–9191) $75/nonmembers, $55/members, published each August. This survey is broken down into 45 industry groups nationally in four regions.

Chapter 9

Computers

Computers

*Clearly few job sources focus on jobs with computers specifically in the non–profit sector. See the **Professional's Job Finder** for a much more extensive set of job sources in computers, data processing, and electronics, albeit they will be largely for positions in the private sector.*

Job ads

Computer (IEEE Computer Society, 10662 Los Vaqueros Cr., Los Alamitos, CA 90720–1264; phone: 714/821–8380) monthly, free/members only. Two to 15 pages with ten to 100 job ads appear under "Career Opportunities." The same ads appear on the IEEE's Web site at URL: **http://www.computer.org**. Updated monthly.

Computing Research Association Index of Jobs is an Internet service that lists jobs in academia relating to research with computers. Go to URL: **http://cra.org/jobs/**, where you can scroll down a list of universities and colleges and click on the one you want to pursue. About 30 institutions are listed and usually about one job is offered in each.

NCSA Job Announcements is an Internet job bank of the National Center for Supercomputing Applications. Go to URL: **http://www.ncsa.uiuc.edu/General/Jobs/00Jobs.html**, and browse through the alphabetical list of job titles for research programmers, network engineers, software developers, and the like, some of which are for faculty and academic research institutions.

Directories

Directory of Computer and High Technology Grants (Research Grant Guides, P.O. Box 1214, Loxahatchee, FL 33470; phone: 561/795–6129; no phone orders, fax orders to 561/795–7794) $59.50 prepaid plus $6/shipping and 6 percent sales tax for Florida residents, 120 pages, published in April of odd–numbered years. Profiles over 500 foundations that offer grants for computers, software, and high–tech office equipment. Each profile includes the address, areas of support, geographic restrictions, grant range, and a list of organizations funded. Arranged by state. Also included is a guide to sites on the Internet that provide information about specific foundations, funding availability, and proposal writing.

Computerworld's The Hundred Best Places to Work (Computerworld, 500 Old Connecticut Path, Framingham, MA 01701; phones: 800/343–6474, 508/879–0700) $10 plus $1.50/postage, 80 pages, published every June. Describes 100 companies, government agencies, and universities that hire information systems specialists. Each entry includes the number of new hires for the previous year plus projected staff changes and salary increases for the coming year.

© CREATIVE MEDIA SERVICES Box 5955 Berkeley, Ca. 94705

National Guide to Funding for Information Technology (The Foundation Center, 79 Fifth Ave., New York, NY 10003–3076; phones: 800/424–9836, 212/620–4230) $115, 414 pages, May 1997. Each of the more than 800 entries includes application information and a list of recent grants awarded for projects involving computer science, engineering and technology, telecommunications, and media.

Chapter 10

Education

Education in general

Be sure to also look up specific specialties in the Index of this book.

Job ads

NESC Newsletter (National Education Service Center, P.O. Box 1279, Dept. NP, Riverton, WY 82501; phone: 307/856–0170) weekly, September through February: $37/one–month subscription, $125/five–month subscription, $10/trial issue. March through August: contact NESC for an order form because you can choose the months for which you wish to receive the newsletter as well as indicate the subject areas in which you are interested. In the course of a year, over 72,000 job ads for teachers and administrators in public and private elementary and secondary schools appear under "Help Wanted," and "Professional Services Offered." Also includes post–secondary positions.

Education Vacancy Bulletin (Career Services, Emporia State University, Campus Box 4014, Emporia, KS 66801–5407; phone: 316/343–5407) weekly March through August, semiweekly the rest of the year, $31.77/six–month subscription, $57.19/annual subscription. Over 150 teaching and administrative positions, including counselors and superintendents, appear in each issue.

The Job Search Handbook for Educators (American Association for Employment in Education, Suite 222, 820 Davis St., Evanston, IL 60201–4445; phone: 847/864–1999) $8, 50 pages, annual. This fabulous resource includes about 40 display ads of school districts interested in hiring teachers. Also included is a list of U.S. state teacher certification offices as well as over a dozen articles on the hiring process in the U.S. and overseas, and a summary of supply/demand report in the U.S., along with salary survey results.

The National Ad Search (P.O. Box 2083, Milwaukee, WI 53201; phones: 800/992–2832, 414/351–1398) 50 issues/year, $40/six–week subscription, $75/three–month subscription, $235/annual subscription, $15/one–week trial subscription. This is a good source for finding classified ads for teaching and administrative positions across the nation. Each issue overflows with 2,000 classified ads reprinted from 75 newspapers around the country. Job ads are divided into 54 disciplines including education. The paper also offers a fax service called National AD–FAX which permits immediate access to all of the paper's ads in any job category for $32 for a four weeks or $45 for six weeks. For $40, they will send the ads from your category to you by first class mail for six weeks.

Alternatively, you can access the same job ads instantly on the Internet. The URL is: **http://nationaladsearch.com**. You can see one ad in each category you choose as a free sample. You can subscribe to this site by credit card, via email, or by calling. You will be charged 10¢ for each ad you view. You must purchase the right to see ads in lots of 100 ads for $10, in advance, with no time limit on using these credits.

Job Search Bulletin Board is a weekly updated gopher site operated by the College of Education, University of Minnesota, where you can find teems of jobs nationwide for elementary level, secondary level, and higher education. Go to URL: **gopher://rodent.cis.umn.edu:11119/**. Select the category of jobs, which will give you a long list of specific job openings by title and location. Click on the title for more details.

Career Focus (New Mexico State University, Placement and Career Services, P.O. Box 30001, Dept. 3509, Las Cruces, NM 88003–0001; phone: 505/646–1631) biweekly, $12.60/six–month subscription. Features brief descriptions of at least 200 jobs openings, largely west of the Mississippi, in education, liberal arts, and other fields. Issues have ranged from 32 to 56 pages.

Job Bulletin #1 (Center Career Services, University of Washington, Box 352190, Seattle, WA 98195–2190; phone: 206/254–0194) weekly, $50/three–month subscription, $25/alumni and current UW students. Includes ads for teachers and administrators at all levels of education. Over 50 ads are in the typical issue. While advertised jobs can be anywhere in the country, most jobs advertised here are located in Oregon and Washington State.

TEACHING Exceptional Children (Council for Exceptional Children, 1920 Association Drive, Reston, VA 22091; phone 703/620–3660) bimonthly, $58/annual nonmember subscription (U.S.), $66/foreign (surface), $95/foreign (airmail), $10.50/single copy, free/members. From six to 30 ads for special education teachers and administrators are listed under "Classified." Includes all levels of education.

Exceptional Children (Council for Exceptional Children, 1920 Association Drive, Reston, VA 22091; phone 703/620–3660) quarterly, $58/annual subscription (U.S.), $66/foreign (surface), $95/foreign (airmail), $15.50/single copy. "Professional Opportunities" carries about 15 ads for positions in all aspects of special education: teaching, administration, university staff.

LDA Newsbriefs (Learning Disabilities Association, 4156 Library Rd., Pittsburgh, PA 15234; phone: 412/341–1515) bimonthly, $13.50/annual nonmember subscription (U.S.), $35/foreign, free/members. "Classified Ads" runs ads for three to ten openings for teachers of students who have learning disabilities.

Reading Today (International Reading Association, 800 Barksdale Rd., Newark, DE 19714; phones: 800/336–7323, ext. 49; 302/731–1600 ext. 245) biweekly, free/members. Includes two to five ads for reading teachers.

Journal of Reading (International Reading Association, 800 Barksdale Rd., Newark, DE 19714; phones: 800/628–7323, ext. 49; 302/731–1600 ext. 245) eight issues/year, $38/annual subscription. Includes occasional ads for reading teachers.

The Reading Teacher (International Reading Association, 800 Barksdale Rd., Newark, DE 19714; phones: 800/628–7323, ext. 49; 302/731–1600 ext. 245) eight issues/year, $38/annual nonmember subscription, free/members. Includes occasional ads for reading teachers.

Update (American Alliance for Health, Physical Education, Recreation and Dance, 1900 Association Dr., Reston, VA 22091; phone: 703/476–3400) bimonthly, $45/annual nonmember institution subscription (individual subscriptions not available), free/members. "Job Exchange" features 30 or more jobs for coaches, athletic directors, and health and physical education teachers. Jobs can be found on the Internet at URL: **http://www.aahperd.org/**, where you can select links to other national organizations listing jobs in physical fitness, recreation, sports, and dance.

The Science Teacher (National Science Teachers Association, 1742 Connecticut Ave., NW, Washington, DC 20002; phone: 703/243–7100) nine issues/year, $55. Three to six ads for science teachers and administrators appear under "Classified."

Expand your mind: Read chapters 1 and 2 first

Science Education News (Directorate for Education and Human Resources Programs, American Association for the Advancement of Science, 1200 New York Ave., NW, Washington, DC 20005; phone: 202/326–6620) six issues/year, free. Under "Opportunities," there are frequent reports that offer internships for teachers. This newsletter can also be found on the Internet at URL: **http://ehr.aas.org/ehr** by selecting "Science Education News."

Minority Funding Report (Government Information Services, Suite 875, 4301 N. Fairfax Dr., Arlington, VA 22203; phone: 703/528–1000) monthly, $128/annual subscription. The "Education Grants Week" section reports on two to four education grants. Another two to ten more grants in housing, health care, and other fields are also reported.

Initiatives (National Association for Women in Education, Suite 210, 1325 18th St., NW, Washington, DC 20036; phone: 202/659–9330) quarterly, $40. Ten to 30 jobs appear under "JOB LINE."

Job services

National Resume Bank (Suite 330, 3637 4th St., North, St. Petersburg, FL 33704; phone: 813/896–3694) $40 to include your resume for an indefinite time period; to update your resume listing, send five copies of your resume with the $5 update fee. To get on this resume database, you must send in your check along with five copies of your resume. Unless you request your name, address, and phone number to be hidden from prospective employers' view, you will be contacted directly by employers interested in you. Includes jobs in education.

National Association of Teachers Agencies (Education Job Search, P.O. Box 223, Georgetown, MA 01833; phone: 508/352–8473, fax: 508/352–8608, email: edjobs@aol.com) price: five to eight percent of your first year salary. Contact EJS for full details on how this service operates. You complete the application form used by this job-matching service. When matched with a teaching or administrative vacancy, your form is sent to the hiring agency which is responsible for contacting you.

CU Career Connection (University of Colorado, Campus Box 133, Boulder, CO 80309–0133; phone: 303/492–4127) $30/four-month fee entitles you to a "passcode" which unlocks this job hotline. You need a touch-tone phone to call and request the field in which you are interested in hearing job openings. The hotline is turned off Monday through Friday, 1:00 a.m. to 4:30 a.m., for daily updating. Over 2,600 jobs are listed in the course of the year.

Faculty Exchange Center (952 Virginia Ave., Lancaster, PA 17603; phone: 717/393–1130) $35/individual membership fee. FEC is a jobs clearinghouse, providing an exchange program, whereby faculty members accept assignment to a host institution while remaining on the payroll of their home

Education in general 89

Drabble reprinted by permission of United Features Syndicate, Inc.
Copyright 1995. All rights reserved.

institution. Each year to facilitate exchange FEC publishes three directories (free to members only), which are of interest to a job seeker: ***Roster of Member Institutions***, published each November, which contains the phone number of the contact person at each member college campus; ***Teacher Exchange Directory***, published each autumn, which contains the names, school addresses, and field of specialty of member instructors; and ***House Exchange Program Directory***, published each spring, which contains information on housing that can be exchanged. Call for further details.

DORS (Defense Outplacement Referral System) (Operation Transition, Defense Manpower Data Center, P.O. Box 130, Seaside CA 93955; phone: 800/727–3677) free; available *only* to military personnel and federal civil service employees, and their spouses; resume kept on file for up to 90 days after separation from the military or civil service. Obtain DORS' "mini–resume" form from a local military installation transition office. You can update your resume for free at a transition office. Over 5,500 employers, including school districts and universities, access this resume database and can conduct their own searches for job candidates.

Directories

National Directory for Employment in Education (American Association for Employment in Education, Suite 222, 820 Davis St., Evanston, IL 60201–4445; phone: 847/864–1999) $20/institutions only, 150 pages, annual. Lists AAEE member institutions.

National Directory of Job and Career Fairs for Educators (American Association for Employment in Education, Suite 222, 820 Davis St., Evanston, IL 60201–4445; phone: 847/864–1999) $10/institutions only, 70 pages, annual. Each entry includes the data and name of the job or career fair, location, sponsoring institution, who may attend, fees, number of employers and candidates expected to attend, chrages and deadlines for employers wishing to exhibit, and contact person.

The Guide to Services and Activities for Teacher Employment (American Association for Employment in Education, Suite 222, 820 Davis St., Evanston, IL 60201–4445; phone: 847/864–1999) $12, 80 pages, annual. Con-

Expand your mind: Read chapters 1 and 2 first

tains detailed information on educational institutions' employment assistance to teacher candidates, a chronological listing of job and career fairs, and the contact information on these institutions offering these services.

Private Independent Schools (Bunting and Lyon, 238 N. Main St., Wallingford, CT 06492; phone: 203/269-3333) $100, 570 pages, published each March. Lists information on about 1,100 private independent schools throughout the world.

National Association for Women in Education Membership Handbook (NAWE, Suite 210, 1325 18th St., NW, Washington, DC 20036; phone: 202/659-9330) free/members only, released each September. Lists member teachers and administrators.

National Clearing House for Professions in Special Education (Council for Exceptional Children, 1920 Association Dr., Reston, VA 22091; phone: 703/264-9477) free. This Internet site offers all kinds of jobs with various agencies and institutions engaged in special education. Go to URL: **http://www.cec.sped.org**, and select "National Clearing House for Professions in Special Education," then click on "Job Search Information" for a state-by-state listing. For jobs specifically with the CEC click on "What's New" and scroll down to "Staff Openings."

Grants for Literacy, Reading & Adult/Continuing Education (The Foundation Center, 79 Fifth Ave., New York, NY 10003-3076; phones: 800/424-9836, within New York State call 212/620-4230) $75 plus $4.50/shipping, 63 pages, published in October of odd-numbered years. Describes recent foundation grants of at least $10,000 given to organizations that support literacy, reading, and adult basic education and continuing education programs. This directory is useful for identifying foundations and grant recipients for which you may wish to work.

Administrators

Job ads

Leadership News (American Association of School Administrators, 1801 N. Moore St., Arlington, VA 22209; phone: 703/528-0700) monthly, free/members only. "Job Bulletin" includes 60 some ads under the following headings: Superintendents, Assistant Superintendents, Central Office, Higher Education, Specialists, Executive Directors, and Principals. These ads and scores of others appear on the Internet at URL: **http://www.aasa.org/**, and selecting "Job Bulletin." There you will find a continuously updated state-by-state listing of jobs.

Education Week (Editorial Projects in Education, Suite 250, 4301 Connecticut, NW, Washington, DC 20008; phone: 202/364-4114) 41 issues/year, $69.94/annual subscription (U.S.), $100.94/annual (Canada), $115.54/else-

Administrators

where (surface mail), $874.14/elsewhere (airmail). About 50 to 100 ads primarily for school superintendents, principals, and administrators (only a few teaching positions) are in "The Marketplace." These jobs and dozens more are also listed on the Internet at URL: **http://www.edweek.org/**, and selecting "Jobs." You then have a choice of either browsing all the listings, or by region, or by title.

AACRAO Data Dispenser (American Association of Collegiate Registrars and Admissions Officers, Suite 330, 1 Dupont Circle, NW, Washington, DC 20036–1171; phone: 202/293–9161) ten issues/year, $30/annual nonmember subscription (U.S.), $40/foreign, free/members. Five to ten ads for university level registrars, admission officers, and administrators appear under "Professional Positions Classifieds."

Employment Opportunities (National Guild of Community School of the Arts, P.O. Box 8018, Englewood, NJ 07631; phone: 201/871–3337) monthly, free/members only. About four job vacancies for administrators in art schools (music, dance, and visual arts education) are announced in the typical issue.

NACAC Bulletin (National Association for College Admission Counseling, 1631 Prince Street, Alexandria, VA 22314–2818; phone: 703/836–2222) ten issues/year, $30/annual nonmember subscription, free/members. Three to five job ads are listed under "Career Corner."

Outlook (American Association of University Women, 1111 16th St., NW, Washington, DC 20036; phone: 202/785–7745) four issues/year, free/members only. The "Classifieds" include ads for three to five administrative openings in higher education.

CUPA News (College and University Personnel Association, Suite 301, 1233 20th St., NW, Washington, DC 20036; phone: 202/429–0311, ext. 329) semimonthly, $75/nonmember annual subscription, $50/members. Six to ten jobs for human resource professionals are listed under "Classified." Some job vacancies are also listed on the Internet at URL: **http://www.cupa.org**.

Spotlight (National Association of Colleges and Employers, 62 Highland Ave., Bethlehem, PA 18017–9085 phones: 800/544–5272, 215/868–1421) 21 issues/year, $72/annual nonmember subscription (also includes *Journal of Career Planning and Employment*), free/members. Under "Jobwire" there are usually five to ten openings for personnel directors, recruiters, and career counselors at universities and colleges.

NASFAA Newsletter (National Association of Student Financial Aid Administrators, Suite 200, 1920 L St., NW, Washington, DC 20036–5020; phone: 202/785–0453) biweekly, free/members only. "Job Classified" carries from ten to 12 ads for financial aid administrators.

NACADA Current Listings (National Academic Advising Association, c/o Bobbie Flaherty, Executive Director, Suite 225, 2323 Anderson Ave., Manhattan, KS 66502; phone: 913/532–5717) is an Internet jobs listing service

Expand your mind: Read chapters 1 and 2 first

at URL: **http://www.ksu.edu/nacada/**. Click on "Placement Service" then "Current Listings." Links to other job listings can be reached by selecting "Job Hunt."

NCURA Newsletter (National Council of University Research Administrators, Suite 220, 1 Dupont Circle, NW, Washington, DC 20036; phone: 202/466-3894) bimonthly, free/members only. About one to four ads for research administrators appear throughout the newsletter.

CASE Job Classifieds is a gopher site operated by the Council for the Support and Advancement of Education that lists mainly administrative positions in higher education. Go to URL: **gopher://gopher.case.org:70/11/currents**, and click on "Here Are the Jobs!," and you'll get a menu of categories to click on for lists of specific job titles.

The Executive Educator (National School Boards Association, 1680 Duke St., Alexandria, VA 22314-9900; phone: 701/838-6722) monthly, $49/annual subscription (U.S.), $58/Canada, $79/elsewhere. About a dozen of elementary and secondary school superintendent positions are advertised under "Jobs."

Job Express (APPA: The Association of Higher Education Facilities Officers, 1643 Prince St., Alexandria, VA 22314; phone: 703/684-1446) semimonthly, $90/annual subscription nonmembers, free/members. Lists six to 12 jobs for control engineers; directors of physical plants; directors of architecture; plant engineers; custodial services; and project, civil, and operating engineers. A weekly listing of two to six jobs also appear on the Internet at URL: **http://www.appa.org**. Select "Job Bank" and then click on "Positions Listed."

ASBO Accents (Association of School Business Officials, International, Membership Department, 11401 N. Shore Dr., Reston, VA 20190-4232; phone 703/478-0405) monthly, $68/annual membership subscription. About ten ads for school administrators appear under "Jobs Bank."

Business Officer (National Association of College and University Business Officers, Suite 500, 1 Dupont Cr., Washington, DC 20036; phone: 202/861-2500) monthly, $50/members only. Ten ads for college and university business officers (fiscal officers, controller, vice chancellors for business affairs, budget and planning) materialize under "Classifieds." Fifteen to 20 job ads can be found on the Internet at URL: **http://www.nacubo.org/**, and selecting "Resource Directory" and then "Employment Opportunities."

Administrators

Position Registry (National Association of College and University Attorneys, Suite 620, 1 Dupont Cr., NW, Washington, DC 20036; phone: 202/833-8390) semimonthly, $60/annual nonmember subscription, $30/members. Three or four attorney positions with universities or colleges are in each issue.

ACPA Ongoing Placement is the Internet job bank for the American College Personnel Association. Go to URL: **http://www.acpa.nche.edu/**, and select "Ongoing Placement" to browse through the 30 or so job titles, most of which are for resident hall directors.

Position Announcements is an Internet job bank for administrative positions in higher education. Go to URL: **http://hubcap.clemson.edu:80/~dducham/pd/jobs/index.html**, and click on "Here" for a listing of several dozen jobs such as student affair coordinator, resident hall directors, and food service managers. Many are a couple of months old.

Job services

Placement Service (Harold Webb Associates, Ltd., P.O. Box 587, Winnetka, IL 60093; phone: 847/446-8637) free. Contact this service for an application form. It places school district superintendents, principals, executive directors, and persons in administrative positions, largely in public schools. Contact for further information.

P.E.N. (National Association of Student Financial Aid Administrators, Suite 200, 1920 L St., NW, Washington, DC 20036-5020; phone: 202/785-0453) available to members only. Accessible by computer modem, this computer job database enables you to locate openings for financial aid administrators. Contact NASFAA for details.

Directories

AACRAO Member Guide (American Association of Collegiate Registrars and Admissions Officers, Suite 330, 1 Dupont Circle, NW, Washington, DC 20036-1171; phone: 202/293-9161) $50/nonmembers, free/members, 200 pages, published every December. Lists some 9,000 members of AACRAO.

NACAC Membership Directory (National Association for College Admission Counseling, 1631 Prince St., Alexandria, VA 22314-2818: phone: 703/836-2222) $50/nonmembers, $10/members, issued each September.

National Association of Student Personnel Administration Membership Handbook (NASPA, Suite 418, 1875 Connecticut Ave, NW, Washington, DC 20009; phone: 202/265-7500) $25/nonmembers, first copy free/members, published every September.

Expand your mind: Read chapters 1 and 2 first

NASFAA National Membership Directory (National Association of Student Financial Aid Administrators, Suite 200, 1920 L St., NW, Washington, DC 20036–5020; phone: 202/785–0453) $60/nonmembers, free/members, issued each January.

1997 Directory (National Association of Colleges and Employers, 62 Highland Ave., Bethlehem, PA 18017–9085 phones: 800/544–5272, 215/868–1421) $47.95 plus $4.50 shipping (U.S., Canada, and Mexico), plus $15 shipping (elsewhere), 368 pages, annual. Includes key contact data on more than 1,700 colleges and 1,400 organizations, plus listings of nearly 6,400 individuals engaged in college placement and human resources work.

CUPA Membership Directory (College and University Personnel Association, 1233 20th St., NW, Washington, DC 20036; phone: 202/429–0311, ext. 392) $150/nonmembers, $25/members, issued annually. Lists human resource administrators at universities and colleges alphabetically and by school within each state.

NCURA Membership Directory (National Council of University Research Administrators, Suite 220, 1 Dupont Circle, NW, Washington, DC 20036; phone: 202/466–3894) free/members only, 272 pages, published every May. Lists some 3,000 administrators.

APPA Membership Directory (APPA: The Association of Higher Education Facilities Officers, 1643 Prince St., Alexandria, VA 22314; phone: 703/684–1446) free/members only, published each April. List some 5,000 individual members representing more than 1,500 universities and colleges, museums, military bases, and other non–profit institutions. The directory is also on the Internet at URL: **http://www.appa.org**, and selecting "Member Services" and then "Member Directory." You'll need a membership user name and passcode to access these selections.

IACLEA Membership Directory (International Association of Campus Law Enforcement Administrators, c/o Peter Berry, 638 Prospect Ave., Hartford, CT 06105; phone: 860/586–7517) $60/nonmembers, free/members, annual.

Buyers Guide and Membership Directory (Association of School Business Officials, International, Membership Department, 11401 N. Shore Dr., Reston, VA 20190–4232; phone 703/478–0405) free/members only, 166 pages, published in the March issue of *School Business Affairs Magazine*. Lists businesses that serve schools as well as school administrators by title.

NACUBO Membership Directory (National Association of College and University Business Officers, Suite 500, 1 Dupont Cr., Washington, DC 20036; phone: 202/861–2500) $115/nonmembers, $45/members, printed every January.

NACUA Membership Directory (National Association of College and University Attorneys, Suite 620, 1 Dupont Cr., NW, Washington, DC 20036; phone: 202/833–8390) free/members only, 306 pages, issued each October. Lists some 2,700 member attorneys.

Elementary and secondary education

World of Learning 1997 (Europa Publications, available from Gale Research, Inc., 835 Penobscot Bldg., Detroit, MI 48226; phone: 800/877–4253) $445, 2,000 pages, annual each February. Lists names, addresses and phone numbers for over 150,000 academic staff and officials at universities, research institutes, libraries, museums, and art galleries throughout the world, plus details on over 400 international organizations concerned with education. Educational institutions and learned bodies are arranged alphabetically by country.

Salary surveys

National Study of Salaries and Wages in Public Schools (Educational Research Service, 2000 Clarendon Blvd., Arlington, VA 22201; phone: 703/243–2100) $60/per volume, published each March. This is the authoritative source of salary data for 33 categories of school personnel. Published in three volumes: salaries scheduled for professional personnel; salaries paid professional personnel; and salaries and wages paid to support personnel.

Administrative Compensation Survey (College and University Personnel Association, 1233 20th St., NW, Washington, DC 20036; phone: 202/429–0311, ext. 392) $300/nonmembers, $80/members, 100 pages, issued annually in January. Salaries of 170 positions in higher education from CEOs to deans to top management.

Chief Executive Compensation and Benefits Survey (College and University Personnel Association, 1233 20th St., NW, Washington, DC 20036; phone: 202/429–0311, ext. 392) $485/nonmembers, $225/members, 100 pages, published in February of odd-numbered years. Reports on pay and benefits for college and university chief executives.

Elementary and secondary education

Also see the "Administrators" and "Education in general" sections earlier in this chapter.

Academic Employment Network is an Internet service that lists by state job opportunities for faculty, staff, and administrative professional in primary and secondary schools. Go to URL: **http://www.acadmeploy.com**, and click on "I'm Looking for a Job!". Then click on the state you wish to search for jobs to get detailed descriptions and contact information. Ads run for 30 days.

Teaching Opportunities (Educator Information Services, 61 Livingston Ave., New Brunswick, NJ 08901; phone: 908/246–7046) nine issues/year, $119.95/annual subscription (individuals), $59.95/six month subscription,

Expand your mind: Read chapters 1 and 2 first

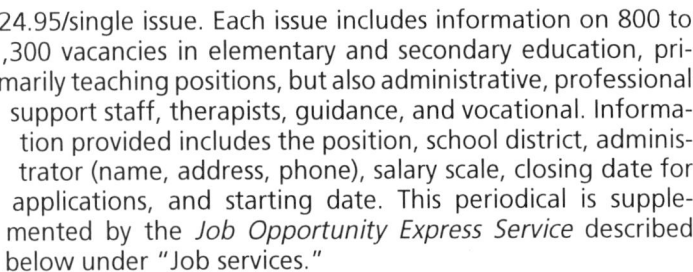

$24.95/single issue. Each issue includes information on 800 to 1,300 vacancies in elementary and secondary education, primarily teaching positions, but also administrative, professional support staff, therapists, guidance, and vocational. Information provided includes the position, school district, administrator (name, address, phone), salary scale, closing date for applications, and starting date. This periodical is supplemented by the *Job Opportunity Express Service* described below under "Job services."

Teacher Magazine (Editorial Projects in Education, Suite 250, 4301 Connecticut Ave., NW, Washington, DC 20008; phone: 202/364–4114) nine issues/year, $17.94/annual subscription (U.S.), $27.12/Canada, $28.20/elsewhere (surface mail), $44.13/elsewhere (airmail). Over 20 positions for elementary and secondary teachers, including summer positions, appear under "The Bulletin Board — Classified Advertising." One hundred to 150 jobs can be found by going to Internet URL: **http://www.edweek.org/**, and selecting "Jobs." You can browse through these listings, or search for positions by region and/or job title.

NASSP NewsLeader (National Association of Secondary School Principals, 1904 Association Drive, Reston, VA 22091; phone: 703/860–0200) monthly during school year, free/members. About five to ten job ads appear throughout the newsletter.

Education Grants Alert (Capitol Publications, Suite 444, 1101 King Street, Alexandria, VA 22314; phones: 800/655–5597, 703/683–4100) weekly, $319/annual subscription. Provides details on private and federal grants for kindergarten through twelfth grade programs.

AEE Job's Clearinghouse (Association for Experiential Education, Suite 100, 2305 Canyon Blvd., Boulder, CO 80302; phone: 303/440–8844) monthly, $80/nonmember annual subscription, $40/members. Ten to 15 openings for elementary and secondary teaching positions and a variety of teaching internships appear in a typical issue. Most of the positions require a background in natural or behavioral science.

Independent School Magazine (National Association of Independent Schools, 1620 L St., NW, Washington, DC 20036–5605; phone: 202/973–9700) three issues/year, $17.50 annual subscription. Approximately 20 to 30 display and classified ads for secondary school positions appear in a typical issue.

NationJob's Education Jobs is a weekly updated Internet job bank listing dozens of vacancies for superintendents, principals, and teachers at the elementary and high school levels. Go to URL: **http://www.nationjob.com/education**, and browse through the alphabetical list of job titles.

Photocopying strictly prohibited

Elementary and secondary education

Job services

National Teachers Clearinghouse (P.O. Box 267, Boston, MA 02117–0267; phone: 617/267–3204) $15.95/current list, $39.95/three-month list, $69.95/six-month list. To receive specific school openings submit the NTC's "Resume Form" which enables you to specify the type of position(s) and geographic location you prefer. Each additional position category is $15. Teaching positions are for kindergarten through community college. Positions are classified into: arts, elementary, counselor, English, foreign languages, mathematics, music, physical and health education, principals, science, social sciences, and special education.

You will receive a report twice a month (February through June, once a month from July through January) of open positions that match your interests and experience. You must contact the school to apply for the position.

Mailing lists for public school districts and private schools are available for purchase. $15/public schools, $15/private schools, $25/both. Lists are printed on self-adhesive labels. A list of all state certification offices is available for $7.

Job Opportunity Express Service (Educator Information Services, 61 Livingston Ave., New Brunswick, NJ 08901; phone: 908/246–7046) $65/basic regular package, $30/five additional notifications. Some job vacancies come in after the periodical *Teaching Opportunities* goes to press. Under the "basic regular package," you'll be notified by phone of up to five late-breaking vacancies that fit your certification(s), grade level preference, and zip code preference. These jobs are not published in *Teaching Opportunities*. Vacancies include elementary and secondary education, primarily teaching positions, but also administrative, professional support staff, therapists, guidance, and vocational. This service supplements the periodical *Teaching Opportunities* described above under "Job ads."

Directories

Directory of Public School Systems in the U.S. (American Association for Employment in Education, Suite 222, 820 Davis St., Evanston, IL 60201–4445; phone: 847/864–1999) $70, 200 pages, annual. Includes nearly 15,000 public school systems. Individual state directories can also be ordered for prices that range from $2 per state (minimum order $7) to $12 per state. Each entry includes the school district name, address, telephone number, hiring official, and grade levels and size of each district.

Handbook of Private Schools (Porter Sargent Publishers, Inc., Suite 1400, 11 Beacon St., Boston, MA 02108; phone: 617/523–1670) $94.50, 1,440 pages, annual. Includes over 1,700 elementary and secondary boarding and day schools: administrators, enrollment breakdown, faculty breakdown, curriculum, financial data, and school history.

Expand your mind: Read chapters 1 and 2 first

Directory for Exceptional Children (Porter Sargent Publishers, Inc., Suite 1400, 11 Beacon St., Boston, MA 02108; phone: 617/523–1670) $64.50, 1,362 pages, 1994. Reports on more than 3,000 schools, facilities, and organizations that serve children and young adults who have developmental, physical and medical, or emotional disabilities.

Petersons's Private Secondary Schools 1996-97 (Peterson's, P.O. 2123, Princeton, NJ 08543–2123; phone: 800/338–3282) $29.95 plus $6.75/shipping, 1,370 pages. Provides detailed information on more than 1,400 secondary institutions worldwide, including military, religious, day, boarding, special needs, and traditional schools, plus complete contact information.

Guide to Summer Camps and Summer Schools (Porter Sargent Publishers, Inc., Suite 1400, 11 Beacon St., Boston, MA 02108; phone: 617/523–1670) $29.50/paperback, $39.50/cloth edition, 492 pages, 1995. Reports on over 1,100 camps and summer schools as well as specialized programs for children with learning, physical, or mental disabilities.

NAIS Directory (National Association of Independent Schools, 1620 L St., NW, Washington, DC 20036–5605; phone: 202/973–9700) free/members, 132 pages, annual. Lists over 1,050 member secondary schools.

Directory of Day Schools in the United States and Canada (Torah Umesorah–National Society for Hebrew Day Schools, 5723 18th Ave., Brooklyn, NY 11204; phone: 718/259–1223) $15, 84 pages, 1997. Lists 620 elementary and high schools .

National Guide to Funding for Elementary and Secondary Education (The Foundation Center, 79 Fifth Ave., New York, NY 10003–3076; phones: 800/424–9836, 212/620–4230) $140 plus $4.50/shipping, 663 pages, published in May of odd–numbered years. Describes the programs of more than 2,100 foundations and corporate direct giving programs that fund elementary and secondary school programs: nursery schools, bilingual education, dropout prevention, educational testing programs, and more. Includes a list of over 6,300 grants that have been funded.

Directory of Education Grants (Research Grant Guides, P.O. Box 1214, Loxahatchee, FL 33470; phone: 561/795–6129; no phone orders, fax orders to 561/795–7794) $59.50 prepaid plus $6 shipping and 6 percent sales tax for Florida residents, 152 pages, published in October of even–numbered years. Profiles of 650 foundations that provide thousands of funding sources for education programs and non–profit health organizations. Each profile lists address, area of support, geographic restrictions, and grant range.

Grants for Elementary & Secondary Education (The Foundation Center, 79 Fifth Ave., New York, NY 10003–3076; phones: 800/424–9836, within New York State call 212/620–4230) $75 plus $4.50/shipping, 345 pages, published in October of odd–numbered years. Describes recent foundation grants of at least $10,000 given to elementary and secondary schools for

Photocopying strictly prohibited

academic programs, counseling, educational testing, drop-out prevention, teacher training and education, salary support, and school libraries. This directory is useful for identifying foundations and grant recipients for which you may wish to work.

Salary survey

An Introduction to the K–8 Principalship (National Association of Elementary School Principals, 1615 Duke St., Alexandria, VA 22314; phone: 703/684–3345) free; you must send a self–addressed stamped (one ounce) number ten business envelope. This brochure includes a few paragraphs about earnings.

Higher education

Also see the section labeled "Administrators" earlier in this chapter and the section called "Trades and vocational education" where you'll find additional job sources for junior colleges.

Job ads

The Chronicle of Higher Education (P.O. Box 1955, Marion, OH 43306–2055; phones: 800/347–6969, 202/466–1000) 48 issues/year, $40.50/six–month subscription, $75/annual subscription. The "Bulletin Board" section contains hundreds of display and classified ads for teaching, research, and administrative positions. Also includes a substantial "positions wanted" section as well as "faculty exchange" and "housing exchange." See *Academe This Week* below for the *Chronicles'* Web site with job listings..

Academe This Week (Chronicle of Higher Education, P.O. Box 1955, Marion, OH 43306–2055; phones: 800/347–6969, 202/466–1000) is the Internet job bank of the *Chronicle of Higher Education*, described above. Search for hundreds of jobs in academia at URL: **http://chronicle.merit.edu/.ads/.links.html**. There browse through the following categories: administrative positions, executive positions, positions outside of academe, as well as the following categories under faculty and research: humanities, social sciences, science and technology, and professional fields. You can also search through five geographic areas: Northeast, Midwest, South, West, and outside the U.S.

Academic Position Network (Suite 815, 245 E. Sixth St., St. Paul, MN 55101; phone: 612/225–1433) is an Internet site that provides hundreds of job listings for faculty, professional staff, administrative positions, graduate fellowships and assistantships, and postdoctoral positions. Go to URL: **http://wwww.umn.edu/apn** and then enter the keywords in the following

Expand your mind: Read chapters 1 and 2 first

categories to conduct your search: particular state (or all), particular field of interest (or all), and particular position (or all). When all the keywords are entered, click on "Begin Search."

Jobs in Higher Education maintained by the Graduate School of Library Science, University of Texas at Austin, is a free Internet site that links you to more than 600 university and college sites with job listings for faculty and staff. Go to URL: **http://volvo.gslis.utexas.edu/**, and select "Academic Advisory Resources on the Internet" and then choose "Jobs in Higher Education." You can select by geographic location or alphabetically for U.S., Canada, United Kingdom, and Australia.

Higher Education Jobs Online is an Internet Job bank provided by Internet Employment Linkage, Inc. Go to URL: **http://www.higheredjobs.com/**, where you can choose either "Search Faculty Positions" or "Search Staff Positions." Whichever you choose, you are then asked to select by academic field or job category, where you will then get a detailed list of job vacancies by title.

Organizations with In-House Job Listings is an Internet site operated by the Department of Agricultural Engineering at the Texas A&M University. Basically it offers a collection of links to the home pages of institutions of higher learning, where you will find job listings. Go to URL: **http://ageninfo.tamu.edu/jobs.html#inhouse**, and choose from the alphabetical list of links.

Black Issues in Higher Education (Cox, Matthews, & Associates, Inc., Suite B-8, 10520 Warwick Ave., Fairfax, VA 22030-3136; phone: 703/385-2981) biweekly, $40/annual subscription. From 200 to 250 ads for faculty positions are listed under "Position Announcements."

The Black Scholar (Black World Foundation, P.O. Box 2869, Oakland CA 94609: phone: 510/547-6633) four issues/year, $30/annual subscription (U.S.), $45/foreign. Fifteen to 30 ads for university faculty and research positions are listed under "Classified Ads."

Affirmative Action Register (Warren H. Green, Inc., 8356 Olive Blvd., St. Louis, MO 63132; phones: 800/537-0655, 314/991-1335) monthly, individuals: $15/annual subscription (first class), $8/six-month subscription (first class); free bulk rate to individuals and to institutional and organizational minority, female, veterans, or disabled candidate sources. Among the hundreds of professional, managerial, and administrative positions are scores of university and college positions. All employers who advertise are committed to an inclusionary hiring process without discrimination. You can also view all the ads in the *Affirmative Action Register* for free on the Internet at URL: **http://www.aar-eeo.com**. You can browse through the available positions alphabetically by employer or by state. Just click on the underlined job description and all the relevant details will appear on your screen.

Photocopying strictly prohibited

Higher education

Journal of Cultural Diversity (Tucker Publications, 5823 Queens Cove, Lisle, IL 60532; phone: 630/969–3809) quarterly, $50/annual subscription, $35/student. Twelve to 22 job ads are listed under "Classified" for university jobs, teaching, nursing, and administration. Jobs are primarily in sociology, ethnic studies, anthropology, and social work.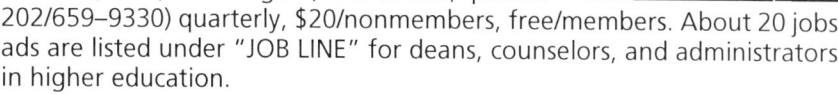

About Women on Campus (National Association for Women in Education, Suite 210, 1325 18th St., NW, Washington, DC 20036; phone: 202/659–9330) quarterly, $20/nonmembers, free/members. About 20 jobs ads are listed under "JOB LINE" for deans, counselors, and administrators in higher education.

The Women's Review of Books (Center for Research on Women, 106 Central St., Wellesley, MA 02181; phone: 617/283–2087) 11 issues/year, $20/annual subscription for individuals and $35 for institutions, add $15 for foreign. "Classified" features 15 to 20 ads for jobs, generally in education or library work, including university teaching, research, and administrative positions.

Women's Studies Job Bank is a gopher service on the Internet operated by the Women's Studies Database at the University of Maryland. For about 40 job listings in academia, mainly for faculty in women's studies, go to URL: **gopher://gopher.inform.umd.edu:70/11/EdRes/Topic/WomenStudies**, and select "Employment."

Careers and the disABLED (Equal Opportunity Publications, Suite 200, 1160 Jericho Turnpike, Huntington, NY 11743; phone: 516/421–9421) quarterly, $8/annual prepaid subscription. About five display ads under "Equal Opportunity & Higher Education Careers" feature positions in higher education for college graduates from employers who certify they are equal opportunity employers who will hire people who have disabilities.

NUCEA News (National University Continuing Education Association, Suite 615, 1 Dupont Cr., Washington, DC 20036; phone: 202/659–3130) monthly, $45/annual nonmember subscription, free/members. Four job ads for continuing education faculty, conference planners, deans, directors, and administrators appear under "Recruiter Advertisements."

Placement Center Job Announcements (Association for Educational Communications and Technology, Suite 820, 1025 Vermont Ave., NW, Washington 20005; phone: 202/347–7834) is a free Internet gopher site for dozens of job announcements for media specialists, librarians, and other vacancies in higher education. Go to URL: **http://www.aect.org/**, and select "Employment." Then click on "gopher://sunbird.usd.edu:7211" and scroll down to "Placement Center (Job Announcements)."

Expand your mind: Read chapters 1 and 2 first

MLA Job Information List (Modern Language Association, 10 Astor Place, New York, NY 10003; phone: 212/614–6321) five issues/year, $30/annual subscription (U.S. and Canada), $47/elsewhere. Each issue contains 200 to 600 university and college job openings for teachers of English composition and literature in the U.S. and Canada, and another 200 to 600 for teachers of foreign languages.

College Language Association Journal (College Language Association, c/o Dr. Cason L. Hill, Morehouse College, Atlanta, GA 30314; phone: 404/681–2800) quarterly, $40/members only (U.S.), $41.50/Canada, $45.50/elsewhere. "CLA Placement Service" includes ads for two to 30 English and modern foreign language teaching positions at private and public two–year and four–year institutions.

Music Faculty Vacancy List (College Music Society, 202 W. Spruce St., Missoula, MT 59807; phones: 800/729–0235, 406/721–9616) monthly, free/annual subscription members only. Lists all types of positions in college music teaching, administration, research, and orchestra performing. The average issue lists 40 to 80 positions. Nonmembers as well as members can purchase mailing labels for $85 per 1,000 address labels of institutions, faculty members, and departments.

The NCAA News (National Collegiate Athletic Association, 6701 College Blvd., Overland Park, KS 66211; phone: 913/339–1906) 46 issues/year, $24/annual nonmember subscription, $12/faculty and students at NCAA member institutions. Around 100 job openings are advertised in "The Market" — athletic directors, trainers, athletic promotions, public relations, sports information, coaches, physical education instructors, and graduate assistants.

Journal of PERD (American Alliance for Health, Physical Education, Recreation, and Dance, 1900 Association Dr., Reston, VA 22091; phone: 703/476–3410) nine issues/year, $100/annual subscription (institutions only, individuals cannot subscribe), free/members. The "Classified" section carries about ten ads for coaches, health, physical education instructors, and athletic directors. Jobs can be found on the Internet at URL: **http://www.aahperd.org/**, where you can select links to other national organizations listing educational jobs in physical fitness, recreation, sports, and dance.

AIN Notes (American Institute of Nutrition, 9650 Rockville Pike, #L–4500, Bethesda, MD 20814; phone: 301/530–7050) quarterly, $30/annual subscription. Four to 12 ads for college level personnel are listed under "Positions Available."

Educational Researcher (American Educational Research Association, 1230 17th St., NW, Washington, DC 20036–3078; phone: 202/223–9485) nine issues/year, $41/annual subscription, free/members. Under "Classifieds," you'll generally find ten ads for faculty and research positions with schools of education and research and development organizations. But the fall issues carry over 20 job ads.

Photocopying strictly prohibited

Anthropology Newsletter (American Anthropological Association, Suite 640, 4350 N. Fairfax Dr., Arlington, VA 22203; phone: 703/528–1902) nine issues/year, Sept.–May, $55/annual subscription nonmembers, free/members. Job ads can range from 80 in the fall to ten in other seasons. The newsletter is also available on the Internet at URL: **http://www.ameranthassn.org**, just click on "Anthropology Newsletter."

Positions for Classicists and Archaeologists (American Philological Association, Department of Classics, Box 117-A, Holy Cross College, Worcester, MA 01610; phone: 508/793–2203) monthly, $25/annual members only subscription; also available for $30, as part of the APA's Placement Service's "Comprehensive Service," which is available only to members of APA or the Archaeological Institute of America (656 Beacon St., Boston, MA 02215). Each issue includes five to 20 ads for classicist and archaeologist faculty and research positions. For a monthly job listing on the Internet go to URL: **http://scholar.cc.emory.edu/**, check out the graphic bookshelf and click on the volume that says "Openings." You'll need a subscriber membership ID to access these listings, which range from two to 25 vacancies.

Perspectives (American Historical Association, 400 A St., SE, Washington, DC 20003; phone: 202/544–2422) nine issues/year, contact for subscription rates. "Employment Information" can carry as many as 100 job ads for history professors, librarians, and public historians. Periodically, an issue will include a salary survey.

History News Dispatch (American Association for State and Local History, Suite 600, 530 Church St., Nashville, TN 37219–2325; phone: 615/255–2971) monthly, $50/members only. About 20 to 35 ads for historians, archivists, and educators appear under "The Marketplace." Includes positions with historical societies, historic sites, libraries, archives, and museums.

IMS Bulletin (Institute of Mathematical Statistics, Suite 7, 3401 Investment Blvd., Hayward, CA 94545; phone: 510/783–8141) bimonthly, $50/annual nonmember subscription, free/members. Ads for 15 to 30 faculty positions fill the "Employment Opportunities" section. These ads also appear online on the Internet at URL: **http://wwwmaths.anu.edu.au/ims/**, and choosing "Employment Opportunities."

Geotimes (American Geological Institute, 4220 King St., Alexandria, VA 22302; phone: 703/379–2480) monthly, $14.95/annual student subscription, $32.95/nonmembers, $24.95/members. Each issue has 20 to 25 classified ads for geologists, geographers, and scientists, generally in higher education. The October issue contains a directory of geology organizations.

ASEE Prism (American Society for Engineering Education, Suite 600, 1818 N St., Washington, DC 20036; phone: 202/331–3500) nine issues/year, free/members only. Jobs are mostly in academia for faculty and research positions. Depending on the season the number of vacancies can range from 20 to 200; a good month of the year is December. These vacancies

Expand your mind: Read chapters 1 and 2 first

prior to publication can be viewed on the Internet at URL: **http://www.asee.org/asee/**. Select "ASEE Publications," then "ASEE Prism," and finally "Positions Open," where you can search or choose.

Academic Physician and Scientist (Lippincott–Raven Publishers, 36th Floor, 1185 Avenue of the Americas, New York, NY 10036; phone: 212/930–9561) bimonthly, free. Each issue contains a motherlode of ads, at least 30 pages of display and classified for academic positions in medicine and science academic positions, averaging about 450 ads. For job postings on the Internet, go to URL: **http://www.acphysci.com**, and select "Classified Ads." Then choose from among "Administration," "Basic Science," and "Clinical Science." From each of these links you choose by specialty and then by title. Sporting the most ads is the "Medicine" specialty in "Clinical Science" with more than 70 listings.

Physics Job Announcements by Thread, an Internet site operated by the Los Alamos National Laboratory, offers more than 120 job listings for faculty and postdoctorates positions at universities and research labs. Go to URL: **http://www.XXX.lanl.gov/Announce/Jobs**, where you can browse for positions by title and geographic region, mostly U.S., but some international.

ACSA NEWS (Association of Collegiate Schools of Architecture, 1735 New York Ave., NW Washington, DC 20006; phones: 800/232–2724, 202/785–2324) nine issues/year, $60/annual member subscription. About 15 to 30 ads for architecture faculty are listed under "Positions Available."

Higher Education Report (Association of Jesuit Colleges and Universities, Suite 405, 1 Dupont Cr., Washington, DC 20036; phone: 202/862–9893) ten issues/year, $17.50/annual subscription (U.S. and Canada). Three to five ads for faculty are listed under "Classifieds."

Academy of Criminal Justice Sciences Employment Bulletin (ACJS, Northern Kentucky University, 402 Nunn Hall, Highland Heights, KY 41099–5998; phones: 800/757–2257, 606/572–5634) monthly from October through April, $15/annual nonmember subscription, free/members. About 40 job ads from academic institutions in criminal justice and criminology are in the typical issue.

The Criminologist (American Society of Criminology, Suite 212, 1314 Kinnear Rd., Columbus, OH, 43212; phone: 614/292–9207) bimonthly, $7.50/annual nonmember subscription (U.S.), $10/foreign, free/members. Ten to 12 jobs for probation officers, police, and faculty are listed under "Positions Announcements."

Employment Bulletin (American Sociological Association, 1722 N St., NW, Washington, DC 20036; phone: 202/833–3410) monthly, $30/nonmember annual subscription, $10/members. This newsletter features about 70 positions in academic, applied, and fellowship settings. Most positions are in sociology, but also related areas such as anthropology and criminology.

Personnel Service Newsletter (American Political Science Association, 1527 New Hampshire Ave., NW, Washington, DC 20036; phone: 202/483–2512) monthly, $35/members only. Each issue has 25 or more job vacancies in political science. Most positions are for faculty and researchers.

Journal of Social Work Education (Council on Social Work Education, 1600 Duke St., Alexandria, VA 22314; phone: 703/683–8080) three issues/year, free/members only. About four vacancies for university teaching positions in social work are in the typical issue.

Social Work Education Reporter (Council on Social Work Education, 1600 Duke St., Alexandria, VA 22314; phone: 703/683–8080) three issues/year, free/members only. About four vacancies for university teaching positions in social work are in the typical issue.

APS Bulletin Board is an Internet job bank site of the American Psychological Society. Go to URL: **http://psych.hanover.edu/APS/** and select "APS Bulletin Board" and then "Complete Listings," where you will find dozens of jobs, mostly for faculty and postdoctoral positions.

AAFCS Action (American Association of Family and Consumer Services, 1555 King St., Alexandria, VA 22314; phones: 800/424–8080, 703/706–4600) five issues/year, free/members only. About seven to 20 vacancies for faculty and administrators in family and consumer sciences appear in "Position Announcements."

Communications of the ACM (Association for Computing Machinery, 17th Floor, 1515 Broadway, New York, NY 10036–5701; phone: 212/626–0500) monthly, $134/nonmembers, free/members. Under "Career Opportunities" there are more than 100 ads, less in the summer, for faculty jobs relating to computing. Also check out the Internet at URL: **http://info.acm.org/**, and select "Career Opportunities and Development," then "Career Opportunities." There you'll find a listing of about 50 positions, most all of them faculty jobs.

Computing Research Association Index of Jobs is an Internet service that lists jobs in academia relating to research with computers. Go to URL: **http://cra.org/jobs/**, where you can scroll down a list of universities and colleges and click on the one you want to pursue. About 30 institutions are listed and usually about one job is offered in each.

Cause Job Posting Service (Association for Managing and Using Information Resources in Higher Education) is an Internet site that lists jobs for primarily administrators of computer networks, information officers, and technical support personnel at academic institutions. Go to URL: **http://cause-www.colorado.edu/pd/jobpost/jobpost.html**, and select "Open Positions." From there you can choose job vacancies under the following categories: "Senior–Level Management" (some 25 positions), "Secondary–Level Management" (25 positions), "Support/Technical Level" (70 positions), and "Other Information Resources" (10 positions).

Expand your mind: Read chapters 1 and 2 first

Financial Management (Financial Management Association International, College of Business Administration, University of South Florida, Tampa, FL 33620; phone: 813/974–2084) quarterly, $80/annual subscription (U.S.), $100/foreign (surface), $160/foreign (airmail). "Placement Clearinghouse" run ads for four to ten business school professor positions. Also includes "Positions Desired" listings. If you are a member or have paid $250 for a user name and password you can find many more jobs on the Internet at URL: **http://www.fma.org**, and selecting "Placement Service" and then "Directory of Positions Available."

Members can also place their resumes into a resume book, by clicking on "Resume."

Academy of International Business Newsletter (Academy of International Business, College of Business Administration, University of Hawaii, 2404 Maile Way, Honolulu, Hawaii 96822–2282; phone: 808/956–3665) quarterly, free/members only. "Job Mart" features five to ten ads for faculty and administrators in business schools.

The Technology Teacher (International Technology Education Association, 1914 Association Dr., Reston, VA 22191–15390; phone: 703/860–2100) eight issues/year, $65/annual nonmember subscription, free/members. Just one or two display ads appear for university faculty.

American Association of Colleges for Teacher Education Briefs (AACTE, Suite 610, 1 Dupont Cr., NW, Washington, DC 20036; phone: 202/293–2450) bimonthly, $30/annual nonmember subscription (U.S.), $40/foreign, free/members. Just one or two ads for deans and faculty are in an issue.

Mechanics (American Academy of Mechanics, Virginia Polytechnic Institute and State University, Department of Engineering, Science, and Mechanics, Blacksburg, VA 24061–0219; phone: 540/231–6841) ten issues/year, free/member individuals, $64/annual subscription nonmember individuals, $80/annual subscription for libraries and schools (North and Latin America), $100/elsewhere schools and libraries. Individuals must live in the Western Hemisphere to subscribe. One to five ads for university faculty are in the typical issue.

NCRE Newsletter (National Council on Rehabilitation Education, c/o Dr. Julie Smart, Department of Special Education, Utah State University, Logan, UT 84322–2870; phone: 801/797–3269) quarterly, free/members only. "Positions" generally lists openings for two rehabilitation education or psychology positions.

Forest Products Journal (Forest Product Society, 2801 Marshall Ct., Madison, WI 53705; 608/231–1361) ten issues/year, $135/annual nonmember subscription, $90/members. "Positions Available" runs job ads for about four faculty and administrators at universities in fields that involve forest products.

Photocopying strictly prohibited

Higher education

Job services

Teachers Registry and Information Service (Council on Social Work Education, 1600 Duke St., Alexandria, VA 22314; phone: 703/683–8080) $137/nonmember seven–month registration fee, $79/nonmember full–time students, $79/members, $44/full–time student members. Fill out the registration form and submit the original plus ten copies. Registration is good for the October through April academic year. Your registration form is put on display at the annual program meeting and sent to schools of social work education actively looking for faculty and administrators. The university contacts you for an interview. In addition, you'll receive announcements of university openings in October, January, and March.

National Faculty Exchange (Academic Resource Network, c/o Betty Worley, President, Suite 140, 4656 W. Jefferson, Fort Wayne, IN 46804; phone: 219/436–2634). Get information about domestic exchange programs for college or university level teachers from their Internet site at URL: **http://arnold.snybuf.edu**.

CLA Placement Service (College Language Association, c/o Dr. Earle D. Clowney, Director, Box 116, Clark Atlanta University, Atlanta, GA 30314; phone: 404/880–8546) free/members only. Submit your resume. When a match is made for an English and modern foreign language teaching position at a private or public two–year or four–year institution, you are sent information about the position. You are responsible for contacting the institution.

Career Opportunities (American Alliance for Health, Physical Education, Recreation, and Dance, 1900 Association Dr., Reston, VA 22091; phone: 703/476–3410) is a free resume service on the Internet. Go to URL: **http://www.aahperd.org/** and click on "American Alliance for Health, Physical Education, Recreation, and Dance," and select "Career Opportunities," where you can submit a resume. Employers will contact you directly.

Resume Book (Financial Management Association International, College of Business Administration, University of South Florida, Tampa, FL 33620; phone: 813/974–2084) $250/nonmembers, free/members. You can place your resume into this resume bank on the Internet at URL: **http://www.fma.org**, and selecting "Resume Book." You will need a user name and password.

ACM Resume Referral Service (Association for Computing Machinery, c/o Resumé Link, P.O. Box 218, Hilliard, OH 43026; phone: 614/777–4000) $87/nonmembers, $26/nonmembers student, free/members. Request the "ACM Resume Database Information Form," complete it and submit it with your payment. To avoid tipping off your current employer that you are looking for another job, you can check a box on the form so your resume will not be released to your present employer. Computer matching is done by Resumé Link, a specialist in electronic job–matching systems. When you

Expand your mind: Read chapters 1 and 2 first

are matched to a job, your resume form is faxed to the prospective employer. This job-matching service checks with you every six months to update your resume. This resume service is available to members only on the Internet at URL: **http://info.acm.org/**, and selecting "Career Opportunities and Development" and then "ACM Resume Referral Service."

Directories

Peterson's Graduate and Professional Programs: An Overview (Peterson's Guides, P.O. 2123, Princeton, NJ 08543-2123; phone: 800/338-3282) $27.95 plus $6.75/shipping, 1,264 pages, annual. Covers graduate and professional programs in 350 fields offered by more than 1,500 accredited U.S. and Canadian colleges and universities.

Peterson's Graduate Programs in the Humanities, Arts & Social Sciences (Peterson's Guides, P.O. 2123, Princeton, NJ 08543-2123; phone: 800/338-3282) $37.95 plus $6.75/shipping, 1,427 pages, annual. Covers more than 10,000 U.S. and Canadian programs in anthropology, architecture, area studies, art and design, communications, criminology, demography, economics, environmental policy, family services, geography, gerontology, history, industrial relations, international affairs, journalism, languages, performing arts, philosophy, political science, psychology, public affairs, social work, sociology, and more.

Peterson's Graduate Programs in the Physical Sciences, Mathematics & Agricultural Sciences (Peterson's Guides, P.O. 2123, Princeton, NJ 08543-2123; phone: 800/338-3282) $34.95 plus $6.75/shipping, 978 pages, annual. Covers more than 3,000 U.S. and Canadian programs in all aspects of the physical sciences, mathematics, horticulture, and agronomy.

Peterson's Graduate Programs in Engineering & Applied Sciences (Peterson's Guides, P.O. 2123, Princeton, NJ 08543-2123; phone: 800/338-3282) $37.95 plus $6.75/shipping, 1,567 pages, annual. Reports on more than 3,400 U.S. and Canadian graduate programs in all aspects of engineering, computer sciences, operations research, technology management, and more.

Peterson's Graduate Programs in the Biological Sciences (Peterson's Guides, P.O. 2123, Princeton, NJ 08543-2123; phone: 800/338-3282) $44.95 plus $7.75/shipping, 2,784 pages, annual. Details nearly 4,000 U.S. and Canadian programs in anatomy, encology, biochemistry, biophysics, biotechnology, botany, ecology, entomology, environmental sciences, genetics, pathology, pharmacology, physiology, zoology, and more.

Guide to Graduate Study in Botany for the United States and Canada (Botanical Society of America, 1735 Neil Avenue, Columbus, OH 43210-1293; phone: 614/292-3519) $12/nonmembers, free/members, 1995. Lists 239 plant science departments in the U.S. and 26 in Canada that offer Ph.D.

Higher education

degrees in some area of the plant sciences. Included are: name and address of institution, name of department, fields of specialization, and titles of recent Ph.D. theses directed for all botanical faculty in the department.

Peterson's Graduate Programs in Business, Education, Health, Information Studies, Law & Social Work (Peterson's Guides, P.O. 2123, Princeton, NJ 08543–2123; phone: 800/338–3282) $27.95 plus $6.75/shipping, 1,978 pages, annual. Profiles 13,000 graduate programs in these fields in the U.S. and Canada.

Peterson's Graduate Programs in Electrical Engineering & Computer Sciences (Peterson's Guides, P.O. 2123, Princeton, NJ 08543–2123; phone: 800/338–3282) $24.95 plus $6.75/shipping, 900 pages, annual. Detailed descriptions on nearly 900 graduate programs in electrical engineering and computer sciences offered by almost 300 U.S. and Canadian colleges and universities.

Peterson's Law Schools (Peterson's Guides, P.O. 2123, Princeton, NJ 08543–2123; phone: 800/338–3282) $21.95 plus $6.75/shipping, 500 pages, annual. Provides in–depth profiles on more than 180 law schools.

Peterson's Nursing Programs (Peterson's Guides, P.O. 2123, Princeton, NJ 08543–2123; phone: 800/338–3282) $24.95 plus $6.75/shipping, 700 pages, annual. Describes more than 2,000 baccalaureate and graduate nursing programs in the U.S. and Canada, includes admission requirements, degrees offered, academic facilities, tuition, financial aid, and admission contacts.

Peterson's Guide to Medical Schools (Peterson's Guides, P.O. 2123, Princeton, NJ 08543–2123; phone: 800/338–3282) $24.95 plus $6.75/shipping, 450 pages, annual. Gives comprehensive descriptions of medical degree programs from more than 140 accredited colleges and universities in the U.S., Puerto Rico, and Canada, plus admission contacts.

Peterson's Top Colleges for Science (Peterson's Guides, P.O. 2123, Princeton, NJ 08543–2123; phone: 800/338–3282) $24.95 plus $6.75/shipping, 804 pages, annual. Provides detailed information on more than 200 U.S. colleges and universities with strong science programs in biology, chemistry, geology, mathematics, and physical sciences.

Peterson's Guide to MBA Programs (Peterson's Guides, P.O. 2123, Princeton, NJ 08543–2123; phone: 800/338–3282) $21.95 plus $6.75/shipping, 1,002 pages, annual. Provides comprehensive information on more than 700 business school graduate programs offered by U.S., Canadian, and selected international institutions of higher learning.

Peterson's Professional Degree Programs in the Visual and Performing Arts (Peterson's Guides, P.O. 2123, Princeton, NJ 08543–2123; phone: 800/338–3282) $24.95 plus $6.75/shipping, 624 pages, annual. Covers all

Expand your mind: Read chapters 1 and 2 first

accredited U.S. and Canadian colleges and universities — more than 400 — offering undergraduate and graduate degrees in dance, music, theater, and the visual arts, including film and photography.

Choose a Christian College (Peterson's Guides, P.O. 2123, Princeton, NJ 08543-2123; phone: 800/338-3282) $14.95 plus $5.75/shipping, 148 pages. Provides full page profiles on more than 140 colleges with a Christian education perspective.

Peterson's Four-Year Colleges (Peterson's Guides, P.O. 2123, Princeton, NJ 08543-2123; phone: 800/338-3282) $24.95 plus $6.75/shipping, 3,176 pages, published each July. Profiles 1,950 accredited institutions in the U.S. that grant baccalaureate degrees. Eight hundred of these schools are described in depth.

Peterson's Two-Year Colleges (Peterson's Guides, P.O. 2123, Princeton, NJ 08543-2123; phone: 800/338-3282) $21.95 plus $6.75/shipping, 912 pages, published each July. Profiles more than 1,500 accredited institutions in the U.S. that grant the associate degree as their highest degree.

Higher Education Directory (Higher Education Publications, Suite 648, 6400 Arlington Blvd., Falls Church, VA 22042; phone: 703/532-2300) $49.50, published each October. Regarded as one of the most authoritative directories of degree-granting, post-secondary institutions accredited by agencies recognized by the U.S. Secretary of Education. They say they are the only directory that follows the U.S. Department of Education guidelines for inclusion.

1996-97 Accredited Institutions of Postsecondary Education (Oryx Press, Suite 700, 4041 N. Central, Phoenix, AZ 85012; phone: 800/279-6799) $64.95 plus $6.50/shipping, 700+ pages, May 1997. Describes more than 5,500 public, private, two-year and four-year colleges and universities, and vocational institutions of higher learning throughout the U.S., plus U.S. sponsored schools in 14 countries. All schools are accredited by national or regional accrediting agencies recognized by the Council on Postsecondary Accreditation.

National Faculty Directory 1997 (Gale Research, Inc., 835 Penobscot Bldg., Detroit, MI 48226; phones: 800/877-4253, 313/961-2242) $710, 3,895 pages in three volumes, July 1996. You can track down any of 650,500 teaching faculty at 3,600 American colleges and universities and 240 Canadian institutions that use English-language instructional materials. The 250-page **1997 Supplement** costs $280.

Washington Education Association Directory (Council for Advancement and Support of Education, Suite 400, 11 Dupont Cr., Washington, DC 20036; phones: 800/554-8536, 202/328-5979) $19, 20 pages, published in winter of even-numbered years. This directory profiles 70 associations that serve and support American higher education, including K-12.

Photocopying strictly prohibited

Higher education

Directory of History Departments and Organizations in the United States and Canada (American Historical Association, 400 A St., SE, Washington, DC 20003; phone: 202/544-2422) $70/nonmembers, $50/members, 870 pages, annual in October. Lists more than 800 history departments and organizations.

Archeological Field Work Opportunities Bulletin (Kendell/Hunt Publishing Co., 4050 Westmark Dr., Dubuque, IA 52004; phones: 800/228-0810, 319/589-1000) $15/nonmembers, $13/members of the Archeological Institute of America; published each December. Gives site, period, date of excavation and field school, application deadline, credits, institutions offering credit, experience required, financial aid, all costs, and volunteer requirements for thousands of digs throughout the U.S. and the world. This is a tremendous resource for contacts in the archeological community.

Archeological Field Work Opportunities is a wonderful Internet networking tool which provides you valued contacts with every major archeological department in academia. Go to URL: **http://durendal.cit.corned.edu**, and click on anyplace on the world map graphic or on the list of archeological digs to get a detailed discussion and fabulous photos of each archeological site in the U.S. and around the world, plus information on the opportunities for volunteers or for field school enrollment.

AAA Guide (American Anthropological Association, Suite 640, 4350 N. Fairfax Dr., Arlington, VA 22203; phone: 703/528-1902) $50/nonmembers, $40/members, 578 pages, published each August. Lists 10,500 individual and institutional members, including universities, museums, and research departments of anthropology in the U.S. and Canada by faculties and specialties, facilities and programs, and information on financial support.

National Guide to Funding in Higher Education (The Foundation Center, 79 Fifth Ave., New York, NY 10003-3076; phones: 800/424-9836, 212/620-4230) $145 plus $4.50/shipping, 1,275 pages, June 1996. Covers nearly 4,500 foundations that have awarded grants to colleges, universities, graduate programs, and research institutes.

AERA Biographical Membership Directory (American Educational Research Association, 1230 17th St., NW, Washington, DC 20036-3078; phone: 202/223-9485) $40/nonmembers, $10/members, annual. Lists more than 22,000 members engaged in educational research.

Financial Management Association International Directory of Members (FMAI, College of Business Administration, University of South Florida, Tampa, FL 33620; phone: 813/974-2084) $100/nonmembers, free/members, 268 pages, published each September. Lists all members of the FMAI, plus contact information.

Expand your mind: Read chapters 1 and 2 first

AECT Membership Directory (Association for Educational Communications and Technology, Suite 820, 1025 Vermont Ave., NW, Washington, DC 20005; phone: 202/347–7834) $40/nonmembers, free/members, 170 pages, published each April. Lists 4,000 members, mostly individuals but some corporate.

NUCEA Membership Directory (National University Continuing Education Association, Suite 615, 1 Dupont Cr., Washington, DC 20036; phone: 202/659–3130) $54.50/nonmembers, $29.50/members, published every October. Essentially a "who's who" in continuing education.

APA Directory of Members (American Philological Association, Department of Classics, Box 117–A, Holy Cross College, Worcester, MA 01610; phone: 508/793–2203) $15/nonmembers, free/members, 141 pages, published in odd–numbered years. Lists about 3,000 academics, mostly professors, some students.

Directory of College Cooperative Education Programs (Oryx Press, Suite 700, 4041 N. Central, Phoenix, AZ 85012; phone: 800/279–6799) $49.95 plus 10 percent/shipping, 232 pages, 1996. Provides details on over 500 cooperative education programs offered at colleges and universities. Each entry includes key contacts and examples of active employers who participate in these programs. Entries are listed by state and indexed by institution and degree programs offered.

Black Professionals in Continuing Education (National University Continuing Education Association, 1 Dupont Cr., Suite 615, Washington, DC 20036; phone: 202/659–3130) $10. Lists individuals who wish to be identified for networking purposes.

NCAA Directory (National Collegiate Athletic Association, 6701 College Blvd., Overland Park, KS 66211; phone: 913/339–1906) $8/nonmembers, $6/members, 250 pages, published every October. Lists addresses and phone numbers of NCAA member institutions. Includes the institution's president, director of athletics, senior woman athletics administrator, and more.

ASEE's Directory of Engineering Graduate Studies and Research (American Society for Engineering Education, Suite 600, 1818 N St., Washington, DC 20036; phone: 202/331–3500) $70/nonmembers, $35/members and students, issued each September. Lists schools by type of program, dean's names, address, phone number, accredited or not, and specific types of engineering.

ASEE's Directory of Engineering Studies and Research Undergraduate Programs (American Society for Engineering Education, Suite 600, 1818 N St., Washington, DC 20036; phone: 202/331–3500) $50/nonmembers, $25/members and students, issued each September. Lists schools by type of program, dean's names, address, phone number, accredited or not, and specific types of engineering.

Higher education

ACSA Annual Directory (Association of Collegiate Schools of Architecture, 1735 New York Ave., NW, Washington, DC 20006; phones: 800/232–2724, 202/785–2324) $17.95, published every November. Includes 115 member schools of architecture with the names of their deans and faculty members. Also available as mailing labels: General School Address list (115 schools) for $50, Administrators (183 names) for $75, Full–Time Faculty (3,000) for $300, and Full– and Part–Time Faculty (5,000+) for $400 (for various foreign continents call for rates).

Directory of Music Faculties in Colleges and Universities, U.S. and Canada (College Music Society, 202 W. Spruce St., Missoula, MT 59802–4202; phones: 800/729–0235, 406/721–9616) $55, 1996–97 edition. Reports on 32,720 music faculty and 1,832 post–secondary institutions.

Art & Design Faculties Directory (College Music Society, 202 W. Spruce St., Missoula, MT 59807; phones: 800/729–0235, 406/721–9616) $55, 1995–96 edition. Reports on art programs and schools throughout the U.S.

American Society of Criminology Membership Directory (American Society of Criminology, Suite 212, 1314 Kinnear Rd., Columbus, OH, 43212; phone: 614/292–9207) free/members only, 118 pages, published in odd–numbered years. Lists more than 2,800 criminologists.

ACJS Membership Directory (Academy of Criminal Justice Sciences, Northern Kentucky University, 402 Nunn Hall, Highland Heights, KY 41099–5998; phones: 800/757–2257, 606/572–5634) $10/nonmembers, free/members, annual. Members are primarily criminologists in higher education.

Directory of Geoscience Departments (American Geological Institute, AGI Publications Center, P.O. Box 205, Annapolis Junction, MD 20701, phone: 301/953–1744) $26 plus $5/shipping, over 480 pages, published every October. Lists 950 geoscience departments in colleges and universities in the U.S., Canada, and Mexico, 12,000 geoscientists, selected foreign geoscience departments, U.S. national laboratories, major museums, field courses, and camps, and earth–science teacher training programs.

Guide to Geoscience Departments in the United States & Canada (American Geological Institute, AGI Publications Center, P.O. Box 205, Annapolis Junction, MD 20701, phone: 301/953–1744) $39.95 plus $6/shipping, over 450 pages, published each October. Lists faculty members with research and teaching specialties at more than 170 schools with geoscience departments. Includes descriptions of research facilities.

Institute of Mathematical Statistics Membership Directory (IMS, Suite 7, 3401 Investment Blvd., Hayward, CA 94545; phone: 510/783–8141) $125/nonmembers, free/members, 1995. Lists more than 4,000 member mathematics and statistics professors with their addresses and telephone numbers.

Expand your mind: Read chapters 1 and 2 first

AACTE Directory (American Association of Colleges of Teacher Education, Suite 610, 1 Dupont Cr., NW, Washington, DC 20036; phone: 202/293–2450) $50/nonmembers, $35/members, annual. Describes programs at colleges of teacher education.

A Guide to College Programs in Hospitality and Tourism (John Wiley & Sons; available from Planning/Communications by special order, toll–free phone: 888/366–5200) $24.95, 512 pages, 1995. This book, by the Council on Hotel, Restaurant, and Institutional Education, describes two–year community college, four–year college, and graduate programs in culinary arts; hotel/motel management, restaurant and food service, and travel and tourism. While it's written for the prospective student, it gives prospective faculty and administrators useful information about the schools and their programs.

AIB Directory of Members (Academy of International Business, College of Business Administration, University of Hawaii, 2404 Maile Way, Honolulu, Hawaii 96822–2282; phone: 808/956–3665) $20/nonmembers, free/members, 107 pages, published in May of even–numbered years. Lists about 2,700 member business school faculty members and administrators.

NCRE Membership Directory (National Council on Rehabilitation Education, c/o Dr. Garth Eldredge, Department of Special Education, Utah State University, Logan, UT 84122–2865; phone: 801/797–3241) $25/nonmembers, free/members, 125 pages, annual in December. Lists more than 500 faculty involved in rehabilitation education.

Forest Products Society Membership Directory (Forest Product Society, 2801 Marshall Ct., Madison, WI 53705; 608/231–1361) free/members only, 86 pages, published each February. Includes job title, address, phone, and employer for each of the 25,000+ members.

APSA Directory of Members (American Political Science Association, 1527 New Hampshire Ave., NW, Washington, DC 20036; phone: 202/483–2512) $55/nonmembers, $35/members, 759 pages, triannual, 1997. Lists some 13,000 political scientists.

Directory of Colleges and Universities with Accredited Social Work Degree Programs (Council on Social Work Education, 1600 Duke St., Alexandria, VA 22314; phone: 703/683–8080) $11.50/nonmembers, $10.50/members, 63 pages, annual in July. Lists about 550 bachelors and masters programs in social work by state.

Grants for Higher Education (The Foundation Center, 79 Fifth Ave., New York, NY 10003–3076; phones: 800/424–9836, within New York State call 212/620–4230) $75 plus $4.50/shipping, 537 pages, in October of odd–numbered years. Describes recent foundation grants of at least $10,000 given to higher education and graduate/professional schools for programs in all disciplines, as well as to academic libraries and student services and organizations. This directory is useful for identifying foundations and grant recipients for which you may wish to work.

Salary surveys

Comparative Costs and Staffing Report for College and University Facilities (APPA: The Association of Higher Education Facilities Officers, 1643 Prince St., Alexandria, VA 22314; phone: 703/684–1446) $90/nonmembers, $35/members, plus $8/shipping, 390 pages, published biennally. This study is based on data collected from over 500 institutions.

The Annual Report on the Economic Status of the Profession (American Association of University Professors, Suite 500, 1012 14th St., NW, Washington, DC 20005; phone: 202/737–5900) $57, published every April. This survey is included in an issue of *Academe* magazine, but is available as a single issue. Reports on wages and benefits by school, state, gender, number of faculty, and number of tenured faculty.

The National Faculty Salary Survey: By Discipline and Rank in Private Four–Year Colleges (College and University Personnel Association, 1233 20th St., NW, Washington, DC 20036; phone: 202/429–0311, ext. 392) $80/nonmembers, $55/members, 90 pages, issued annually in January. Gives the range and average salaries for full–time faculty.

The National Faculty Salary Survey: By Discipline and Rank in Public Four–Year Colleges (College and University Personnel Association, 1233 20th St., NW, Washington, DC 20036; phone: 202/429–0311, ext. 392) $80/nonmembers, $55/members, 90 pages, issued annually in January. Gives the range and average salaries for full–time faculty.

APSA Survey of Political Science Departments (American Political Science Association, 1527 New Hampshire Ave., NW, Washington, DC 20036; phone: 202/483–2512) $20, annual. Gives salary information and enrollment trends of four–year institutions offering political science.

Statistics on Social Work Education in the United States: 1996 (Council on Social Work Education, 1600 Duke St., Alexandria, VA 22314; phone: 703/683–8080) $17.25, annual in June. Surveys of accredited bachelor and masters degree programs in social work, giving faculty salaries by rank, ethnicity, gender, highest earned degree, primary responsibility, and level of program.

Trades and vocational education

Job ads

The Community College Times (American Association of Community Colleges, Suite 410, 1 Dupont Cr., NW, Washington, DC 20036; phones: 800/250–6557, 202/728–0200) biweekly, $52/annual nonmember subscrip-

Expand your mind: Read chapters 1 and 2 first

tion (U.S.), $62/foreign, free/members. "Careerline" has 5 to 6 pages of ads for teaching and administrative positions at junior and community colleges.

Techniques (American Vocational Association, 1410 King St., Alexandria, VA 22314; phones: 800/826–9972, 703/683–3111) eight issues/year, $35/annual nonmember subscription, free/members. "Marketplace" carries ads for three or four vocational educators, administrators, and teacher educators at secondary and post–secondary institutions. This publication will occasionally run a salary survey, called ***Data File***. Call to find out which back issues contains one.

NAABAVE news & notes (National Association for the Advancement of Black Americans in Vocational Education, c/o Dr. Warner Dickerson, 3476 Renault, Memphis, TN 38118; phones: 901/362–8654, or 313/494–1660, ask for Dr. Ethel Washington) semiannual, free/members only. "Job Opportunity" will have one to five notices of job vacancies in vocational teaching and administration. Jobs do not appear in every issue and when they do, the ads are sometimes out of date.

Connect (Vocational Industrial Clubs of America, P.O. Box 3000, Leesburg, VA 22075; phone: 703/777–8810) nine/issues during the school year, $8.50/annual subscription/nonmembers, free/members. Each issue provides tips for postsecondary and college instructions on finding jobs in the vocational educational field. Jobs in the vocational field can be found on the Internet at URL: **http://www.vica.org**. Scrolling down and clicking on "VICA News" will list a couple of job vacancies with VICA, but scads of jobs in vocational education can be found at the links site, "Vocational/Technical Links," which links you up with loads of institutions advertising jobs.

Next (Vocational Industrial Clubs of America, P.O. Box 3000, Leesburg, VA 22075; phone: 703/777–8810) quarterly during the school year, $8.50/annual subscription/nonmembers, free/members. Each issue provides tips for finding vocational jobs, developing interviewing skills, and preparing resumes.

Directories

AACC Membership Directory (American Association of Community Colleges, Suite 410, 1 Dupont Cr., NW, Washington, DC 20036; phones: 800/250–6557, 202/728–0200) $60/nonmembers, $45/members, annual. Lists presidents and 15 key administrators at each of the AACC's 1,100 member community colleges.

Who's Who in Community Colleges (American Association of Community Colleges, Suite 410, 1 Dupont Cr., NW, Washington, DC 20036; phones: 800/250–6557, 202/728–0200) $10; 491 pages, last published in 1993. For each institution, this directory gives basic information plus the names of the top twelve administrators.

Trades and vocational education

National VICA Staff Directory (Vocational Industrial Clubs of America, P.O. Box 3000, Leesburg, VA 22075; phone: 703/777–8810) is a free directory of contacts in vocational education on the Internet. Go to URL: **http://www.vica.org**, and scroll down to "Vica Directory."

American Trade Schools Directory (Croner Publications, Suite 1–D, 10951 Sorrento Valley Rd., San Diego, CA 92121; phones: 800/441–4033, 619/546–1894) $110 plus $9.95 shipping, over 600 pages, includes updates ten times a year. Brief profiles on over 12,000 trade, technical, and vocational schools in the U.S. and Puerto Rico. Includes more than 320 occupational categories.

Directory of Accredited Institutions (Career College Association, Suite 980, 750 First Street, NE, Washington, DC 20002–4241; phone: 202/336–6700) free, 60 pages, annual. Lists some 600 trade, technical, and vocational schools accredited by the Accrediting Council for Independent Colleges and Schools (ACICS).

Expand your mind: Read chapters 1 and 2 first

Chapter 11

Emergency management

Emergency management

Job ads

The NCCEM Bulletin (National Coordinating Council on Emergency Management, Unit N, 7297 Lee Highway, Falls Church, VA 22042; phone: 703/533–7672) monthly, free/members only, $75/annual dues. Jobs listed under "Personnel Corner." About one job ad every three months.

Directory

The NCCEM Membership Directory (National Coordinating Council on Emergency Management, Unit N, 7297 Lee Highway, Falls Church, VA 22042; phone: 703/533–7672) $10, published every January.

Chapter 12

Environment

Environment

*Also see the chapters on "Science," "Forestry and horticulture," and "Parks and recreation." Additional job sources that focus on environmental positions in government and the private sector appear in the **Government Job Finder** and the **Professional's Job Finder** respectivvely.*

Job ads

The Job Seeker (Route 2, Box 16, Warrens, WI 54666; phone: 608/378–4290) bimonthly, $60/annual subscription, $36/six–month subscription, $19.50/three–month subscription. Lists 200 environmental and natural resource vacancies in every aspect of these fields, including environmental education. For an additional $10, you can get nine special supplementary issues, December through April, that feature summer jobs not listed in the *Job Seeker*. A sample of these job ads is available each week on the Internet at URL: **http://www.msildaugh.com/jobseeker/index.html**.

Environmental Health Perspectives Bulletin Board is an Internet site that gives you job listings that include environmental, biological, and physiological fields. Go to URL: **http://ehPhet1.niehs.nih.gov/docs/bboard/bbboard.html**, and select "Position Announcements," where you can browse through about 20 job notices.

Environmental Career Opportunities (Brubach Publishing Company, P.O. Box 560, Standardsville, VA 22973; phone: 202/861–0592) $29/two–month subscription, $49/four months, $69/six months, $129/annual, $8.95/single issue. You'll find announcements for more than 300 positions in all aspects of the environmental field: advocacy, communications, and fundraising; research and education; legislative assistants; environmental policy, legislation, and regulation; conservation and resource management; environmental engineering, risk assessment, and impact analysis; government agencies; and internships.

Environmental Opportunities (P.O. Box 4379, Arcata, CA 95518; phone: 707/826–1909) monthly, $47/annual subscription, $26/six–month subscription, $50/annual subscription (Canada), $60/annual subscription elsewhere. Over 125 jobs, internships, seasonal work, educational offerings, and conferences. Includes administrative positions, fisheries, wildlife, forestry, research, parks, outdoor recreation, and ecology. Write for free sample copy.

Environmental Job Opportunities is an Internet gopher job bank of the e–zine, *New Environmentalist Journal,* where you can find about a dozen environmental–related jobs. Go to URL: **gopher://manning.cais.com:70/**, select "The New Environmentalist," and then "Environmental Job Opportunities."

Environmental Careers Organization is a terrific Internet site for paid internship jobs. Go to URL: **http://www.eco.org/**, and select "Paid Internships." Then under "Current Openings" select the region of the country you want to browse for positions. There are some very substantial jobs here, for geologists, GIS technicians, biologists, and cartographers, among others.

EarthWorks includes *Job Scan* (Student Conservation Association, P.O. Box 550, Charlestown, NH 03603; phone: 603/543–1700) monthly, $31.95/nonmember annual subscription, $24.95/member annual subscription. About 70 jobs in a typical issue plus 20 to 30 internships.

The Caretaker Gazette (1845 NW Deane St., Pullman, WA 99163; phone: 509/332–0806) bimonthly, $24/annual subscription. Among its 80 job announcements are jobs and internships in forestry, fisheries, environment, and caretaking.

Virginia Coast Reserve Gopher Service Job Bank is an Internet job listing of environmentally–related science disciplines, such as organismal physiologists, ecologists, wildlife biologists. Go to URL: **gopher://atlantic.evsc .virginia.EDU:70/11/Opportunities**, and select "Jobs." Most are for faculty and postdoctoral positions; some of the listed jobs are out of date.

Environmental Careers Bulletin (Suite 327, 11693 San Vicente Blvd., Los Angeles, CA 90047; no phone orders) monthly, free, but when you write for a subscription you must provide your job title, college major, college degree, and year degree was received. From 20 to 50 display ads for

Photocopying strictly prohibited

Environment

environmental positions, largely private sector, but with some in the non–profit sector, appear in the typical issue. Details on this company's environmental job fairs held around the country are included.

The Wildlifer (The Wildlife Society, 5410 Grosvenor Ln., Bethesda, MD 20814; phone: 301/897–9708) bimonthly, free/members only; $39/annual dues, $20/students. About 20 positions in conservation, wildlife, and natural resources appear under "Positions Available."

Journal of the National Technical Association (Peterson's Magazine Group, 202 Carnegie Center, Princeton, NJ 08540; phones: 800/338–3282 ext. 533, 609/243–9111 ext. 533) spring, summer, and autumn issues, $16.90/each, $50.70/annual subscription. Ten to 40 vacancies for health physicists, biologists, engineers, and environmental scientists appear in display ads.

Water Environment Technology (Water Environment Federation, 601 Wythe St., Alexandria, VA 22314; phone: 703/684–2400) monthly, contact for current rates. Jobs listed under "Classifieds." About 10 to 15 job ads are in the typical issue. You can see 20 to 30 job ads at their Web site at URL: **http://www.wef.org** and selecting "Member Networking" and then choosing "Job Bank." Positions include faculty and research in public works, environmental science, wastewater and water engineering, and sewer maintenance.

Environmental Protection Magazine (Stevens Publishing Corp., Customer Service, P.O. Box 2604, Waco, TX 76702; phone: 817/662–7000) monthly, $99/annual subscription (U.S.), $124/Canada and Mexico, $134/elsewhere. Between eight and ten job ads appear per issue.

The Conservogram (Soil and Water Conservation Society, 7515 NE Ankeny Rd., Ankeny, IA 50021–9764; phone: 515/232–1080) ten issues/year, $49/annual subscription members only. Jobs listed under "Classified Advertising." About five to ten job ads per issue.

E Magazine (Earth Action Network, 28 Knight St., Norwalk, CT 06851; phone: 203/854–5559) bimonthly, $20/annual subscription (U.S.), $25/Mexico and Canada, $30/elsewhere. Five to ten job openings are in "Classified–Job Opportunities."

Ecological Society of America Newsletter (ESA, Suite 400, 2010 Massachusetts Ave., NW, Washington, DC 20036; phone: 202/416–6182) six issues/year, $5/annual subscription nonmembers, free/members. Ten to 15 ads for ecotoxicologists, plant ecologists, and ecologists appear under "Job Announcements." Most positions are with universities or other institutions.

For a clean mind and clean air: Read chapters 1 and 2 first

Newsletter of the Ecological Society of America (ESA, Suite 420, 2010 Massachusetts Ave., NW, Washington, DC 20036; phone: 202/833–8773) five issues/year, free. Fifteen to 25 ads for ecotoxicologists, plant ecologists, and ecologists appear under "Job Announcements."

Resource Recycling (P.O. Box 10540, Portland, OR 97206; phone: 503/227–1319) monthly, $47/annual subscription. About two recycling and solid waste management positions are listed under "Positions Available."

AEE Job's Clearinghouse (Association for Experiential Education, Suite 100, 2305 Canyon Blvd., Boulder, CO 80302; phone: 303/440–8844) monthly, $80/nonmember annual subscription, $40/members. Ten to 15 job openings and internships for environmental educators with emphasis on wilderness experience are among the 60 to 125 ads in a typical issue.

Job services

The Nature Conservancy Job Hotline (The Nature Conservancy, 1815 N. Lynn St., Arlington, VA 22209) free, updated every Friday. Call 703/247–3721 any old time (does not require a touch–tone phone) and you'll hear the following: how many jobs are on the hotline today, their job titles, and a detailed description of each job's requirements plus to whom you should send your resume and cover letter. Jobs include research, field work, administration, science positions, land conservation, and everything else in the environmental field.

Environmental Action Job Book (Environmental Action Foundation, Suite 600, 6930 Carroll Ave., Takoma Park, MD 20912; phone: 301/891–1100) free. This up–to–date book of environmental jobs and internships can be seen only at the Environmental Action Foundation's office.

Environmental Careers Organization Placement Service (286 Congress St., Boston, MA 02110; phone: 617/426–4375) free. This service finds temporary employment for college graduates and people thinking of changing careers that ranges from three months to two years. There is also a possibility of permanent placement. Request an application form; do *not* send your resume. The national office in Boston sends it to a regional office where you are placed into the applicant pool. Positions are with corporations, consulting firms, government agencies, and non–profit organizations.

Diversity Initiative Program Placement Service (Environmental Careers Organization, 286 Congress St., Boston, MA 02110; phone: 617/426–4375) free/one year. This service places minority college students and graduates in internships. Send in a completed application form, *not* your resume, to the national office in Boston. The national office sends it to a regional office where you are placed into the applicant pool. Positions are with non–profit organizations, government agencies, corporations, and consulting firms.

Photocopying strictly prohibited

Environment

Resource Assistant Program (The Student Conservation Association, P.O. Box 550, Charlestown, NH 03603; phone: 603/543-1700) free. Although this program places you in a nonpaying three-month volunteer position, you can use the contacts you make to gain an advantage when applying for a paying job from one of these employers. You do receive free travel, lodging, food, and basic living expenses. The program places volunteers with the National Park Service, U.S. Forest Service, U.S. Fish and Wildlife Service, Bureau of Land Management, state park and wildlife agencies, and private natural resource agencies. Positions are in the fields of wildlife and fisheries, forestry, recreation management, geology, archaeology, engineering and surveying, interpretation, visitor assistance, back country and wilderness management, trail maintenance and construction, hydrology and water resources, range management and plant taxonomy, and environmental education. Contact the SCA for an application and more information.

The Environmental Careers Organization operates a job-matching service via the Internet at URL: **http://www.eco.org/welcome.html**. Click on "Our Program" to access the service which covers a wide range of positions in the environment including engineering, planning, computer sciences, and mostly earth sciences. If you select "National Environmental Careers Conference," you'll find links to a good number of companies that may have job openings posted on their home pages and to environmental organizations and agencies.

Directories

World Directory of Environmental Organizations (California Institute of Public Affairs, P.O. Box 189040, Sacramento, CA 95818; phone: 916/442-2472) $50 plus 7.25 percent sales tax for California residents, foreign: $63/surface mail, $70/airmail; 232 pages, 1996. Describes more than 3,000 government agencies, research institutes, and citizens' and professional associations in the U.S. and around the globe. Divided into 50 topics with index, glossary, and bibliography of related directories and databases.

Environmental Telephone Directory (Government Institutes, Suite 200, 4 Research Place, Rockville, MD 20850; phone: 301/921-2355) $67 plus $6/shipping, 256 pages, 1996. Detailed information — including phone numbers — on state and federal government agencies that deal with the environment; identifies the environmental aides of U.S. Senators and Representatives. Also available on the *GI Environmental Database CD ROM* described below.

For a clean mind and clean air: Read chapters 1 and 2 first

Directory of Environmental Information Sources (Government Institutes, Suite 200, 4 Research Place, Rockville, MD 20850; phone: 301/921–2355) $79 plus $6/shipping, 322 pages, published in September of odd-numbered years. Includes federal and state government resources, professional, scientific, and trade organizations; newsletters, magazines, and databases. Also available on the *GI Environmental Database CD ROM* described immediately below.

GI Environmental Database CD ROM (Government Institutes, Suite 200, 4 Research Place, Rockville, MD 20850; phone: 301/921–2355) $149 plus $6/shipping. This Windows™ CD–ROM includes the *Environmental Telephone Directory* and *Directory of Environmental Information Sources* described above as well as an environmental regulatory glossary, environmental acronyms, and a customized spell-checking dictionary that can be added to popular word processing programs.

Environmental Guide to the Internet (Government Institutes, Suite 200, 4 Research Place, Rockville, MD 20850; phone: 301/921–2355) $49 plus $6/shipping, 236 pages, 1996. Gives detailed information on electronic journals, Web sites, and discussion groups.

Conservation Directory (National Wildlife Federation, 8925 Leesburg Pike, Vienna, VA 22184; phones: 800/822–9919, 703/796–4000): $60/nonmembers, $54.50/members, $49/student, annual. Lists organizations, agencies, and officials concerned with environmental education and conservation. Includes index that list organizations by their particular interests.

Gale Environmental Sourcebook (Gale Research, Inc., 835 Penobscot Bldg., Detroit, MI 48226; phone: 800/877–4253) $85, 934 pages, 1994. Gives you full descriptions and contact information on more than 9,000 environmental organizations, publications, programs, and information services. Includes alphabetical and subject indexes.

Directory of Natural Science Centers (Natural Science for Youth Foundation, 130 Azalea Dr., Roswell, GA 30075; phone: 770/594–9367) $78.50/nonmembers, $49.95/for educational professionals, 600 pages, 1997. Gives details on over 1,350 nature centers.

The Wildlife Society Membership Directory and Certification Registry (The Wildlife Society, 5410 Grosvenor Ln., Bethesda, MD 20814; phone: 301/897–9770) $5/nonmembers, free/members, published each September. Members are professionals in conservation, wildlife, and natural resources.

International Environment Resources is an Internet site with a large international collection of links to the home pages of environmental organizations and companies. Go to URL: **http://www.contact.org/environs.htm**, and browse the alphabetical listing.

The New Careers Directory: Internships and Professional Opportunities in Technology and Social Change (Student Pugwash USA, Suite 814, 815 15th St., NW, Washington, DC 20005; phone: 202/393–6555) $18, $10/stu-

Environment

dents, add $3/shipping. Offers full details on where and how to apply for internships and entry-level jobs with non-profits and government agencies in the environment and energy, development, communications, peace/security, health, law, and general science.

Summer Jobs for Students (Peterson's Guides; available from Planning/Communications' catalog at the end of this book) $16.95, 320 pages, published each November. Describes over 20,000 summer job openings in the United States and Canada with environmental programs, resorts, camps, amusement parks, expeditions, theaters, national parks, and government. Each detailed employer description includes salary and benefits, employer background, profile of employees, and whom to contact to apply.

Grants for Environmental Protection & Animal Welfare (The Foundation Center, 79 Fifth Ave., New York, NY 10003-3076; phones: 800/424-9836, within New York State call 212/620-4230) $75 plus $4.50/shipping, 250 pages, published in October of odd-numbered years. Describes recent foundation grants of at least $10,000 given for environmental protection and legal agencies, for pollution abatement and control, conservation, and environmental education. This directory is useful for identifying foundations and grant recipients for which you may wish to work.

National Guide to Funding for the Environment and Animal Welfare (The Foundation Center, 79 Fifth Ave., New York, NY 10003-3076; phones: 800/424-9836, within New York State call 212/620-4230) $95 plus $4.50/shipping, 527 pages, May 1996. Describes more than 1,700 foundations and corporate direct giving programs for projects involved in conservation, ecological research, waste reduction, advocacy, animal protection and welfare, and wildlife preservation.

California Environmental Directory: A Guide to Organizations and Resources (California Institute of Public Affairs, P.O. Box 189040, Sacramento, CA 95818; phone: 916/442-2472) $40, 128 pages, May 1993. A guide to nearly 1,000 government agencies, university programs, and major associations concerned with air quality, soil, law, health, the desert, the coast, and much more.

California Water Resources Directory: A Guide to Organizations and Information Resources (California Institute of Public Affairs, P.O. Box 189040, Sacramento, CA 95818; phone: 916/442-2472) $25, 1991, 120 pages. Includes nearly 1,000 governmental and non-governmental organizations that deal with water policy, development, supply, and conservation as well as related health, environmental quality, energy, and economic aspects.

For a clean mind and clean air: Read chapters 1 and 2 first

Environmental Grantmaking Foundations (Environmental Data Research Institute, P.O. Box 22770, Rochester, NY 14692–2770; phones: 800/724–1857, 716/473–3090) $84, plus $6 shipping (U.S.), plus $12 shipping (surface Canada), plus $14 shipping (airmail Canada), 900 pages, April 1996. Get full details on over 700 of the most significant independent, community, and corporate foundations in the U.S. and Canada that give environmental grants. Each foundation profile includes key individuals, history and philosophy, financial data, program and funding analysis, sample grants, application process, emphases, and limitations.

Experience–Based Training and Development: Directory of Programs (Association for Experiential Education, Suite 100, 2305 Canyon Blvd., Boulder, CO 80302; phone: 303/440–8844) $15/nonmembers, $12.50/members, 98 pages, 1997. Description of more than 90 training and development programs in the U.S. and abroad that emphasize environmental concerns.

Chapter 13

Finance and accounting

Finance and accounting

Job ads

In Search Of (American Academy of Actuaries, 1100 17th St., NW, Washington, DC 20036; phone: 202/223–8196) bimonthly, $295/members only. Fifty job ads for actuarial positions appear throughout.

Credit Union Magazine (Credit Union National Association, P.O. Box 431 Madison, WI 53701–0431; phones: 800/356–9655, 608/231–4000) monthly, $36/annual subscription. "Classified–Career Opportunities" features announcements for ten or more positions of all types with credit unions.

Credit Union Management (Credit Union Executives Society, P.O. Box 14167, Madison, WI 53714–0167; phones: 800/252–2664, 608/271–2664) monthly, $54/annual nonmember subscription, $40/members. The "Classifieds" feature about five ads for financial CEOs, marketers, operations, data processing, and accountants.

The Accounting Review (American Accounting Association, 5717 Bessie Dr., Sarasota, FL 34233; phone: 941/921–7747) quarterly, $90/annual nonmember subscription (to be increased in 1997), free/members (annual dues: $85; members can opt for this periodical, *Accounting Horizons*, or *Issues in Accounting Education* as part of their membership; if they want

two of these, dues are $95; to get all three, dues are $100). Under "Placement Ads," you'll find job descriptions for around 60 university faculty positions in accounting.

Accounting Horizons (American Accounting Association, 5717 Bessie Dr., Sarasota, FL 34233; phone: 941/921–7747) quarterly, $60/annual nonmember subscription, free/members (annual dues: $85; members can choose this periodical, *The Accounting Review*, or *Issues in Accounting Education* as part of their membership; if they want two of these, dues are $95; to receive all three, dues are $100). Under "Placement Ads," you'll find job descriptions for 30 to 50 university faculty positions in accounting.

Issues in Accounting Education (American Accounting Association, 5717 Bessie Dr., Sarasota, FL 34233; phone: 941/921–7747) published in spring and autumn, $30/annual nonmember subscription, free/members (annual dues: $85; members can select this periodical, *Accounting Horizons*, or *The Accounting Review* as part of their membership; if they want two of these, dues are $95; to get all three, dues are $100). Under "Placement Ads," you'll find job descriptions for 70 or more university faculty positions in accounting.

ACA News (American Compensation Association, 14040 N. Northsight Blvd., Scottsdale, AZ 85260; phone: 602/951–9191) 10 issues/year, $50/nonmember annual subscription, free/members. Twenty to 30 job openings for compensation and benefits analysts, some in the non–profit sector, appear each issue in the "Career Marketplace."

Directories

American Academy of Actuaries Yearbook (American Academy of Actuaries, 1100 17th St., NW, Washington, DC 20036; phone: 202/223–8196) $25/nonmembers, free/members, 97 pages, published every January. Lists the 300 members alphabetically.

Directory of Actuarial Membership (American Academy of Actuaries, 1100 17th St., NW, Washington, DC 20036; phone: 202/223–8196) $100/nonmembers, free/members, annual. Includes contact information on over 10,000 members.

Credit Union Executive Society Annual Membership Directory (Credit Union Executives Society, P.O. Box 14167, Madison, WI 53714; phones: 800/252–2664, 608/271–2664) free/members only, $415/annual dues, published annually. Includes details on operations management of credit unions.

Photocopying strictly prohibited

Finance and accounting

Financial Marketing Association Directory (Credit Union Executives Society, P.O. Box 14167, Madison, WI 53714; phones: 800/252-2664, 608/271-2664) free/members only, $415/annual dues, issued annually. Details on marketing directors of credit unions.

Salary surveys

Compensation in the Accounting/Financial Field (Abbott, Langer & Associates, 548 First St., Crete, IL 60417; phone: 708/672-4200) $495, annual. In-depth analysis of salary and benefits for 22 different positions from junior accountants to chief financial officers in education, non-profit organizations, business, industry, and government.

The Actuarial Salary Survey (American Academy of Actuaries, 1100 17th St., NW, Washington, DC 20036; phone: 202/223-8196) free, 24 pages, published each December. Presents salaries by practice area, geographic location, and education.

REIT Executive Compensation Survey (National Association of Real Estate Investment Trusts Membership Directory, 1129 20th St., NW, Washington, DC 20036; phone: 202/785-8717) contact for current costs, issued biennially. Covers executive compensation within the real estate investment trust industry for the top five positions.

Bank on it: Read chapters 1 and 2 first

Chapter 14

Forestry and horticulture

Forestry and horticulture

*Also see listings in the "Environment" and "Parks and recreation" chapters. The **Professional's Job Finder** and **Government Job Finder** contain substantially more extensive sets of job sources in these fields.*

Job ads

AABGA Newsletter (American Association of Botanical Gardens and Arboreta, 786 Church Rd., Wayne, PA 19087; phone: 610/688–1120) monthly, available only to members, $55/annual dues, $25/students. About 15 positions in public horticulture ranging from gardener to director appear under "Positions Available."

Internship Directory (American Association of Botanical Gardens and Arboreta, 786 Church Rd., Wayne, PA 19087; phone: 610/688–1120) $5/nonmember, $4/members, published each October. This is a very extensive state–by–state listing of summer internships available in public horticulture and private estates.

ASHS Newsletter (American Society for Horticultural Science, 600 Cameron St., Alexandria, VA 22314–2562; phone: 703/836–4606) monthly, free/members only. About 20 research or teaching positions in horticultural science are under "Opportunities."

HortOpportunities (American Society for Horticultural Science, 600 Cameron St., Alexandria, VA 22314–2562; phone: 703/836–4606) biweekly, $45/nonmember three–month subscription, $49/Canada, $55/elsewhere, $25/member three–month subscription, $29/Canada, $35/elsewhere. This jobs–only newsletter features from 40 to 70 detailed listings for professors, researchers, nursery operators, and other horticultural–related positions. Members may place free "Position Wanted" ads. This publication is also available on the Internet at URL: **http://www.ashs.org**, and clicking on "HortOpportunities."

Job services

Jobs Hotline (American Association of Botanical Gardens and Arboreta, 786 Church Rd., Wayne, PA 19087; phone: 610/688–1120) free. Call 610/688–9127 weekdays 5 p.m. to 9 a.m. (eastern time) and 24 hours on weekends for a tape recording that describes four to eight jobs in public horticulture.

Florapersonnel (1740 Lake Markham Rd., Sanford, FL 32771; phone: 407/320–8177) free. The job seeker completes Florapersonnel's form and submits it along with her resume. Resumes are kept on file indefinitely. When a match is made, Florapersonnel contacts the job seeker and, if the job seeker gives the okay, Florapersonnel gives her name and resume to the potential employer who then contacts the employer. (Normally, we don't list "headhunters" in this book, but the horticulture field has so few job sources that it seems essential to include this listing.) Jobs range from greenhouse growers to directors. Includes nursery, floral, landscape, and irrigation.

Photocopying strictly prohibited

Directories

AABGA Membership Directory (American Association of Botanical Gardens and Arboreta, 786 Church Rd., Wayne, PA 19087; phone: 610/688–1120) members/only, annual dues: $55, $25/students. Lists institutional members of AABGA.

ASHS Membership Directory (American Society for Horticultural Science, Suite 400, 113 S. West St., Alexandria, VA 22314; phone: 703/836-4606) $50/non-members, free/members, 280 pages, published each October. Lists information about ASHS's 5,000 members, primarily individuals.

Salary survey

AABGA Salary Survey (American Association of Botanical Gardens and Arboreta, 786 Church Rd., Wayne, PA 19087; phone: 610/688–1120) $40/nonmembers, $30/members, published in odd–numbered years. Contains salary information for 22 job categories in botanical gardens in the U.S. and Canada. You can also buy a subset of the survey by job area for just $10.

Chapter 15

Foundations and grants

Foundations and grants

Also see the "Philanthropy" chapter for additional job sources. Many directories of grant opportunities have been written for specific individual states. These are described in Chapter 30 under "Job and grant sources by state." In addition, be sure to check the Index for grant sources that are listed under a specific discipline elsewhere in this book.

Job ads

Foundation News and Commentary (Council on Foundations, 1828 L St., NW, Washington, DC 20036; phone: 202/466–6512) bimonthly, $48/nonmember annual subscription (U.S. and Canada), $98/elsewhere (airmail), free/members. About two to three job ads for executive directors and coordinators with foundations appear in display ads and in the classifieds section. Includes "Positions Wanted." Check "People" section for notices of those leaving and arriving in jobs.

Minority Funding Report (Government Information Services, Suite 875, 4301 N. Fairfax Dr., Arlington, VA 22203; phone: 703/528–1000) monthly, $128/annual subscription. The "Education Grants Week" section reports on two to four education grants. Another two to ten more grants in housing, health care, and other fields are also reported.

Foundation Giving Watch (Taft Group, 835 Penobscot Bldg., 645 Griswold St., Detroit, MI 48226–4094; phones: 800/877–8238, 313/961–2242) monthly, $149/annual subscription. This newsletter is a great source of up-to-date foundation funding opportunities with reports on new foundations, new grant programs, changing funding priorities, and community or regional funding news. Eight pages are devoted to new and updated profiles of foundations.

Corporate Philanthropy Report (Capitol Publications, Suite 444, 1101 King St., Alexandria, VA 22314; phone: 800/655–5597) monthly, $205/annual subscription. "Spotlight" reports details on funders within a specific category.

Education Grants Alert (Capitol Publications, Suite 444, 1101 King St., Alexandria, VA 22314; phone: 800/655–5597) weekly, $319/annual subscription. Provides regular updates on hard-to-find funding sources and numerous grant notices.

Health Grants & Contracts Weekly (Capitol Publications, Suite 444, 1101 King St., Alexandria, VA 22314; phone: 800/655–5597) weekly, $369/annual subscription. Updated information on health-related grant sources from the federal government and non-profits.

Foundation & Corporate Grants Alert (Capitol Publications, Suite 444, 1101 King St., Alexandria, VA 22314; phone: 800/655–5597) monthly, $279/annual subscription. Updates on latest grant information from corporations and foundations.

Federal Grants & Contracts Alert (Capitol Publications, Suite 444, 1101 King St., Alexandria, VA 22314; phone: 800/655–5597) weekly, $389/annual subscription. Updates on a broad spectrum of funding opportunities for non-profits from federal agencies.

Directories

Foundation Grants to Individuals (The Foundation Center, 79 Fifth Ave., New York, NY 10003–3076; phones: 800/424–9836, 212/620–4230) $65, 630 pages, published in May of odd-numbered years. This book offers everything you need to start your grant search: details on over 3,300 independent and corporate foundations that make grants to individuals. For each foundation, you'll find the contact person, application procedures, financial data, and giving preferences. Since relatively few foundations will issue a grant to an individual, this book is *the essential source* for any individual seeking a grant.

For a firm foundation, read chapters 1 and 2 first

Foundations and grants

Sources of Foundations (Capitol Publications, Suite 444, 1101 King St., Alexandria, VA 22314; phone: 800/655-5597) $475 plus $6/shipping, annual each April. This CD-ROM lists more than 13,000 private and corporate foundations, plus the names of more than 63,000 directors, officers, and trustees. Specify format you desire: Macintosh or Windows™.

Foundations On-Line (Northern California Community Foundation, Inc.) free. Go to Internet URL: **http://www.foundations.org** where you will find this "Directory of Charitable Foundations" Click on "Go to Directories and More!" Here you can select "Foundations and Grantmakers Directory and Home Page Gateway" which links you to over 50 foundations located throughout the country.

The Foundation Center offers a Web site with links to many foundations. Go to URL: **http://www.fdncenter.org** and look under the heading "Grantmaker Information." Selecting "Private Foundations on the Internet" will let you search links to over 100 private foundations. Picking "Corporate Grantmakers on the Internet" gets you to links to about 50 of them. You can also select "Grantmaking Public Charities on the Internet" and "Community Foundations on the Internet." You can search any of these databases by subject and/or location.

The Grants Database (Oryx Press, Suite 700, 4041 N. Central, Phoenix, AZ 85012-3397; phones: 800/279-6799, 602/265-2651). Constantly updated by Oryx Press, this database is one of the most comprehensive sources of information on funding programs on biomedical, health care, and humanities subjects. It includes details on research grants, award competitions, scholarships, arts contests, internships, visiting professorships and lectureships, and more. You can access this database through DIALOG. For information, call 800/334-2564.

Corporate Foundations & Giving (Capitol Publications, Suite 444, 1101 King St., Alexandria, VA 22314; phone: 800/655-5597) $259 plus $6/shipping, annual each April. This CD-ROM provides detailed information on more than 4,000 corporate givers, with contact names. Specify format you desire: Macintosh or Windows™.

Giving by Industry (Capitol Publications, Suite 444, 1101 King St., Alexandria, VA 22314; phone: 800/655-5597) $198 plus $6/shipping, 350 pages, 1996. Provides more than 200 profiles of leading corporate giving programs in primary industries.

Show me the money...please

The Grantseeker's Guide to Essential Internet Sites (Capitol Publications, Suite 444, 1101 King St., Alexandria, VA 22314; phone: 800/655–5597) $75 plus $6/shipping, 150 pages, 1996. Lists more than 230 essential Internet sites detailing funding opportunities from foundations, corporations, associations, and federal agencies.

Grant Source: Computers in the Classroom (Capitol Publications, Suite 444, 1101 King St., Alexandria, VA 22314; phone: 800/655–5597) $75 plus $6/shipping, 1995. Lists more than 45 funding sources from foundations, corporations, and federal agencies .

Grant Source: Dropout Prevention and Student Retention (Capitol Publications, Suite 444, 1101 King St., Alexandria, VA 22314; phone: 800/655–5597) $75 plus $6/shipping, 1995. Lists more than 50 funding sources from foundations, corporations, and federal agencies .

Grant Source: Student Leadership (Capitol Publications, Suite 444, 1101 King St., Alexandria, VA 22314; phone: 800/655–5597) $75 plus $6/shipping, 1995. Lists more than 50 funding sources from foundations, corporations, and federal agencies.

Grant Source: Teen Pregnancy and Sex Education (Capitol Publications, Suite 444, 1101 King St., Alexandria, VA 22314; phone: 800/655–5597) $75 plus $6/shipping, 1995. Lists more than 50 funding sources from foundations, corporations, and federal agencies.

Grant Source: Crime Prevention in Schools and Communities (Capitol Publications, Suite 444, 1101 King St., Alexandria, VA 22314; phone: 800/655–5597) $75 plus $6/shipping, 1995. Lists hundreds of funding options from foundations, corporations, and federal agencies.

Grant Source: Parental Involvement in Education (Capitol Publications, Suite 444, 1101 King St., Alexandria, VA 22314; phone: 800/655–5597) $75 plus $6/shipping, 1995. Lists more than 50 funding sources from foundations, corporations, and federal agencies.

Grant Source: Math and Science (Capitol Publications, Suite 444, 1101 King St., Alexandria, VA 22314; phone: 800/655–5597) $75 plus $6/shipping, 1995. Lists more than 60 funding sources from foundations, corporations, and federal agencies.

GRINDEX (American Anthropological Association, Suite 640, 4350 N. Fairfax Dr., Arlington, VA 22203; phone: 703/528–1902) is a key to grants and support for anthropology students, faculty, and practitioners. *GRINDEX* cross–indexes 225 agencies by program, geographical area, topic, and users' need. *GRINDEX* is available in each September issue of the *Anthropological Newsletter*, $9/individual issue, and on the Internet at URL: **http://www.ameranthassn.org** and clicking on "Grants and Supports."

Annual Register of Grant Support (R.R. Bowker; available from Reed Elsevier, P.O. Box 31, New Providence, NJ 07974; phone: 800/521-8110) $199.95 plus 7 percent shipping and handling, published each September. Describes over 3,000 sources of grant funding: traditional sources (private,

For a firm foundation, read chapters 1 and 2 first

Foundations and grants

corporate, and public) plus non-traditional sources (educational associations, unions, special interest groups, church organizations, community trusts, and more). Areas covered include: multiple special purpose, humanities, international affairs, special populations, urban and regional affairs, education, sciences, social sciences, physical sciences, life sciences, and technology and industry. Includes all the information you need to write your grant proposal.

The Foundation Directory (The Foundation Center, 79 Fifth Ave., New York, NY 10003-3076; phones: 800/424-9836, 212/620-4230) $190/softcover, 2,068 pages, annual in March. Includes entries on over 7,700 foundations that hold assets of at least $2 million or annually distribute $200,000 or more in grants. Each entry includes financial data, purpose and activities, types of support, limitations, and application information.

The Foundation Directory, Part 2 (The Foundation Center, 79 Fifth Ave., New York, NY 10003-3076; phones: 800/424-9836, 212/620-4230) $185/softcover, 1,127 pages, annual in March. Includes entries on over 4,500 foundations with grant programs of $50,000 to $200,000. Each entry includes financial data, purpose and activities, types of support, limitations, application information, and a list of sample grants.

The Foundation Directory, Supplement (The Foundation Center, 79 Fifth Ave., New York, NY 10003-3076; phones: 800/424-9836, 212/620-4230) $135/softcover, 626 pages, annual in September. Includes updated information on more than 12,000 foundations, and lists for the first time many new foundations.

The Foundation 1,000 (The Foundation Center, 79 Fifth Ave., New York, NY 10003-3076; phones: 800/424-9836, 212/620-4230) $295, 2,956 pages, annual each November. Contains 1,000 extremely detailed profiles of foundations that run several pages. This is probably the most thorough analysis of foundations available anywhere.

America's New Foundations (Taft Group, 835 Penobscot Bldg., 645 Griswold St., Detroit, MI 48226-4094; phones: 800/877-8238, 313/961-2242) $180, 1,450 pages, annual. Profiles over 3,000 private company and community foundations that give over $100,000 annually. Each listing includes the foundation's priorities, recipient types, financial information, names of officers and directors and a list of major grant recipients.

Foundation Reporter (Taft Group, 835 Penobscot Bldg., 645 Griswold St., Detroit, MI 48226-4094; phones: 800/877-8238, 313/961-2242) $375, 1,965 pages, annual. Provides detailed profiles of 1,000 leading foundations: foundation philosophy, financial summary, typical grant recipients, extensive list of recent grants, new programs supported and programs being phased out, and biographical information on foundation officers and directors.

Show me the money...please

Guide to U.S. Foundations (The Foundation Center, 79 Fifth Ave., New York, NY 10003–3050; phones: 800/424–9836, 212/620–4230) $225, 4,235 pages, annual in April. These two volumes report fundamental information on over 38,800 U.S. foundations. Each entry includes the name and address, contact person, and total grants during the past year. The contents of this book are also available by computer modem via DIALOG File 26 and 27. DIALOG File 27 enables you to generate lists of foundations by grant subject area. Contact DIALOG at 800/334–2564 for information on using these databases. Contact the Foundation Center's Online Support Staff at 212/620–4230 to learn more about which online utilities provide "gateway" access, or for free materials to help you search these database files.

National Directory of Corporate Giving (The Foundation Center, 79 Fifth Ave., New York, NY 10003–3076; phones: 800/424–9836, 212/620–4230) $195, 1,092 pages, published in October of odd–numbered years. Presents profiles on more than 2,600 corporate foundations plus an additional 650+ direct giving programs: application procedures, key personnel, types of support awarded, giving limitations, and purpose and activity statements. Also includes a "Current Giving" section which lists recent grant recipients by subject area.

Corporate Foundation Profiles (The Foundation Center, 79 Fifth Ave., New York, NY 10003–3076; phones: 800/424–9836, 212/620–4230) $155, 778 pages, February 1995. This book offers four to six–page analyses of 235 of the U.S.'s top corporate foundations and grant makers whose annual giving is at least $1.25 million.

Directory of Corporate and Foundation Givers (Taft Group, 835 Penobscot Bldg., 645 Griswold St., Detroit, MI 48226–4094; phones: 800/877–8238, 313/961–2242) $240, two volumes, 4,100 pages, annual. These tomes detail over 4,500 private foundations, 3,500 corporate giving programs, 1,500 corporate foundations, and 2,000 corporate direct givers that distribute at least $250,000 in grants each year. Included in each entry are contact information, eligibility requirements, giving priorities, grant types, and financial data. Each entry also includes biographies of the officers and directors, and the recipients of the ten largest grants. Nine indexes help you locate potential funders by grant type, recipient type, headquarters state, industry, and operating location.

Prospector's Choice (Taft Group, 835 Penobscot Bldg., 645 Griswold St., Detroit, MI 48226–4094; phones: 800/877–8238, 313/961–2242) $845, electronic publication on Windows™ CD–ROM format only. This gigantic reference work gives you more than 10,000 profiles of top private foun-

For a firm foundation, read chapters 1 and 2 first

Foundations and grants

dations and corporate giving programs, and its search features allows you to pinpoint the exact information you want.

Grants on Disc (Taft Group, 835 Penobscot Bldg., 645 Griswold St., Detroit, MI 48226-4094; phones: 800/877-8238, 313/961-2242) $695, electronic publication on Windows™ CD-ROM format only. This work will give you detailed information on approximately 270,000 grants per year; and who made them, with addresses, phone and fax numbers.

Corporate Giving Yellow Pages (Taft Group, 835 Penobscot Bldg., 645 Griswold St., Detroit, MI 48226-4094; phones: 800/877-8238, 313/961-2242) $99, 350 pages, annual. Lists the contact person (with address and phone number) at each of over 3,500 corporate giving programs and corporate foundations.

Corporate Giving Directory (Taft Group, 835 Penobscot Bldg., 645 Griswold St., Detroit, MI 48226-4094; phones: 800/877-8238, 313/961-2242) $410, 1,875 pages, annual. Get full details on the 1,000 largest corporate givers, including contact names, deadlines, total assets and giving, average grant size, and names of recent grant recipients. Learn also which organizations give to your type of cause, which organizations give in your geographic area, and which organizations offer the type and level of grant support you need.

International Foundation Directory 1996 (Gale Research, Inc., 835 Penobscot Bldg., Detroit, MI 48226-4094; phone: 800/877-4253) $190, 815 pages, 1996. Covers more than 1,200 foundations, trusts, and similar non-profit institutions in 50 countries.

Directory of International Corporate Giving in America and Abroad (Taft Group, 835 Penobscot Bldg., 645 Griswold St., Detroit, MI 48226-4094; phones: 800/877-8238, 313/961-2242) $199, 930 pages, annual. Over 650 foreign and U.S. multinational corporations are profiled. Included in each listing are the contact name for grants, average grant size, names of recent grant recipients, application procedures, and typical grants.

Foundations & Grantmakers Directory is an Internet directory of charitable grantmakers at URL: **http://www.foundations.org/grantmakers.html**. Browse through alphabetically for the links to their home pages.

Directory of Biomedical and Health Care Grants (Oryx Press, 4041 N. Central, Phoenix, AZ 85012-3397; phones: 800/279-6799, 602/265-2651) $84.50, 672 pages, annual. Furnishes details on over 3,100 funding sources: full program descriptions, contact names (with address and phone number), application procedures, deadlines, and any special restrictions.

National Directory of Grants & Aid to Individuals in the Arts, International (Washington International Arts Letter, P.O. Box 12010, Des Moines, IA 50312; phone: 319/358-6777) $30/nonmembers, $22/members, 260 pages, spring 1997. Grant information from foundations, government sources, individuals, and donors that support the arts.

Show me the money...please

Financial Aid for African Americans (Reference Service Press, Suite 4, 5000 Windplay Dr., El Dorado Hills, CA 95762; phone: 916/939–9620) $34.95/prepaid plus $4.50 for shipping, 380 pages, published in January of odd–numbered years. Provides details on over 1,200 grants, fellowships, loans, awards, and internships set aside for African American students. Indexed by program title, sponsoring organization, residency requirements, subject interests, and deadline date.

Financial Aid for Hispanic Americans (Reference Service Press, Suite 4, 5000 Windplay Dr., El Dorado Hills, CA 95762; phone: 916/939–9620) $34.95/prepaid plus $4.50 for shipping, 410 pages, published in January of odd–numbered years. Provides details on over 1,300 grants, fellowships, loans, awards, and internships set aside for Hispanic students. Indexed by program title, sponsoring organization, residency requirements, subject interests, and deadline date.

Financial Aid for Asian Americans (Reference Service Press, Suite 4, 5000 Windplay Dr., El Dorado Hills, CA 95762; phone: 916/939–9620) $30/prepaid plus $4.50 for shipping, 380 pages, published in January of odd–numbered years. Provides details on over 1,000 grants, fellowships, loans, awards, and internships set aside for Asian American students. Indexed by program title, sponsoring organization, residency requirements, subject interests, and deadline date.

Financial Aid for Native Americans (Reference Service Press, Suite 4, 5000 Windplay Dr., El Dorado Hills, CA 95762; phone: 916/939–9620) $34.95/prepaid plus $4.50 for shipping, 425 pages, published in January of odd–numbered years. Provides details on over 1,300 grants, fellowships, loans, awards, and internships set aside for Native American students. Indexed by program title, sponsoring organization, residency requirements, subject interests, and deadline date.

Financial Aid for Veterans, Military Personnel, and Their Dependents (Reference Service Press, Suite 4, 5000 Windplay Dr., El Dorado Hills, CA 95762; phone: 916/939–9620) $39.50/prepaid plus $4 shipping, 325 pages, published in January of even–numbered years. Provides details on over 900 scholarships, fellowships, loans, grants, awards, and internships established for military–related personnel.

Financial Aid for the Disabled and Their Families (Reference Service Press, Suite 4, 5000 Windplay Dr., El Dorado Hills, CA 95762; phone: 916/939–9620) $47.50/prepaid plus $4 shipping, 350 pages, published in January of even–numbered years. Provides details on nearly 900 grants, fellowships, loans, awards, and internships designed primarily or exclusively for the disabled and members of their families. Indexed by program title, sponsoring organization, residency requirements, subject interests, and deadline date.

For a firm foundation, read chapters 1 and 2 first

Foundations and grants

Grants for Minorities (The Foundation Center, 79 Fifth Ave., New York, NY 10003–3076; phones: 800/424–9836, within New York State call 212/620–4230) $75 plus $4.50/shipping, 384 pages, published in October of odd–numbered years. Describes recent foundation grants of at least $10,000 for ethnic groups and minority populations, including African–Americans, Hispanics, Asian–Americans, Gays and lesbians, Native Americans, immigrants, and refugees. This directory is useful for identifying foundations and grant recipients for which you may wish to work.

Financial Aids for Women (Reference Service Press, Suite 4, 5000 Windplay Dr., El Dorado Hills, CA 95762; phone: 916/939–9620) $45/prepaid plus $4 shipping, 520 pages, published in January of odd–numbered years. Provides details on over 1,700 grants, fellowships, loans, awards, and internships designed primarily or exclusively for women. Indexed by program title, sponsoring organization, residency requirements, subject interests, and deadline date.

Grants for Women & Girls (The Foundation Center, 79 Fifth Ave., New York, NY 10003–3076; phones: 800/424–9836, within New York State call 212/620–4230) $75 plus $4.50/shipping, 270 pages, published in October of odd–numbered years. Describes recent foundation grants of at least $10,000 given for education, career guidance, vocational training, equal rights, rape prevention, shelter programs for victims of domestic violence, health programs, abortion rights, pregnancy programs, athletics and recreation, arts programs, and social research. This directory is useful for identifying foundations and grant recipients for which you may wish to work.

Directory of Grants in the Humanities (Oryx Press, Suite 700, 4041 N. Central, Phoenix, AZ 85012–3397; phones: 800/279–6799, 602/265–2651) $84.50, 720 pages, annual. Includes details on 4,000 corporate, private, and government support for competitions and awards, performances, productions, exhibits, conferences, scholarships, internships, graduate assistantships, and more: full program descriptions, contact names (with address and phone number), deadlines, and any special restrictions.

Funding Sources for Community and Economic Development (Oryx Press, Suite 700, 4041 N. Central, Phoenix, AZ 85012–3397; phones: 800/279–6799, 602/265–2651) $64.95, 520 pages, 1997. Includes details on 2,000 corporate, private, and government funding sources for special school programs, health care, business development, civic affairs, and arts and humanities projects .

Grants–at–a–Glance (Association for Women in Science, Suite 650, 1200 New York Ave., NW, Washington, DC 20005; phone: 202/326–8940) $8/nonmembers, $7/members, 100 pages. Lists over 400 awards, fellowships, and scholarships for women in

Show me the money...please

engineering, mathematics, and a wide variety of scientific fields at all levels of undergraduate and graduate studies.

Directory of Building and Equipment Grants (Research Grant Guides, P.O. Box 1214, Loxahatchee, FL 33470; phone: 561/795-6129; no phone orders, fax orders to 561/795-7794) $59.50 prepaid plus $6/shipping and 6 percent sales tax for Florida residents, 148 pages, published in late autumn of odd-numbered years. Profiles on 600 foundations, as well as federal programs, that issue thousands of grants for construction, renovation, and equipment.

Directory of Operating Grants (Research Grant Guides, P.O. Box 1214, Loxahatchee, FL 33470; phone: 561/795-6129; no phone orders, fax orders to 561/795-7794) $59.50 prepaid plus $6/shipping and 6 percent sales tax for Florida residents, 150 pages, published annually in February. Profiles over 670 foundations that support general ongoing operating expenses. Listed by state, information includes: address, phone number, grant range, contact person, and list of recent organizations funded.

Directory of Computer and High Technology Grants (Research Grant Guides, P.O. Box 1214, Loxahatchee, FL 33470; phone: 561/795-6129; no phone orders, fax orders to 561/795-7794) $59.50 prepaid plus $6/shipping and 6 percent sales tax for Florida residents, 120 pages, published in April of odd-numbered years. Profiles over 500 foundations that offer grants for computers, software, and high-tech office equipment. Each profile includes the address, areas of support, geographic restrictions, grant range, and a list of organizations funded. Arranged by state. Also included is a guide to sites on the Internet that provide information about specific foundations, funding availability, and proposal writing.

Directory of Health Grants (Research Grant Guides, P.O. Box 1214, Loxahatchee, FL 33470; phone: 561/795-6129; no phone orders, fax orders to 561/795-7794) $59.50 prepaid plus $6/shipping and 6 percent sales tax for Florida residents, 148 pages, published in autumn of odd-numbered years. Profiles of 750 foundations that provide 3,200 funding sources to non-profit health organizations. Each profile lists address, area of support, geographic restrictions, and grant range.

Directory of Social Service Grants (Research Grant Guides, P.O. Box 1214, Loxahatchee, FL 33470; phone: 561/795-6129; no phone orders, fax orders to 561/795-7794) $59.50 prepaid plus $6/shipping and 6 percent sales tax for Florida residents, 164 pages, published in the summer of odd-numbered years. Profiles of more than 900 foundations that offer thousands of funding sources to non-profit social service organizations. Each profile lists address, area of support, geographic restrictions, and grant range.

For a firm foundation, read chapters 1 and 2 first

Foundations and grants

Directory of Education Grants (Research Grant Guides, P.O. Box 1214, Loxahatchee, FL 33470; phone: 561/795-6129; no phone orders, fax orders to 561/795-7794) $59.50 prepaid plus $6/shipping and 6 percent sales tax for Florida residents, 152 pages, published in October of even-numbered years. Profiles of 650 foundations that provide thousands of funding sources for education programs and non-profit health organizations. Each profile lists address, area of support, geographic restrictions, and grant range.

Directory of Grants for Organizations Serving People with Disabilities (Research Grant Guides, P.O. Box 1214, Loxahatchee, FL 33470; phone: 561/795-6129; no phone orders, fax orders to 561/795-7794) $59.50 prepaid plus $6/shipping and 6 percent sales tax for Florida residents, 216 pages, published in the spring of odd-numbered years. Profiles of 847 foundations that provide 2,700 funding sources for disability programs. Each profile lists address, area of support, geographic restrictions, and grant range.

Salary survey

Grantmakers Salary Report (Council on Foundations, 1828 L St., NW, Washington, DC 20036; phone: 202/466-6512) $65/nonmembers, $30/members, 160 pages, annual. Provides information on compensation for 37 distinct salary positions, including executive, program officer, communications assistant, donor relations associate, and human resources director.

Show me the money...please

Chapter 16

Health care

Health care in general

*See the **Professional's Job Finder** for a much more extensive listing of job sources in private sector health care. The listings in this chapter focus on non–profit positions. Virtually all of the job sources described in this chapter include teaching or research positions even if the description doesn't mention this fact.*

Job ads

Health & Medicine (Magellan Internet Guide) free. To find a number of Internet sites with job ads on them, go to URL: **http://magellan.mckinley.com/netscape.cgi/Health** and select "Career & Employment." You'll find brief reviews and links to around 15 Web sites that feature job ads in health care.

Medical AdMart appears on the Internet at URL: **http://www.medical–admart.com/**. Choose "Select Magazine" and then "Select Category" to access the 370+ vacancies for physicians, veterinarians, nurses, and other medical professionals. About 20 percent of the positions are in the non–profit sector.

Health care in general

Experimental Medicine Job Listings offers dozens of vacancies in experimental medicine, mostly research. Go to Internet URL: **http://www.medcor.mcgill.ca/EXPMED/DOCS/jobs.html** and select "Positions" to enter the job database. You can browse or search by employer or country. Ninety percent of the positions are in education, especially postdoctoral research.

The Nation's Health (American Public Health Association, 1015 15th St., NW, Washington, DC 20005; phone: 202/789–5600) 11 issues/year, $15/annual subscription (U.S.), $18/foreign. Jobs listed under "Job Openings" in the "Classified Advertising" section. Typical issue announces about 50 job openings. Jobs are also listed on the Internet at URL: **http://www.apha.org**. Click on "About APHA," then "Job Openings," and finally "APHA Job Openings."

Hospitals and Health Networks (American Hospital Publishing, P.O. Box 92567, Chicago, IL 60675; phone: 800/621–6902) bimonthly, $65/annual subscription. From five to 15 positions, mostly for hospital administrators, but also for a handful of maintenance, and patient care positions (doctors, nurses, etc.) appear under "Classified."

Rural Health Care (National Rural Health Association, Suite 301, 1 W. Armour Blvd., Kansas City, MO 64111; phone: 816/756–3140) bimonthly, $74/annual nonmember subscription, free/members. About 25 physician and nursing positions appear under "Classified."

American Journal of Health Promotion (Suite 104, 1660 Cass Lake Rd., Keego Harbor, MI 48320; phone: 810/682–0707) bimonthly, $69/annual subscription. Five to ten positions for wellness program administrators and postdoctoral research fellowships appear under "Opportunities Available."

AABB Weekly Report (American Association of Blood Banks, 8101 Glenbrook Rd., Bethesda, MD 20814; phone: 301/907–6977) 46 issues/year, $128/nonmember annual subscription, $98/members. Under "Classified Advertising" you'll find ads for five to ten vacancies for medical blood technicians, blood bank directors, medical directors, and medical technicians with specialties in transfusion medicine and blood banking.

Transfusion (American Association of Blood Banks, 8101 Glenbrook Rd., Bethesda, MD 20814; phone: 301/907–6977) eleven issues/year, $150/annual subscription (U.S.), $195/foreign. Under "Classified," you'll find two to 15 ads for medical blood technicians, blood bank directors, medical directors, and medical technicians with specialties in transfusion medicine and blood banking.

College Health Job Line (American College Health Association, P.O. Box 28937, Baltimore, MD 21240; phone: 410/859–1500, fax 410/850–0823) free/members only, updated every Friday. This is a fax-on-demand service in which you can fax a request for a list of from four to ten job openings for directors, administrators, physicians, nurses, and health educators with college health centers.

Read chapters 1 and 2 first — doctor's orders

News Briefs (American Association of Blood Banks, 8101 Glenbrook Rd., Bethesda, MD 20814; phone: 301/907–6977) 11 issues/year, free/members only. Under "Referral Exchange" you'll find ads for five to ten vacancies for medical blood technicians, blood bank directors, medical directors, and medical technicians with specialties in transfusion medicine and blood banking.

Academic Physician and Scientist (Lippincott–Raven Publishers, 36th Floor, 1185 Avenue of the Americas, New York, NY 10036; phone: 212/930–9561) bimonthly, free. Each issue contains about 450 display and classified ads for teaching and research positions in academic medicine. These ads are also available on the Internet for free at URL: **http://www.acphysci.com**. You can browse through the job ads under "Administration," "Basic Science," and "Clinical Science."

Academic Medicine (Association of American Medical Colleges, 2450 N Street, NW, Washington, DC 20037; phone: 202/828–0416) monthly, $70/annual nonmember subscription (U.S.), $120/foreign, free/members. About 15 display ads in the back of the magazine tout job opportunities for deans and presidents of medical schools, student health center administrators, and university physicians.

The Neuroscience Newsletter (Society for Neuroscience, Suite 500, 11 Dupont Cr., NW, Washington, DC 20036; phone: 202/462–6688) bimonthly, free/members only. Thirty to 40 vacancies for faculty and researchers dominate the "Positions Available" section of this attractive newsletter.

Journal of Nuclear Medicine (Society of Nuclear Medicine, 1850 Samuel Morse Dr., Reston, VA 20190; phone: 703/708–9000) monthly, $140/annual nonmember subscription, free/members. About 25 positions for physicians, technologists, and radiologists are advertised.

Update (Medical Group Management Association, 104 Inverness Terrace East, Englewood, CO 80112–5306; phone: 303/799–1111) monthly, free/members only. A typical issue contains about 60 medical management positions are in "Update Classified Advertising." Anybody can access some of the jobs that appear in *Update* on the Internet at URL: **http://mgma.com/classifieds**. Positions include administrative and executive jobs with HMOs, medical schools, and private practices.

AMHA Newsletter (Association of Mental Health Administrators, Suite 500, 60 Revere Dr., Northbrook, IL 60062; phone: 847/480–9626) semimonthly, $46/six month nonmember subscription, free/members. 4 or 5 job ads appear under "Executive Classified Service" for administrative positions in behavioral health facilities.

Emergency Medical Services (Summer Communications, Inc., 7626 Densmore Ave., Van Nuys, CA 91406–2088) monthly, $21.97/annual subscription (U.S.), $37/foreign. Just two to four ads for positions for paramedics and emergency physicians appear under "Employment Opportunities" and in display ads throughout, includes jobs overseas.

Photocopying strictly prohibited

Health care in general

Jobs in Dietetics: National Edition (P.O. Box 3537, Santa Monica, CA 90408–3537; phone: 310/453–5375) monthly, with mid–month job updates, $96/annual subscription, $58/three–month subscription, $42/two–month subscription, $25/one–month subscription; California residents must add 8.25 percent sales tax. About 400 dietitian, nutritionist, and food service professional jobs — outside California — are announced in a typical issue. About ten to 20 percent of the jobs are in education, public health and community nutrition, and research. These jobs are for registered dietitians or certified dietary managers or people with a B.A. in nutrition from an accredited program. Individuals with degrees from alternative, non–accredited nutrition programs are usually unqualified for these positions. Your first issue will include a sheet that names additional sources of private sector and government positions.

Journal of the American Dietetic Association (ADA, 216 W. Jackson Blvd., Chicago, IL 60606; phone: 312/899–0040) monthly, $100/nonmember annual subscription, free/members. About 40 ads for dietitians appear under "Classified Advertising" each issue.

California Jobs in Dietetics (P.O. Box 3537, Santa Monica, CA 90408–3537; phone: 310/453–5375) biweekly, $48/six–issue subscription, $84/annual subscription. California residents add 8.25 percent sales tax. Almost ten percent of the 230 dietitian and nutritionist jobs in a typical issue are listed under "Public Health & Community Nutrition." These jobs are for registered dietitians or certified dietary managers or people with a B.A. in nutrition from an accredited program. Individuals with degrees from alternative, non–accredited nutrition programs are usually unqualified for these positions. Your first issue will include a sheet that names additional sources of government and non–profit sector positions in California and nationally.

Career Mart (American College of Healthcare Executives, 1 N. Franklin St., Chicago, IL 60606; phone: 312/424–2800) monthly, free/members only, $35/member six–month subscription. Typical issue includes more than 150 upper–level health care management positions listed under "Career Mart."

NHO Newsline (National Hospice Organization, Suite 901, 1901 N. Moore St., Arlington, VA 22209; phone: 703/243–5900) bimonthly, free/members only; $55/annual dues. Fewer than ten display ads appear for administrative, nursing, social workers, spiritual care, etc. in hospices.

ADVANCE for Health Information Professionals (Merion Publications, 650 Park Ave., West, King of Prussia, PA 19406–4025; phones: 800/355–5627, 610/265–7812) biweekly, free to qualified professionals, contact publisher for subscription application. Under "Classified Employment Opportunities" you'll find a handful of faculty positions for instructors of health information technology and medical records technology. You'll also find around 70 job ads for medical records coding specialists, medical records supervisors/directors/assistants, DRG managers, abstracters, oncology data managers, transcriptionists, and tumor registrars.

Read chapters 1 and 2 first — doctor's orders

FASEB Newsletter (Federation of American Societies for Experimental Biology, Suite L–2310, 9650 Rockville Pike, Bethesda, MD 20814; phone: 301/530–7027) eight issues/year, $60/nonmembers, free/members. "Positions and Opportunities" features about six openings for professors and research assistants.

ADVANCE for Respiratory Care Practitioners (Merion Publications, 650 Park Ave., West, King of Prussia, PA 19406–4025; phones: 800/355–5627, 610/265–7812) biweekly, free to qualified professionals, contact publisher for subscription application. Under "Classified Employment Opportunities" you'll find around 120 job ads for respiratory therapists, respiratory technicians, electroencephalograph technicians, home care therapists, pulmonary technologists, directors of respiratory care, neonatal respiratory therapists, and polysomnographic technologists. A handful of ads appear for faculty positions in cardio–respiratory care, directors of clinical education, and respiratory therapy.

NAHC Report (National Association for Home Care, 227 Seventh St., SE, Washington, DC 20003; phone: 202/547–5277) weekly, $325/annual nonmember subscription, free/members. Two to ten ads for health care directors and supervisors appear under "Classifieds."

Journal of School Health (American School Health Association, 7263 State Route 43, Kent, OH 44240; phone: 330/678–1601) ten issues/year, $85. Two or three vacancies for professors and camp nurses are in the typical issue.

Journal of Perinatology (Mosby Yearbook, 11830 Westline Industrial Dr., St. Louis, MO 63146; phone: 314/453–4406) quarterly, $70/annual subscription. The "Classified" section has around ten positions for nutritionists, perentologists (prenatal), and nurses.

Journal of Environmental Health (National Environmental Health Association, Suite 970, South Tower, 720 S. Colorado Blvd., Denver, CO 80222; phone: 303/756–9090) ten issues/year, $90/nonmember annual subscription, $75/members, $25/students. Jobs listed under "Opportunities." Five to ten job ads appear in the typical issue for sanitarians, toxicologists, health planners, and related positions.

Career Services Bulletin (American College of Sports Medicine, 401 W. Michigan St., Indianapolis, IN 46202–3233; phone: 317/637–9200) monthly, $20/annual nonmember subscription, $10/members. Around 50 positions in sports medicine and exercise science appear throughout, many on university faculties.

American Journal of Obstetrics and Gynecology (Mosby Year Book, Journal Subscription Services, 11830 Westline Industrial Dr., St. Louis, MO 63146; phone: 800/453–4351) monthly, $144/annual subscription, $66/students. Close to 60 practitioner and faculty positions appear in display ads.

Health care in general

Opportunities in Dermatology (American Academy of Dermatology, 930 N. Meacham Rd., Schaumburg, IL 60168; phone: 847/330–0230) monthly, $125/annual non-member subscription, $75/members. Your subscription gets you four different editions: *Clinical Positions Available, Dermatologists Seeking Clinical Positions, Academic Positions Available,* and *Dermatologists Seeking Academic Positions.* Hundreds of positions are listed state–by–state in each "positions available" edition. Only about 70 dermatologists are listed in the "seeking positions" editions.

The New Careers Directory: Internships and Professional Opportunities in Technology and Social Change (Student Pugwash USA, Suite 814, 815 15th St., NW, Washington, DC 20005; phone: 202/393–6555) $18, $10/students, add $3/shipping, 1996. Offers full details on where and how to apply for internships and entry–level jobs in health care and related fields.

Job services

National Hospice Organization Job Bank (NHO, Suite 901, 1901 N. Moore St., Arlington, VA 22209; phone: 703/243–5900) free/members only; $55/annual dues. Join NHO and you can call this job hotline where you can hear nine to 20 job descriptions. Updated each Friday. Positions include: administrative, nursing, social workers, spiritual care, etc.

Jobs for Dietitians Career Counseling Hotline (P.O. Box 3537, Santa Monica, CA 90408–3537; phone: 310/453–5375) available only to subscribers to either the national or California edition of *Jobs for Dietitians* described above under "Job ads." Hotline number is given in the newsletter.

ACHE ONLINE (American College of Healthcare Executives, 1 N. Franklin St., Chicago, IL 60606; phone: 312/424–2800) free/members only. Online job database available through CompuServe. Includes over 150 job vacancies in the public and private sectors.

FSG Online Jobs in Biotechnology, Pharmaceuticals and Medicine (Franklin Search Group, 5632 SW 88th Terrace, Cooper City, FL 33328; phone: 305/434–4840) free. Go to Internet URL: **http://www.medmarket.com/tenants/fsg/** and pick "Search jobs" to examine over 70 vacancies, largely in biotechnology and pharmaceuticals. You can enter a keyword to search or browse by selecting "List All Open Positions." You can place your resume in this firm's resume bank by clicking on "Post Resume." You can submit your resume electronically, by fax, or by real mail. You can keep your identity confidential. About 30 percent of the positions are in education, research, or other aspect of the non–profit sector.

Read chapters 1 and 2 first — doctor's orders

Directories

Job Opportunities in Health Care (Peterson's Guides; available from Planning/Communications' catalog at the end of this book) $21.95, 305 pages, published each September for the next year. Features brief descriptions of over 1,500 high-growth hospitals and health-care companies, plus in-depth reports on a few of the entries. Briefly describes each hospital or company, number of employees, expertise needed, and person to contact about job vacancies. Actual vacancies cannot be guaranteed, but this serves as a good directory of potential employers in all aspects of health care.

Directory of Biomedical and Health Care Grants 1995 (Oryx Press, 4041 N. Central, Phoenix, AZ 85012-3397; phones: 800/279-6799, 602/265-2651) $84.50, 672 pages, 1994. Furnishes details on over 3,100 funding sources: full program descriptions, contact names (with address and phone number), application procedures, deadlines, and any special restrictions.

Directory of Health Grants (Research Grant Guides, P.O. Box 1214, Loxahatchee, FL 33470; phone: 561/795-6129; no phone orders, fax orders to 561/795-7794) $59.50 prepaid plus $6 shipping and 6 percent sales tax for Florida residents, 148 pages, published in autumn of odd-numbered years. Profiles 750 foundations that provide 3,200 funding sources to non-profit health organizations. Each profile lists address, area of support, geographic restrictions, and grant range.

Allied Health and Rehabilitation Professions Education Directory 1996-1997 (American Medical Association, Order Processing, P.O. Box 7046, Dover, DE; phone: 800/621-8335) $54.95/nonmembers, $39.95/members, 350 pages, 1996. Covers 4,674 education programs sponsored by 2,200 accredited, post-secondary institutions. Describes each occupation, work environment, entry-level salaries, and more.

Eat Right America (American Dietetic Association) free. Go to the Internet at URL: **http://www.eatright.org/** and select "Find a Dietitian." You can search for professional dietitians by location, type of services, and area of expertise.

Encyclopedia of Medical Organizations and Agencies (Gale Research, Inc., 835 Penobscot Bldg., Detroit. MI 48226-4094; phone: 800/877-4253) $230, 1,550 pages, 1996. Provides information on nearly 14,000 major public and private organizations and agencies concerned with medical information, funding, research, education, planning, advocacy, advice, and service. A good source of information on potential employers as well as identifying desirable places to work.

Medical and Health Information Directory (Gale Research, Inc., 835 Penobscot Bldg., Detroit. MI 48226-4094; phone: 800/877-4253) $569/three-volume set, 4,152 pages, 1996. *Volume 1: Organizations, Agencies, and Institutions* ($235, 1,854 pages) details over 19,200 national, international, and state professional and voluntary organizations, as well as foundations

Health care in general

and grant–issuing organizations, research centers, and medical and allied health schools. It's a good source for finding health care associations for which to work. *Volume 2: Publications, Libraries, and Other Information Sources* ($235, 926 pages) reports on over 11,000 libraries, audiovisual producers and services, publications, publishers, and databases. *Volume 3: Health Services* ($235, 1,372 pages) gives current data on more than 27,600 clinics, treatment centers, care programs, counseling/diagnostic services, and other health services arranged into 31 subject chapters.

AABB Membership Directory (American Association of Blood Banks, 8101 Glenbrook Rd., Bethesda, MD 20814; phone: 301/907–6977) $50 plus $4/shipping, issued in December of even–numbered years.

American College of Physician Executives Membership Directory (American College of Physician Executives, Suite 200, 4890 W. Kennedy Blvd., Tampa, FL 33609; phone: 813/287–2000) free/members only, annual.

Membership Directory of the American College Health Association (ACHA, P.O. Box 28937, Baltimore, MD 21240; phone: 410/859–1500) free/members only, 115 pages, annual each September. Lists about 2,500 individual members and 910 institutional members.

Directory of American Medical Education (Association of American Medical Colleges, 2450 N Street, NW, Washington, DC 20037; phone: 202/828–0416) $50/ nonmembers, $25/members, 489 pages, annual. Lists 125 medical schools and key personnel contacts.

Hospital Blue Book (Blue Book's, 2100 Powers Ferry Rd., Atlanta, GA 30339; phones: 800/533–8484, 770/955–5656) $224, released each March. Includes over 100 medical schools with contact names, addresses, and phones. Also includes extensive listings of 8,000 U.S. and Canadian hospitals, 137,000 special services, 126,000 key employees, total number of beds, facility type, plus 500 multi–hospital and health care system with address, phone and 2,800 key contact persons. The Southern edition costs $99.

AHA Guide to the Health Care Field (American Hospital Association, Attn: AHA Order Processing Department, 1 N. Franklin, Chicago, IL 60606; phone: 800/242–2626) $250/nonmembers, $95/members, annual. Provides details on hospitals, health care systems, health care organizations, agencies, and providers. Also available on computer disk, $2,000/nonmembers, $1,800/members.

HCIA Directory of Health Care Professionals (HCIA, 300 E. Lombard St., Baltimore, MD 21202; phone: 800/568–3282) $299/nonmembers plus $7.95 shipping and handling, $259/members plus $7.95 shipping and handling, annual. Lists some 6,500 hospitals in the United States, with key contact names, addresses, and bed numbers.

Read chapters 1 and 2 first — doctor's orders

American College of Healthcare Executives Directory (American College of Healthcare Executives, 1 N. Franklin St., Chicago, IL 60606; phone: 312/424–2800) $150/nonmembers, $100/members, published in the even–numbered years. Also available on CD–ROM; contact for price. Lists over 23,000 health care executives in public and private sectors.

National Guide to Funding in Health (The Foundation Center, 79 Fifth Ave., New York, NY 10003–3076; phones: 800/424–9836, 212/620–4230) $150, 1,142 pages, published in April of odd–numbered years. Entries for each of the 3,300+ foundations and corporate giving programs include application information, list of recent grant recipients, and over 13,000 sample grants.

AIDS Funding: A Guide to Giving by Foundations and Charitable Organizations (The Foundation Center, 79 Fifth Ave., New York, NY 10003–3076; phones: 800/424–9836, 212/620–4230) $75, 206 pages, published in December of odd–numbered years. Entries for each of the 600+ foundations, public charities, and corporate giving programs include application information and a list of recent grant recipients.

Association of Academic Health Centers Directory (AAHC, Suite 720, 1400 16th St., NW, Washington, DC 20036; phone: 202/265–9600) $20/nonmembers, free/members, issued each January.

Membership Directory for the Society of Nuclear Medicine (Society of Nuclear Medicine, 1850 Samuel Morse Dr., Reston, VA 20190; phone: 703/708–9000) $150/nonmembers, free/members; published in the summer of odd–numbered years.

FASEB Directory of Members (Federation of American Societies for Experimental Biology, Suite L–2310, 9650 Rockville Pike, Bethesda, MD 20814; phone: 301/530–7027) $60/nonmembers prepaid (U.S.), $65/Mexico and Canada, $71/elsewhere, $16/members, $$21/Mexico and Canada, $27/elsewhere, 450 pages, annual. Includes members of the Federation of American Societies for Experimental Biology.

Grants for Health Programs for Children and Youth (The Foundation Center, 79 Fifth Ave., New York, NY 10003–3076; phones: 800/424–9836, within New York State call 212/620–4230) $75 plus $4.50/shipping, 183 pages, published in October of odd–numbered years. Describes recent foundation grants of at least $10,000 given to hospitals and health care facilities, social service agencies, and education institutions for research, program development, general operating support, education programs, treatment for drug and alcohol abuse, pregnancy, and children with disabilities. This directory is useful for identifying foundations and grant recipients for which you may wish to work.

Grants for Public Health & Diseases (The Foundation Center, 79 Fifth Ave., New York, NY 10003–3076; phones: 800/424–9836, within New York State call 212/620–4230) $75 plus $4.50/shipping, 192 pages, published in October of odd–numbered years. Describes recent foundation grants of at

Photocopying strictly prohibited

Health care in general

least $10,000 for public health programs and diseases including genetic diseases; birth defects; cancer; AIDS; nerve, muscle, and bone diseases, allergies, and other diseases; prevention of sexually transmitted diseases; and epidemiology. This directory is useful for identifying foundations and grant recipients for which you may wish to work.

Grants for Hospitals, Medical Care & Research (The Foundation Center, 79 Fifth Ave., New York, NY 10003–3076; phones: 800/424–9836, within New York State call 212/620–4230) $75 plus $4.50/shipping, 402 pages, published in October of odd–numbered years. Describes recent foundation grants of at least $10,000 given to hospitals, clinics, nursing homes, health care facilities, health support services, public health programs, reproductive health care, and medical research centers. This directory is useful for identifying foundations and grant recipients for which you may wish to work.

Grants for Medical & Professional Health Education (The Foundation Center, 79 Fifth Ave., New York, NY 10003–3076; phones: 800/424–9836, within New York State call 212/620–4230) $75 plus $4.50/shipping, 92 pages, published in October of odd–numbered years. Describes recent foundation grants of at least $10,000 given to graduate and professional schools of medicine, dentistry, nursing, and public health for general support, faculty development, symposiums, and conferences. This directory is useful for identifying foundations and grant recipients for which you may wish to work.

Salary surveys

Hospital Salary & Benefits Report (Hospital & Healthcare Compensation Service, P.O. Box 376, Oakland, NJ 07436; phone: 201/616–5722) $250 plus $7.50/shipping prepaid, 300 pages, published each July. Reports on salary and bonus payments, perquisites, and other data for over 125 job titles in management and administration, nursing, rehabilitation and mental health, social work, laboratory, medical records and library, dietary, pharmacy, and technical. Data reported by principal cities, geographic regions, nationally, hospital bed sizes, and gross annual revenue categories. Includes for–profit, government, and non–profit facilities.

Nursing Home Salary & Benefits Report (Hospital & Healthcare Compensation Service, P.O. Box 376, Oakland, NJ 07436; phone: 201/616–5722) $250 plus $7.50/shipping prepaid, 288 pages, published each April. Reports on salary and bonuses for 25 management and 33 nonmanagement positions, both nationally and in nine regions.

Hospice Salary & Benefits Report (Hospital & Healthcare Compensation Service, P.O. Box 376, Oakland, NJ 07436; phone: 201/616–5722) $195 plus $7.50/shipping prepaid, 268 pages, published each November. Reports on

Read chapters 1 and 2 first — doctor's orders

salary and bonus payments for 29 management jobs and 40 nonmanagement positions nationally. Includes non-profit, for-profit, and government facilities.

Homecare Salary & Benefits Report (Hospital & Healthcare Compensation Service, P.O. Box 376, Oakland, NJ 07436; phone: 201/616-5722) $250 plus $7.50/shipping prepaid, 420 pages, published each November. Reports on salary and bonus payments for 29 management jobs and 40 nonmanagement positions nationally.

Management Company Report (Hospital & Healthcare Compensation Service, P.O. Box 376, Oakland, NJ 07436; phone: 201/616-5722) $495 plus $7.50/shipping prepaid, 180 pages, published each January. Reports on salary and bonuses for 80 job titles for management employees, both nationally and regionally, in hospitals, nursing homes, and home health management companies.

Dentists

Job ads

Journal of Dental Education (American Association of Dental Schools, Suite 600, 1625 Massachusetts Ave., NW, Washington, DC 20036; phone: 202/667-9433) monthly, $75/annual subscription (U.S.), $100/Canada, $125/elsewhere, free/members. Around 20 vacancies for dental school faculty appear under "Classified."

Bulletin of Dental Education (American Association of Dental Schools, Suite 600, 1625 Massachusetts Ave., NW, Washington, DC 20036; phone: 202/667-9433) monthly, $18/nonmember annual subscription (U.S.), $24/foreign, free/members. Twenty to 25 job ads for dental school faculty, administrators, and professors appear under "Classifieds."

Journal of Dentistry for Children (American Society of Dentistry for Children, 211 E. Chicago Ave., Chicago, IL 60611; phone: 312/943-1244) bimonthly, $65/annual nonmember subscription (U.S.), $150/foreign, contact for member rates. About 11 positions and practices for sale appear under "Opportunities for Pedodontists." Also "positions wanted."

Journal of Dental Research (International and American Association for Dental Researchers, 1619 Duke St., Alexandria, VA 22314; phone: 703/548-0066) 16 issues/year, $350/annual nonmember subscription, $41/members, $16/student members. The inside front cover runs one to four classified ads for dental researchers.

Photocopying strictly prohibited

Directories

Directory of Institutional Members (American Association of Dental Schools, Suite 600, 1625 Massachusetts Ave., NW, Washington, DC 20036; phone: 202/667–9433) $50/nonmembers, $25/members, 144 pages, annual. Lists some 55 dental schools, plus contact information for deans and administrative stafs.

1997 Membership Directory (International and American Association for Dental Researchers, 1619 Duke St., Alexandria, VA 22314; phone: 703/548–0066) free/members (nonmembers call for price), 304 pages, updated in December every two or three years. Lists contact information for more 11,000 dental researchers.

Salary survey

Faculty Salary Survey (American Association of Dental Schools, Suite 600, 1625 Massachusetts Ave., NW, Washington, DC 20036; phone: 202/667–9433) $50/nonmembers, $25/members, 1996. Extensive survey of salaries and benefits for university and college professors, instructors, and teachers engaged in dental education.

Doctors

Job ads

New England Journal of Medicine (Massachusetts Medical Society, 1440 Main St., Boston, MA 02114; phone: 617/893–3800) weekly, $115/annual subscription. Among the 300 to 500 physician positions advertised in the "Classifieds" section and in display ads throughout the magazine are many teaching and research positions.

JAMA: The Journal of the American Medical Association (American Medical Association, Order Department, P.O. Box 109046, Chicago, IL 60610–9046; phones: 800/262–2350, 312/670–7827) weekly, $125/annual nonmember subscription, free/members. "Physician Recruitment Advertising" offers openings for 120 to 200 physicians of all types. You can also see these ads on the Internet at URL: **http://ama–assn.org/** by first selecting "Scientific Journals and News." Next select "Physician Recruitment." You'll be asked to complete a free, one-time registration to access this area. Do it! Then you can browse through the ads or choose any of the more than 20 disciplines to browse through job ads for a specialty.

Read chapters 1 and 2 first — doctor's orders

American Family Physician (American Academy of Family Physicians, 8880 Ward Pkwy., Kansas City, MO 64114; phone: 800/274-2237 ext. 3166) 16 issues/year, $75/physicians annual subscription, $47/students, residents, health care professionals. "AFP Classified Information" overflows with over 300 available positions, including around 40 faculty openings.

Annals of Internal Medicine (American College of Physicians, P.O. Box 7777, Philadelphia, PA 19175; phone: 800/523-1546) $103/annual nonmember subscription (U.S.), $120/Canada (includes GST), $163/elsewhere; $72/nonmember physicians, $52/nonmember medical students, free/members. From 100 to 150 vacancies for physicians in internal medicine appear under "Classified."

Opportunities (American Academy of Orthopaedic Surgeons, 6300 N. River Rd., Rosemont, IL 60018-4262; phone: 847/823-7186) is an Internet jobs database provided to members of the AAOS. Go to URL: **http://www.aaos.org**, and select "Member Services," then "Placement Service," and finally "Opportunities." There it will ask for your membership ID number to access it. You won't need an ID number to check out the scads of links to similar sites under "Orthopaedic Yellow Pages."

Journal of the American Medical Women's Association (AMWA, Suite 400, 801 N. Fairfax St., Alexandria, VA 22314; phone: 703/838-0500) bimonthly, $50/annual nonmember subscription, (U.S.), $55/foreign, free/members. The "Classifieds" carry 30 to 40 job openings for physicians of all types.

Journal of the National Medical Association (SLACK, Inc., 6900 Grove Rd., Thorofare, NJ 08086; phone: 609/848-1000) monthly, $90/annual subscription. About 20 openings for pathologists, surgeons, staff, and faculty appear under "Positions Available."

The New Physician (American Medical Student Association, 1902 Association Dr., Reston, VA 22091; phone: 703/620-6600) nine issues/year, $25/annual nonmember subscription, free/members. Five to ten residency positions appear under "Classifieds/Opportunities."

ACPM News (American College of Preventive Medicine, Suite 206, 1660 L St., NW, Washington, DC 20036; phone: 202/466-2044) quarterly, $25/annual nonmember subscription, free/members. The "Classified" section contains two or three job vacancies for faculty, health educators, epidemiologists, MPH qualified health professionals, and fellowships. About the same number of jobs are listed on the Internet at URL: **http://www.acpm.org/acpm/**, and selecting "Employment Opportunities."

The DO (American Osteopathic Association, 142 Ontario St., Chicago, IL 60611-2864; phone: 312/280-5800) monthly, $55/annual subscription (U.S.), $70/foreign. About 125 openings for osteopaths appear under "Classifieds-Opportunities."

Photocopying strictly prohibited

ACOInformation (American College of Osteopathic Internists, Suite 670, 5301 Wisconsin Ave., NW, Washington, DC 20015; phones: 800/327-5183, 202/237-8980) monthly, free/members only. About half of the ten vacancies listed under "Professional Opportunities" are for positions at teaching hospitals and other educational institutions.

American Academy of Otolaryngology–Head and Neck Surgery Bulletin (AAO-HNS, 1 Prince St., Alexandria, VA 22314; phone: 703/836-4444) monthly, $65/annual subscription nonmembers, free/residents, $25/corresponding members and allied health members. "Employment Classifieds" publish 200+ positions for otolaryngologists.

AGA News (American Gastroenterological Association, 7910 Woodmont Ave., Bethesda. MD 20814; phone: 301/654-2055) monthly, free/members only. "Personnel" describes around 40 positions for gastroenterological physicians, researchers, and assistants.

Archives of Dermatology (American Medical Association, Order Department, P.O. Box 109046, Chicago, IL 60610-9046; phones: 800/262-2350, 312/670-7827) monthly, $140/annual subscription. From 50 to 75 job openings for practitioners, businesses, and faculty appear under "Classified Advertising." You can also see these ads on the Internet at URL: **http://ama-assn.org/** by first selecting "Scientific Journals and News." Next select "Physician Recruitment." You'll be asked to complete a free, one-time registration to access this area. Do it! Then you can browse through the ads or choose any of the more than 20 specialities to browse through job ads for a specialty.

The Dendrite (American Academy of Neurology, 2221 University Ave., SE, Minneapolis, MN 55414; phone: 612/623-8115) monthly, free/members only. From 60 to 100 positions plus 30 fellowships, 15 placement firms, and "positions wanted" fill each issue.

Archives of Neurology (American Medical Association, Order Department, P.O. Box 109046, Chicago, IL 60610-9046; phones: 800/262-2350, 312/670-7827) monthly, $160/annual subscription. Fifty to 100 positions for neurologists, residencies, administration, and faculty are published under "Classified Advertising." You can also see these ads on the Internet at URL: **http://ama-assn.org/** by first selecting "Scientific Journals and News." Next select "Physician Recruitment." You'll be asked to complete a free, one-time registration to access this area. Do it! Then you can browse through the ads or choose any of the more than 20 specialities to browse through job ads for a specialty.

Read chapters 1 and 2 first — doctor's orders

Obstetrics and Gynecology (Elsevier Science, 655 Avenue of the Americas, New York, NY 10010; phone: 212/989–5800) monthly, $148/annual subscription, $92/interns and residents. Sixty to 70 small display ads for job openings appear toward the end of each issue.

Archives of Physical Medicine and Rehabilitation (W.B. Saunders Company, Periodicals, 6277 Sea Harbor Drive, Orlando, FL 32887–4800; phone: 800/654–2452) monthly, $150/annual subscription, $65/residents and students. Sixty to 80 openings for physicians, rehabilitation practitioners, occupational therapists, psychologists, and speech therapists appear under "Classified Advertising."

CAMS Newsletter (Chinese American Medical Society, 281 Edgewood Ave., Teaneck, NJ 07666; phone: 201/833–1506) quarterly, free/members only, $100/annual dues. Twelve to 15 practitioner and academic positions appear under "Positions Available."

Journal of American Medical Women's Association (AMWA, Suite 400, 801 N. Fairfax St., Alexandria, VA 22314; phone: 703/838–0500) quarterly, $255/member physicians, $70/member nonphysicians. Nonmembers call for subscription rate. About five job ads appear in a typical issue.

Archives of Ophthalmology (American Medical Association, Order Department, P.O. 109046, Chicago, IL 60610–9046; phones: 800/262–2350, 312/670–7827) monthly, $120/annual subscription (U.S.). Around 30 openings for practitioners, residencies, faculty, and businesses appear under "Classified Advertising." You can also see these ads on the Internet at URL: **http://ama–assn.org/** by first selecting "Scientific Journals and News." Next select "Physician Recruitment." You'll be asked to complete a free, one–time registration to access this area. Do it! Then you can browse through the ads or choose any of the more than 20 specialities to browse through job ads for a specialty.

Journal of Visual Impairment and Blindness (AFB Press, American Foundation for the Blind, Suite 300, 11 Penn Plaza, New York, NY 10001; phone: 212/502–7600) monthly, $74/annual subscription (U.S.), $99/foreign. "Classified" contains five to seven ads for practitioners, teachers (elementary school through university), researchers, and administrators interested in working with the blind.

Journal of Perinatology (Mosby Yearbook, 11830 Westline Industrial Dr., St. Louis, MO 63146; phone: 314/453–4406) quarterly, $70/annual subscription. The "Classified" section has around ten positions for nutritionists, perentologists (prenatal), and nurses.

Job services

National Physicians Register (Suite 422J, 8 Park Plaza, Boston, MA 02116; phone: 800/342–1007) free. A physician submits a copy of her resume and gives her geographic preference and type of position sought. NPR creates a synopsis of the resume and assigns a code number to it. These synopses are published with code numbers rather than the physician's name in a bulletin sent bimonthly to 9,300 hospitals, clinics, group practices, and health maintenance organizations. The potential employer tells NPR which doctors interest it and NPR sends the contact information to the employer. Then, the employer can ask for a copy of her resume. (Employers usually ask for 20 to 50 persons per week at this service.) However, if the physician tells NPR that he doesn't want his name given out, NPR sends the job seeker a letter telling him a particular facility is interested in him and that he should contact the potential employer directly. Between 500 and 2,000 physicians are registered at any one time, although that number is growing. Serves both M.D. and osteopathic physicians.

Physician Recruitment (American Medical Association, Order Department, P.O. Box 109046, Chicago, IL 60610–9046; phones: 800/262–2350, 312/670–7827) free. You can see ads for physician positions, including for positions at Veterans Administration hospitals, on the Internet at URL: **http://ama–assn.org/** by first selecting "Scientific Journals and News." Next select "Physician Recruitment." You'll be asked to complete a free, one–time registration to access this area. Do it! Then you can browse through the ads or choose any of the more than 20 specialities to browse through job ads for a specialty.

AMA/FREIDA, AMA Fellowship & Residency Electronic Interactive Database Access System (American Medical Association, Order Processing, P.O. Box 7046, Dover, DE; phone: 800/621–8335) $599/members, $1,199/nonmembers, available on 3.5 inch and 5.25 inch MS–DOS disks and in a Macintosh version. The only official listing of residency and fellowship programs accredited by the Accreditation Council for Graduate Medical Education, these disks provide detailed information on over 75 percent of the residency and fellowship programs available.

National Resident Matching Program (2450 N Street, NW, Washington, DC 20037; phone: 202/828–0676) contact for rates. Matches graduating medical students with residencies. Fourth year medical students register with their school to participate.

Teratology Society Recruitment Service (Teratology Society, c/o Dr. Alan Hoberman, Argus Research Lab, Inc., 905 Sheehy Dr., Building A, Horsham, PA 19044; phone: 215/443–8710) free/members; call to see if it's now available to nonmembers as well. Complete the service's resume form. This service sends your form to all registered employers. It is kept on file for a year or until you find a new job, whichever comes first. Positions are for physicians and scientists who do clinical, pre–clinical work, or research on birth defects.

Placement Service (American Academy of Orthopaedic Surgeons, 6300 N. River Rd., Rosemont IL 60018–4262; phone: 847/823–7186) $300, which provides you a listing in the booklet, *Positions Wanted*; and gets you an annual subscription to the booklet *Practice Opportunities*. Each booklet is

Read chapters 1 and 2 first — doctor's orders

updated and published every January, April, July, and October. You can download a listing form for *Positions Wanted* on the Internet at URL: **http://www.aaos.org**, and selecting "Member Services," then "Placement Service," then "I want to find a job," and finally "Positions Wanted Listing Form." An online job database is available by clicking on "Opportunities," but you'll need a membership ID number to access it. Be sure to check out the dozens of links to similar sites under "Orthopaedic Yellow Pages."

Directories

AMA Physician Select (American Medical Association, Order Department, P.O. Box 109046, Chicago, IL 60610–9046; phones: 800/262–2350, 312/670–7827) free. This interactive directory is available on the Internet at URL: **http://ama–assn.org/** and choosing "AMA Physicians Select." You can search by name or by medical specialty. The entries for the 650,000 licensed physicians include contact information and their specialties. This is a valuable tool particularly for networking purposes.

American Medical Association Directory of Physicians in the U.S. (AMA, Order Processing, P.O. Box 7046, Dover, DE; phone: 800/621–8335) $545, four volumes; $745/CD–ROM version, October 1996. Reports details on over 735,000 physicians in the U.S. Each entry includes primary and secondary practice specialties, office address, medical school and year graduated, and type of practice. Includes alphabetical and geographical indexes.

Graduate Medical Education Directory, 1996–1997 (American Medical Association, Order Processing, P.O. Box 7046, Dover, DE; phone: 800/621–8335) $62.95/nonmembers, $46.95/members; on CD–ROM: $149.95/nonmembers, $119.95/members. Provides information on over 7,400 ACGME–accredited programs and more than 1,600 GME teaching institutions. Includes telephone numbers of graduate medical education program directors and accredited programs. Also features state licensure requirements and fees and a complete list of U.S. medical schools.

Yearbook and Directory of Osteopathic Physicians (American Osteopathic Association, 142 Ontario St., Chicago, IL 60611–2864; phone: 312/280–5800) $95, annual. In nearly 800 pages, this directory offers both alphabetical and geographical listings of osteopathic physicians plus osteopathic hospitals, research centers, and postdoctoral training programs.

Optics Education Directory (International Society for Optical Engineering, P.O. Box 10, Bellingham, WA 98227; phone: 360/676–3290) annual, free. Lists colleges and universities worldwide offering educational programs in optics and related fields.

CAMS Membership Directory (Chinese American Medical Society, 281 Edgewood Ave., Teaneck, NJ 07666; phone: 201/833–1506) free/members only, $100/annual dues, issued in even–numbered years.

Photocopying strictly prohibited

ACPM Membership Directory (American College of Preventive Medicine, Suite 403, 1015 15th St., NW, Washington, DC 20005; phone: 202/789–0003) $20/nonmembers, free/members, 110 pages, published in the summer of odd–numbered years. Lists about 2,100 physicians engaged in preventive medicine.

Membership Directory for the Society of Nuclear Medicine (Society of Nuclear Medicine, 1850 Samuel Morse Dr., Reston, VA 20190; phone: 703/708–9000) $150/nonmembers, free/members, published in the summer of odd–numbered years.

Directory of the American Academy of Orthopaedic Surgeons (AAOS, 6300 N. River Rd., Rosemont IL 60018–4262; phone: 847/823–7186) $50 plus $8 shipping/nonmembers, free/members, 400 pages, annual in late spring. Lists contact information for 20,000 member orthopaedic surgeons.

Salary survey

Physician Salary Survey Report (Hospital & Healthcare Compensation Service, P.O. Box 376, Oakland, NJ 07436; phone: 201/616–5722) $250 prepaid plus $7.50/shipping, 324 pages, published each February. For physicians employed by hospitals, group practice, and health maintenance organizations. Reports on salary and benefits nationally and in nine regions for 49 physician specialties. Also reports on hours worked, housing and meal allowances, incentive bonuses, and more. Includes physicians at medical schools, non–profit, government, and for–profit facilities.

Nurses

Job ads

American Journal of Nursing (Lippincott–Raven Publishers, P.O. Box 50480, Boulder, CO 80321; phones: 800/627–0484, 303/604–1464) monthly, $35/annual subscription (U.S.), $60/Canada, $71/elsewhere. Over 70 nursing and nursing administrative and academic positions, plus privately–operated placement services, appear in the "Classifieds Ads." You can access these job ads on the Internet at URL: **http://www.ajn.org** and then selecting "AJN Career Guide." At the bottom of the page is a U.S. map divided into regions. Click on the region in which you want to work and you'll see a list of employers from which to choose. The job descriptions are quite detailed. In addition, under "Nationwide Opportunities," you can select an employer listed to see its job openings.

Nurse Practitioner Journal (Springhouse Corp., P.O. Box 5053, Brentwood, TN 37024; phones: 800/490–6580, 615/322–3322) monthly, $45/annual subscription, $27/students. You'll find around 60 to 70 job openings in

Read chapters 1 and 2 first — doctor's orders

display ads and under "Positions and Opportunities" for nurse practitioners, pediatric, psychiatric, ob/gyn, geriatric, family, public health, occupational medicine, and faculty positions.

Nursing Outlook (Mosby Yearbook, Westline Industrial Dr., St. Louis, MO 63146; phone: 800/325–4177) bimonthly, $38/annual subscription (U.S.), $64.20/Canada, $60/elsewhere . "Advertising–Classifieds" includes ten ads for nursing administrators, nurse educators, and deans of nursing schools.

ABNF Journal (Tucker Publications, Association of Black Nursing Faculty in Higher Education, 5823 Queens Cove, Lisle, IL 60532; phone: 630/969–3809) bimonthly, $85/nonmembers, $40/students, free/members. The "Classifieds" carry ads for 15 to 22 nursing positions at universities and colleges.

Minority Nurse Newsletter (Tucker Publications, 5823 Queens Cove, Lisle, IL 60532; phone: 630/969–3809) quarterly, $40/annual subscription, $30/students. The "Classifieds" carry ads for five to ten ads for nursing positions in hospitals, home health care agencies, and schools of nursing.

NANPRH Newsletter (National Association of Nurse Practitioners in Reproductive Health, Suite 800, 1090 Vermont Ave., NW, Washington, DC 20005; phone: 202/408–7025) three issues/year, $75/annual subscription. About 50 openings for nurse practitioners appear under "Job Openings." Most openings are with affiliates of Planned Parenthood.

The American Nurse (American Nurses Association, Suite 100 West, 600 Maryland Ave., SW, Washington, DC 20024–2571; phone: 800/274–4262) ten issues/year, $20/annual nonmember subscription, $10/students, free/members. "Positions Available" features about 10 job openings for nursing faculty including positions overseas.

Nursing Research (Lippincott–Raven Publishers, American Journal of Nursing Co., 555 W. 57th St., New York, NY 10019; phones: 800/627–0484, 212/582–8820) bimonthly, $35/annual subscription (U.S.), $60/foreign. About ten research positions appear under "Classified Advertising."

Nurse Educator (Lippincott–Raven Publishers, P.O. Box 1590, Hagerstown, MD 21741; phone: 800/777–2295) bimonthly, $67/annual subscription (U.S.), $97/foreign. About five university positions appear under "Classified."

The Journal of Nursing Administration (Lippincott–Raven Publishing, P.O. Box 1590, Hagerstown, MD 21741; phone: 800/777–2295) 11 issues/year, $72/annual subscription (U.S.), $116/foreign. Twenty positions for nurse administrators appear under "Classified."

Nursing and Health Care (National League for Nursing, 350 Hudson St., New York, NY 10014; phone: 800/669–1656) ten issues/year, $40/annual subscription. The "Classified" section features five to 10 pages of ads for hospital nursing staff as well as academic positions.

Photocopying strictly prohibited

Journal of Nursing Education (SLACK, Inc., 6900 Grove Rd., Thorofare, NJ 08086–9447; phone: 800/257–8290) nine issues/year, $64/annual subscription (U.S.), $83/Canada plus 7 percent GST tax, $102/elsewhere. About six job openings appear under "Classified Marketplace."

Directories

Toll-Free Instant RSVP Nursing Career Directory (Springhouse Corp., 1111 Bethlehem Pike, Springhouse, PA 19477; phones: 800/331–3170, 215/646–8700) free, published each January. This directory lists over 600 hospitals and health centers that are looking for nursing professionals. Job openings are listed under each hospital. This service gives you a phone number to call to submit your qualifications and specialty interests over the phone, or you can send in the reader service card from the directory. The *RSVP* line calls the nurse recruiters at the facilities of your choice. The nurse recruiter sends you an application form. There is a possibility that this service will be discontinued in 1997.

Peterson's Nursing Programs (Peterson's Guides, P.O. 2123, Princeton, NJ 08543–2123; phone: 800/338–3282) $24.95 plus $6.75/shipping, 700 pages, annual. Describes more than 2,000 baccalaureate and graduate nursing programs in the U.S. and Canada, includes admission requirements, degrees offered, academic facilities, tuition, financial aid, and admission contacts.

Salary survey

Nursing Department Compensation Report (Hospital & Healthcare Compensation Service, P.O. Box 376, Oakland, NJ 07436; phone: 201/616–5722) $195 plus $7.50/shipping prepaid, published each November. This comprehensive salary and wage study of nurses and aides employed by hospitals, nursing homes, home care agencies, and hospices reports data on base salaries, bonuses and perquisites, hourly rates and more, by state, geographic region, nationally, and by major cities.

Pharmaceuticals

Job ads

Jobs in Pharmacy Related Fields — Academic, Industry, Government (david_bourne@uokhsc.edu) free. Go to URL: **http://www.cpb.uokhsc .edu/Pharmacy/jobs/jobs.html** where you'll find links to over 20 web sites with job vacancies in the pharmaceutical field.

Read chapters 1 and 2 first — doctor's orders

American Association of Colleges of Pharmacy News (AACP, 1426 Prince St., Alexandria, VA 22314; phone: 703/739–2330) 11 issues/year, $25/annual subscription. Half of the newsletter is devoted to ten to 20 job vacancy notices for pharmacy educators and instructors.

Directories

Profile of Faculty (American Association of Colleges of Pharmacy, 1426 Prince St., Alexandria, VA 22314; phone: 703/739–2330) $25/nonmembers, free/members, published each February.

FASEB Directory of Members (Federation of American Societies for Experimental Biology, Suite L–2310, 9650 Rockville Pike, Bethesda, MD 20814; phone: 301/530–7027) $60/nonmembers prepaid (U.S.), $65/Mexico and Canada, $71/elsewhere, $16/members of the American Society for Pharmacology and Experimental Therapeutics, 450 pages, annual. Lists contact information for members of the federation.

Research

Also see the "Research" chapter.

Job ads

Cancer Research Journal (American Association for Cancer Research, Suite 816, 620 Chestnut St., Philadelphia, PA 19106–3483; phone: 215/440–9300) semimonthly, $460/annual nonmember subscription (U.S.), $550/foreign, free/members. The "Employment Register" features notices from about 130 job seekers who advertise their availability, plus ads for around 100 research positions, generally postdoctoral.

Directory

Directory of Members: American Association for Cancer Research (AACR, Suite 816, 620 Chestnut St., Philadelphia, PA 19106–3483; phone: 215/440–9300) $50/nonmembers, free/members, annual. Lists contact information for more than 12,000 physicians engaged in cancer research.

Photocopying strictly prohibited

Therapy-mental

Also see the "Social services" chapter.

Job ads

The APA Monitor (American Psychological Association, 750 First St., NE, Washington, DC 20002–4242; phone: 202/336–5500) monthly, $27.50/nonmember annual subscription (U.S.), $39.50/foreign, free/members. Jobs listed under "Position Openings." From 400 to 800 job ads for psychologists and support staff grace the pages of a typical issue. These job vacancies are also displayed on the Internet at URL: **http://www.apa.org/**. Select "Classified Ads" or "Employment Opportunities" to access the job listings which are listed by state.

APS Bulletin Board is an Internet job bank site of the American Psychological Society. Go to URL: **http://psych.hanover.edu/APS/** and select "APS Bulletin Board" and then "Complete Listings," where you will find dozens of jobs, mostly for faculty and postdoctoral positions.

Psychiatric News (American Psychiatric Association, 1400 K St., NW, Washington, DC 20005; phone: 202/682–6250) bimonthly, $40/annual nonmember subscription (U.S.), $60/foreign, free/members. Display ads and the "Classified Notices" feature 300 to 350 job vacancies for staff psychiatrists and psychologists, administrative staff, and support staff.

National Council News (National Community Mental Healthcare Council, Suite 320, 12300 Twinbrook Pkwy, Rockville, MD 20852; phone: 301/984–6200) 11 issues/year, $60/nonmember annual subscription, free/members. Jobs listed in "JOBank" insert. The typical issue features 20 to 30 job ads for social workers and counselors, psychiatrists, psychologists, clinical workers, and administrative positions.

Communiqué (National Association of School Psychologists, Suite 402, 4340 East–West Hwy., Bethesda, MD 20919; phone: 301/657–0207) eight issues/year, $30/annual nonmember subscription, free/members. About 20 job vacancies for psychologists in elementary schools through colleges appear under "Employment Notices." You are instructed to contact these employers to learn of any job openings they currently have.

Journal of the American Academy of Child & Adolescent Psychiatry (Williams & Wilkins, 351 W. Camden St., Baltimore, MD 21202; phones: 800/638–6423, 410/528–4000) monthly, $109/annual subscription (U.S.), $234/foreign, $25/single issue price. Ten to 15 display ads appear for child and adolescent psychiatrists including: medical directors, division chiefs, and residency programs.

Read chapters 1 and 2 first — doctor's orders

Psych Discourse (The Association of Black Psychologists, P.O. Box 55999, Washington, DC 20040–5999; phone: 202/722–0808) monthly, $95/nonmembers, free/members of ABP, $15/single issue. From 20 to 40 job ads are in the typical issue, usually for faculty positions.

AMHCA Advocate (American Mental Health Counselors' Association, Suite 304, 801 N. Fairfax St., Alexandria, VA 22314; phones: 800/326–2642, 703/548–6002) ten issues/year, $25/nonmember annual subscription, included in membership package. Jobs listed under "Classifieds." About four job ads in the usual issue.

AACAP News (American Academy of Child and Adolescent Psychiatry, 3615 Wisconsin Ave., NW, Washington, DC 20016; phones: 800/333–7636, 202/966–7300) bimonthly, $109/annual subscription, $74/professionals in training. You'll generally find ten to 15 ads under "Positions" for practitioner and academic positions.

Family Therapy News (American Association for Marriage and Family Therapy, 1100 17th St., NW, Washington, DC 20036; phone: 202/452–0109) bimonthly, $35/nonmember annual subscription, $20/members. "Classified Ads" has about 25 openings for marriage and family therapists including practitioners, researchers, pastoral counselors, faculty, and practices for sale.

ABA Newsletter (Association for Behavior Analysis, Attn: Patty DeLoach, 213 West Hall, Western Michigan University, Kalamazoo, MI 49008–5052; phone: 616/387–4495) three issues/year, $30/annual nonmember subscription, free/members. "Positions available" lists from five to ten openings for psychologists, therapists, consultants, and faculty.

Job services

APA JobBank (American Psychiatric Association, 1400 K St., NW, Washington, DC 20005; phone: 202/682–6108) free/members only. Complete this job–matching service's "profile" form. When matched with a vacancy, you are sent information on the employer. You are responsible for contacting the employer. Profiles are kept on file indefinitely.

American Psychological Association Resume Database (American Psychological Association, 750 First St., NE, Washington, DC 20002–4242; phone: 202/336–5500) contact Resumé–Link (614/777–4000) for nonmember fees, $20/members, $10/student members. Request the "APA Resume Database Information Form," complete it and submit it with your payment. To avoid tipping off your current employer that you are looking for another job, you can check a box on the form so your resume will not be released to your present employer. Computer matching is done by Resumé–Link, a specialist in electronic job–matching systems. When you are matched to a job, your resume form is faxed to the prospective employer. This job-matching service checks with you every six months to update your resume.

Directories

APA Membership Directory (American Psychological Association, 750 First St., NE, Washington, DC 20002–4242; phone: 202/336–5500) $70/nonmembers, $50/members, published every four years, 1996. Provides names, phone numbers, and educational backgrounds of APA members.

APA Membership Register (American Psychological Association, 750 First St., NE, Washington, DC 20002–4242; phone: 202/336–5500) $35/nonmembers, $22.50/members, published every year except the year in which the *APA Membership Directory*, described immediately above, comes out. Provides names and phone numbers of APA members.

Mental Health Directory (Center for Mental Health Services, Knowledge Exchange Network, P.O. Box 42490, Washington, DC 20015; phone: 800/789–2647) free. This directory includes hospitals, group homes, halfway houses, and other mental health organizations by city and state.

National Community Mental Healthcare Council 1996 Membership Directory (National Community Mental Healthcare Council, Suite 320, 12300 Twinbrook Pkwy., Rockville, MD 20852; phone: 301/984–6200) $40/nonmembers, $15/members. Lists some 900 community-based mental health care and substance abuse provider organizations.

Association of State and Provincial Psychology Boards Membership Roster (Association of State & Provincial Psychology Boards, P.O. Box 4389, Montgomery, AL 36103; phone: 334/832–4580) $4, prepaid. Lists addresses and phone numbers of state and provincial psychology licensing boards in the U.S. and Canada.

Association for Behavior Analysis Membership Directory (ABA, Attn: Patty DeLoach, 213 West Hall, Western Michigan University, Kalamazoo, MI 49008–5052; phone: 616/387–4495) $16 (U.S.), $21/foreign, 160 pages, issued each December. Lists the names, addresses, phones, fax numbers, and specialties for each of its 2,500 members.

Grants for Mental Health, Addictions & Crisis Services (The Foundation Center, 79 Fifth Ave., New York, NY 10003–3076; phones: 800/424–9836, within New York State call 212/620–4230) $65 plus $4.50/shipping, 183 pages, published in October of odd-numbered years. Describes recent foundation grants of at least $10,000 given to hospitals, health centers, residential treatment facilities, group homes, and mental health associations for addiction prevention and treatment, for hotline/crisis intervention services, and for public education and research. This directory is useful for identifying foundations and grant recipients for which you may wish to work.

Read chapters 1 and 2 first — doctor's orders

Therapy–physical

Also see the "Social services" chapter.

Job ads

ASHA Leader (American Speech–Language–Hearing Association, 10801 Rockville Pike, Rockville, MD 20852; phones"800/638-8255, 301/897-5700) biweekly, $60/annual nonmember subscription, free/members; note: your subscription is actually for two publications, the other being *ASHA* which no longer carries job ads and comes out quarterly. Around 200 ads in the "ASHA Classifieds" describe openings for speech–language pathologists, audiologists, speech scientists, and speech and hearing professors. These ads also appear on the Internet at URL: **http://www.asha.org** by selecting "Classifieds."

Counseling Today (American Counseling Association, 5999 Stevenson Ave., Alexandria, VA 22304-3300; phone: 703/823-9800, ext. 222) monthly, $37/annual subscription. "Employment Classifieds" describe around 20 vacancies for psychologists and counselors in private practice, agencies, and universities.

PT Bulletin (American Physical Therapy Association, Suite 400, 333 N. Fairfax St., Alexandria, VA 22314; phone: 800/826-4150) weekly, free/members only. About 400 ads for physical therapists, PT assistants, rehabilitation directors, and physical medicine in the fields of: acute care, long-term care, geriatrics, orthopedics, sports medicine, industrial rehabilitation, home health care, and hand therapy.

OT Week (American Occupational Therapy Association, 4720 Montgomery Ln., Bethesda, MD 20814; phones: 800/344-7832, 301/652-2682) weekly, $80/nonmember annual subscription, free/members. Around 225 job openings for occupational therapists fill this tabloid.

AATA Newsletter (American Art Therapy Association, 1202 Allanson Rd., Mundelein, IL 60060; phone: 847/949-6064) quarterly, $26/annual nonmember subscription (U.S.), $38/foreign, free/members. Positions for art therapists in rehabilitation medical facilities and universities appear under "Opportunities" when available.

Art Therapy: Journal of the American Art Therapy Association (AATA, 1202 Allanson Rd., Mundelein, IL 60060; phone: 847/949-6064) quarterly, $50/annual nonmember subscription (U.S.), $74/foreign, free/members. Positions for art therapists in rehabilitation medical facilities and universities.

Update (American Alliance for Health, Physical Education, Recreation and Dance, 1900 Association Dr., Reston, VA 22091; phone: 703/476-3400) bimonthly, $45/annual nonmember institution subscription (individual sub-

Therapy–physical

scriptions not available), free/members. "Job Exchange" features 30 or more jobs largely with universities as well as numerous graduate assistantships and grants. These job listings are also available on the Internet at URL: **http://www.aahperd.org/**. There you can select links to other national organizations that list job vacancies in physical therapy.

Journal PERD (American Alliance for Health, Physical Education, Recreation and Dance, 1900 Association Dr., Reston, VA 22091; phone: 703/476–3400) nine issues/year, $100/annual nonmember institution subscription (individual subscriptions not available). The "Classifieds" feature about five positions with camps and universities. These job listings are also available on the Internet at URL: **http://www.aahperd.org/**. There you can select links to other national organizations that list job vacancies in physical therapy.

Journal of Cognitive Rehabilitation (NeuroScience Publishers, 6555 Carrollton Ave., Indianapolis, IN 46220; phone: 317/257–9672) bimonthly, $35/annual subscription (U.S.), $40/Canada, $50/elsewhere. You'll find about five ads for administrators and speech pathologists, psychologists, physical therapists, and occupational therapists under "Job Positions."

NCRE Newsletter (National Council on Rehabilitation Education, c/o Dr. Julie Smart, Department of Special Education, Utah State University, Logan, UT 84322–2870; phone: 801/797–3269) quarterly, free/members only. "Positions" generally lists openings for two rehabilitation education or psychology positions.

Job service

American Speech–Language–Hearing Association Resume Database (ASHA, 10801 Rockville Pike, Rockville, MD 20852; phones: 800/638–8255, 301/897–5700) $160/nonmember annual fee, $20/members, $10/student members. Request the "ASHA Resume Database Information Form," complete it and submit it with your payment. To avoid tipping off your current employer that you are looking for another job, you can check a box on the form so your resume will not be released to your present employer. Computer matching is done by Resumé–Link, a specialist in electronic job–matching systems. When you are matched to a job, your resume form is faxed to the prospective employer. This job–matching service checks with you every six months to update your resume.

Directories

ASHA Membership Directory (American Speech–Language–Hearing Association, 10801 Rockville Pike, Rockville, MD 20852; phones: 800/638–8255, 301/897–5700) $60/nonmembers, $40/members, last published in 1995.

Read chapters 1 and 2 first — doctor's orders

Members can access this entire directory of 87,000 names on the Internet at URL: **http://www.asha.org**. Select "For ASHA Members" and then provide your ASHA membership number as a password.

Professional Services Board List of Accredited Clinics in Audiology and Speech–Language Pathology (American Speech–Language–Hearing Association, 10801 Rockville Pike, Rockville, MD 20852; phones: 800/638–8255, 301/897–5700) free, 40 pages, updated monthly. Although you can receive this list by mail, the association prefers that you request it by fax (dial 202/274–4520) and it will be faxed to you. You can also obtain this list via the Internet at URL: **http://www.asha.org**. Click on "Consumer Information" and then "Professional Services Board." Organized by state, each entry includes the names, addresses, phone numbers, and contact person at ASHA accredited clinics offering audiology and/or speech–language pathology services.

NCRE Membership Directory (National Council on Rehabilitation Education, c/o Dr. Garth Eldredge, Department of Special Education, Utah State University, Logan, UT 84122–2865; phone: 801/797–3241) $25/nonmembers, free/members, 125 pages, issued every December. Lists more than 500 faculty involved in rehabilitation education.

Membership Directory (American Art Therapy Association, 1202 Allanson Rd., Mundelein, IL 60060; phone: 847/949–6064) $65/nonmembers, $19/members, 319 pages, published in August of even–numbered years. Lists 4,751 individuals engaged in art therapy.

American Horticultural Therapy Association Annual Membership Directory (AHTA, 362–A Christopher Ave., Gaithersburg, MD 20879; phone: 301/948–3010) free/members only, 200 pages, issued each January. Lists over 800 individuals engaged in horticultural therapy.

Salary surveys

AOTA Annual Professional Income (American Occupational Therapy Association, 4720 Montgomery Ln., Bethesda, MD 20814; phones: 301/652–2682) $8/nonmembers, free/members, 1997. Gives salary breakdowns for occupational therapists and occupational therapy assistants by experience, settings, state, and more.

Membership Survey Report (American Art Therapy Association, 1202 Allanson Rd., Mundelein, IL 60060; phone: 847/949–6064) $2.32/nonmembers, 32¢/members, issued in June of odd–numbered years. Presents data on salaries by areas of specialization, educational degree, work setting, and age of the clients served.

Photocopying strictly prohibited

Chapter 17

Housing, planning, and development

Housing, planning, and development

*Also see the entries for each of these specialties in the **Government Job Finder.***

Job ads

Planners Network (Planners Network, c/o Pratt GCPE, 200 Willoughby Ave., Brooklyn, NY 11205; phone: 718/636–3461) bimonthly, free/members only; annual dues: $15/students and persons with incomes below $25,000, $25/incomes between $25,000 and $50,000, $45/incomes over $50,000. Jobs listed under "Job." Typical issue features about five to 20 jobs in housing, community development, organizing, and university faculty and research.

The NonProfit Times (Suite 318, 240 Cedar Knolls Rd., Cedar Knolls, NJ 07927; phone: 201/734–1700) monthly, $59/annual subscription (U.S.), $89/Canada, $129/elsewhere, free/qualified full–time non–profit executives, write for qualification form. "The National NonProfit Employment Marketplace" carries 20 to 30 ads for all sorts of positions related to planning, economic development, and public administration. Go to the Web site at URL: **http://www.nptimes.com/** for a host of valuable links to other non-profits.

Shelterforce (National Housing Institute, 439 Main St., Orange, NJ 07050; phone: 201/678-3110) bimonthly, $18/annual individual subscription (U.S.), $30/libraries, institutions, and law firms (U.S.); add $8/Canada, add $15/elsewhere. Under "Jobs" you'll find five to ten positions largely with non-profit economic/community development agencies, housing authorities, and in organizing. Includes positions ranging from entry level to executive directors. The National Housing Institute may add the job listings to its Web site at URL: **http://www.nhi.org**.

Roundup (National Low-Income Housing Information Service, 1012, Suite 1200, 14th St., NW, Washington, DC 20005; phone: 202/662-1530 ext. 226) ten issues/year, available free as part of membership in the Low Income Housing Information Service for $35/annual individual membership, $10/low-income individual membership. "Job Openings" carries ads for about eight positions in community and economic development, housing, organizing, and rural development.

Preservation Magazine (National Trust for Historic Preservation, 1785 Massachusetts Ave., NW, Washington, DC 20036; phone: 202/588-6075), bimonthly, $4.50/individual back issue, free subscription/members only, $20/annual dues (individual), $24/annual dues (family). Five job ads listed under "Marketplace" for positions in the preservation field.

Chamber Jobwatch (Association of Chamber of Commerce Executives, 4232 King St., Alexandria, VA 22302; phone: 703/998-0072) semimonthly, $80/annual nonmember subscription, $40/members. Each issue features 20 or more job ads for executives and management personnel for chambers of commerce, including executive directors, government relations staff, marketing, community development, and communications.

Council News (American Economic Development Council, Suite 540, 9801 W. Higgins, Rosemont, IL 60018; phone: 847/692-9944) semimonthly, available to members only, annual membership: $280, plus $30 processing fee first year only; $190, plus $30 processing fee first year only, when another person in your office is already a member. Jobs listed under "Career Opportunities." About six job ads are in the typical issue.

Economic Developments (National Council for Urban Economic Development, Suite 700, 1730 K St., NW, Washington, DC 20006; phone: 202/223-4735) 24 issues/year, free/members only; $295/annual dues. Jobs listed under "Job Mart." Typical issue sports three to ten job ads.

City Limits (40 Prince St., New York, NY 10012; phone: 212/925-9820) ten issues/year; $25/annual subscription for individuals and community groups, $35/all others. About ten positions ranging from grant writers to administrators for housing, social work, community development, and neighbor-

Housing, planning, and development

hood organizations in New York City are listed under "Job Ads." A handful of job listings also appear on the Internet at URL: **http://www.citylimits.org**, and scrolling down to "Job Listings."

Development Times (National Congress for Community Economic Development, Suite 325, 11 Dupont Cr, Washington, DC 20036; phone: 202/234–5009) 8 times/year, $39/annual subscription. Five to seven jobs in community development are listed under "Employment Opportunities."

GIS Jobs Clearinghouse (Remote Sensing Laboratory, University of Minnesota) free. This Web site offers over 70 jobs in its job database that is updated monthly. Go to Internet URL: **http://www.gis.umn.edu/rsgisinfo/jobs.html** and select "Current or Previous Month" to browse or search by job title. Positions are in the geographic information system field.

AAG Newsletter (Association of American Geographers, 1710 16th St., NW, Washington, DC 20009; phone: 202/234–1450) monthly, free/members only. From 25 to 50 positions, primarily academic, are listed under "Jobs in Geography."

Job Openings for Economists (American Economic Association, Suite 305, 2014 Broadway, Nashville, TN 37203; phone: 615/322–2595) bimonthly, $25/annual nonmember subscription (U.S.), $34/foreign, $15/AEA regular members, $7.50/AEA junior members. Among the 150 plus jobs in a typical issue are a number in the non–profit sector including university faculty.

NEA Job Placement Bulletin (National Economic Association, School of Business, University of Michigan, Ann Arbor, MI 48109–1234; phone: 313/763–0121) quarterly, free/members only. Ten to 20 jobs in government and education appear in the typical issue.

Public Sector Job Bulletin (P.O. Box 1222, Newton, IA 50208–1222; phone: 515/791–9019) biweekly, $22/annual subscription, $14/six months. Among the 30 to 60 job openings in each issue are a growing number of positions in economic development and housing with non–profit entities.

AIC Newsletter (American Institute of Constructors, 466 94th Ave. North, St. Petersburg, FL 33702; phone: 813/578–0317) bimonthly, free/members only. Each issue has ads for "constructors" (estimators, project managers, project engineers, faculty, etc.) scattered throughout. Check out the Internet at URL: **http://www.aicnet.org** for possibly more job vacancy listings. The constructors were still constructing the site when we went to press.

Plan ahead by reading chapters 1 and 2 first

Urban Affairs Newsletter (University of Delaware, Newark, DE 19716; phone: 302/831–2394) five issues/year, free/members only. Jobs listed under "Positions Available." About three to ten job ads are printed in a typical issue. Lists university teaching positions in urban affairs and related areas.

The New Careers Directory: Internships and Professional Opportunities in Technology and Social Change (Student Pugwash USA, Suite 32, 1638 R St., NW, Washington, DC 20009; phone: 202/328–6555) $18, $10/students; add $3 shipping, last published in 1993. Offers full details on where and how to apply for internships and entry-level jobs in development.

Job services

Resume Referral Service (American Economic Development Council, Suite 540, 9801 W. Higgins, Rosemont, IL 60018; phone: 847/692–9944) $100/non-members for 12 months, free to members. Return form with ten copies of your resume. AEDC lets you know when it matches your qualifications with a potential employer, but it is up to the employer to contact you for the interview. Once you are in the resume referral service you will be sent by first class mail job listings from hiring organizations as they come into the AEDC office. You are responsible for contacting prospective employers. Ads will be mailed within a week of receipt.

CEUD Online (National Council for Urban Economic Development, Suite 700, 1730 K St., NW, Washington, DC 20006; phone: 202/223–4735) free. Go to Internet URL: **http://cued.org/** and select "Personnel Agency" to enter this database of economic and community development positions. Select "CUED Economic Development Internships" to learn how to apply for the internships listed.

Economic Development Career Center (National Council for Urban Economic Development, Suite 700, 1730 K St., NW, Washington, DC 20006; phone: 202/223–4735) members only, $119.95/annual dues, can join at this site. This job database for economic development positions is located at Internet URL: **http://IEDN.com/iedn/careercenter/**. Also includes a ***Directory of Consultants*** in economic development.

Building Industry Exchange. Go to Internet URL: **http://www.building.org/centers/career/begin.html** and select "A/E/C Classified Advertising, Career, & Employment" to access a database with 40 to 60 jobs in construction including estimators, sales, executives, crafts, and project managers. About ten percent of the positions are for faculty.

Directories

Directory of State Housing Coalitions (National Low–Income Housing Information Service, Suite 1200, 1012 14th St., NW, Washington, DC 20005; phone: 202/662–1530) $5, 26 pages, most recent edition published May 1991. Includes 87 organizations with synopses of 41 of them.

Affordable Housing Directory (Business Communication Services, Suite 502, 657 Mission St., San Francisco, CA 94105; phone: 415/546–7255) $75, over 100 pages, published each January. Includes contact information on hundreds of firms that specialize in affordable housing including non–profit and for–profit developers, attorneys, accountants, planners, architects, management agents, and sources of debt and equity funding. Entries are indexed by region.

American Planning Association Membership Directory (American Planning Association, Suite 1600, 122 S. Michigan Avenue, Chicago, IL 60603; phone: 312/431–9100; $39.95 plus $5.95 shipping, last published in summer 1995. Alphabetical listing of 29,000 professional planners and planning commissioners plus geographical index and specialty index. Includes names, addresses, phone, and email addresses. You can also find the city in which an APA member lives by accessing this directory at APA's web site at URL: **http://www.planning.org**. This directory, however, will not give you the member's address or telephone number.

AICP Roster (American Institute of Certified Planners, c/o American Planning Association, 1776 Massachusetts Ave., NW, Washington, DC 20036; phone: 202/872–0611) $30/nonmember, $20/APA member, free/AICP members, 180 pages, published in even–numbered years. AICP is an institute within the American Planning Association. This directory lists the 9,000+ AICP members alphabetically and by city within each state. Although AICP membership is achieved by passing a demanding test, it does not indicate that AICP members are better qualified nor more competent than other professional planners. Since titles are listed, this is a good source to identify directors of non–profits engaged in housing and community development as well as related fields.

CUED Directory (National Council for Urban Economic Development, Suite 700, 1730 K St., NW, Washington, DC 20006; phone: 202/223–4735) $200/nonmembers, free/members, 271 pages, published each September. Give contact information on the members of the National Council for Urban Economic Development; includes economic and community development professionals working in government, with non–profits, and in the private sector. The 1,600 entries are listed alphabetically within states.

National Directory for Community Economic Development (National Congress for Community Economic Development, Suite 325, 11 Dupont Cr., Washington, DC 20036; phone: 202/234–5009) $49, published in April of even–numbered years. Lists 1,700 organizations, mostly non–profit, in

Plan ahead by reading chapters 1 and 2 first

the community development field, profiles their services and activities, and provides names of key contact personnel, addresses, phone and fax numbers.

Trends & Economic Development Organizations: A Directory (National Council for Urban Economic Development, Suite 700, 1730 K St., NW, Washington, DC 20006; phone: 202/223-4735) $225/nonmembers, $145/members, published in May of even-numbered years. Profiles 137 economic development organizations from 51 metropolitan areas, including 43 city agencies, 20 county agencies, and 40 private sector organizations.

Who's Who in Economic Development (American Economic Development Council, Suite 540, 9801 W. Higgins, Rosemont, IL 60018; phone: 847/692-9944) free/members only, published each August. Geographical and alphabetical listings of members throughout the world. Also includes geographical and alphabetical lists of certified economic developers.

Directory of Partners (Alliance for National Renewal Partners, Suite 300, 1445 Market St., Denver, CO 80202-1728; phone: 303/571-4343) is an Internet directory and collection of links of non-profit organizations dedicated to renewal of the community. There's a wide range of groups here, most of them involved in community economic and social development, creating affordable housing, and combating racial injustice. Go to URL: **http://www.ncl.org/anr/**, and select "Directory of Partners" for an alphabetical list of members, which you access by clicking on the letters of the alphabet graphic. The directory supplies street and email addresses, phone and fax numbers, and key contact names. When an entry is underlined, it is linked to its home page.

GIS World GeoDirectory (GIS World, Inc., Suite 250, 155 E. Boardwalk Dr., Fort Collins, CO 80525-9945; phone: 970/223-4848) $149.95 plus 10 percent shipping in U.S. and Canada (plus 3 percent sales tax for Colorado residents; GST for Canadian residents), add 20 percent shipping elsewhere, published every October, three volumes (also available on CD-ROM for $149.95) which can be purchased individually for $69.95: I: Data Sources; II: **Academic Institutions**; III: Venders, Providers, and Services. Includes descriptions of geographic information system companies and schools including contact names, plus a directory of GIS service providers including consultants, system integrators, and application developers.

Guide to Program in Geography in the United States and Canada: AAG Handbook and Directory of Geographers (Association of American Geographers, 1710 16th St., NW, Washington, DC 20009; phone: 202/234-1450), $40/nonmembers, $20/members and students, 825 pages, annual in August. Lists all universities and colleges with geography departments and some 17,400 geographers

Photocopying strictly prohibited

Housing, planning, and development

Directory of Black Economists (National Economic Association, School of Business, University of Michigan, Ann Arbor, MI 48109-1234; phone: 313/763-0121) $25/nonmembers, free/members, published in odd-numbered years.

American Institute of Constructors Directory of Members (AIC, 466 94th Ave. North, St. Petersburg, FL 33702; phone: 813/578-0317) free/members only, 60 pages, published each July. Lists some 2,100 member constructors (estimators, project managers, project engineers), giving addresses and phone numbers. You can obtain a mailing list of the members on 3.5-inch disk for $75.

Urban Affairs Directory (University of Delaware, Newark, DE 19716; phone: 302/831-2394) $25, published in odd-numbered years. Lists academic programs in universities and colleges that specialize in urban affairs and related issues.

National Guide to Funding for Community Development (The Foundation Center, 79 Fifth Ave., New York, NY 10003-3076; phones: 800/424-9836, 212/620-4230) $135, 808 pages, May 1996. Each of the more than 2,500 entries for foundations, corporate direct giving programs, and public charities includes application information and a list of recent grants awarded for projects covering community improvement; economic development; housing development, construction, and rehabilitation; homeless shelters; low-cost temporary housing; and community service clubs.

Grants for Community Development, Housing & Employment (The Foundation Center, 79 Fifth Ave., New York, NY 10003-3076; phones: 800/424-9836, within New York State call 212/620-4230) $75 plus $4.50/shipping, 448 pages, published in October of odd-numbered years. Describes recent foundation grants of at least $10,000 given to community organizations, government agencies, and universities for a wide range of social services, housing and urban development programs, including business services and federated giving programs. This directory is useful for identifying foundations and grant recipients for which you may wish to work.

Grants for Homeless (The Foundation Center, 79 Fifth Ave., New York, NY 10003-3076; phones: 800/424-9836, within New York State call 212/620-4230) $75 plus $4.50/shipping, 86 pages, published in October of odd-numbered years. Describes recent foundation grants of at least $10,000 given to shelters and temporary housing services, legal rights and advocacy programs, food services and health care, and to services for homeless families, youth, and children. This directory is useful for identifying foundations and grant recipients for which you may wish to work.

Plan ahead by reading chapters 1 and 2 first

Grants for Public Policy and Public Affairs (The Foundation Center, 79 Fifth Ave., New York, NY 10003–3076; phones: 800/424–9836, within New York State call 212/620–4230) $75 plus $4.50/shipping, 353 pages, published in October of odd–numbered years. Describes recent foundation grants of at least $10,000 for government and public administration, public affairs, leadership development, foreign policy, international peace and security, and a wide range of public policy studies. This directory is useful for identifying foundations and grant recipients for which you may wish to work.

Salary surveys

Planners' Salaries and Employment Trends, 1995 (American Planning Association, Suite 1600, 122 S. Michigan Ave., Chicago, IL 60603; phone: 312/4312–9100) $28, $14/subscribers to APA's Planning Advisory Service, plus $5/shipping, 25 pages, 1996. Reports on salaries for professional urban and regional planners by type of employer (foundations and universities, municipal, state, federal, and consultant/business), experience, education, position, jurisdiction's size, race, sex, and by state. Excerpts from this survey appear on APA's Web site at URL: **http://www.planning.org/**. See the site map to locate it.

CUED Salary Survey (National Council for Urban Economic Development, Suite 700, 1730 K St., NW, Washington, DC 20006; phone: 202/223–4735) $75/nonmembers, $60/members, published in December of even–numbered years. Covers community and economic development officials.

1996–1997 Compensation and Benefits Survey (American Economic Development Council, Suite 540, 9801 W. Higgins Rd., Rosemont, IL 60018; phone: 847/692–9944) contact for current price. Profiles organization background, base salary, and benefits for economic development professionals.

Annual Graduating Senior Placement Survey (American Institute of Constructors, 466 94th Ave., North, St. Petersburg, FL 33702; phone: 813/578–0317) $25/nonmembers, free/members, published each October. Reports on the salaries of seniors in construction who graduated in the previous academic year.

Chapter 18

Legal services

Legal services

The ***Professional's Job Finder*** and the ***Government Job Finder*** both contain much more extensive sets of entries for attorneys and related professions.

Job ads

Opportunities in Public Interest Law (ACCESS: Networking in the Public Interest, Suite 838, 1001 Connecticut Ave., NW, Washington, DC 20036; phone: 202/785–4233) published every February and October, $42.90/each edition. Each issue features details on hundreds of positions in non–profit and government public interest law.

Clearinghouse Review (National Clearinghouse for Legal Services, 2nd Floor, 205 W. Monroe, Chicago, IL 60606; phone: 312/263–3830) monthly, $300/annual subscription (U.S.), $95/foreign. About 25 ads for attorneys and paralegals, largely with non–profits, and faculty appear under "Job Market."

National and Federal Legal Employment Report (Federal Reports, Inc., Suite 408, 1010 Vermont Ave., NW, Washington, DC 20005; phones: 800/296–9611, 202/393–3311) monthly. Subscription rates for individuals: $39/three–month, $69/six–month, $125/annual subscription; rates for institutions: $50, $90, $160, respectively plus 75¢/month for postage. The

typical issue contains descriptions of 500 to 600 attorney and law-related positions primarily in the federal government, state and local government, public defender and legal aid offices, Capitol Hill, colleges and universities, international organizations, law firms, and private employers (including corporations and associations). Includes legal positions in the Washington, D.C. area, throughout the U.S., and abroad.

PiES Job Alert! (Public Interest Clearinghouse, 100 McAllister St., San Francisco, CA 94102–4978; phone: 415/255–1714) semimonthly, three-month subscriptions: $40/employed; $20/unemployed or students; annual subscription: $190/schools and institutions. Over 50 professional and support positions are described per issue for work with legal aid offices, progressive law firms, and other kinds of law/advocacy-related public interest organizations. About half the positions are located in the San Francisco Bay area; the rest are from across the country.

Lawyers Job Bulletin Board (Federal Bar Association, Publications Department, Suite 408, 1815 H St., N.W., Washington, DC 20006; phone: 202/638–0252) monthly, $30/nonmember annual subscription, $20/nonmember students, $20/members. Typical issue features 25 job openings primarily with the federal government, although about 10 percent of the ads are for positions with District of Columbia area courts, private firms, and non-profits.

Legal Times (1730 M St., NW, Washington, DC 20036; phone: 202/457–0686) weekly, $175/annual subscription. The classifieds section contains job vacancies largely in the DC area, but also nationally, for attorneys, paralegals, legal assistants, and legal secretaries.

Cornerstone (National Legal Aid and Defender Association, 8th Floor, 1625 K St., NW, Washington, DC 20006; phone: 202/452–0620) quarterly, $20/nonmember subscription, free/members. "Job Listings" usually includes 15 to 20 job announcements.

ABA Journal (American Bar Association, Attn: Order Fulfillment, 750 N. Lake Shore Dr., Chicago, IL 60611; phone: 312/988–5555) monthly, free/members, $66/annual nonmember subscription. In the "Legal Mart" you'll find a section labeled "The Fine Print" which contains ads for about five or so teaching or administrative positions at law schools.

ALA Management Connections Bulletin (Association of Legal Administrators, Suite 325, 175 E. Hawthorn Pkwy., Vernon Hills, IL 60061–1428; phone: 847/816–1212) weekly, $150/nonmember six-month subscription, $100/members. This is the print version of the *ALA Management Connec-*

Legal services

tion job hotline described below under "Job services." In it you will find job ads for law office managers with non–profits and public interest groups, although the vast majority of positions advertised are with private firms. You can place a "Position Wanted" ad of your own for $75/nonmembers, $50/members. This ad will be recorded on *ALA Management Connections* and appear in the *ALA Management Connections Bulletin.* Contact the Association of Legal Administrators for details.

Summer Legal Employment Guide (Federal Reports, Inc., Suite 408, 1010 Vermont Ave., NW, Washington, DC 20005; phones: 800/296–9611, 202/393–3311) $16/individuals, $18/institutions, plus $2.50 shipping, 32 pages, annual. Describes federal summer legal intern and law clerk programs for law students with more than 125 government, international, and non–profit organizations. Since these internships go quickly, contact *Federal Reports* about a copy by mid–autumn of the year before you want a summer internship.

The Insider's Guide to Private/Nonprofit Legal Employers: Washington, DC Metro Area (Federal Reports, Inc., Suite 408, 1010 Vermont Ave., NW, Washington, DC 20005; phones: 800/296–9611, 202/393–3311) $24.95/individuals, $39.95/institutions, plus $2.50/shipping, 1996. Gives detailed information on over 350 corporations, law firms, and non–profits in the Washington, D.C. metropolitan area that hire attorneys.

Gopher Menu: Justice Department is an Internet site that provides some 300 job listings for accountants, attorneys, file clerks, legal secretaries, paralegals, and many other jobs relating to work in law. Go to URL: **gopher://justice2.usdoj.gov/**, then select "Justice Department Careers Opportunities," and click on "DOJ Job Vacancies."

Job services

CU Career Connection (University of Colorado, Campus Box 133, Boulder, CO 80309–0133; phone: 303/492–4127) $30/four–month fee entitles you to a "passcode" which unlocks this job hotline. You need a touch–tone phone to call and request the field in which you are interested in hearing job openings. The hotline is turned off Monday through Friday, 1:00 a.m. to 4:30 a.m., for daily updating. Over 2,600 jobs are listed in the course of the year.

ALA Management Connections (Association of Legal Administrators, Suite 325, 175 E. Hawthorn Pkwy., Vernon Hills, IL 60061–1428; phone: 847/816–1212) free, updated weekly. To hear job descriptions for law office managers with law departments of public interest and non–profit agencies (as well as mostly private sector positions), call 708/445–6777 anytime. You'll need a touch–tone phone. Press "3" after the message starts so you can hear the instructions. You can place a "Position Wanted" ad of your own for $75/nonmembers, $50/members. This ad will be

Reading chapters 1 and 2 first is bono, pro

recorded on *ALA Management Connections* and appear in the *ALA Management Connections Bulletin* described above under "Job ads." Contact the Association for Legal Administrators for details.

Directories

Directory of Legal Aid and Defender Offices in the U.S. and Territories (National Legal Aid and Defender Association, 8th Floor, 1625 K St., NW, Washington, DC 20006; phone: 202/452–0620) $60/nonmember, $15/member, 263 pages, annual. Divided into a civil section and a defender section; offices in each section are listed by state.

Peterson's Law Schools (Peterson's Guides, P.O. 2123, Princeton, NJ 08543–2123; phone: 800/338–3282) $21.95 plus $6.75/shipping, 500 pages, annual. Provides in–depth profiles on more than 180 law schools.

Salary surveys

Compensation of Legal & Related Jobs (non–law firms) (Abbott, Langer & Associates, 548 First St., Crete, IL 60417; phone: 708/672–4200) $575/entire set; Vol. 1: Supervisory and Managerial Attorneys, $225; Vol. 2: Non–supervisory attorneys, $235; Vol. 3: Legal Administrators/Paralegal Assistants/Legal Secretaries, $225; annual. Findings are presented by job type, geographic area, experience, education, size of firm, and more. Includes non–profit organizations.

Legal Salary Survey (David J. White & Associates, 809 Ridge Rd., Wilmette, IL 60091; phone: 800/962–4947) $195, published each October 6. Reports on salaries for attorneys employed by law firms, corporations, and insurance companies: by experience and region.

Honor thy copyright: Photocopying is not allowed

Chapter 19

Media

Media

*See the **Professional's Job Finder** for a much more extensive collection of job sources for media careers, some of which include positions in the non-profit sector.*

Job ads

AEJMC News (Association for Education in Journalism and Mass Communication, University of South Carolina, LeConte College, Room 121, Columbia, SC 29208–0251; phone: 803/777–2005) bimonthly, $10/annual subscription (U.S.), $15/foreign (surface mail), $20/foreign (airmail). The "Placement Service" carries 20 to 90 ads for college/university faculty positions in journalism and mass communication.

College Broadcaster Magazine (National Association of College Broadcasters, 71 George St., Box 1824, Providence, RI 02912–1824; phone: 401/863–2225) quarterly, $20/student nonmember annual subscription, $30/professional nonmember, free/members. Fifty jobs and 20 internships in all areas of the media industry appear in the "Classifieds."

Jobs for Journalist Listings and Current News (Society of Professional Journalists, P.O. Box 77, Greencastle, IN 46135; phone: 317/653–3333) weekly, $100/nonmember six–month subscription, $25/members; $200/nonmember annual subscription, $50/members; contact for details on receiving this by email. The typical issue is filled with over 150 job ads with newspapers, radio, television, and online services, plus internships, fellowships, and public relations positions.

Entertainment Employment Journal (Suite 320, 5632 Van Nuys Blvd., Van Nuys, CA 91401; phone: 818/901–6330) semiweekly, $95/annual subscription (U.S.), $110/annual subscription (Canada), $60/six–month subscription (U.S.), $35/three–month subscription (U.S.). From 50 to 75 jobs in all aspects of the media and entertainment industries fill these pages.

Spectra (Speech Communication Association, Bldg. E, 5105 Backlick Rd., Annandale, VA 22003; phone: 703/750–0533) 12 issues/year, available only with membership (dues $110/ regular members, $45/student members). The "Classifieds" carry ads for about 50 university faculty positions in journalism, communications, and broadcasting. Members who pay an extra $45 to subscribe to the SCA's *Placement Service*, described below, receive a first class subscription.

Public Relations Career Opportunities (Suite 1190, 1575 I St., NW, Washington, DC 20005; phone: 202/408–7904) biweekly, $97/nonmember three–month subscription, $147/nonmember six months, $217/nonmember annual; members of Public Relations Society of America: $67/three months, $117/six months, $187/annual. Each issue includes 150 to 200 job vacancies listed by region. About half the jobs are with non–profit organizations and educational institutions. Jobs include everything from copywriters to public relations managers.

Religious Broadcasting (National Religious Broadcasters, 7839 Ashton Ave., Manassas, VA 20109; phone: 703/330–7000) 10 issues/year, $24 annual nonmember subscription (U.S.), $30/Canada, $48/elsewhere, free/members. Five to ten positions for everything in radio and television are described under "Classified." Also includes positions sought. About five to ten other jobs and about 15 internships can be found on the Internet at URL: **http://www.nrb.com**, and clicking on "Classified." Jobs are listed for six weeks.

National Diversity Journalism Job Bank offers hundreds of ads for everything in journalism: journalism professors, journalism watchdog groups, reporters, editors, copy editors, graphic artists, and page designers. Go to Internet URL: **http://www.newsjobs.com/** and select "The Jobs" to access the job database. To place your resume in the National Diversity Journalism Job Bank, pick "How to Send Resumes." Click on "Other Job Banks" to access an extensive set of links to — no surprise here — other job banks on the Internet.

The Independent Film & Video Monthly (Foundation for Independent Video and Film, 304 Hudson St., New York, NY 10013; phone: 212/807–1400) monthly, $45/nonmember subscription, $25/nonmember students, free/members of the Association of Independent Video and Filmmakers, individual issues available at newsstands for $3.75. The "Classifieds" feature around

Photocopying strictly prohibited

Media

30 job ads in all facets of film and video production. Job ads appear under "Opportunities–Gigs," "Postproduction," and "Preproduction–Development." Freelancers can advertise their availability under "Freelancers." Jobs available include faculty positions. There's also a "Notices –Competitions" section and a "Resources–Funds" section where you can learn about grant opportunities as well as identify funders in this field for which you may wish to work.

SCREENsite: Employment Office Opportunities is an Internet site for film and television positions, largely faculty and academic positions in film and TV studios. Go to URL: **http://www.sa.ua.edu/TCF/teach/employ/index.htm**, and select "Film/TV Positions" for a list of about 15 to 20 job vacancies.

Employment Bulletin Board features over 150 job ads for a full panoply of positions in the broadcasting industry. Go to Internet URL: **http://www.tvjobs.com/bulletin.htm** where you can choose from the following categories (the number of jobs posted the week of January 1, 1997 is given): education (5), television (over 100 jobs), radio (15), cable (10), multimedia (2), corporate industrial (4), and post–production (20). Each job listing includes the date it was posted and the closing date for applications. This site requires a Web browser like Netscape or Internet Explorer that supports tables.

PR Marcom Jobs West – Southern California (Rachel P.R. Services , Suite 200C, 1650 S. Pacific Coast Highway, Redondo Beach, CA 90277; phones: 310/792–1313 inside California; 800/874-8577 elsewhere in the U.S.) bi-weekly, $39/three–month subscription, $59/four months, $69/six months, $99/annual, specify whether you wish to receive your newsletter by fax or first class mail. About 100 job announcements, virtually all for positions in Southern California, fill this newsletter.

PR Marcom Jobs West – Northern California (Rachel P.R. Services, Suite 200C, 1650 S. Pacific Coast Highway, Redondo Beach, CA 90277; phones: 310/792–1313 inside California; 800/874-8577 elsewhere in the U.S.) bi-weekly, $39/three–month subscription, $59/four months, $69/six months, $99/annual, specify whether you wish to receive your newsletter by fax or first class mail. About 100 job announcements, virtually all for positions in Northern California and the Pacific Northwest, fill this newsletter.

PR Marcom Jobs East (Rachel P.R. Services, Suite 1600, 208 E. 51st St., New York, NY 10022; phone: 212/962–9100) biweekly, $39/three–month subscription, $59/four months, $69/six months, $99/annual, specify whether you wish to receive your newsletter by fax or first class mail. About 100 job openings for positions in New York, New Jersey, Boston, Washington DC, and surrounding states, fill this newsletter.

PR Marcom Jobs Mid-America (Rachel P.R. Services, Suite 1600, 208 E. 51st St., New York, NY 10022; phone: 212/962–9100) biweekly, $39/three–month subscription, $59/four months, $69/six months, $99/annual, specify whether you wish to receive your newsletter by fax or first class mail. About 100 job openings for positions in the Midwest, Southeast, South, and Rocky Mountain regions, fill this newsletter.

Publishers' Auxiliary (National Newspaper Association, Suite 550, 1525 Wilson Blvd., Arlington, VA 22209; phone: 703/907–7900) biweekly, $60/annual nonmember subscription, free/members. Under "Help Wanted" you'll find about half a dozen positions for editors, writers, sales, circulation, financial, newspaper management, and university faculty. Includes "situations wanted."

The Quill (Society of Professional Journalists, P.O. Box 77, Greencastle, IN 46135; phone: 317/653–3333) nine issues/year, $27/annual nonmember subscription, free/members. The "Classifieds" section has four or five positions in all aspects of the print and broadcast media, including faculty.

Placement Center Job Announcements (Association for Educational Communications and Technology, Suite 820, 1025 Vermont Ave., NW, Washington, DC 20005; phone: 202/347–7834) is a free Internet gopher site for dozens of job announcements for media specialists, librarians, and other vacancies in higher education. Go to URL: **http://www.aect.org/**, and select "Employment." Then click on "gopher://sunbird.usd.edu:7211" and scroll down to "Placement Center (Job Announcements)."

Guild News (Graphic Artists Guild of New York, 11 W. 20th St., New York, NY 10011; phone: 212/463–7730) quarterly, $15/nonmembers, free/members. Three or four positions for graphic artists appear under "Job Opportunities."

The New Careers Directory: Internships and Professional Opportunities in Technology and Social Change (Student Pugwash USA, Suite 814, 815 15th St., NW, Washington, DC 20005; phone: 202/393–6555) $18, $10/students; add $3 shipping. Offers full details on where and how to apply for internships and entry–level jobs with socially responsible organizations, including the news media.

Job Services

Jobphone (Editorial Freelancers Association, 71 W. 23rd St., New York, NY 10010; phone: 212/929–5400). Call the *Jobphone* at 212/929–5411, to hear a recording that briefly describes about 20 to 40 freelance writing, editing, proofreading, indexing, and translating opportunities. Listings are updated weekly. Only EFA members who subscribe to this service can call another phone number to get details (such as pay and whom to contact) on the listed jobs. Members can subscribe to *Jobphone* for $20/year. Write for membership rates (they're too complicated to explain here).

Placement Service (Speech Communication Association, Bldg. E, 5105 Backlick Rd., Annandale, VA 22003; phone: 703/750–0533) $45 annual fee/members only. This placement service for aspiring broadcast journalists and announcers provides three benefits: a first class subscription to the SCA's newsletter, *Spectra*, described above; a file service containing a member's vitae and letters of recommendation that can be sent to any employer at the member's request; and special placement meetings with employers at the SCA annual conventions.

Job Bank Gratis (Rachel P.R. Services, Suite 200C, 1650 S. Pacific Coast Highway, Redondo Beach, CA 90277; phones: 310/792–1313 inside California, 800/874–8577 elsewhere in the U.S.) $10/year. If you wish to use this job matching service, your resume will be placed in the *Job Bank Gratis* database and matched to job openings that are *not* advertised in any of the *PR Marcom Jobs* newsletters they publish. When a match is made this service contacts you and you take the next step of contracting the prospective employer.

Directories

The Source (Rachel P.R. Services, Suite 200C, 1650 S. Pacific Coast Highway, Redondo Beach, CA 90277; phones: 310/792–1313 inside California; 800/874–8577 elsewhere in the U.S.) $29, 75 pages, published in even–numbered years with monthly updates sent to you free. Provides details on 3,500 job sources in public relations, journalism, advertising, and marketing: job banks, trade publications, job hotlines, freelance cooperatives, Internet sites, executive recruiters, employment agencies, and associations.

Station Handbook Manual Radio Edition (National Association of College Broadcasters, 71 George St., Box 1824, Providence, RI 02912–1824; phone: 401/863–2225) $25/nonmembers, free/members. Lists employers and companies by address and phone. Also available on diskette for $25; contact for details.

Station Handbook Manual T.V. Edition (National Association of College Broadcasters, 71 George St., Box 1824, Providence, RI 02912–1824; phone: 401/863–2225) $25/nonmembers, free/members. Lists employers and companies by address and phone. Also available on diskette for $25; contact for details.

Mailing List (National Association of College Broadcasters, 71 George St., Box 1824, Providence, RI 02912–1824; phone: 401/863–2225) is a free membership list available on a gopher site at URL: **gopher://rodent.cis.umn.edu:11152/**. Scroll down to "Mailing List" and then click on "NACB (National Association College Broadcasters) Mailing List." This site also provides links to other radio gophers by clicking on "Other Radio and TV Gophers on the Net."

EFA Membership Directory (Editorial Freelancers Association, 71 W. 23rd St., New York, NY 10010; phone: 212/929–5400) $28/nonmembers, free/members, 145 pages, published every February. Gives details on its 1,000 members available for freelance work in writing, proofreading, editing, translating, and indexing.

Executive Recruiter Labels (Rachel P.R. Services, Suite 200C, 1650 S. Pacific Coast Highway, Redondo Beach, CA 90277; phones: 310/792–1313 inside California, 800/874–8577 elsewhere in the U.S.) $19/set of labels. Provides a set of mailing labels for over 100 key executive recruiters who make placements in advertising, public relations, journalism, and marketing for positions paying over $35,000 annually.

Women in Communications Membership and Resource Directory (Association for Women in Communications, Inc., Suite 6, 1244 Ritchie Hwy, Arnold, MD 21012–1887; phone: 410/544–7442) free/members, nonmembers, call for price, annual each February. Members are in all aspects of media and communications including print and broadcast journalism, public relations, advertising, and marketing. Directory includes a yellow pages resource section where members and nonmembers place a 50–word listing of their business product or service.

Directory of Religious Broadcasting (National Religious Broadcasters, 7839 Ashton Ave., Manassas, VA 20109; phone: 703/330–7000) $69.95/nonmembers, $25/members, 350 pages, issued each January. Lists 4,000 stations, plus radio show producers, and other key personnel.

Christian Radio Talk Show Directory (James Lloyd, P.O. Box 3, Ashland, OR 97520; phone: 541/899–8888) $19.95 plus $2.75/shipping, prepaid only. Lists information on over 600 radio talk shows with a Christian slant.

Grants for Film, Media & Communications (The Foundation Center, 79 Fifth Ave., New York, NY 10003–3076; phones: 800/424–9836, within New York State call 212/620–4230) $75 plus $4.50/shipping, 145 pages, published in October of odd–numbered years. Describes recent foundation grants of at least $10,000 given for film, video, documentaries, radio, television, printing, publishing, and censorship issues. This directory is useful for identifying foundations and grant recipients for which you may wish to work.

Salary surveys

Women in Communications Job & Salary Survey Results (Women in Communications Foundation, 6900 Newman Rd., Clifton, VA 20124; phone: 703/359–9000) contact for pricing and availability. Includes salary levels in print and broadcast media, corporate, non–profit, advertising and public relations, government, education, and freelance.

Photocopying strictly prohibited

Marketing

AEJMC Salary Survey (Association for Education in Journalism and Mass Communication, University of South Carolina, LeConte College, Room 121, Columbia, SC 29208–0251; phone: 803/777–2005) $15, annual. Salary and demographic survey of journalism/communication faculty.

Marketing

Job ads

Marketing News (American Marketing Association, Suite 200, 250 S. Wacker Dr., Chicago, IL 60606–5819; phones: 800/262–1150, 312/648–0536) biweekly, $60/annual nonmember subscription, $30/members. The "Marketplace" features 25 jobs in marketing and marketing research including university faculty.

Job service

American Marketing Association Academic Placement Service (American Marketing Association, Suite 200, 250 S. Wacker Dr., Chicago, IL 60606–5819; phone: 312/648–0536) $95 11–month fee/nonmembers, $75 11–month fee/members. The job seeker completes an "applicant's" form, which serves as a resume. Every quarter, resumes are circulated to universities that subscribe to this service. Schools are responsible for contacting potential employees for an interview. Every quarter, a set of open positions is sent to registrants who are free to contact the universities directly.

Directories

Journalism and Mass Communication Directory (Association for Education in Journalism and Mass Communication, University of South Carolina, LeConte College, Room 121, Columbia, SC 29208–0251; phone: 803/777–2005) $25 (U.S.), $35/foreign (surface mail), $50/foreign (airmail), 334 pages, published each September. Lists 450 journalism schools, AESMC members, and foundations: includes phone numbers, addresses, faculty names, courses, and degrees offered.

The Christian Media Directory (James Lloyd, P.O. Box 3, Ashland, OR 97520; phone: 541/899–8888) $35 plus $2.75/shipping, prepaid only. Lists over 8,000 producers, publishers, recording labels, studios, all–Christian music and radio stations, film and video companies, television stations, and more — all with a Christian slant.

Chapter 20

Museums and libraries

Museums

Also see entries later in this chapter under "Libraries."

Job ads

AVISO (American Association of Museums, Suite 200, 1225 I St., NW, Washington, DC 20005; phone: 202/289-9122) monthly, $33/annual nonmember subscription (U.S.), $48/foreign, free/members. "Placement" contains 90 ads for curators, registrars, directors, development officers, internships, and all other museum positions.

ASTC Newsletter (Association of Science/Technology Centers, Suite 500, 1025 Vermont Ave, NW, Washington, DC 20005; phone: 202/783-7200) bimonthly, $35/annual nonmember subscription (U.S.), $45/foreign, free/members. Ten to 15 positions with museums and teaching positions are under "Positions Available." For more jobs, about ten to 15, see the Internet at URL: **http://www.astc.org/astc/**. Click on "Career Corner" and then "Job Bank" for five categories of jobs and one for internships.

Jobs in Interpretation (National Association for Interpretation, P.O. Box 1892, Ft. Collins, CO 80522; 970/484-8283) weekly, members get their first five issues free in any format: available in print ($6/issue nonmember,

$3/issue members), by fax or email ($5/issue nonmembers, $2/issue members). These are jobs and internships for "interpreters," communicators who combine an understanding of natural or cultural history with sharing their knowledge with others. Employed by parks, historical sites, museums, nature centers, zoos, public forests, and resident camps.

American Visions (Vision Foundation, P.O. Box 37049, Washington, DC 20078–4741; phones: 800/998–0864, 202/496–9593) bimonthly, $18/annual subscription (U.S.), $30/foreign. The "Queries and Announcements" section features two or three librarian and museum curator positions, generally dealing with African American culture, history, or art.

Directories

The Official Museum Directory (R.R. Bowker; available from Reed Elsevier, P.O. Box 31, New Providence, NJ 07974; phone: 800/521–8110) $210/nonmembers, $149.95/members of the American Association of Museums; plus 7 percent shipping and handling, 2,050 pages, two volumes, published each November. Provides details on over 7,300 U.S. museums, art associations, art museums and galleries, arts and crafts museums, folk art museums, children and junior museums, college and university museums, company museums, general museums, planetariums, zoos, aquariums, arboreta, and 75 other types of institutions. Includes a buyers guide and products directory.

Museums of the World (K.G. Saur, Reed Elsevier, P.O. Box 31, New Providence, NJ 07974; phone: 800/521–8110) $355 plus 7 percent/shipping, 672 pages, 1996, next edition due in November, 1997. Includes 24,000 museums in 191 nations organized by country and city within individual nations with addresses, phone numbers, description of holdings, facilities, museum directors, and more. Includes a subject index plus name indices for museums and personnel.

Museums/Galleries Yellow Pages resides on the Internet at URL: **http://www.imagesite.com/muse/museylpgs.html** with a directory of contact information for museums and art galleries.

The Museum Professional sits at Internet URL: **http://www.sirius.com/~robinson/musprof.html** where it offers links to the home pages of museums, museum organizations, and other art and education sites.

Directory of Historical Organizations, Societies, and Agencies in the United States and Canada (Sage Publications, 2455 Teller Rd., Thousand Oaks, CA 91320; phone: 805/499–9774) call for price, scheduled for publication in summer of 1997. Includes history–related organizations with brief descriptions of staff.

International Directory of the Arts (R.R. Bowker, available from Reed Elsevier, P.O. Box 31, New Providence, NJ 07974; phone: 800/521–8110) $275 plus 7 percent/shipping, 1,450 pages, published in even–numbered

Read the instructions — chapters 1 and 2 — first

years. Offers more than 130,000 names and addresses of museums and public galleries, auctioneers, restorers, antique trade and numismatics, art publishers and journals, associations, universities, and academies, and galleries throughout the world.

NAI Membership Directory (National Association for Interpretation, P.O. Box 1892, Ft. Collins, CO 80522; 970/491-6434) free/members only, 200 pages, published each spring. Lists all 3,000 members (names, addresses, job titles) plus interpretive consultants and a suppliers registry that lists companies and individuals serving the interpretive profession.

ASTC Directory (Association of Science/Technology Centers, Suite 500, 1025 Vermont Ave., NW, Washington, D.C. 20005; phone: 202/783-7200) $40/nonmembers, $25/members, 200 pages, published annually in the summer. Lists about 450 member science museums, aquariums, zoos, and science centers, plus 50 more associate members which are companies that supply museums.

Museums From A to Z is an Internet directory for art museums worldwide. Go to URL: **http://www.vol.it/UK/EN/ARTE**, and select "Museums from A to Z," where you will get an alphabetical (surprise!) and detailed listing of museums.

Salary surveys

Association of Art Museum Directors Salary Survey (American Association of Museums, Suite 200, 1225 I St., NW, Washington, DC 20005; phone: 202/289-1818) $30/nonmembers, $25/AAMD members, published each May. Reports salary information and position descriptions for 37 professional positions in U.S. art museums by region, budget, and nationally.

1997 ASTC Salary Survey (Association of Science/Technology Centers, Suite 500, 1025 Vermont Ave., NW, Washington, D.C. 20005; phone: 202/783-7200) $150/nonmembers, $100/members, published periodically in May. Survey by size of museum budget of salaries and benefit packages of museum officers and other management personnel.

Libraries

*For a much more extensive listing of job sources for public libraries, see the **Government Job Finder**.*

Job ads

Library JobSearch (University of Illinois, Graduate School of Library Information Sciences) free. Go to Internet URL: **http://carousel.lis.uiuc.edu/**

No photocopying please

~jobs/ where you can browse through hundreds of job ads in library and information services. You can also search by keyword, job title, city, state, and/or employer.

American Libraries (American Library Association, 50 E. Huron St., Chicago, IL 60611; phones: 800/545-2433 (outside Illinois), 800/545-2444 (Illinois only), 800/545-2455 (Canada only), 312/280-4211) 11 issues/year, $50/annual subscription for libraries, subscription included in membership package. Jobs listed under "Career Leads." The typical issue features 75 to 100 job ads.

Job notices can be obtained three weeks prior to publication in *American Libraries* in **Career Leads Express**, which is a copy of the uncorrected galleys of job notices that will appear in the next issue of *American Libraries*. *Career Leads Express* is available to nonmembers and members alike for $1/issue, prepaid only. With your check, send a self-addressed stamped (two ounces postage) #10 envelope to AL Leads Express, 50 E. Huron, Chicago, IL 60611. Typical issue includes 75 or more positions.

Library Journal (Cahners Publishing Company, P.O. 8035, Boulder, CO 80306; phone: 800/677-6694) 21 issues/year, $94.50/annual subscription (U.S.), $116/Canada, $159/elsewhere (airmail). Jobs listed under "Classified Advertising." Fifty to 70 ads for librarian positions grace the pages of a typical issue.

College & Research Libraries News (Association of College and Research Libraries, 50 E. Huron St., Chicago, IL 60611; phones: 800/545-2433, 312/944-6795) monthly, $35/annual nonmember subscription (U.S.), $40/Canada and Mexico, $45/elsewhere, free/members. From 30 to 60 classified and display job ads for academic librarians appear in a typical issue. These ads also appear on the Internet at URL: **http://www.ala.org/acr/.html**, and selecting "Job Ads," then clicking on "C&RL News Classified Advertising Archives," which gives you a selection of issues to scroll down to.

School Library Journal (Cahners Publishing, P.O. Box 57559, Boulder, CO 80322; phone: 800/456-0409) monthly, $79.50/annual subscription (U.S.), $105/Canada, $125/elsewhere. About 15 librarian positions with public libraries and university, elementary, and secondary school libraries appear under "Classifieds."

Library Hotline (P.O. Box 6457, Torrance, CA 90504; phone: 800/278-2991) 50 issues/year, $74/annual subscription (U.S.), $97/foreign. Thirty percent of the 25 to 30 vacancies listed for librarians are with government agencies, universities, schools, and other non-profit entities.

History News Dispatch (American Association for State and Local History, Suite 600, 530 Church St., Nashville, TN 37219-2325; phone: 615/255-2971) monthly, $50/members only. About 20 to 35 ads for historians, archivists, and educators appear under "The Marketplace." Includes positions with historical societies, historic sites, libraries, archives, and museums.

Read the instructions — chapters 1 and 2 — first

Placement Center Job Announcements (Association for Educational Communications and Technology, Suite 820, 1025 Vermont Ave., NW, Washington, DC 20005; phone: 202/347-7834) is a free Internet gopher site for dozens of job announcements for media specialists, librarians, and other vacancies in higher education. Go to URL: **http://www.aect.org/**, and select "Employment." Then click on "gopher://sunbird.usd.edu:7211" and scroll down to "Placement Center (Job Announcements)."

Journal of Academic Librarianship (JAI Press Inc., 55 Old Post Rd. #2, Greenwich, CT 06830-1678; phone: 203/661-7602, email: 102062.2522@compserve.com) bimonthly, $60/annual subscription (U.S.), $80/foreign. Two or three ads for university librarians appear under "Classified Ads."

Institutional Library Mail Jobline (c/o Gloria Spooner, Library Consultant, State Library of Louisiana, P.O. Box 131, Baton Rouge, LA 70821-0131; phone: 504/342-4931) monthly, free. Send self-addressed stamped envelope for copy. Lists institutional library positions in U.S. and its territories.

MLA News (Medical Library Association, Suite 300, 6 N. Michigan Ave., Chicago, IL 60602; phone: 312/419-9094) ten issues/year, $48.50/nonmember annual subscription (U.S.), $61.50/foreign, free/members. From 10 to 15 ads appear in the "Employment Opportunities" for librarian posts in the health sciences. These ads may also be purchased two weeks before they are published through the service *Advanced Employment Opportunities* listed directly below.

Advanced Employment Opportunities (Medical Library Association, Suite 300, 6 N. Michigan Ave., Chicago, IL 60602; phone: 312/419-9094) $25/nonmembers, $15/members. Over a six-month period you are sent a listing of job ads from *MLA News*, listed directly above, two weeks before it is published. Job ads for all kinds of public, academic, and medical library positions can be accessed on the Internet at URL: **http://www.kumc.edu/MLA**. Select "Career Services" and then "Employment Opportunities." Listings are updated twice a month.

ASIS Jobline (American Society for Information Science, Suite 501, 8720 Georgia Ave., Silver Spring, MD 20910-3602; phone: 301/495-0900) monthly, free/members only. About 15 job ads appear in the typical issue.

Job Postings (ALISE, c/o of University of Michigan: School of Information, Attn: Emily K. Lenhart, 304 West Hall, 550 E. University Ave., Ann Arbor, MI 48109-1092; phone: 313/936-9812) free. This job bank service on the Internet can be reached at URL: **http://www.si.umich.edu/ALISE/**, and selecting "Job Postings," where you'll find a detailed listing of 30 to 40 library positions in academia.

ARL Career Resources (Association of Research Libraries, Suite 800, 21 DuPont Cr., Washington, D.C. 20036; phone: 202/296-2296) free, on the Internet at URL: **http://arl.cni.org/**. Scroll down and click on "ARL Career

No photocopying please

Libraries

Resources," and you'll find 75 to 80 job announcements for administrators, librarians, archivists, and curators that you can search for either by geographic region or by job title.

New England Library Jobline (GSLIS, New England Library Jobline, Simmons College, 300 The Fenway, Boston, MA 02115). Call 617/521–2815 to hear a 24–hour tape recording of library and information science positions requiring an M.L.S. degree. Updated each Wednesday.

Information Outlook (Special Libraries Association, 1700 18th St., NW, Washington, DC 20009; 202/234–4700) monthly, $65/annual subscription, $75/foreign. From five to ten positions in library services are listed under "Positions Open." SLA members with a password can view these jobs on the Internet at URL: **http://www.sla.org/professional**, and selecting "SLA Job Search–Online," and then clicking on the ball graphic.

Job services

SpeciaLine Employment Clearinghouse Job Hotline (Special Libraries Association, 1700 18th St., NW, Washington, DC 20009; 202/234–4700). Call 202/234–3632 for a 24–hour tape recording of jobs with special libraries.

Career Hotline/Job Database Service (American Association of Law Libraries, Suite 940, 53 W. Jackson, Chicago, IL 60604; phone: 312/939–4764). Call the 24–hour Career Hotline, 312/939–7877, for a recording of brief job descriptions of law librarian positions and where to apply. This is the index to the AALL's *Job Database Service* which is updated weekly by Friday noon. AALL members can request a free printout of all job listings by calling 312/939–4764 or faxing a request to 312/431–1097. Nonmembers can obtain a printout for free. There are typically 10 to 20 jobs listed at any one time.

MLA Job Line (Medical Library Association, Suite 300, 6 N. Michigan Ave., Chicago, IL 60602–4805; phone: 312/419–9094) free. Call 312/553–4636 for a 24 hour tape–recording of 15 or more jobs in the medical library field. Updated weekly. On your touch–tone phone, be ready to select type of job, part of the country, and salary range desired.

Directories

Who's Who in Special Libraries (Special Libraries Association, 1700 18th St., NW, Washington, DC 20009; 202/234–4700) $65/nonmembers, free/members, published each autumn. Includes alphabetical and geographical lists of special libraries as well as a buyers guide with contact information on products and services.

Directory of Special Libraries and Information Centers (Gale Research, Inc., 835 Penobscot Bldg., Detroit, MI 48226; phone: 800/233–4253) $515,

Read the instructions — chapters 1 and 2 — first

2,663 pages in two volumes, annual. Provides comprehensive information on 22,400 information centers, archives, and special and research libraries in the U.S., Canada, and elsewhere.

Subject Directory of Special Libraries (Research, Inc., 835 Penobscot Bldg., Detroit, MI 48226; phone: 800/233–4253) $800/three volumes, annual. These volumes contain the same material as the *Directory of Special Libraries and Information Centers,* but rearranged into 14 subject areas in three volumes, available individually: Business, Government, and Law Libraries, $310; Computers, Engineering, and Science Libraries, $310; Health Sciences Libraries, $310.

New Special Libraries (Gale Research, Inc., 835 Penobscot Bldg., Detroit, MI 48226; phone: 800/233–4253) $420, 930 pages, annual. Furnishes comprehensive information on special libraries in the U.S., Canada, and elsewhere not included in Gale's *Directory of Special Libraries and Information Centers* described above.

Membership List (Association of College and Research Libraries, Data Processing Unit, 50 E. Huron St., Chicago, IL 60611; phones: 800/545–2433, 312/944–6795) $80/1,000 cheshire labels, $90/1,000 pressure–sensitive labels, databank updated continuously. Membership list includes 11,000 members; you can get specialized lists by zip code.

National Guide to Funding for Libraries and Information Services (The Foundation Center, 79 Fifth Ave., New York, NY 10003–3076; phones: 800/424–9836, 212/620–4230) $95, 234 pages, published in April of odd–numbered years. Furnishes essential data on over 600 foundations and corporate direct giving programs. Each entry includes application information, types of support, and recent grants.

Grants for Libraries & Information Services (The Foundation Center, 79 Fifth Ave., New York, NY 10003–3076; phones: 800/424–9836, within New York State call 212/620–4230) $75 plus $4.50/shipping, 130 pages, published in October of odd–numbered years. Describes recent foundation grants of at least $10,000 given for public, academic, research, special, and school libraries for archives and information centers, consumer information, and philanthropy information centers. This directory is useful for identifying foundations and grant recipients for which you may wish to work.

Directory of the Medical Library Association (MLA, Suite 300, 6 N. Michigan Ave., Chicago, IL 60602; phone: 312/419–9094) $150/nonmembers, free/members, add $4/shipping, published each September.

Membership Directory of Association for Library and Information Science Education (ALISE, c/o of University of Michigan: School of Information, Attn: Emily K. Lenhart, 304 West Hall, 550 E. University Ave., Ann Arbor, MI 48109–1092; phone: 313/936–9812) $50, 128 pages, published each January. Lists 2,208 librarians and information science specialists, plus contact information.

No photocopying please

Libraries

ARL Member Libraries (Association of Research Libraries, Suite 800, 21 DuPont Cr., Washington, D.C. 20036; phone: 202/296–2296) free, on the Internet at URL: **http://arl.cni.org/**. Scroll down and click on "ARL Member Libraries," and there you will get a detailed listing in alphabetical order of all 120 member institutions.

Salary surveys

ALISE Library and Information Science Education Statistical Report (Association for Library and Information Science Education, c/o of University of Michigan: School of Information, Attn: Emily K. Lenhart, 304 West Hall, 550 E. University Ave., Ann Arbor, MI 48109–1092; phone: 313/936–9812) $54/nonmember (U.S.), $56/foreign, published each May. Includes a salary survey of teachers in member schools.

ARL Annual Salary Survey 1995-96 (Association of Research Libraries, Suite 800, 21 DuPont Cr., Washington, D.C. 20036; phone: 202/296–2296) $65 plus $6 shipping/nonmember, $35 plus $6 shipping/member, 1995. Survey list of salaries by position and expertise, gender and race, geographic region, and size of library. Survey is based on 12,000 professional positions in ARL's 120 member libraries.

MLA Salary Survey (Medical Library Association, Suite 300, 6 N. Michigan Ave., Chicago, IL 60602; phone: 312/419–9094) $60/nonmembers, $35/members, add $3.50/shipping, April 1995, next edition in 1998. Association members: medical librarians/health information professionals in medical libraries in hospitals, medical schools, and other institutions. These are cross referenced by region, type of institution, position, gender, and number of people supervised.

Chapter 21

Parks and recreation

Parks and recreation

*Also see listings in the "Environment" and "Forestry and horticulture" chapters. You'll find many more job sources for both of these fields described in the **Government Job Finder**.*

Job ads

NRPA Job Bulletin (National Recreation and Park Association, Suite 300, 2775 South Quincy St., Arlington, VA 22206; phone: 703/820–4940) 22 issues/year, $50/nonmember annual subscription, $35/members. Typical issue includes 30 positions for parks directors, maintenance, lifeguards, therapeutic recreation specialists, plus internships and seasonal jobs.

Opportunities (Natural Science for Youth Foundation, 130 Azalea Dr., Roswell, GA 30075; phones: 800/992–6793, 404/594–9367) bimonthly, $35/annual subscription, $10/single issue, included in membership package. "Positions available " lists details on 45 to 70 jobs for naturalists, curators, raptor rehabilitators, and administrative positions, largely at nature centers.

Job service

NRPA/World Net (National Recreation and Park Association, Suite 300, 2775 South Quincy St., Arlington, VA 22206; phone: 703/820–4940) $75/annual subscription for nonmember individuals, $225/nonmember agencies, $50/member individuals, $150/member agencies. This computer information and communications network includes *NRPA Job Bulletin.* Updated biweekly.

Directories

Parks Directory of the United States (Omnigraphics, Inc., 2500 Penobscot Bldg., Detroit, MI 48226; phones: 800/234–1340, 313/961–1340) $145 plus shipping, 831 pages, 1995. Get full contact information and a detailed description of 4,700 national and state parks, recreation areas, historic sites, battlefields, monuments, forests, preserves, memorials, seashores, trails, urban parks, wildlife refuges, and other designated recreational areas in the U.S. that are administered by national and state park agencies. Indexed by classification, special features, and name.

Workamper News (201 Hiram Rd., Heber Springs, AR 72543; phone: 800/446–5627) bimonthly, contact for current subscription rates. Lists over 300 different employers who are actively seeking employees for public parks and campgrounds as well as commercially–operated parks, resorts, campgrounds with positions available at all levels, from housekeeping and grounds maintenance to upper management. All levels of jobs are available, ranging from housekeeping and grounds maintenance to upper management. Also operates a 24–hour **Job Hotline** with about 15 jobs on it daily. Updated on Tuesdays. The number is published in *Workamper News* and changes with each issue.

NCAA Directory (National Collegiate Athletic Association, 6701 College Blvd., Overland Park, KS 66211; phone: 913/339–1906) $8/nonmembers, $6/members, released every October. Includes key personnel at 1,000 NCAA member schools.

Compendium of Special Recreation for People with Disabilities (Special Recreation, Inc., 362 Koser Ave., Iowa City, IA 52246–3038; phone: 319/337–7578) $49.95/nonmembers plus $2.50/postage, 354 pages, 1994. Gives details on 1,500 organizations involved in recreation for people who have disabilities. Includes foundations and social service agencies.

Directory of Natural Science Centers (Natural Science for Youth Foundation, 130 Azalea Dr., Roswell, GA 30075; phone: 770/594–9367) $78.50/nonmembers, $49.95/for educational professionals, 600 pages, 1997. Gives details on over 1,350 nature centers.

Coach says read chapters 1 and 2 first

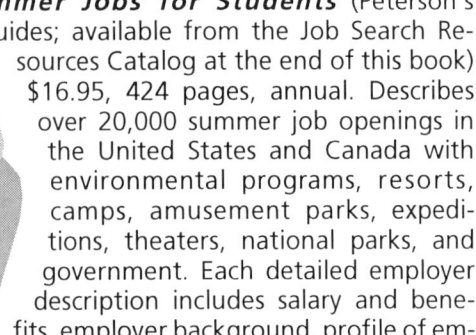

Summer Jobs for Students (Peterson's Guides; available from the Job Search Resources Catalog at the end of this book) $16.95, 424 pages, annual. Describes over 20,000 summer job openings in the United States and Canada with environmental programs, resorts, camps, amusement parks, expeditions, theaters, national parks, and government. Each detailed employer description includes salary and benefits, employer background, profile of employees, and whom to contact to apply.

Grants for Recreation, Sports & Athletics (The Foundation Center, 79 Fifth Ave., New York, NY 10003–3076; phones: 800/424–9836, within New York State call 212/620–4230) $75 plus $4.50/shipping, 161 pages, published in October of odd–numbered years. Describes recent foundation grants of at least $10,000 given to clubs, leagues, camps, parks, scouting, social service agencies, and community organizations for recreation, athletics, and physical fitness. This directory is useful for identifying foundations and grant recipients for which you may wish to work.

Salary Survey

National Comprehensive Salary and Benefits Study (National Recreation and Park Association, Suite 300, 2775 South Quincy St., Arlington, VA 22206; phone: 703/820–4940) $30/nonmembers, $21/members, 56 pages, 1993. Reports on salary ranges by job title and by region. Includes information on salary increases, overtime, car allowances, and other benefits.

Camps and camping

*For a much greater selection of job sources, see the **Professional's Job Finder**.*

Job ads

Camping Magazine (American Camping Association, 5000 State Road 67 North, Martinsville, IN 46151; phones: 800/428–2267, 317/342–8456) bimonthly, $18.95/annual nonmember subscription (U.S.), $25/Canada, $31.50/elsewhere, free/members. About 25 job vacancies for camp directors, counselors, activity specialists, instructors, lifeguards, and nurses appear under "Classifieds–Help Wanted" plus ads for camp planners and ads for camps for sale or lease. Also "Positions Wanted."

AEE Job's Clearinghouse (Association for Experiential Education, Suite 100, 2305 Canyon Blvd., Boulder, CO 80302; phone: 303/440–8844) monthly, $80/nonmember annual subscription, $40/members. Dozens of ads for summer camp counselors and outdoor therapists to work with troubled youths are among the 32 pages of opportunities in a typical issue.

Directories

Guide to Accredited Camps (American Camping Association, 5000 State Road 67 North, Martinsville, IN 46151; phones: 800/428–2267, 317/342–8456) nonmembers: $16.95/print, $19.95/disk, members: $15.25/print, $17.05/disk, published in even–numbered years. Provides contact names, phones, and addresses, for over 2,000 accredited camps. Entries include session lengths, camper ages, price range, special focus, activities and programs offered, and programs for campers who have disabilities.

Guide to Summer Camps and Summer Schools (Porter Sargent Publishers, Inc., Suite 1400, 11 Beacon St., Boston, MA 02108; phone: 617/523–1670) $29.50/paperback, $39.50/cloth edition, 492 pages, last edition 1995–96. Reports on over 1,100 camps and summer schools as well as specialized programs for children with learning, physical, or mental disabilities.

Coaching and sports

Job ads

Athletics Employment Weekly (RDST Enterprises, Route 2, Box 140, Carthage, IL 62321; phone: 217/357–3615) weekly, $50/six–month subscription, $80/annual subscription. A typical issue features 75 to 100 coaching, training, and administrative positions in athletics, for two to four year colleges nationwide. Also includes academic advisors and counselors.

The NCAA News (National Collegiate Athletic Association, 6701 College Blvd., Overland Park, KS 66211; phone: 913/339–1906) 46 issues/year, $24/annual nonmember subscription, $12/faculty and students at NCAA member institutions. Around 100 job openings are advertised in "The

Coach says read chapters 1 and 2 first

Market" — athletic directors, trainers, athletic promotions, public relations, sports information, coaches, physical education instructors, and graduate assistants.

Update (American Alliance for Health, Physical Education, Recreation and Dance, 1900 Association Dr., Reston, VA 22091; phone: 703/476-3400) eight issues/year, $45/annual nonmember subscription, included in $85/annual membership. "Job Exchange" features 30 or more jobs largely with camps and universities as well as numerous graduate assistantships and grants. Jobs can also be found on the Internet at URL: **http://www.aahperd.org/**, where you can select links to other national organizations listing jobs in physical fitness, recreation, sports, and dance.

Job service

Resume Databank (Black Coaches Association, P.O. Box 4040, Culver City, CA 90231-4040; phones: 888/667-3222, 310/342-8253) is a free resume service on the Internet. Go to URL: **http://www.bca.org/**, and select "Resume Databank." Then to submit a resume click on "Submit Resume to Databank," download the application form and mail it to the BCA. Employers need to register to browse the resume databank.

Directories

National Directory of College Athletics (Men) (Collegiate Directories, Inc., P.O. Box 450640, Cleveland, OH 44145; phones: 800/426-2232, 216/835-1172) $28.95 plus $2.50/shipping, published each August. Provides details on over 2,100 senior and junior college men's athletic departments in the U.S. and Canada.

National Directory of College Athletics (Women) (Collegiate Directories, Inc., P.O. Box 450640, Cleveland, OH 44145; phones: 800/426-2232, 216/835-1172) $22.95 plus $2.50/shipping, published each August. Provides details on over 2,000 senior and junior college women's athletic departments in the U.S. and Canada.

National Directory of High School Coaches (Athletic Publishing Company, P.O. Box 931, Montgomery, AL 36101; phone: 334/263-4436) $49.95, issued every September. Lists more than 186,000 high school coaches at 22,600 high schools.

Clell Wade Coaches Directory (P.O. Box 177, Cassville, MO 65625; phone: 417/847-2783) $9.95/state or regional edition, prepaid, published each September. Published in 41 state or regional editions for high schools and junior high schools, one edition of North American colleges, and four editions of Canadian high schools and colleges, this series of directories covers high school and college athletic programs and their personnel.

Photocopying strictly prohibited

Coaching and sports

NCAA Directory (National Collegiate Athletic Association, 6701 College Blvd., Overland Park, KS 66211; phone: 913/339–1906) $8/nonmembers, $6/members, 250 pages, released every October. Includes key personnel at 1,000 NCAA member schools.

Blue Book of College Athletics for Senior, Junior and Community Colleges (Athletic Publishing Company, P.O. Box 931, Montgomery, AL 36177–9643; phone: 334/263–4436) $32.95, published each September. Provides details on over 1,800 colleges and universities with athletic programs, athletic conferences, and related associations in the U.S. and Canada, with some in Mexico and Puerto Rico.

The American Football Coaches Association Directory (Collegiate Directories, Inc., P.O. Box 450640, Cleveland, OH 44145; phones: 800/426–2232, 216/835–1172) $22.95 plus $2.50/shipping, 176 pages, published each September. This is an excellent source of potential employers. There's a lot more in here than just the association's members (their phone numbers are not given). It also includes contact information on professional leagues and teams as well as senior and junior college conferences, bowl games, and related professional associations.

The American Baseball Coaches Association Directory (Collegiate Directories, Inc., P.O. Box 450640, Cleveland, OH 44145; phones: 800/426–2232, 216/835–1172) $22.95 plus $2.50/shipping, 176 pages, published each September. This is an excellent source of potential employers. There's a lot more in here than just the association's members (their phone numbers are not given). It also includes contact information on professional leagues and teams as well as senior and junior college conferences, tournaments, and related professional associations.

Coach says read chapters 1 and 2 first

Chapter 22

Philanthropy

Philanthropy

Also see the "Grants and foundations" chapter.

Job ads

The Chronicle of Philanthropy (1255 23rd St., NW, Washington, DC 20037; phones: 800/347–6969, 202/466–1200) 24 issues/year, $67.50/annual subscription, $36/six–month subscription. The "Professional Opportunities" section runs ads for 60 to 90 job openings in all aspects of the non–profit world, from fundraisers to CEOs. Includes lots of fundraiser and director of development positions. Also included is a section filled with new grants listed by foundation (includes address and phone) which you can use to identify foundations at which you may wish to work or from which you may wish to seek a grant. You can also use this list to identify non–profit organizations receiving these grants for which you may wish to work. Each issue also includes an extensive "Directory of Services" filled with ads from companies for which you may wish to work.

Philanthropy Journal Online (Philanthropy Journal) free. Go to Internet URL: **http://www.philanthropy–journal.org** and select "Jobs." You can browse through detailed descriptions of about 25 openings, largely with foundations and colleges, mostly for executive director and other administrative positions related to foundation administration or fundraising.

Philanthropy

Corporate Giving Watch (Taft Group, 835 Penobscot Bldg., 645 Griswold St., Detroit, MI 48226–4094; phones: 800/877–8238, 313/961–2242) monthly, $140/annual subscription. Learn about new corporate grant programs, changes in giving priorities, and changes in corporate program officers. Eight pages are devoted to new and updated corporate profiles.

AHP Connect (Association for Healthcare Philanthropy, Suite 400, 313 Park Ave., Falls Church, VA 22046; phone: 703/532–6243) eight issues/year, $60/annual nonmember subscription, free/members. Six to ten vacancies for health care or hospital fundraisers appear under "Positions Available."

Directories

Charitable Organizations of the U.S. (Gale Research, Inc., 835 Penobscot Bldg., Detroit, MI 48226; phone: 800/877–4253) $150, 565 pages, 1992. Detailed profiles on more than 800 charitable organizations in the U.S., with contact information on their leadership, spokespersons, and sponsors. Includes data on sources of income, expenses for administration, fund raising programs, and percentage of program payout based on total income.

Charities USA is a gateway Internet site, where you are sure to find among the 400 links to charitable organizations many philanthropic organizations. Go to URL: **http://www.charitiesusa.com/**, and select among the following: Animal, Children, Christian Services, Conservation and Preservation, Education, Health, Human and Civil Rights, Human Service, Medical Research, Military & Veterans, Women, and World Service.

AHP Membership Directory and Buyers' Guide (Association for Healthcare Philanthropy, Suite 400, 313 Park Ave., Falls Church, VA 22046; phone: 703/532–6243) $125/nonmembers, free/members, 130 pages, issued each January. Lists some 2,500 individual and 150 corporate members.

Fund Raiser's Guide to Religious Philanthropy (Taft Group, 835 Penobscot Bldg., 645 Griswold St., Detroit, MI 48226–4094; phones: 800/877–8238, 313/961–2242) $160, 1,000 pages, annual. About 1,020 of the most important funding sources of religious and religiously–affiliated organizations are detailed.

Salary survey

AHP Total Compensation Report (Association for Healthcare Philanthropy Foundation, Suite 400, 313 Park Ave., Falls Church, VA 22046; phone: 703/532–6243) $150/nonmembers, free/members, published in odd–numbered years. Reports on salaries by position and bed size, type of institution, gender, as well as on age, size of staff, insurance, retirement benefits, perquisites, and vacation time. There are two reports, for the United States and for Canada; ask for the one you want.

Donate your time to read chapters 1 and 2 first

Chapter 23

Records management and archives

Records management and archives

*Also see the chapter on "Museums and libraries." See the **Government Job Finder** for a more extensive set of job sources.*

Job ads

Archival Outlook (Society of American Archivists, Suite 504, 600 S. Federal, Chicago, IL 60605; phone: 312/922–0140) published in alternating months with *SAA Employment Bulletin*, free/members only. Jobs listed under "Employment Opportunities." About 20 job ads per issue.

SAA Employment Bulletin (Society of American Archivists, Suite 504, 600 S. Federal, Chicago, IL 60605; phone: 312/922–0140) published in alternating months with *Archival Outlook*, available to members for $24/year; nonmembers can purchase individual issues for $6 each. Lists only jobs. About 20 jobs ads per issue.

AIC Newsletter (American Institute for Conservation of Historic and Artistic Works, Suite 301, 1717 K St., NW, Washington, DC 20006; phone: 202/452-9545) bimonthly, free/members only. Jobs listed under "Positions Available." Around 20 job ads per issue, largely for conservators.

Journal of the American Health Information Management Association (AHIMA, Suite O1400, 919 N. Michigan Ave., Chicago, IL 60611-1683; phone: 312/787-2672, ext. 253) monthly, $72/nonmember annual subscription, free/members. Around 10 to 15 classified ads for medical record administrators, technicians, coders, and reviewers are in the typical issue.

OAH Newsletter (Organization of American Historians, 112 N. Bryan St., Bloomington, IN 47408; phone: 812/855-7311) quarterly, free/members only. From five to ten positions for government, public, and U.S. historians; archivists; and university faculty appear under "Professional Opportunities."

OAH Job Registry (Organization of American Historians, 112 N. Bryan St., Bloomington, IN 47408; phone: 812/855-7311). You can find the latest job openings for archivists, historians, and university faculty on this Internet service. Go to URL: **http://www.indiana.edu./~oah**, and click on "Professional Opportunities in American History" and then "Current Employment Listings," where you'll find six to 12 listings.

Directories

AIC Directory (American Institute for Conservation of Historic and Artistic Works, Suite 301, 1717 K St., NW, Washington, DC 20006; phone: 202/452-9545) $58/nonmembers, free/members, published each August. Members listed alphabetically, geographically, and by specialty.

Directory of Individual and Institutional Members (Society of American Archivists, Suite 504, 600 S. Federal, Chicago, IL 60605; phone: 312/922-0140) $50/nonmembers, $10/members, 170 pages, annual. Gives name, address, phone, and email for archivists and private, government, and non-profit archival institutions.

Read chapters 1 and 2 first

Chapter 24

Religion

Religion

Also see the "Social services" chapter.

Job ads

Christianity Today (Christianity Today, Inc., P.O. Box 11618, Des Moines, IA 50340; phones: 800/999–1704, 630/260–6200) 14 issues/year, $24.95/annual subscription (U.S.), $32.95/foreign. "The Marketplace–Employment" features 65 to 70 ads for ministers, caseworkers, missionaries, professors, editors, lawyers, and broadcasters.

Your Church (Christianity Today, Inc., P.O. Box 11618, Des Moines, IA 50340; phones: 800/999–1704, 630/260–6200) bimonthly, free. In a typical issue, "Employment" will feature 50 or more ads for ministers, caseworkers, missionaries, professors, editors, lawyers, and broadcasters.

National Catholic Reporter (P.O. Box 419281, Kansas City, MO 64141; phones: 800/444–8910, 816/531–0538) weekly, semiweekly during the summer months, 44 issues/year, $36.95/annual subscription. Over 40 positions in religion (teachers, directors of lay ministries, directors of religious activities and chaplain services, counselors, musicians, etc.) appear under "NCR Classifieds." Included employment wanted ads.

Religion

Catholic Digest (P.O. Box 51549, Boulder, CO 80322; phone: 800/678–2836) monthly, $19.95/annual subscription. The "Vocation Guide" includes 25 display ads from different religious orders.

Pastoral Music (National Association of Pastoral Musicians, 225 Sheridan St., NW, Washington, DC 20011; phone: 202/723–5800) bimonthly, $24/annual nonmember subscription, free/members. "Hotline" runs 25 or more ads for church and synagogue musicians, ministers, and directors of music and liturgy.

Pastoral Music Notebook (National Association of Pastoral Musicians, 225 Sheridan St., NW, Washington, DC 20011; phone: 202/723–5800) bimonthly, free/members only; $48/annual dues. "Hotline" runs 25 or more ads for church and synagogue musicians, ministers, and directors of music and liturgy.

Higher Education Report (Association of Jesuit Colleges and Universities, Suite 405, 1 Dupont Cr., Washington, DC 20036; phone: 202/862–9893) ten issues/year, $17.50/annual subscription (U.S. and Canada). Three to five ads for faculty are listed under "Classifieds."

MinistryLink is the Internet site to search out if you are looking for a job with a Roman Catholic parish or school. Go to URL: **http://www.csbsju.edu/sot/MinistryLink/**, and select "Positions Available," and there you can search by keyword, category, or region. Alternatively, you can browse through the dozens of positions for ministers, music directors, principals, teachers, liturgists, and youth coordinators.

Christian Connection Classifieds is an interdenominational Internet site where you can find ten to 15 positions for ministers, school administrators, and missionaries. Go to URL: **http://tcm.nbs.net/~cc/chjob.html**, and browse.

Religious Broadcasting (National Religious Broadcasters, 7839 Ashton Ave., Manassas, VA 20109; phone: 703/330–7000) 10 issues/year, $24 annual nonmember subscription (U.S.), $30/Canada, $48/elsewhere, free/members. Five to ten positions for everything in radio and television are described under "Classified." Also includes positions sought. About five to ten other jobs and about 15 internships can be found on the Internet at URL: **http://www.nrb.com**, and clicking on "Classified." Jobs are listed for six weeks.

Jewish Monthly (B'nai B'rith International, 1640 Rhode Island Ave., NW, Washington, DC 20036; phone: 202/857–6645) bimonthly, $12/annual subscription, $2/single issue. One or two jobs for rabbis and camp counselors appear in the "Classifieds." A few more jobs are listed on the Internet. Go to URL: **http://bnaibrith.org**, and select "Job Openings," which is updated as jobs become available.

Follow the righteous path to chapters 1 and 2 first

The Christian Reader (Christianity Today, Inc., P.O. Box 37629, Boone, IA 50037; phones: 800/223–3161, 630/260–6200) bimonthly, $17.50/annual subscription (U.S.), $22.50/foreign. "Classifieds–Employment" runs two or three ads for positions with Christian publishers.

Job services

Job Hotline (National Association of Pastoral Musicians, 225 Sheridan St., NW, Washington, DC 20011; phone: 202/723–5800) monthly, $25/nonmembers, $15/members. These are the same 25 or more vacancies for church and synagogue musicians, ministers, and directors of music and liturgy that appear in *Pastoral Music Notebook* and *Pastoral Music* described above under "Job ads." However, NPM members can access them before publication by calling this live job hotline.

Presbyterian Association of Musicians Referral Service (100 Witherspoon, Louisville, KY 40202–1396; phone: 502/569–5288) $20/members only, annual. Churches that wish to hire musicians submit a job description which is then mailed to subscribing members. Listings are mailed on the first Monday of every month.

Christian Placement Service (Intercristo, 19303 Fremont Avenue N, Seattle, WA 98133; phones: 800/426–1342, 800/251–7740) $42.50/three–month subscription, $19.50/renewal subscription. You must fill out a personal profile application form which includes selecting up to four occupations, three geographic preferences, compensation, denomination, experience, education, skills, and more. This will put you into an extensive database connected to ministries all over the world from which you will be matched with jobs available and be sent four printouts that match your qualifications and interests. There are literally thousands of jobs available which are updated frequently. If you are interested in integrating your faith with your employment this is the service to join.

National Association of Temple Administrators Placement Service (NATA, Suite 6K, 310 E. 70th St., New York, NY 10021; phone: 212/861–5728) $100/year nonmember registration fee, free/members. Positions filled are with reform Jewish congregations. You submit a copy of your resume to the service. When the service receives a job description from a congregation for an administrator, it sends a notice to all registrants. You contact the service and ask it to send your resume to the congregation which is then responsible for contacting you for the next step in the hiring process. About 25 to 30 jobs a year are listed with this service.

North American Association of Synagogue Executives Placement Service (NAASA, c/o United Synagogue of Conservative Judaism, 155 Fifth Ave., New York, NY 10010; phone: 212/533–7800, ext. 2250) free/members only. You submit your own resume and the service's completed form. Figuring out how this service works is even more difficult than reading the Torah without vowels. If you are a member, or wish to join one of NAASE's assemblies, you should inquire directly. Jobs are with conservative synagogues.

Directories

National Directory of Churches, Synagogues, and Other Houses of Worship (Gale Research, Inc., 835 Penobscot Bldg., Detroit, MI 48226; phone: 800/877–4253) $310/four volume set, $85/per volume, 4,057 pages total, 1993. With a volume for each of four geographic regions, this tome describes over 350,000 houses of worship in the U.S. You'll find each congregation's name, address, phone, size, denomination, date established, and leader's name.

Directory of Religious Organizations in the United States (Gale Research, Inc., 835 Penobscot Bldg., Detroit, MI 48226; phone: 800/877–4253) $130, 728 pages, 1992. Details about 2,500 nondenominational, interdenominational, and inter–faith organizations that provide services, information, or support for religious bodies: churches, denominations, sects, and cults. You'll learn the name and phone number of each organization's chief executive officer, its goals and activities, and its products, including publications, audio and video tapes, and radio and television programs. This is a good source to identify potential employers in the "affiliated" religion industry.

The Official Catholic Directory (R.R. Bowker; available from Reed Elsevier, P.O. Box 31, New Providence, NJ 07974; phone: 800/521–8110) $204.95 plus 7 percent shipping and handling, call for special clergy rate, 2,200 pages, annual. Lists more than 60,000 leaders in the Roman Catholic Church in the U.S.A. including: parish clergy, chancery officials, colleges and universities, novitiates and provincialities, seminaries, and foreign missions.

Catholic World Wide Web Directory is a huge collection of links to a countless number of Roman Catholic parishes, orders, and organizations. Go to URL: **http://www.catholic.org/**, and select "Catholic Web Directory." Then choose among the following: "Religious Orders," "Catholic Parishes on the Web," and "Catholic Organizations."

Directory of Religious Broadcasting (National Religious Broadcasters, 7839 Ashton Ave., Manassas, VA 20109; phone: 703/330–7000) $69.95/nonmembers, $25/members, 350 pages, issued each January. Lists 4,000 stations, plus radio show producers, and other key personnel.

The Christian Media Directory (James Lloyd, P.O. Box 3, Ashland, OR 97520; phone: 503/488–1405) $35 plus $2.75/shipping, prepaid only. Lists over 7,000 producers, publishers, recording labels, studios, all–Christian music and radio stations, film and video companies, television stations, and more.

Follow the righteous path to chapters 1 and 2 first

The Gospel Voice (Music City News, Suite 601, 50 Music Square West, Nashville, TN 37203; phone: 615/329–2200) $2. Each year the April issue of *Music City News* includes *The Gospel Voice,* a directory of the gospel music industry that offers information on record labels, artists, radio and television shows, and music publishers.

The Religious Funding Resource Guide (ResourceWomen, 4527 S. Dakota Ave., NE, Washington, DC 20017; phone: 202/832–8071) $75 + $7/postage, $90/libraries and universities + $7/postage, 526 pages, published each February. Packed with details on 38 religious funders who issue grants to community–based, social justice, and social service organizations working for change in their communities. Includes current application forms, guidelines, and grant lists, calendar of deadline, information on denominational structures and how to address clergy, and strategies for seeking funds from religious sources.

National Guide to Funding in Religion (The Foundation Center, 79 Fifth Ave., New York, NY 10003–3076; phones: 800/424–9836, 212/620–4230) $140 plus $4.50/shipping, 865 pages, published in April of odd–numbered years. Presents details on 4,200 foundations and corporate direct giving programs that have a history of funding churches, missionary societies, religious welfare, and religious education programs.

Fund Raiser's Guide to Religious Philanthropy (Taft Group, 835 Penobscot Bldg., 645 Griswold St., Detroit, MI 48226–4094; phones: 800/877–8238, 313/961–2242) $160, 1,000 pages, annual. About 1,020 of the most important funding sources of religious and religiously–affiliated organizations are detailed.

Grants for Religion, Religious Welfare & Religious Education (The Foundation Center, 79 Fifth Ave., New York, NY 10003–3076; phones: 800/424–9836, within New York State call 212/620–4230) $75 plus $4.50/shipping, 305 pages, published in October of odd–numbered years. Describes recent foundation grants of at least $10,000 given to synagogues, churches, missionary societies, religious orders, and associations and organizations concerned with religious welfare and education. This directory is useful for identifying foundations and grant recipients for which you may wish to work.

Choose a Christian College (Peterson's Guides, P.O. 2123, Princeton, NJ 08543–2123; phone: 800/338–3282) $14.95 plus $5.75/shipping, 148 pages. Provides full page profiles on more than 140 colleges with a Christian education perspective.

Salary survey

Presbyterian Association of Musicians Referral Service Salary Survey (100 Witherspoon, Louisville, KY 40202–1396; phone: 502/569–5288) $2, annual. Salary guidelines, sample contracts, and code of ethics included.

No photocopying, please

Chapter 25

Research

Research

Also see the "Foundations and grants" chapter as well as the "Job and grant sources by state" section of Chapter 30.

Job ads

Professional Staff Position Listings (National Research Council, Office of Human Resources, GR 145, 2101 Constitution Ave., NW, Washington, DC 20418; phone: 202/334–2000) weekly, free. Send a self–addressed #10 business envelope stamped with two ounces of postage for each issue you'd like to receive. About 40 vacancies are described in each issue. Half of the positions are for research in a wide variety of agencies including social science, science or engineering, agriculture, environment, life sciences, medicine, mathematics, transportation. The NRC shares an Internet site with the National Academy of Sciences, National Academy of Engineering, and Institute of Medicine, each of which offers scads of research positions. Go to URL: **http://www2.nas.edu/ohr/** and browse through the job titles that interest you.

SRA News (Society of Research Administrators, Suite 300, 1200 19th St., NW, Washington, DC 20036; phone: 202/857–1141) bimonthly, free/members only. The "Classifieds" carry two or three ads for administrator positions for all types of research projects and programs. Many more ads can be found on the Internet at URL: **http://web.fie.com/cws/sra/sra.htm**, and selecting "Job Ads." You need to be a member with user name and password to access this resource.

NCURA Newsletter (National Council of University Research Administrators, Suite 220, 1 Dupont Cr., NW, Washington, DC 20036; phone: 202/466–3894)bimonthly, free/members only. About one to four ads for research administrators appear throughout the newsletter.

Computing Research Association Index of Jobs is an Internet service that lists jobs in academia relating to research with computers. Go to URL: **http://cra.org/jobs/**, where you can scroll down a list of universities and colleges and click on the one you want to pursue. About 30 institutions are listed and usually about one job is offered in each.

ACA Newsletter (American Crystallographic Association, P.O. Box 96, Ellicott Station, Buffalo, NY 14205–0096; phone: 716/856–9600, ext. 321) quarterly, available only to members, included in dues. "Positions Available" features about ten job ads for chemistry, physics, and structural biologist positions in research laboratories and universities. Check out the Internet for about ten to 15 job listings by going to URL: **http://www.hwi.buffalo.edu/aca/**. Select "Web Page Directory" and then "ACA Jobs and Ends."

Physics Job Announcements by Thread, an Internet site operated by the Los Alamos National Laboratory, offers more than 120 job listings for faculty and postdoctorate positions at universities and research labs. Go to URL: **http://www.XXX.lanl.gov/Announce/Jobs**, where you can browse for positions by title and geographic region, mostly U.S., but some international.

Job service

Talent Pool is an Internet resume database service of Recruitment On–Line Inc. for such research positions as geometric modelers, technical writers, and market analysts. Go to URL: **http://www.helpwanted.com**, and get detailed directions on how to submit a free two–page resume that is kept on file for three months. You will need to submit it as an HTML document or text only document by attaching it to your email application sent to resume@helpwanted.com. This resume bank is not available to the general public; only those agencies and company recruiters who have access will be able to review your resume.

Directories

Directory of Research Grants, 1995 (Oryx Press, Suite 700, 4041 N. Central, Phoenix, AZ 85012–3397; phones: 800/279–6799, 602/265–2651) $135, 1,208 pages, 1995. Describes over 6,000 sources of research funding in dozens of disciplines and subject areas.

Research Centers Directory (Gale Research, Inc., 835 Penobscot Bldg., Detroit, MI 48226–4094; phone: 800/877–4253) $500, 2,500 pages in two volumes, published in odd–numbered years. Provides details on more than 14,000 non–profit research units in all fields including university research parks and technology transfer centers. Entries are grouped into chapters covering five broad categories: life sciences; physical sciences and engineering, private and public policy, social and cultural studies, and multidisciplinary and coordinating centers. Includes separate personal name index, which lists center directors and other important contacts.

NCURA Membership Directory (National Council of University Research Administrators, Suite 220, 1 Dupont Circle, NW, Washington, DC 20036; phone: 202/466–3894) free/members only, 272 pages, published every May. Lists some 3,000 administrators.

SRA Membership Directory (Society of Research Administrators, Suite 300, 1200 19th St., NW, Washington, DC 20036; phone: 202/857–1141) free/members only, 250 pages, issued each March. Lists 2,900 individuals and 120 institutions.

World Directory of Crystallographers (American Crystallographic Association, P.O. Box 96, Ellicott Station, Buffalo, NY 14205–0096; phone: 716/856–9600, ext. 321) $10/members only, April 1997. Lists about 2,300 members of the ACA, which includes chemists, physicists, and structural biologists.

Salary surveys

Compensation in Research & Development (Abbott, Langer & Associates, 548 First St., Crete, IL 60417; phone: 708/672–4200) $650/entire set, 768 pages; Part I: Directors/Managers/Supervisors, $250; Part II: Engineers/Scientists/Technologists, $250; Part III: Technicians, $250. Reports on 16 job categories from entry–level technician to research and development director.

Compensation & Benefits in Independent Laboratory, Testing, and Inspection Firms (Abbott, Langer & Associates, 548 First St., Crete, IL 60417; phone: 708/672–4200) $395, 1996. Reports on salaries and benefits for executive, professionals, laboratory staff, and field technicians by job functions, employer size, location, experience, education, and more.

Research your way to chapters 1 and 2 first

Chapter 26

Safety

Safety

*If criminal justice is your thing, see the **Government Job Finder** for a much more extensive set of job sources.*

Job ads

NELS—National Employment Listing Service (Criminal Justice Center, Sam Houston State University, Huntsville, TX 77341–2296; NELS' phone: 916/392–2550). Formerly a jobs newsletter, ***NELS*** is now a bulletin board service you can access via your modem at 916/392–4640. After completing the online registration process, you can find the NELS "catalog" in the database section of the main menu. Also available via ftpmail on the Internet by sending an email message to "ftpmail@search.org". Then type: "get nels_cat.txt". You'll receive the current NELS "catalog" within 24 hours by email. It runs 20 to 60 printed pages. You can print it or just browse through it on your computer screen. The *NELS* "catalog" usually contains descriptions of 100 to over 200 vacant positions in four categories: Academics and research (criminal justice); Law enforcement and security (police officers, document examiners, print examiners, criminologists, public service aides, jailers); Community services and corrections (correctional trainees, psychologists, social workers, physicians, speech pathologists,

Safety

communications, clerical, counselors, probation officers); and Institutional corrections (correctional officers, psychologists, nurses, chaplains, cooks, therapists, pharmacists, trades and laborers).

The Criminologist (American Society of Criminology, Suite 212, 1314 Kinnear Rd., Columbus, OH, 43212; phone: 614/292–9207) bimonthly, $7.50/annual nonmember subscription (U.S.), $10/foreign, free/members. Ten to 12 jobs for probation officers, police, and faculty are listed under "Positions Announcements."

Law Enforcement News (John Jay College of Criminal Justice, Suite 438, 899 Tenth Ave., New York, NY 10019; phone: 212/237–8442) bimonthly, $22/annual subscription (U.S.), $37/foreign. Vacancies are offered under "Jobs."

Employment Bulletin (American Sociological Association, 1722 N St., NW, Washington, DC 20036; phone: 202/833–3410) monthly, $30/nonmember annual subscription, $10/members. This newsletter features about 70 positions in academic, applied, and fellowship settings. Most positions are in sociology, but also related areas such as anthropology and criminology.

Directories

American Society of Criminology Membership Directory (American Society of Criminology, Suite 212, 1314 Kinnear Rd., Columbus, OH, 43212; phone: 614/292–9207) free/members only, 118 pages, published in odd–numbered years. Lists more than 2,800 criminologists.

Crime, Law Enforcement & Abuse Prevention (The Foundation Center, 79 Fifth Ave., New York, NY 10003–3076; phones: 800/424–9836, within New York State call 212/620–4230) $75 plus $4.50/shipping, 191 pages, published in October of odd–numbered years. Describes recent foundation grants of at least $10,000 for crime prevention, rehabilitation services for offenders, courts and the administration of justice, law enforcement agencies, and protection against and prevention of neglect, abuse, or exploitation. This directory is useful for identifying foundations and grant recipients for which you may wish to work.

The safe way is to read chapters 1 and 2 first

Chapter 27

Science

Science in general

*Also see the "Museums and libraries" and "Research" chapters in this book. For a much more extensive listing of science and engineering job sources, see the **Professional's Job Finder**. The job sources presented in this chapter focus on academic and research laboratory employment.*

Job ads

Science (American Association of the Advancement of Science, 1200 New York Ave., NW, Washington, DC 20005; phones: 800/731–4939, 202/326–6500) 51 issues/year, $87/annual subscription (U.S.), call for foreign rates. "Personnel Placement" overflows with around 200 to 400 advertisements for scientists of all types, although most ads seem to be for biologists and scientists in academia.

Nature (Macmillan Magazines, P.O. Box 5054, Brentwood, TN 37025; phone: 800/524–0384) weekly, $145/annual individual subscription (U.S.), $155/Canada and Mexico, $80/students (U.S.), $86/students (Canada and Mexico), include student identification with your order. Job ads for over 300 scientists of all sorts appear in "Nature Classified." The majority of openings are for academic or research positions. Advertised jobs include

Science in general

virtually everything in science throughout the U.S. and the world. You can also access the jobs openings on the Internet by visting URL: **http://www.nature.com** and then choosing "International Science Jobs."

Met–Jobs: Meteorology and Atmospheric Science and Employment Opportunities is one of the biggest Internet sites for jobs in science we've come across. Each month the site lists from 200 to 500 jobs, and notwithstanding its title most are in the earth sciences. Go to URL: **http://www.eskimo.com/~tsmith/mail/mj–arc.html**, and select the category: Select "MET–JOBS" for 10 to 15 jobs for meteorology and atmospheric science professionals, select "GISRL–JOBS" for 25 to 100 jobs for geographic informations systems professionals, select "GIVENG–JOBS" for 50 to 150 jobs for civil engineers, and select "GEOSCI–JOBS" for 125 to 200 jobs for geoscientists.

AWIS Magazine (Association for Women in Science, Suite 650, 1200 New York Ave., NW, Washington, DC 20005; phone: 202/408–0742) bimonthly, $60/nonmember annual subscription, free/members. From 10 to 25 ads for life, physical, social, and mathematical sciences and engineering appear under "Employment Opportunities."

Geotimes (American Geological Institute, 4220 King St., Alexandria, VA 22302; phone: 703/379–2480) monthly, $14.95/annual student subscription, $32.95/nonmembers, $24.95/members. Each issue has 20 to 25 classified ads for academic positions. The October issue contains a directory of geology organizations.

GSA Today (Geological Society of America, P.O. Box 9140, Boulder, CO 80301; phones: 800/472–1988, 303/447–2020) monthly, $45/annual nonmember subscription, free/members. Four or five openings in the earth sciences appear under "Classifieds–Positions Open." Scores of job announcements can be found on the Internet at URL: **http://www.geosociety.org**, scrolling down to "Membership," and then clicking on "Employment Service," which will give you the listings alphabetically by university.

ACA Newsletter (American Crystallographic Association, P.O. Box 96, Ellicott Station, Buffalo, NY 14205–0096; phone: 716/856–9600, ext. 321) quarterly, available only to members, included in dues. "Positions Available" features about ten job ads for chemistry, physics, and structural biologists positions in research laboratories and universities. Check out the Internet for about ten to 15 job listings by going to URL: **http://www.hwi.buffalo.edu/aca/**. Select "Web Page Directory" and then "ACA Jobs and Ends."

The New Careers Directory: Internships in Technology and Social Change (Student Pugwash USA, Suite 814, 815 15th St., NW, Washington, DC 20005; phone: 202/393–6555) $18, $10/students; add $3 shipping. Offers full details on where and how to apply for internships and entry–level jobs in science and society.

Use the scientific method and read chapters 1 and 2 first

Job services

Employment Matching Service (Geological Society of America, P.O. Box 9140, Boulder, CO 80301–9140; phones: 800/472–1988, 303/447–2020) $60/annual nonmember fee, $30/members. Registrants complete a form and include a two-page resume. Employers receive printouts of these forms throughout the year and are responsible for contacting applicants directly.

Medzilla Jobs and Employment Resources in Biotechnology, Medicine, and Science (The Franklin Search Group, 14522 54th Place West, Edmonds, WA 48026–3811) is an Internet site provides both a job bank and a resume database. To get to the job bank go to URL: **http://www.chemistry.com/**, and select "Search Jobs." Enter keywords for the field and type of work you want (such as "Biology" and "Research") and then click on "Submit Search." To enter your resume in the free resume database select "Apply for Jobs and Post Your Resume."

Directories

IDEAAAS: Sourcebook for Science, Mathematics, and Technology Education (The Learning Team, 84 Business Park Dr., Armonk, NY 10504; phones: 800/793–8326, 914/273–2226) $28.95, 245 pages, 1995. Details 1,500 professional societies, teacher organizations, regional education laboratories, education associations, curriculum developers, museums, zoos, aquariums, planetariums, science centers, research institutes, federal and state agencies, scholarship programs, and community organizations involved in the fields of science, mathematics, and technology. Resources are presented by state. Especially valuable for anybody involved in kindergarten through high school education.

Directory of Geoscience Departments (American Geological Institute, AGI Publications Center, P.O. Box 205, Annapolis Junction, MD 20701, phone: 301/953–1744) $34.50 plus $6 shipping/nonmembers, $27.50 plus $6 shipping/members, 480+ pages, published every October. Lists more than 1,000 geoscience departments in colleges and universities and more than 13,000 geoscientists, as well as selected foreign geoscience departments, U.S. national laboratories, major museums, field courses, and camps, and earth-science teacher training programs.

GSA Membership Directory (Geological Society of America, P.O. Box 9140, Boulder, CO 80301; phones: 800/472–1988, 303/447–2020) $19.20/members only, usually issued each spring.

Photocopying strictly prohibited

World Directory of Crystallographers (American Crystallographic Association, P.O. Box 96, Ellicott Station, Buffalo, NY 14205–0096; phone: 716/856–9600, ext. 321) $10/members only, April 1997. Lists about 2,300 members of the ACA, which includes chemists, physicists, and structural biologists.

Grants for Science & Technology Programs (The Foundation Center, 79 Fifth Ave., New York, NY 10003–3076; phones: 800/424–9836, within New York State call 12/620–4230) $75 plus $4.50/shipping, 206 pages, published in October of odd–numbered years. Describes recent foundation grants of at least $10,000 for education and research in computer science and technology; scientific societies, associations and institutes; science museums; planetariums; and libraries. This directory is useful for identifying foundations and grant recipients for which you may wish to work.

Salary surveys

Careers in Biotechnology (Industrial Biotechnology Association, 1625 K St., NW, Washington, DC 20006; phone: 202/857–0244) contact for price, most recently published in 1990. In addition to explaining this emerging field in some detail, this directory describes the training needed, sources of additional information, relevant associations, sample job ads and job descriptions, a guide to recruiters for biotechnology jobs, and results of a salary survey. Specialties included in biotechnology are chemists, chemical engineers, physicists, engineers, biologists, and geneticists.

Medzilla: The Salary Survey (The Franklin Search Group, 14522 54th Place West, Edmonds, WA 48026–3811) is an Internet site salary survey of jobs in biotechnology, medicine, and science. It was conducted in 1995 from 1,200 responses. Go to URL: **http://www.medzilla.com/survey.html**, and choose the results by clicking on the degree: B.S., M.S., Ph.D., M.B.A, etc.

Biological sciences

Job ads

Academic Physician and Scientist (Lippincott–Raven Publishers, 36th Floor, 1185 Avenue of the Americas, New York, NY 10036; phone: 212/930–9561) bimonthly, free/qualified persons, write for application. Each issue contains at least 30 pages of display and classified ads for academic positions in medicine and science, averaging 450 ads per issue. For job postings on the Internet, go to URL: **http://www.acphysci.com**, and select "Classified Ads." Then choose from among "Administration," "Basic Science," and

Use the scientific method and read chapters 1 and 2 first

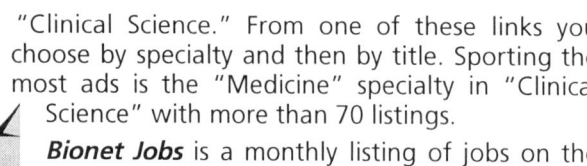

"Clinical Science." From one of these links you choose by specialty and then by title. Sporting the most ads is the "Medicine" specialty in "Clinical Science" with more than 70 listings.

Bionet Jobs is a monthly listing of jobs on the Internet at URL: **http://www .bio.net/hypermail/ Employment/**. You select "Read the most recent Employment/bionet jobs" and get a listing of some 200 jobs, mostly for postdoctoral and research positions in the biological sciences.

ASM News (American Society for Microbiology, 1325 Massachusetts Ave., NW, Washington, DC 20005; phone: 202/737-3600) monthly, $37/annual nonmember subscription, free/members. You'll find between 20 to 30 job opportunities for biologists, molecular biologists, and microbiologists under "Employment."

Career Connection offers hundreds of positions in the bioinformatics, biochemistry, and molecular biology on the Internet at URL: **http://www .ebi.ac.uk/htbin/biojobs.pl**. You can search by keyword or by category.

BioSpace Career Center runs over 50 job ads in bioscience at its Internet site at URL: **http://www .biospace.com/g/synd/career/**. You can browse or search by employer, region, or occupation.

Positions in Bioscience and Medicine is an Internet job bank for faculty, postdoctoral, and research positions from around the world. It can be reached at URL: **http://www.inofrmatik.uni-rostock.de/HUM-MOLGEN/**. Search and click on "Positions" in the left-hand column; then enter keywords in the following: "Type of Work," "Subject," and "Continent;" and then click on "Go Get It."

Journal of National Technical Association (Peterson's Magazine Group, 202 Carnegie Center, Princeton, NJ 08540; phones: 800/338-3282 ext. 533, 609/243-9111 ext. 533) spring, summer, and autumn issues, $16.90/each, $50.70/annual subscription. Ten to 40 jobs ads appear throughout the magazine for biology, engineering, science, and technology positions.

The FASEB Journal (Federation of American Societies for Experimental Biology, 9650 Rockville Pike, Bethesda, MD 20814-3998; phone: 301/530-7020) monthly, $118/nonmember annual subscription (U.S.), $138/Canada and Mexico, $170/elsewhere, $49/members (U.S.), $69/Canada and Mexico, $110/elsewhere. About 20 ads for life science positions, mostly at the doctoral level, appear under "Employment Opportunities." An equal number of "Position Desired" ads also appear.

ASC Bulletin (American Society of Cytopathology, Suite 201, 400 W. 9th St., Wilmington, DE 19801; phone: 302/429-8802) eight issues/year, $25/nonmembers annual subscription, free/members. Around five to 10 positions for cytopathologists and cytotechnologists are in the "Classifieds."

Photocopying strictly prohibited

Biological sciences

The Physiologist (American Physiological Society, 9650 Rockville Pike, Bethesda, MD 20814–3991; phone: 301/530–7180) bimonthly, $25/nonmember annual subscription (U.S.), $35/foreign, free/members. "Positions Available" carries ads for five or six university teaching and research positions. The last three listings of classified job ads appear on the Internet at URL:**gopher://oac.hsc.uth.tmc.edu:3300/00/employ/list**.

Nature Bio/Technology (Nature Publishing Company, 345 Park Ave. South, New York, NY 10010; phone: 800/524–0328) monthly, $59/annual subscription (U.S., Canada). Around 20 to 25 job ads are under "Classified."

ESA Newsletter (Entomological Society of America, 9301 Annapolis Rd., Suite 300, Lanham, MD 20706–3115; phone: 301/731–4535) monthly, $15/nonmember annual subscription, $8/members, $2/single copies. "Opportunities" lists ten to 15 jobs for entomologists, biologists, geneticists, and toxicologists.

SOT Newsletter (Society of Toxicology, Suite 302, 1767 Business Center Dr., Reston, VA 20190; phone: 703/438–3115) five issues/year, free, available only to members. "Placement Service" typically has about eight job ads for toxicologists.

American Journal of Botany (Botanical Society of America, 1735 Neil Ave., Columbus, OH 43210–1293; phone: 614/292–3519) monthly, $155/annual subscription (U.S.), $165/Canada, $180/elsewhere. Four to eight ads for botanists and biologists appear under "Positions Available."

Plant Science Bulletin (Botanical Society of America, 1735 Neil Ave., Columbus, OH 43210–1293; phone: 614/292–3519) quarterly, $15/annual nonmember subscription. About five job ads in botany and biology, mostly academic, are in the typical issue.

SIM News (Society for Industrial Microbiology, Suite 92A, 3929 Old Lee Hwy., Fairfax, VA 22030; phone: 703/691–3357) bimonthly, free/members, $6/per copy nonmembers. One or two ads for microbiologists are in "Placement."

Genetic Engineering News (Mary Ann Lieberc Publications, 2 Madison Ave., Larchmont, NY 10538; phone: 914/834–3100) 21 issues/year, $228/annual subscription, free/qualified professionals. Five to ten ads for biochemists, bioengineers, and biologists appear under "Classified."

Job services

FASEB Career Resources (Federation of American Societies for Experimental Biology, 9650 Rockville Pike, Bethesda, MD 20814–3998; phone: 301/530–7020) free. FASEB offers several job services under this rubric. *CAREERS OnLine* is an electronic database of job vacancies in biomedical careers. You can view the job vacancies at Internet URL: **http://www.faseb.org/careers** and choosing "Applicant Service" and then "CAREERS HardCopy OnLine" under which you will find ads for five to 15 positions,

Use the scientific method and read chapters 1 and 2 first

mostly in education and research. In addition, you can place your resume in CAREERS OnLine, an electronic resume database that employers can search for potential employees. Your resume is specially coded to retain confidentiality and keep your current employer from discovering you're looking for a new job. When an employer finds someone it wants to contact for an interview, this service will ask you for permission to give your name to the employer. Contact FASEB or visit its web site for full details.

SOT Mid–Year Placement Service (Society of Toxicology, Suite 302, 1767 Business Center Dr., Reston, VA 20190; phone: 703/438–3115) $50/nonmembers, $45/postdoctoral nonmembers, $40/full–time student nonmembers, $25/full and associate members, $20/postdoctoral members, $15/full–time student members. You must already have your Ph.D. or be within 12 months of receiving it. Resume forms for participating in this program become available each July 1 and are due back by mid–August. In early September, all participating employers are sent a packet with the completed resume forms of all the job candidates while job candidates are sent a packet with all positions registered with this service. You're responsible for contacting employers about specific jobs. You can use a pseudonym on the resume form to protect your confidentiality. SOT operates a similar placement program at its annual spring convention. Contact SOT for fees and deadlines (resume forms usually are due by early February). Completing this service's narrative resume form and computer form puts your resume among those that employers see at the *SOT Placement Service* which is conducted at SOT's annual conference, usually held in March. If you attend the conference, you can be interviewed right there. If you do not attend the conference, an employer may still contact you to arrange an interview and you can obtain a copy of the jobs posted at the conference by requesting them from SOT after the conference has ended.

BioMedNet Job Exchange is a huge Internet site with an international scope for all kinds of jobs in the biological sciences. Go to URL: **http://BioMedNet.com**, click on "Visitors," and then select "Jobs." You will then be confronted with a world map graphic, and moving the cursor to North America and double clicking will get you — hold your breath now — 777 jobs when we last looked. The site requires you to complete an online application before you browse this free service.

American Society for Microbiology Placement Service (ASM, 1325 Massachusetts Ave., NW, Washington, DC 20005; phone: 202/737–3600) $50/nonmember annual fee, $30/members, $15/student members. You fill out their registry form. When there is a match, your form is sent to the employer who is responsible for contacting you.

SIM Placement Service (Society for Industrial Microbiology, Suite 92A, 3929 Old Lee Hwy., Fairfax, VA 22030; phone: 703/691–3357) free/members only. You submit your own resume. When a job match is made, you

Photocopying strictly prohibited

Biological sciences

are notified and are responsible for contacting the potential employer. Positions include microbiologists, quality assurance, fermentation, bioremediation, process control, and research.

Questionnaire on Employment Status of Women in Physiology (American Physiological Society, Membership Services, 9650 Rockville Pike, Bethesda, MD 20814; phone: 301/530–7172) free/female members only. You complete the resume questionnaire which is kept on file indefinitely. When a university department chair is hiring faculty, she can request copies of these questionnaires as part of the faculty search.

Directories

FASEB Directory of Members (Federation of American Societies for Experimental Biology, 9650 Rockville Pike, Bethesda, MD 20814; phone: 301/530–7000) $60/nonmembers (U.S.), $65/Canada and Mexico, $71/elsewhere, $16 (U.S.)/members, $21/members Canada and Mexico, $27/members elsewhere, 450 pages, annual. Includes contact information on members of the American Physiological Society, American Society for Biochemistry and Molecular Biology, American Society for Pharmacology and Experimental Therapeutics, American Association of Pathologists, American Institute of Nutrition, American Association of Immunologists, and American Society for Cell Biology, Biophysical Society, American Association of Anatomists, and the Protein Society.

Society of Toxicology Membership Directory (Society of Toxicology, Suite 302, 1767 Business Center Dr., Reston, VA 20190; phone: 703/438–3115) free/members only, issued each July.

SIM Membership Directory (Society for Industrial Microbiology, Suite 92A, 3929 Old Lee Hwy., Fairfax, VA 22030; phone: 703/691–3357) free, available only to members, issued in odd–numbered years.

Membership Directory (Genetics Society of America, 9650 Rockville Pike, Bethesda, MD 20814; phone: 301/571–1825) free/members only, issued in the spring of even–numbered years. Includes members of GSA, American Society of Human Genetics, and the American Board of Medical Genetics.

Botanical Society of America Directory (BSA, 1735 Neil Ave., Columbus, OH 43210–1293; phone: 614/292–3519) $10/nonmembers, free/members, published in the spring of even–numbered years.

Salary survey

Salaries of Scientists, Engineers, and Technicians (Commission on Professionals in Science and Technology, Suite 300, 1100 New York Ave., NW, Washington, DC 20005; phone: 202/326–7080) $100/nonmembers, $75/members, published in even–numbered years in February. Reports the results of about 50 salary surveys.

Use the scientific method and read chapters 1 and 2 first

Chemistry

Also see listings under "Engineers" in this chapter.

Job ads

Chemical & Engineering News (American Chemical Society, (American Chemical Society, Department L–0011, Columbus, OH 43210; phones: 800/333–9511, 800/227–5558) weekly, call for rates. "Classifieds" contain around 25 to 30 private sector positions as another 25 to 30 positions in academia. That address is not a typographical error.

Chemical Engineering (McGraw–Hill, P.O. Box 440, Hightstown, NJ 08520; phones: 800/257–9402, 609/426–7070) monthly, $29.50/annual subscription (U.S.), $35.50/Canada, call for rates to other countries. You'll find 15 to 20 vacancies for chemical, process, mechanical, and environmental engineers under "Employment Opportunities."

Clinical Laboratory News (American Association for Clinical Chemistry, 2101 L St., NW, Suite 202, Washington, DC 20037; phones: 800/892–1400, 202/857–0717) monthly, $30/annual nonmember subscription, free/members. About six positions for clinical chemists and clinical laboratory personnel are printed under "Classified." "Positions Wanted" ads also appear.

Job services

Year–Round Professional Data Bank (American Chemical Society, 1155 16th St., NW, Washington, DC 20036; phone: 800/227–5558, press code 3 and then 1) free/members only. Complete the "Professional Information Summary Form" which is then entered into ACS's *Professional Data Bank*. When a job match is made, your entry is sent to the employer who is responsible for contacting you. Each month all registrants' forms are sent to participating employers.

Confidential Employment Listing Service (American Chemical Society, 1155 16th St., NW, Washington, DC 20036; phone: 800/227–5558 press code 3 and then 1) $40/annual fee, members only. This is a part of the ACS's *Year–Round Professional Data Bank*. You provide a list of employers who should *not* receive your qualifications. Information about you that is sent to employers does not include your name or other personal information. Interested employers contact ACS which then contacts you. If you are interested, you contact the employer.

American Association for Clinical Chemistry Employment Service (AACC, Suite 202, 2101 L St., NW, Washington, DC 20037; phones: 800/892–1400, 202/857–0717) $65/annual nonmember fee, $40/members; add $25 for AACC to type your form for you. You complete the AACC "Candidate

Registration Form" which is then placed in the AACC's *Resume Book* which is distributed to over 100 employers at AACC's annual national conference as well as throughout the year. Interested employers contact you directly. Interviewing is available at the annual conference which is held at the end of July. In addition, registrants receive the AACC *Jobs Packet* which gives details on up to 150 job openings for clinical laboratory professionals at all levels. Between August and July you will be sent new position postings as AACC receives them. You can register online via the Internet URL: **http://www.aacc.org** and submit your resume online. If this service is not listed on the home page yet, select "What's New" and you'll find the spot at which to register online.

Chemistry & Industry Magazine Job Search is located on the Internet at URL: **http://ci.mond.org/jobs/home.html**. Select "Search" to access the job database where there are hundreds of positions for chemists advertised. You can search posted jobs by keyword. This site also includes a job-matching service which you can access by clicking on "Sign Up." You are contacted when a match is made and are responsible for contacting the employer.

Salary surveys

Salaries (American Chemical Society, Membership Services, P.O. Box 9389, Minneapolis, MN 55440–9389; phones: 800/800/227–5558) $150, 150 to 200 pages, published in early autumn. Results of salary survey of ACS members by education, type of employer, experience, and many other criteria.

Starting Salaries of Chemists and Chemical Engineers (American Chemical Society, Membership Services, P.O. Box 9389, Minneapolis, MN 55440–9389; phones: 800/800/227–5558) $29.95, 90 pages, published in December. Reports on salaries for new graduates in chemistry and chemical engineering by degree earned.

Engineers

Also see entries under "Chemistry" and "Physics" in this chapter.

Job ads

Prism (American Society for Engineering Education, Suite 600, 1818 N Street, NW, Washington, DC 20036; phone: 202/331–3500) nine issues/year, $75/annual nonmember subscription, free/members. Around 30 to 75 vacancies in private industry and academia are published under "Classified."

Use the scientific method and read chapters 1 and 2 first

Minority Engineer (Equal Opportunity Publications, Suite 200, 1160 E. Jericho Turnpike, Huntington, NY 11743; phone: 516/421–9421) three issues/year, $17/annual subscription, free/minority engineering professionals and minority college students within two years of graduation (must complete detailed form). Around 20 to 30 vacancies for engineers are scattered throughout.

Woman Engineer (Equal Opportunity Publications, Suite 200, 1160 Jericho Turnpike, Huntington, NY 11743; phone: 516/421–9421) three issues/year, $17/annual subscription. Over 20 display ads throughout this magazine feature positions in all areas of engineering.

SWE Magazine (Society of Women Engineers, 120 Wall Street, New York, NY 10005; phone: 212/509–9577) bimonthly, $30/nonmember annual subscription, free/members. Ten to 25 ads for all types of engineers appear under "Classified/Recruitment Advertising," mostly academic positions.

The Career Engineer (National Society of Black Engineers, 1454 Duke St., P.O. Box 25588, Alexandria, VA 22313–5588; phone: 703/549–2207) monthly, $30/nonmember annual subscription, free/members. Scattered throughout the typical issue are 20 to 25 job adds for engineers of all types.

NSBE Magazine (National Society of Black Engineers, 1454 Duke St., P.O. Box 25588, Alexandria, VA 22313–5588; phone: 703/549–2207) five issues/year; $20/nonmember annual subscription, included in membership package. Forty engineering positions are advertised in every issue including college and university teaching positions.

Nuclear News (American Nuclear Society, 555 N. Kensington Ave., La Grange Park, IL 60526; phone: 708/352–6611) 13 issues/year, $88/nonmember annual subscription. "Employment" runs about 10 job vacancy announcements for nuclear engineers, quality assurance engineers, and mechanical engineers.

Chemical Engineering Progress (American Institute of Chemical Engineers, 345 E. 47th St., New York, NY 10017; phone: 212/705–8100) monthly, $85/annual nonmember subscription (U.S.), $140/foreign, free/members. Between 70 and 90 job ads for chemical engineers grace the "Classified Advertising." In even–numbered years, one of the summer issues contains a synopsis of the *AIChE Salary Survey Report*, described below under "Salary surveys."

InTech (Instrument Society of America, 67 Alexander Dr., Research Triangle Park, NC 27709; phone: 919/549–8411) monthly, free, available only to members. "Special Classifieds" include 5 to 10 job ads for engineers.

Engineers

Microwaves and RF (Penton Publications, Subscriptions, P.O. Box 96732, Chicago, IL 60693; phone: 216/931–9188) 13 issues/year, $75/annual subscription, free to qualified professionals. Three to ten display ads for engineers, primarily in microwave technology and instrumentation (some management) appear throughout.

Advanced Materials and Processes (ASM International, 9639 Kinsman, Materials Park, OH 44073–0002; phone: 216/338–5151) monthly, $150/annual nonmember subscription (U.S.), $175/foreign, free/members. From ten to 20 ads for metallurgists and materials engineers — including academic positions — are under "Classified." Includes positions wanted. Job ads are also available at their home page at URL: http://**www.asm-intl.org**.

ASME News (American Society of Mechanical Engineers, 22 Law Drive, Fairfield, NJ 07007; phones: 800/843–2763, 212/705–7722) monthly, free, available only to members. Around two positions for mechanical engineers appear in "Opportunities."

The Environmental Engineer (American Academy of Environmental Engineers, Suite 100, 130 Holiday Ct., Annapolis, MD 21401; phone: 410/266–3311) quarterly, $20/annual subscription (U.S. and Canada), $30/elsewhere. Typical issue features two to four display ads for jobs.

Cost Engineering (American Association of Cost Engineers International, Suite 100, 209 Prairie Ave., Morgantown, WV 26505; phones: 800/858–2678, 304/296–8444) monthly, $52/nonmember annual subscription, free/members. Scattered throughout are four to eight ads for cost engineers, control managers, and cost estimators and controllers. Members only can view job vacancies on the Internet at URL: **http://www.aacei.org** by selecting "Employment."

Job services

ENR Web Site (McGraw–Hill, P.O. Box 518, Hightstown, NJ 08520; phones: 800/257–9402, 212/512–3549) free. Go to Internet URL: **http://www.enr.com** and select "Find a Job" to access ENR's database of 200 to 400 engineering positions. About 10 percent of the jobs are in education and non–profits.

SAE Resume Database (SAE International: The Engineering Society for Advancing Mobility Land Sea Air and Space, 400 Commonwealth Dr., Warrendale, PA 15096; phone: 412/776–4841, ext. 369) $30/nonmember fee for three months, free/members. The job candidate completes the service's "Resume Database System" information form. To avoid tipping off your current employer that you are looking for another job, you can check a box on the form so your resume will not be released to your present employer. Computer matching is done by Resumé Link, a specialist in electronic job–matching systems. Employers subscribe to this database

Use the scientific method and read chapters 1 and 2 first

system and are able to search it by over 40 search criteria. When you are matched to a job, your resume form is faxed to the prospective employer, who is responsible for contacting the job seeker for an interview. Among the thousands of job candidates listed are mechanical, civil, electrical, aeronautical, and chemical engineers, plus physicists, chemists, and others who work closely with engineers.

Society of Women Engineers Resume Database (Society of Women Engineers, 120 Wall Street, New York, NY 10005; phone: 212/509–9577) $100/nonmember annual fee, $30/nonmember students, free/members. Request the "SWE Resume Referral Service Information Form," complete it and submit it with your payment. To avoid tipping off your current employer that you are looking for another job, you can check a box on the form so your resume will not be released to your present employer. Computer matching is done by Resumé Link, a specialist in electronic job-matching systems. When you are matched to a job, your resume form is faxed to the prospective employer. This job-matching service checks with you every six months to update your resume.

ASM International Resume Database (ASM International, 9639 Kinsman, Materials Park, OH 44073–0002; phone: 216/338–5151) $50/nonmember annual fee, $15/nonmember students, free/members. Request the "ASM Resume Referral Service Information Form," complete it and submit it with your payment. To avoid tipping off your current employer that you are looking for another job, you can check a box on the form so your resume will not be released to your present employer. Computer matching is done by Resumé Link, a specialist in electronic job-matching systems. When you are matched to a job, your resume form is faxed to the prospective employer. This job-matching service checks with you every six months to update your resume.

Resume Referral Service (Instrument Society of America, 67 Alexander Dr., Research Triangle Park, NC 27709; phone: 919/549–8411) free/members only. The resume service form you complete is kept on file for three months. When a match is achieved, you are contacted. Positions included are engineers and technicians.

AIChE Resume Referral Service (American Institute of Chemical Engineers, 345 E. 47th St., New York, NY 10017; phone: 212/705–7525) $150/nonmember six-month fee, $25/nonmember students, free/members. Request the "AIChE Resume Referral Service Information Form," complete it and submit it with your payment. To avoid tipping off your current employer that you are looking for another job, you can check a box on the form so your name will not be released to your present employer. Computer matching is done by Resumé Link, a specialist in electronic job-matching systems. When you are matched to a job, your resume form is faxed to the prospective employer. You should write for AIChE's short booklet called *AIChE Career Services for Chemical Engineers* which describes additional job services for AIChE members.

Materials Research Society Resume Database (Materials Research Society, c/o Resumé Link, P.O. Box 218, Hilliard, OH 43026; phone: 614/777–4000) $100/nonmember annual fee, $25/nonmember students, free/members. Request the "MRS Resume Referral Service Information Form," complete it and submit it with your payment. To avoid tipping off your current employer that you are looking for another job, you can check a box on the form so your resume will not be released to your present employer. Computer matching is done by Resumé Link, a specialist in electronic job–matching systems. When you are matched to a job, your resume form is faxed to the prospective employer. This job–matching service checks with you every six months to update your resume.

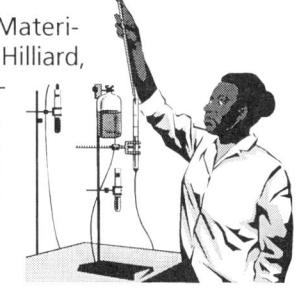

TMS Resume Database (Minerals, Metals, and Materials Society, 420 Commonwealth Dr., Warrendale, PA 15086; phone: 412/776–9080) $100/nonmember annual fee, $25/nonmember students, free/members. Request the "TMS Resume Referral Service Information Form," complete it and submit it with your payment. To avoid tipping off your current employer that you are looking for another job, you can check a box on the form so your resume will not be released to your present employer. Computer matching is done by Resumé Link, a specialist in electronic job–matching systems. When you are matched to a job, your resume form is faxed to the prospective employer. This job–matching service checks with you every six months to update your resume.

ASEE Prism (American Society for Engineering Education, Suite 600, 1818 N St., Washington, DC 20036; phone: 202/331–3500) nine issues/year, free/members only. Jobs are mostly in academia for faculty and research positions. Depending on the season the number of vacancies can range from 20 to 200; a good month of the year is December. These vacancies prior to publication can be viewed on the Internet at URL: **http://www.asee.org/asee/**. Select "ASEE Publications," then "ASEE Prism," and finally "Positions Open," where you can search or choose.

OPTICS.ORG (International Society for Optical Engineering, P.O. Box 10, Bellingham, WA 98227–0010; phone: 360/676–3290) free. Go to Internet URL: **http://optics.org/** and select "Employment Center" and then "Find a Job" to access the job database. Updated monthly, there are close to 40 jobs, including teaching and research positions, in optics, optoelectronics, lasers, holography, research and development, and related fields.

You can place your resume in the resume database which employers search directly (hence you cannot protect yourself from your current employer finding you), at the Internet site by selecting "Post a Resume." You must submit your resume electronically at this site. It will be kept in the resume database for two months.

Use the scientific method and read chapters 1 and 2 first

Placement Exchange (International Society for Optical Engineering, P.O. Box 10, Bellingham, WA 98227–0010; phone: 360/676–3290) free. Submit your resume to be put in resume books available to employers at SPIE's symposia. Jobs, including faculty and research positions, are in optics, optoelectronics, lasers, holography, research and development, and related fields.

American Association of Cost Engineers International Resume Service (AACE, Suite 100, 209 Prairie Ave., Morgantown, WV 26505; phones: 800/858–2678, 304/296–8444) free/members only. A member submits his resume which is kept in the database for six months. When a match is made, the resume is given to the potential employer who is responsible for contacting the job candidate.

Directories

ASCE Membership Directory (American Society of Civil Engineers, P.O. Box 831, Somerset, NJ 08875; phone: 800/548–2723) $100/nonmembers, $25/members, 1,060 pages, published early in odd–numbered years. Gives contact information on over 140,000 civil engineers.

Who's Who in Engineering (American Association of Engineering Societies, Suite 608, 1111 19th St., NW, Washington, DC 20036–3690; phones: 800/658–8897, 202/296–2237) $225/nonmembers, $140/members, 1,026 pages, 1995. Includes biographies of more than 15,000 engineers listed alphabetically with geographic and specialization indices.

International Directory of Engineering Societies and Related Organizations (American Association of Engineering Societies, Suite 608, 1111 19th St., NW, Washington, DC 20036–3690; phones: 800/658–8897, 202/296–2237) $190/nonmembers, $130/members. 350 pages, 1996. Provides information on over 1,270 engineering and technical organizations in the U.S. and overseas including publications, and organizational objective. Indexed by organization in English and native languages, as well as by acronyms, engineering disciplines, and geographic region.

The Biotechnology Directory (Stockton Press, 345 Park Avenue South, New York, NY 10010; phones: 800/221–2123 (outside New York state), 212/689–9200) $275 plus $6/shipping, published every November. Includes the often hard–to–find government departments engaged in biotechnology as well as over 7,000 companies, research centers, and academic institutions involved in the field.

ASEE's Directory of Engineering Graduate Studies and Research (American Society for Engineering Education, Suite 600, 1818 N St., Washington, DC 20036; phone: 202/331–3500) $70/nonmembers, $35/members and students, issued each September. Lists schools by type of program, dean's names, address, phone number, accredited or not, and specific types of engineering.

Engineers

ASEE's Directory of Engineering Studies and Research Undergraduate Programs (American Society for Engineering Education, Suite 600, 1818 N St., Washington, DC 20036; phone: 202/331–3500) $50/nonmembers, $25/members and students, issued each September. Lists schools by type of program, dean's names, address, phone number, accredited or not, and specific types of engineering.

Directory of Undergraduate Programs in Engineering and Engineering Technology (American Society for Engineering Education, Suite 200, 11 Dupont Cr., Washington, DC 20036; phone: 202/986–8500) $49.95/nonmembers, $24.95/members and students, plus $3 shipping, annual. Lists school information by type of program and specific types of engineering.

Salary surveys

Annual Salary Survey by Engineering Manpower Consortium (American Society of Mechanical Engineers, 22 Law Drive, Fairfield, NJ 07007; phones: 800/843–2763, 212/705–7782) annual, free/members only.

ASCE Salary Survey (American Society of Civil Engineers, 1801 Alexander Bell Dr., Reston, VA 20191; phone: 703/295–6000) $32/nonmembers, $24/members, 96 pages, 1995. Reports on salaries of civil engineers by location and other factors.

AIChE Salary Survey Report (American Institute of Chemical Engineers, 345 E. 47th St., New York, NY 10017; phone: 212/705–7523) $100/nonmembers, $50/members, 66 pages, published in June of even–numbered years. A synopsis is included in a summer issue of *Chemical Engineering Progress* described above under "Job ads."

Engineers: A Quarterly Bulletin on Careers in the Profession (American Association of Engineering Societies, Suite 608, 1111 19th St., NW, Washington, DC 20036–5703; phones: 800/658–8897, 202/296–2237) $25/nonmember annual subscription, $15/members, $8/nonmember single issue, $5/members, published quarterly. Offers detailed, timely articles and data on trends in engineering salaries, employment, enrollments, degrees, and women and minorities in the profession.

Salaries of Engineers in Education (American Association of Engineering Societies, Suite 608, 1111 19th St., NW, Washington, DC 20036–5703; phones: 800/658–8897, 202/296–2237) $120/nonmembers, $75/members, 100 pages, published in July of even–numbered years. Details the median, quartile, decile, and mean salaries of engineers in educational institutions, quantified by academic rank, length of contract, and years of experience.

Engineers' Salaries: Special Industry Report (American Association of Engineering Societies, Suite 608, 1111 19th St., NW, Washington, DC 20036–5703; phones: 800/658–8897, 202/296–2237) $927.50/nonmembers, $174/members, 230 pages, published each July. Extremely detailed

Use the scientific method and read chapters 1 and 2 first

breakdown of engineering salaries according to industry type and geographic location, company size, years of experience, highest degree held, and supervisory status.

Professional Income of Engineers (American Association of Engineering Societies, Suite 608, 1111 19th St., NW, Washington, DC 20036–3690; phones: 800/658–8897, 202/296–2237) $120/nonmembers, $75/members, 190+ pages, published annually in July. This is an abridged version of *Engineers' Salaries: Special Industry Report* without the detailed breakdowns of salary differences based on education.

American Association of Cost Engineers International Salary Survey (AACE, Suite 100, 209 Prairie Ave., Morgantown, WV 26505; phones: 800/858–2678, 304/296–8444) $7.50, published in autumn of odd–numbered years. This salary and demographic survey is based on the input of 1,400 cost professionals.

Mathematics

Job ads

AMSTAT News (American Statistical Association, 1429 Duke St., Alexandria, VA 22314–3402; phone: 703/684–1221) monthly, $45/nonmember annual subscription, free/members. The number of job ads for statisticians, biostatisticians, and educators that are printed in "Professional Opportunities" typically varies between 30 and 100.

Employment Information in the Mathematical Sciences (American Mathematical Society, PO Box 6248, Providence, RI 02904; phones: 800/321–4267, 401/455–4000) published monthly in October through January and in March, $105/annual subscription, $45/student or unemployed. Dozens upon dozens of job vacancies for mathematics–related positions for Ph.D. level mathematicians in universities and research centers. Even more voluminous listings of job vacancies can be found on the Internet at URL: **http://www.ams.org/**, and selecting "Professional Information and Services," then "Employment Information and Services." Then you have a choice of "Employment Listings" and "Post–Doctoral Listings."

SIAM News (Society for Industrial and Applied Mathematics, 3600 University City Science Center, Philadelphia, PA 19104–2688; phone: 215/382–9800) eight issues/year, $24/annual nonmember subscription (U.S.), $30/foreign, free/members. Fifty to 60 job ads for mathematics and engineering professionals appear under "Professional Opportunities."These same ads appear on the Internet at URL: **http://www.siam.org/career.htm**, and selecting "Membership Information," then "SIAM News," and finally "Professional Opportunities."

Photocopying strictly prohibited

Jobs in Mathematics is an Internet site where you can find jobs and internships. Go to URL: **http://www.cs.dartmouth.edu/~gdavis/policy/jobmarket.html** and select "JobOpenings." Select "Jobs in Academia" for links to lots of sites where you can find positions in the academic world. Pick "Summer Internships" to discover links to summer positions.

Directory

Directory of Members (American Statistical Association, 1429 Duke St., Alexandria, VA 22314–3402; phone: 703/684–1221) $25/members only, published in May of 1997 and every three years thereafter. Includes contact information on members of the ASA, Biometric Society (Eastern and Western North American Regions), Institute of Mathematical Statistics, and Statistical Society of Canada.

Physics

Also see entries under "Engineers" in this chapter.

Job ads

Physics Today (American Institute of Physics, 500 Sunnyside Blvd., Woodbury, NY 11797–2999; phone: 800/344–6902) monthly, $69/annual nonmember subscription (U.S.), $84/ foreign, free/members. Over 80 percent of the 115 job openings advertised under "Information Exchange" are for teaching and research positions for physicists, engineers, and chemists.

The Physics Teacher (American Institute of Physics, 1 Physics Ellipse, College Park, MD 20740–3845; phone: 301/209–3322) monthly, nonmembers/contact for subscription rate, members/$79 annual subscription. Includes one to two teaching jobs in a typical issue.

Physics Job Announcements by Thread, an Internet site operated by the Los Alamos National Laboratory, offers more than 120 job listings for faculty and postdoctorates positions at universities and research labs. Go to URL: **http://www.XXX.lanl.gov/Announce/Jobs**, where you can browse for positions by title and geographic region, mostly U.S., but some international.

American Institute of Physics Career Services (AIP Career Services, 1 Physics Ellipse, College Park, MD 26740; phone: 301/209–3190) free. Go to Internet URL: **http://www.aip.org/careers/** and select "Access Job Opportunities." You have three choices for seeing non–profit sector positions: (1)

Use the scientific method and read chapters 1 and 2 first

"Industry, Government, Non–Profit, Other," (25 jobs listed), (2) "Bachelor Positions" (20 jobs listed), and (3) "Academic Positions" (100 listed). Job listings are updated every two or three days.

YSNjobs offers a database of physics positions that you have to download from its Internet site. Go to URL: **http://www.physics.uiuc.edu/ysn/httpd/htdocs/ysnarchive/joblist.html** and click on a specific issue to download the file.

Physics World Jobs is an Internet Job bank for physics jobs in institutions of higher learning and research centers worldwide. Go to URL: **http://www.iop.org/cgi-bin/Jobs/main**, and select "All Current Vacancies" for about 35 vacancies.

Accelerator Job Listings on the Web offers job postings for physicists as well as links to many laboratories. Go to Internet URL: **http://beam.slac.stanford.edu/www/library/definitions/jobs.html** where you can browse through dozens of job postings or search by job title, occupation, or employer. About 80 percent of the advertised positions are education or research.

AAS Job Register (American Astronomical Society, Suite 400, 2000 Florida Ave., NW, Washington, DC 20009; phone: 202/328–2010) monthly, free/members only. The entire issue is packed to the gills with ads for astronomy and astrophysicist positions with universities or laboratories. More job opportunities can be found at the society's Internet site at URL: **http://www.aas.org/JobRegister/aasjobs.html**. Select "Browse Page" to get a listing of some 40 to 50 jobs and fellowships.

Sky Watch '97 (Sky Publishing Corp., P.O. Box 9111, Belmont, MA 02178; phone: 617/864–7360) $3.95/U.S., 130 pages, published each September. Lists planetariums in the United States.

Job services

Employment Referral Service (Career Services Division, American Institute of Physics, 1 Physics Ellipse, College Park, MD 20740; phone: 301/209–3190), $25/year (U.S.), $35/foreign. Pay your fee and you'll receive the ERS' resume form which you complete and submit with one copy of your resume. Your resume will be kept on file for one year. Contact ERS for details on how this job-matching service works, including whether you can exclude certain organizations from accessing your resume. You also receive a one-year subscription to the monthly publication, *Career Opportunities*, which contains job announcements for physicists.

Physics Jobs On-Line is an Internet site that provides job listings and allows you to post a job wanted notice. Go to URL: **http://www.tp.umu.se/TIP-TOP/FORUM/JOBS**, and you'll get a listing of about 80 jobs in physics by connecting to listings of permanent jobs, postdoctoral opportunities, summer jobs, and internships. To post a "Jobs Wanted" announcement the job seeker must first register with a user name and password, which the site will tell you how to obtain.

Directories

American Physical Society Membership Directory (American Physical Society, American Institute of Physics, 1 Physics Ellipse, College Park, MD 20740–3844; phone: 301/209–3280), $50/nonmembers, free/members, 663 pages, published in December of odd–numbered years. Lists about 40,000 members.

Directory of the American Association of Physics Teachers (AAPT, 1 Physics Ellipse, College Park, MD 20740–3845; phone: 301/209–3322) free/members only, 240 pages, published in even–numbered years.

AAS Membership Directory (American Astronomical Society, Suite 400, 2000 Florida Ave., NW, Washington, DC 20009; phone: 202/328–2010) $20/nonmembers, free/members, 240 pages, issued each January. Lists more than 6,000 individual and corporate members.

Salary survey

Salary Report (American Institute of Physics, Education and Employment Statistics Division, 1 Physics Ellipse, College Park, MD 20740; phone: 301/209–3070) $15, published in April of odd–numbered years. Salary and benefits are reported by location, employment sector, gender, experience, and degree.

Utilities

For a much more extensive listing of job sources, see both the ***Government Job Finder*** *and the* ***Professional's Job Finder.***

Job ads

Public Utilities Fortnightly (Public Utilities Reports, Inc., Suite 401, 8229 Boone Blvd., Vienna, VA 22182; phone: 703/847–7720) bimonthly, $177/annual subscription. Includes a few job ads.

APGA Newsletter (American Public Gas Association, Suite 102, 11094–D Lee Hwy, Fairfax, VA 22030; phone: 703/352–3890) biweekly, free/members only. Jobs listed under "Position Available." Few job ads; job ads not in every issue.

Use the scientific method and read chapters 1 and 2 first

Chapter 28

Social sciences

Social sciences

Also see the "Housing, planning, and development" chapter and the "Education" chapter.

Job ads

Anthropology Newsletter (American Anthropological Association, Suite 640, 4350 N. Fairfax Dr., Arlington, VA 22203; phone: 703/528–1902) nine issues/year, $55/annual subscription, free/members. "Placement" runs around 15 to 80 ads for faculty and research positions. The largest number of ads appear in the fall. These ads can also be found on the Internet at URL: **http://www.ameranthassn.org** and clicking on "Career Placement."

SAA Bulletin (Society for American Archaeology, Suite 12, 900 2nd Street, NE, Washington, DC 20002; phone: 202/789–8200) five issues/year, $30/institutional subscription, free/members only, annual dues: $110, $50/students. About six ads for archaeologists and anthropologists, usually with preservation agencies, are listed under "Positions Open." You can view these ads on the Internet at URL: **http://www.sscf.ucsb.edu/SAABulletin/**. Select "View the most recent issue" and then click on "Positions Open" from the numbered list. You can also view ads from previous issues.

Practicing Anthropology (Society for Applied Anthropology, P.O. Box 24083, Oklahoma City, OK 73124; phone: 405/843–5113) quarterly, $30/nonmember annual subscription (U.S.), $35/foreign, free/members. Two or three display ads for anthropologists and sociologists are in the typical issue.

SFAA Newsletter (Society for Applied Anthropology, P.O. Box 24083, Oklahoma City, OK 73124; phone: 405/843–5113) quarterly, free/members only. Four or five display ads for anthropologists and sociologists are in the typical issue.

History News Dispatch (American Association for State and Local History, Suite 600, 530 Church St., Nashville, TN 37219–2325; phone: 615/255–2971) monthly, $50/members only. About 20 to 35 ads for historians, archivists, and educators appear under "The Marketplace." Includes positions with historical societies, historic sites, libraries, archives, and museums.

Personnel Service Newsletter (American Political Science Association, 1527 New Hampshire Ave., NW, Washington, DC 20036; phone: 202/483–2512) monthly, $35/members only. Each issue has 25 or more job vacancies in political science. Most positions are for faculty and researchers.

Employment Bulletin (American Sociological Association, 1722 N St., NW, Washington, DC 20036; phone: 202/833–3410) monthly, $30/nonmember annual subscription, $10/members. This newsletter features about 70 positions in academic, applied, and fellowship settings. Most positions are in sociology, but also related areas such as anthropology and criminology.

The Rural Sociologist (Rural Sociological Society, c/o Rabel J. Bundge, Treasurer, Department of Sociology, Room 510, Arentzen Hall, Western Washington University, Bellingham, WA 98225–9081; phone: 360/650–7521) quarterly, $18/annual nonmember subscription, free/members. "Announcements" carries two or three positions for faculty and researchers. "Grants and Fellowships" includes announcements for four or five opportunities.

Job services

Placement Service (American Anthropological Association, 4350 N. Fairfax Dr., Suite 640, Arlington, VA 22203; phone: 703/528–1902) $110/nonmember annual fee, $35/members. There are three aspects to this service. First, you will receive a small newsletter with all the job ads that will appear three weeks later in the *Anthropology Newsletter* described above under "Job ads." Second, you are requested to complete a short resume form which is sent to prospective employers prior to the AAA's annual convention in late autumn. Interested employers will contact you to arrange an interview at the annual meeting. Third, you are sent a list of job openings from employers who will be interviewing at the annual meeting. You may contact them to arrange an interview there.

Check out chapters 1 and 2 first

Dial-a-Job and *Dial-an-Internship* (National Association for Interpretation, P.O. Box 1892, Ft. Collins, CO 80522; 303/491–6434) Call 303/491–7410 24 hours a day for a recording of full–time, seasonal, and temporary jobs in environmental education, interpretation, and related fields including historians, archaeologists, museum personnel, and publication designers. The tape runs from 10 to 30 minutes. Updated weekly. For internships, call 303/491–6784 24 hours a day. The tape runs from 5 to 20 minutes. Updated weekly.

Directories

AAA Guide (American Anthropological Association, Suite 640, 4350 N. Fairfax Dr., Arlington, VA 22203; phone: 703/528–1902) $50/nonmembers, $35/members, 588 pages, annual each September. Lists universities, museums, and departments of anthropology in the U.S. and Canada by faculties and specialties, facilities and programs, and information on financial support.

Directory of Historical Organizations, Societies, and Agencies in the United States and Canada (Sage Publications, 2455 Teller Rd., Thousand Oaks, CA 91320; phone: 805/499–9774) call for price, scheduled for publication in summer of 1997. Includes history–related organizations with brief descriptions of staff.

Directory of Members (American Society for Eighteenth–Century Studies) is an online directory on the Internet at URL: **http://www.press.jhu.edu/associations/asecs/**. Click on "Membership" and then "Membership Directory." You must be a member and have your log–in name and password to access this directory. There is an online registration form you can fill out. The directory is updated continuously and lists some 2,500 professors and scholars in the U.S. and abroad.

APSA Directory of Members (American Political Science Association, 1527 New Hampshire Ave., NW, Washington, DC 20036; phone: 202/483–2512) $55/nonmembers, $35/members, 759 pages, triannual, 1997. Lists some 13,000 political scientists.

Grants for Social and Political Science Programs (The Foundation Center, 79 Fifth Ave., New York, NY 10003–3076; phones: 800/424–9836, within New York State call 212/620–4230) $75 plus $4.50/shipping, 198 pages, published in October of odd–numbered years. Describes recent foundation grants of at least $10,000 for research and education in political science, sociology, anthropology, psychology, economics, behavioral science, population studies, international studies, ethnic studies, women's studies, urban and rural studies, poverty studies, and law. This directory is useful for identifying foundations and grant recipients for which you may wish to work.

Please do not photocopy

Social sciences

Archeological Field Work Opportunities Bulletin (Kendell/Hunt Publishing Co., 4050 Westmark Dr., Dubuque, IA 52004; phones: 800/228–0810, 319/589–1000) $15/nonmembers, $13/members of the Archeological Institute of America; published each December. Gives site, period, date of excavation and field school, application deadline, credits, institutions offering credit, experience required, financial aid, all costs, and volunteer requirements for thousands of digs throughout the U.S. and the world. This is a tremendous resource for contacts in the archeological community.

Archeological Field Work Opportunities is a wonderful Internet networking tool which provides you valued contacts with every major archeological department in academia. Go to URL: **http://durendal.cit.corned.edu**, and click on anyplace on the world map graphic or on the list of archeological digs to get a detailed discussion and fabulous photos of each archeological site in the U.S. and around the world, plus information on the opportunities for volunteers or for field school enrollment.

Salary survey

APSA Survey of Political Science Departments (American Political Science Association, 1527 New Hampshire Ave., NW, Washington, DC 20036; phone: 202/483–2512) $20, annual. Gives salary information and enrollment trends of four-year institutions offering political science.

Check out chapters 1 and 2 first

Chapter 29

Social services

Social services

*Also see the job sources described in this book's "Health care" chapter, the **Government Job Finder's** "Social services" and "Public health and health care" chapters, and in the **Professional's Job Finder's** "Social services" and "Health care" chapters.*

Job ads

NASW News (National Association of Social Workers, Suite 700, 750 First St., NE, Washington, DC 20002; phone: 800/638–8799) 10 issues/year, $25/nonmember subscription, included in membership package. Jobs listed under "The Classifieds." The typical issue is filled to the brim with over 200 job ads in the arenas of social work, human services, mental health, public health, and social services.

Human Services & Liberal Arts Careers (KB Enterprise/NHSE, 13137 Penndale Ln., Fairfax, VA 22033; phone: 703/378–0439) weekly, $42/six consecutive issues, $45/six issues every other week, $60/12 consecutive issues, $65/12 issues every other week; contact for rates for longer periods of time. From 250 to 330 short descriptions of job openings appear in every issue. The jobs listed are paid ads from employers, come from the Sunday edition of leading newspapers across the country, and Internet postings. The vast majority of the positions advertised are for social workers, thera-

Social services

pists, child care, and other social service positions. Most positions require only a few years experience or are entry level. A large percentage of the jobs is for positions in the non–profit sector.

Social Service Jobs (Employment Listings for Social Services, 10 Angelica Dr., Framingham, MA 01701; phone: 508/626–8644) biweekly, $42/six issues, $62/twelve issues, $118/annual subscription. Typical issue features 140+ positions listed by geographic region.

Social Work and Social Services Jobs Online (George Warren Brown School of Social Work, Washington University) offers hundreds of positions for free via the Internet. Go to URL: **http://www.gwbssw.wustl.edu/~gwbhome/jobs/swjobs.html** and select "Jobs Database." You can search by state or browse. Also check out the links by selecting "Job Resources Links," which gets you to home pages of social service organizations that offer more jobs.

TFA Employment Opportunities Bulletin (email address only: RBWEINSTOCK@gallua.gallaudet.edu) irregular, free, delivered only by email. Each emailing features offerings of three to 15 positions in human services, sign language interpreting, social work, counseling, psychology, school administration, teaching, and other areas of working with people who are deaf or hard of hearing.

Professional Opportunities Bulletin (Association Jewish Family and Children's Agencies, Suite 11, 3086 State Highway 27, Kendall Park, NJ 08824; phones: 800/634–7346, 908/821–0909) bimonthly, free. Each issue lists vacancies for social workers, family and childrens' services, family and children therapists, and group home staff for agencies in the Association's network. Includes executive director, senior management, and direct client contact positions.

FSA Today (Family Service America, Inc., 11700 W. Lake Park Dr., Milwaukee, WI 53224; phone: 414/359–1040) monthly, $25/six–month subscription, free/members. Each issue under "Management Opportunities" has job ads for management positions in social work including executive directors. This organization also has services that consist of a resume critique ($25/nonmembers, free/members) and CEO candidate consultation ($100/nonmembers, free/members). Call for further details.

Job Opportunities Bulletin (National Collaboration for Youth, Suite 601, 1319 F St., NW, Washington, DC 20004; phone: 202/347–2080) monthly, $2/issue nonmembers, free/members, purchase only by issue, no subscription available. Each issue includes 30+ job ads for administrative, executive, financial, and youth coordinator positions in youth development agencies.

Job Opportunities in the National Assembly Network (The National Assembly, Suite 601, 1319 F St., NW, Washington, D.C. 20004; phone: 202/347–2080, email: Emcornell@aol.com) monthly, $5 individual issue/nonmembers, free/members. Lists 80 to 100 job opportunities from 50 social

Work your way to chapters 1 and 2 first

service agencies, including United Way of America, Family Service America, YMCA, YWCA, Volunteers of America, Catholic Charities USA, American Red Cross, and Travelers Aid International.

Directory of Internships in Youth Development (National Collaboration for Youth, Suite 601, 1319 F St., NW, Washington, DC 20004; phone: 202/347–2080) free, annual. This directory is available strictly on NCY's Internet site at URL: **http://www.nassembly.org/nonprofit**. Simply select "Internships" to get to this detailed listing of over 800 paid and unpaid internship opportunities in 244 youth-serving organizations in 43 states. Includes opportunities to work directly with young people such as counseling troubled youth, teaching skills, supervising recreational activities, child care, and conducting public relations and fund raising events.

Youth Today (American Youth Work Center, 1200 17th St., NW, Washington, DC 20036; phone: 202/785–0764) bimonthly, free. Nearly ten ads appear under "Classifieds — Job Opportunities" for all sorts of positions in youth work including organizers, management, camps, and outreach coordinators.

Job Exchange (Association for Education and Rehabilitation of the Blind, Suite 320, 206 N. Washington St., Alexandria, VA 22314; phone: 703/836–6060) monthly, available only to members: first six months free, $10/year thereafter. From 40 to 60 vacancies for administrators and practitioners (orientation and mobility specialists, teachers of persons with visual impairments, etc.) grace a typical issue.

Volta Voices (Alexander Graham Bell Association, 3417 Volta Place, NW, Washington, DC 20007; phone: 202/337–5220) bimonthly, $50/annual nonmember subscription, free/members. The "Classified" section carries ads for about ten positions for audiologists, teachers of persons with hearing impairments, interpreters, and administrators.

Volta Review (Alexander Graham Bell Association, 3417 Volta Place, NW, Washington, DC 20007; phone: 202/337–5220) five issues/year, $50/annual nonmember subscription, free/members and parents of a hearing-impaired child. The "Classified" section carries ads for about ten positions for audiologists, teachers of persons with hearing impairments, interpreters, and administrators.

American Annals of the Deaf (Kendall School, Outreach Services KDES–PAS–6, 800 Florida Ave., NE, Washington, DC 20002; phone: 202/651–5340) five issues/year, $50/annual subscription U.S.), $55/Canada, $65/elsewhere. One or two ads for teachers of children with hearing impairments appear as classifieds or display ads.

Counseling Today (American Counseling Association, 5999 Stevenson Ave., Alexandria, VA 22304–3300; phones: 800/633–4931 703/823–9800, ext. 222) monthly, $37/annual subscription (U.S.), $73/foreign. "Employment Classifieds" describe around 20 vacancies for psychologists and counselors in private practice, agencies, and universities.

Photocopying strictly prohibited

Social services

Journal of Psychiatric Services (American Psychiatric Association, 1400 K St., NW, Washington, DC 20005; phone: 202/682–6228) monthly, $45/annual subscription (U.S.), $65/foreign. Jobs listed under "Classified Advertising." Typical issue runs 25 to 65 job ads.

Special Recreation Digest (Special Recreation, Inc., 362 Koser Ave., Iowa City, IA 52246–3038; phone: 319/337–7578) quarterly, $39.95/annual subscription. Fifteen activity or recreation positions such as therapists, coordinators, and administrators appear under "Recreation."

The Counselor (National Association of Alcoholism and Drug Abuse Counselors, Suite 900, 1911 N. Fort Myer Dr., Arlington, VA 22209; phone: 703/741–7686) bimonthly, $42/nonmember annual subscription, free/members. Jobs listed under "Employment Classifieds." Typical issue features over 10 job ads, usually for upper level counselors with medical facilities.

With One Voice (Alliance for Rehabilitation Counseling, Suite 102, 8807 Sudley Rd., Manassas, VA 20110–4719; phone: 703/361–2077) bimonthly, free/members of the National Rehabilitation Counseling Association and of the American Rehabilitation Counseling Association. Jobs listed under "Job Openings." Some issues have no jobs listed. Few job ads.

AAMR News & Notes (American Association on Mental Retardation, Suite 846, 444 North Capitol St., NW, Washington, DC 20001–1512; phones: 800/424–3688, 202/387–1968) bimonthly, $40/annual subscription (U.S.), $46/Canada, $55/elsewhere, free/members. A typical issue lists five to 20 ads for administrators, direct care workers, psychologists, speech pathologists, and occupational therapists. Also check out job listings on the Internet at URL: **http://www.aamr.org**, and scroll down to "Career Opportunities."

Mental Retardation (American Association on Mental Retardation, Suite 846, 444 North Capitol St., NW, Washington, DC 20001–1512; phones: 800/424–3688, 202/387–1968) bimonthly, $89/nonmember annual subscription (U.S.), $95/Canada, $104/elsewhere. Jobs listed under "The Exchange." Five to 20 ads an issue.

TASH Newsletter (The Association for Persons with Severe Handicaps, Suite 210, 29 W. Susquehanna Ave., Baltimore, MD 21204; phones: 410/828–8274, **TDD**: 410/828–1306) 11 issues/ year, free/members only; individual issues available for $5/nonmembers. Job are not advertised in every issue. When included, about two to five jobs are listed under "Positions Open."

Family Therapy News (American Association for Marriage and Family Therapy, 1100 17th St., NW, Washington, DC 20036; phone: 202/452–0109) bimonthly, $35/nonmember annual subscription, $20/members. "Classified Ads" has about 25 openings for marriage and family therapists including practitioners, researchers, pastoral counselors, faculty, and practices for sale.

Work your way to chapters 1 and 2 first

Job Training and Placement Report (Joe Jones Publishing, P.O. Box 5000, Iola, WI 54945; phone: 715/445–5000) monthly, $129/annual subscription (U.S.), $139/foreign. 25 to 30 positions for professionals who train and place people with disabilities appear under "Position Openings." The number of job vacancies described in this relatively new section is increasing each month.

Medical Rehab Report (American Rehabilitation Association, Suite 200, 1910 Association Dr., Reston, VA 20191; phones: 800/368–3513, 703/648–9300) monthly, free/members only. Three to six job ads appear in a typical issue.

Rehabilitation Management Magazine (Curant Communications, Suite 202, 4676 Admiralty Way, Marina Del Rey, CA 90292; phone: 310/306–2206) bimonthly, free. Each issue features five or six display ads from employers as well as four pages of display ads from recruiters. Jobs are for managers and directors of rehabilitation facilities as well as for physical and occupational therapists.

Journal of Rehabilitation (National Rehabilitation Association, 633 S. Washington St., Alexandria, VA 22314; phone: 703/836–0850) quarterly, $50/annual subscription (U.S.), $60/Canada, $75/elsewhere, free/members. About ten openings are touted under "Classified."

Contemporary Rehab (National Rehabilitation Association, 633 S. Washington St., Alexandria, VA 22314; phone: 703/836–0850) eight issues/year, free/members only. Two to eight job openings are advertised under "Classified."

Contemporary Long-Term Care (Bill Communications, 355 Park Ave. South, New York, NY 10010; phone: 212/592–6200) monthly, $72/annual subscription (U.S.), $89.95/Canada, $185/elsewhere. The "Classifieds" runs ads for around 30 positions for administrators, managers, marketing, sales representatives, and nursing directors.

Personnel Bulletin (Evangelical Lutheran Church in America, 8765 W. Higgins Rd., Chicago, IL 60631; phone: 773/380–2690) monthly, $5/annual subscription. The entire issue is filled with about 25 job vacancies for administrators for nursing homes and hospitals, counselors, professors, and the whole gamut of social services. Employers are all affiliated with the Lutheran Church.

Long-Term Care Administrator (American College of Health Care Administrators, 325 S. Patrick St., Alexandria, VA 22314; phone: 703/739–7913) quarterly, $45/annual nonmember subscription, free/members. Two to five openings for long-term care administrators at nursing homes and hospices are advertised under "Professional Referral Service."

NAHC Report (National Association for Home Care, 227 Seventh St., SE, Washington, DC 20003; phone: 202/547–5277) weekly, $325/annual nonmember subscription, free/members. Two to ten ads for health care directors and supervisors appear under "Classifieds."

Photocopying strictly prohibited

Social services

Journal of Long-Term Care Administration (American College of Health Care Administrators, 325 S. Patrick St., Alexandria, VA 22314; phone: 703/739–7913) quarterly, $70/annual nonmember subscription, free/members. A display ad for nursing home administrators, directors of nursing, and medical directors makes it into an issue occasionally.

AAHSA Currents (American Association of Homes and Services for the Aging, Suite 500, 901 E Street, NW, Washington, DC 20004; phone: 202/783–2242) monthly, free/members only. "Job Mart" carries about ten ads for administrative positions with residential facilities for senior citizens plus five or six "Positions Wanted."

Aging Today (American Society on Aging, Suite 511, 833 Market St., San Francisco, CA 94103; phone: 415/882–2910) bimonthly, $30/annual nonmember subscription, free/members, $100/annual dues. Two to four display ads for positions in caring for older people are in a typical issue.

AEE Job's Clearinghouse (Association for Experiential Education, Suite 100, 2305 Canyon Blvd., Boulder, CO 80302; phone: 303/440–8844) monthly, $80/nonmember annual subscription, $40/members. Lists dozens of ads for outdoor therapists to work with troubled youths.

Job services

CU Career Connection (University of Colorado, Campus Box 133, Boulder, CO 80309–0133; phone: 303/492–4127) $30/four-month fee entitles you to a "passcode" which unlocks this job hotline. You need a touch-tone phone to call and request the field in which you are interested in hearing job openings. The hotline is turned off Monday through Friday, 1:00 a.m. to 4:30 a.m., for daily updating. Over 2,600 jobs are listed in the course of the year.

Job Bank (National Association of Activity Professionals, Suite 900, 1401 I St., NW, Washington, DC 20005; phone: 202/218–4120) free. Your resume is kept on file for a year. When a match is made, a copy is sent to the employer who is responsible for contacting you. Jobs include activity directors and their assistants, largely at nursing homes.

Directories

National Directory of Private Social Agencies (Croner Publications, Suite 1–D, 10951 Sorrento Valley Rd., San Diego, CA 92121; phones: 800/441–4033, 619/546–1894) $90 plus $9.95 shipping. Includes updates ten times a year. Lists more than 15,000 private social agencies: phone and hotline numbers, contact person, services provided, population served, locations where services provided, and more.

Work your way to chapters 1 and 2 first

Fund Raiser's Guide to Human Service Funding (Taft Group, 835 Penobscot Bldg., 645 Griswold St., Detroit, MI 48226–4094; phones: 800/877–8238, 313/961–2242) $130, 1,450 pages, annual. Over 1,850 funders of human service agencies are detailed in 33 different categories of human services. Included in each entry are the funders' human service priorities, grant types, types of recipients, names of officers and directors, application procedures, and a list of recent grants.

National Guide to Funding for Children, Youth, and Families (The Foundation Center, 79 Fifth Ave., New York, NY 10003–3076; phones: 800/424–9836, 212/620–4230) $150, 1,095 pages, published in April of odd–numbered years. Each of the 3,400 entries includes application information and a list of recent grants for child development, disadvantaged youth, family planning, homelessness, and many other concerns.

National Guide to Funding in Substance Abuse (The Foundation Center, 79 Fifth Ave., New York, NY 10003–3076; phones: 800/424–9836, 212/620–4230) $95, 238 pages, April 1995. Each of the 600+ entries includes application information and a list of recent grants awarded to non–profits engaged in fighting such substance abuse problems as alcohol and drug abuse, smoking addiction, and drunk driving.

Directory of Social Service Grants (Research Grant Guides, P.O. Box 1214, Loxahatchee, FL 33470; phone: 561/795–6129; no phone orders, fax orders to 561/795–7794) $59.50 prepaid plus $6 shipping and 6 percent sales tax for Florida residents, 164 pages, published in the summer of odd–numbered years. Profiles of more than 900 foundations that provide thousands of funding sources to non–profit social service organizations. Each profile lists address, area of support, geographic restrictions, and grant range.

Directory of Grants for Organizations Serving People with Disabilities (Research Grant Guides, P.O. Box 1214, Loxahatchee, FL 33470; phone: 561/795–6129; no phone orders, fax orders to 561/795–7794) $59.50 prepaid plus $6 shipping and 6 percent sales tax for Florida residents, 216 pages, published in the spring of odd–numbered years. Profiles of 847 foundations that provide 2,700 funding sources for disability programs. Each profile lists address, area of support, geographic restrictions, and grant range.

Funding in Aging: A Guide to Giving by Foundations, Corporations, and Charitable Organizations (The Foundation Center, 79 Fifth Ave., New York, NY 10003–3076; phones: 800/424–9836, 212/620–4230) $95, 294 pages, October 1996. Describes federal and state programs, private foundations, and corporations that support aging projects. Each of the 1,000 entries includes application information and a list of recent grants.

Directory of Member Agencies (Family Service America, 11700 W. Lake Park Dr., Milwaukee, WI 53224; phone: 414/359–1040) free/members only, issued each February. Presented by state, these are social service agencies that tend to employ social workers.

Photocopying strictly prohibited

Social services

American Public Welfare Directory (APWA, Suite 500, 810 First St., NE, Washington, DC 20002; phone: 202/682–0100) $80/nonmembers, $75/members, plus $5 shipping if not prepaid, published every August. Lists federal social service agencies, state and local social service agencies by state, Canadian provincial, and federal agencies.

Charities USA is a gateway Internet site, where you are sure to find among the 400 links to charitable organizations many social service organizations. Go to URL: **http://www.charitiesusa.com/**, and select among the following: Animal, Children, Christian Services, Conservation and Preservation, Education, Health, Human and Civil Rights, Human Service, Medical Research, Military & Veterans, Women, and World Service.

Directory of Experiential Therapy and Adventure–Based Counseling Programs (Association for Experiential Education, Suite 100, 2305 Canyon Blvd., Boulder, CO 80302; phone: 303/440–8844) $15/nonmembers, $12.50/members; add $4.50 shipping, 101 pages. This is a state–by–state listing of 257 adventure and experiential alternative organizations with programs for people with special needs which use adventure programming as part of their therapeutic process.

Directory of Therapeutic Adventure Professionals (Association for Experiential Education, Suite 100, 2305 Canyon Blvd., Boulder, CO 80302; phone: 303/440–8844) $15.50/nonmembers, $10/members; add $4.50 shipping, 135 pages, 1996. Lists 130 individuals who use adventure activities in therapeutic settings.

Experience–Based Training and Development: Directory of Programs (Association for Experiential Education, Suite 100, 2305 Canyon Blvd., Boulder, CO 80302; phone: 303/440–8844) $15/nonmembers, $12.50/members, 98 pages, 1997. Describes over 90 training and development programs in the U.S. and abroad.

Directory of Member Agencies (Child Welfare League of America, 3rd Floor, 440 First St., NW, Washington, DC 20001; phone: 202/638–2952) $35/nonmembers, free/members, 271 pages, published in the spring every other year. Lists some 900 member child welfare agencies: key contact names, addresses, telephone numbers, fax numbers.

Directory of Victim Assistance Programs (National Organization for Victim Assistance, 1757 Park Rd., NW, Washington, DC 20010–2101; phone: 202/232–6682) $50, 1997. Listings of thousands of victim assistance programs in the U.S. Also available on an IBM–formatted 3.5–inch floppy disk in Wordperfect.

National Organization for Human Service Education Membership Directory (NOHSE, c/o Dr. Maryanne Woodside, University of Tennessee, 533 Andy Holt Tower, Knoxville, TN 37996–0150; phone; 423/974–2268) free/members only, 45 pages, published in the spring of odd–numbered years. Lists more than 600 human service educators and practicitioners.

Work your way to chapters 1 and 2 first

National Directory for Elder Care Information and Referral (National Association of Area Agencies on Aging, Suite 100, 1112 16th St., NW, Washington, DC 20036; phone: 202/296–8130) $48, 171 pages, published in January of odd–numbered years. Lists 664 state and area agencies on aging as well as providers of services to elderly persons.

College and Career Programs for Deaf Students (Gallaudet Research Institute, 800 Florida Ave., NE, Washington, DC 20002; phone: 202/651–5575) $16.45, last edition 1995. Describes programs at colleges that provide services for deaf and hard of hearing persons.

Directory of Services for Blind and Visually Impaired Persons in the United States and Canada (American Foundation for the Blind, Suite 300, 11 Penn Plaza, New York, NY 10001; phone: 212/502–7600) $79.95/print edition plus $7/shipping, 550 pages, 1993, new edition in 1997; $100/CD-ROM plus $7/shipping, annual Lists details on over 3,000 local, state, regional, and national services including medical and research organizations, schools, clinics, rehabilitation services, and producers of alternate media and products for people with blindness.

Rehabilitation Source Book (American Rehabilitation Association, Suite 200, 1910 Association Dr., Reston, VA 20191; phones: 800/368–3513, 703/648–9300) $125, 450 pages, published every other January. Lists contact information for 6,000 rehabilitation facilities.

Senior Citizen Services (Gale Research, Inc., 835 Penobscot Bldg., Detroit, MI 48226; phone: 800/877–4253) $100/set of four volumes: Northeast, Southeast, Midwest, West; $40/each volume individually; 1993. Features information on 16,000 regional and local government and private agencies and organizations that furnish services for America's older citizens including adult day care, case management, respite care, and home delivered meals. A good source for identifying potential employers and learning about them.

The National Directory of Managed & Integrated Care Organizations (Managed Care Information Center, 3100 Highway 238, Wall Township, NJ 07719-1442; phones: 800/516–4343, 908/681–1133) $275 plus $7.50 shipping, annual. Lists over 1,850 managed care organizations and integrated care organizations, details on each organization's name and address, telephone and fax numbers, and key contacts. An electronic version on Windows™–formatted 3.5–inch floppy disk is available for $795 and with it you get a semiannual update.

Healthcare Blue Book (Blue Book's, 2100 Powers Ferry Rd., Atlanta, GA 30339; phones: 800/533–8484, 770/955–5656) $219.50, annual. Includes details on over 16,500 nursing homes and long–term care facilities with contact names of 63,000 key personnel, 2,000 ambulatory surgery centers with over 4,000 contact names, 9,000 home–care health agencies with over

Photocopying strictly prohibited

Social services

16,000 key contacts, over 1,600 hospices with over 2,600 key personnel, and 2,000 managed care providers (HMO, PPO, POS) with more than 5,000 contact names.

National Home Care and Hospice Directory (National Association for Home Care, 227 Seventh St., SE, Washington, DC 20003; phone: 202/547–5277) $135/nonmembers, $50/members, add $6/shipping, 912 pages, issued each winter. This directory lists the nation's home care and hospice providers by city and state as well as 18,500 home care providers including visiting nurse associations, homemaker–home health aide agencies, large chain providers, and HMO–based and for–profit agencies. It also includes the names, addresses, and phones for home care agency directors and an updated list of state associations in home care. Each entry includes the name of the executive director, types of services provided, and geographic area served.

Grants for Social Services (The Foundation Center, 79 Fifth Ave., New York, NY 10003–3076; phones: 800/424–9836, within New York State call 212/620–4230) $75 plus $4.50/shipping, 505 pages, published in October of odd–numbered years. Describes recent foundation grants of at least $10,000 to human service organizations for children's and youth services, family services, personal social services, emergency assistance, residential or custodial care, and services to promote the independence of specific population groups such as people who have developmental disabilities or persons who are homeless. This directory is useful for identifying foundations and grant recipients for which you may wish to work.

Grants for Aging (The Foundation Center, 79 Fifth Ave., New York, NY 10003–3076; phones: 800/424–9836, within New York State call 212/620–4230) $75 plus $4.50/shipping, 114 pages, published in October of odd–numbered years. Describes recent foundation grants of at least $10,000 for advocacy and legal rights, housing, education and community services, employment, health and medical care, recreation, arts and culture, volunteer services, and social research. This directory is useful for identifying foundations and grant recipients for which you may wish to work.

Grants for Alcohol & Drug Abuse (The Foundation Center, 79 Fifth Ave., New York, NY 10003–3076; phones: 800/424–9836, within New York State call 212/620–4230) $75 plus $4.50/shipping, 77 pages, published in October of odd–numbered years. Describes recent foundation grants of at least $10,000 for counseling, education, treatment, medical research, residential care, halfway houses, and programs on alcohol and drug abuse prevention. This directory is useful for identifying foundations and grant recipients for which you may wish to work.

Grants for Children & Youth (The Foundation Center, 79 Fifth Ave., New York, NY 10003–3076; phones: 800/424–9836, within New York State call 212/620–4230) $75 plus $4.50/shipping, 584 pages, published in October of odd–numbered years. Describes recent foundation grants of at least $10,000 to support neonatal care, child welfare, adoption, foster care, services for abused children, research on child development, pregnancy

Work your way to chapters 1 and 2 first

counseling and adolescent pregnancy prevention, prevention and rehabilitation of juvenile delinquency, and youth centers and clubs. This directory is useful for identifying foundations and grant recipients for which you may wish to work.

Grants for Physically & Mentally Disabled (The Foundation Center, 79 Fifth Ave., New York, NY 10003–3076; phones: 800/424–9836, within New York State call 212/620–4230) $75 plus $4.50/shipping, 198 pages, published in October of odd–numbered years. Describes recent foundation grants of at least $10,000 to schools, hospitals, and primary care facilities for research, medical and dental care, employment and vocational training, education, diagnosis and evaluation, recreation and rehabilitation, and legal aid. This directory is useful for identifying foundations and grant recipients for which you may wish to work.

Salary surveys

Residential Services and Developmental Disabilities in the United States (American Association on Mental Retardation, Suite 846, 444 North Capitol St., NW, Washington, DC 20001–1570; phones: 800/424–3688, 202/387–1968) $44.95 plus $4/shipping, 1992 (new edition scheduled for late 1997, call for availability and price). Reports on wages and benefits of direct care workers based on a study of over 1,000 public and private residential facilities by state.

Salaries and Benefits in Youth Development Agencies (National Collaboration for Youth, Suite 601, 1319 F St., NW, Washington, DC 20004; phone: 202/347–2080) $34.95, 106 pages, published each September. Includes salaries and benefits with non–profit agencies that serve children, youth, and their families.

Income and Compensation Salary Survey (National Association of Alcoholism and Drug Abuse Counselors, Suite 900, 1911 N. Fort Myer Dr., Arlington, VA 22209; phone: 703/741–7686) $50/nonmembers, $25/members, 76 pages, annual. Reports on counselor benefits and salaries by education and geographically.

Compensation Report on Management Employees in Hospital, Nursing Home, and Home Care Management Companies (Hospital & Healthcare Compensation Service, P.O. Box 376, Oakland, NJ 07436; phone: 201/616–5722) $485/prepaid plus $7.50/shipping, half price if purchased along with any other of this company's reports, published each January. Reports on salary and bonus payments for exempt management positions at nursing homes hospitals, and home care management companies nationally and by region.

Nursing Home Salary and Benefits Report (Hospital & Healthcare Compensation Service, P.O. Box 376, Oakland, NJ 07436; phone: 201/616–5722) $240 prepaid, 288 pages, annual in April. Reports on salary and bonus

Social services

payments for 25 management and 32 nursing, therapy, dietary, and clerical positions, both nationally and by nine regions. Includes 22 fringe benefits and bonus information.

Hospice Salary & Benefits Report (Hospital & Healthcare Compensation Service, P.O. Box 376, Oakland, NJ 07436; phone: 201/616–5722) $185 prepaid plus $7.50/shipping, published in October. Reports on salary and bonus payments for 67 management, nursing, therapy and clerical jobs according to auspices, revenue size, state, geographical region, and principal city. Includes data on fringe benefits and perquisites.

Home Care Salary & Benefits Report (Hospital & Healthcare Compensation Service, P.O. Box 376, Oakland, NJ 07436; phone: 201/616–5722) $240/prepaid plus $7.50/shipping, published every October. Reports on salary and bonus payments for 69 management, nursing, therapy, and clerical jobs according to five classifications: revenue size, states, geographical region, principal city, and nationally. Includes data on 19 fringe benefits and perquisites.

1995 Salary Survey (American Rehabilitation Association, Suite 200, 1910 Association Dr., Reston, VA 20191; phones: 800/368–3513, 703/648–9300) $150/nonmembers, $100/members, 144 pages. Covers more than 40 full–time positions common to medical, vocational, and residential facilities.

Salaries and Benefits in the Youth Development Field (The National Assembly, Suite 601, 1319 F St., NW, Washington, D.C. 20004; phone: 202/347–2080, email: Emcornell@aol.com) $33/nonmembers, $27/members, 84 pages, 1995. Survey of salaries, benefits, and minimum educational requirements for part–time and full–time youth development professionals in selected community–based agencies nationwide.

CWLA CEO Compensation and Benefits Study (Child Welfare League of America, 3rd Floor, 440 First St., NW, Washington, DC 20001; phone: 202/638–2952) $12.95, 1993. Detailed study of CEO salaries and benefit packages for child welfare agencies by state, metropolitan statistical area, type of agency, agency income, and size of agency staff.

CWLA Salary Survey (Child Welfare League of America, 3rd Floor, 440 First St., NW, Washington, DC 20001; phone: 202/638–2952) $34.95, 1995. Detailed survey of employment compensation levels at child welfare agencies.

Work your way to chapters 1 and 2 first

Chapter 30

Savvy job and grant sources for each state

In addition to using the job-search tools that focus on your profession, the savvy job seeker also uses resources geared strictly for finding non-profit and education jobs in the states or metropolitan areas where you want to work. You should, of course, look at the local classifieds — and thanks to the Internet you can get these online from about half the newspapers in the country. Fortunately, there are also a good many sources of job openings that are local, regional, or statewide in coverage that get you to the jobs the local classifieds never carry. This chapter explains what those job sources are, identifies them for each state and major metropolitan area, and introduces you to the free job bank that every state operates, but which few habitually-employed workers ever use. It also reports on directories of foundations and other funding sources.

Web sites with job listings for individual states have proliferated like crazy. Best of all, any job seeker now can dip into the job database that every state operates. As recently as 1995, you had to make like Blanche Dubois and depend on the kindness of strangers — namely the sometimes unfriendly employees at a state-run Job Service office — to get this information. Today, you can ask your computer, an inert object that is often

City and state job-finding tools

friendlier that some people who work at employment service offices, to do the searching for you. The Internet actually brings one of the most important parts of the Job Service office right into your home or office.

The job sources in this chapter include periodicals, job–matching services, job hotlines, online job and resume databases, salary surveys, and state directories of non–profit organizations and foundations. The scope of most of these job sources is broad: they cover everything in the non–profit sector rather than a single occupation.

City and state job-finding tools

State–operated Job Service offices. Perhaps the most underutilized "free lunch" ever offered to job seekers is the Job Service that every state government operates. Although the quality of their service varies widely, each Job Service office provides employment assistance that includes career counseling and a job database. Some also offer job–matching services.

Popularly known as the "unemployment office," a state Job Service office can put you in contact with job vacancies that range from low–paid and entry–level jobs to top–level positions.

Each Job Service office maintains a constantly updated list of job openings from throughout the state. The vast majority of states let you access this list via computer. You can usually obtain a full job description from the Job Service office for those positions that interest you.

The entries in this chapter note if a state's Job Service office also provides additional job search assistance such as job–matching services.

You should be able to find the address and phone number for a nearby Job Service office in your local telephone directory. In case you can't, this chapter offers information that enables you to locate each state's employment services, including Job Service offices, by mail, phone, or on the Internet. You should write or call directly for more information from the states of your choice. Please note that while most states call these "Job Services," some assign a different moniker like "Employment Security Department." So before you turn to your local phone directory to find the Job Service office nearest you, be sure to see the entry in this chapter for your state to learn what your state calls its Job Service offices. Dartmouth College maintains a list of the addresses and phone numbers for every Job Service office in the nation at Internet URL: **ftp://listserv–ftp.dartmouth.edu/pub/listserv/fedjobs/General/stateadr.txt**. Offices are listed by state. This is a very large file that takes a few minutes to load when you visit the site. It's worth the wait.

Every Job Service office participates in the U.S. Department of Labor's job database, **America's Job Bank**. Formerly called the *Interstate Job Bank*, this computerized network links the nation's 1,800 Job Service Offices with

By–pass the State of Confusion: Read chapters 1 and 2 first

a pool of at least 250,000 current job vacancies — ten percent of which are positions with non–profits and educational institutions. Nearly all allow job seekers to access this database from the Job Service office.

Today you can bypass the trip to a Job Service office and access this free database from your own computer by going to Internet URL: **http://www.ajb.dni.us**. In addition to the Internet, *America's Job Bank* is available on computer systems in public libraries, colleges, high schools, shopping malls, and other places of public access via a kiosk system with touch screens and on personal computers. Job openings include all types of work including technical, blue collar, professional, clerical, and management.

Using *America's Job Bank*, you can conduct a nationwide search three ways. Select "Menu Search" to conduct a self–directed job search in which you can seek vacancies by occupation and state, if desired. This type of search requires the use of an Internet browser that is compatible with HTML 3.0 such as Netscape Navigator version 2.0 or higher or Microsoft's Internet Explorer version 2.0 or higher. If you don't have a compatible browser you can still choose "Keyword Search" which will let you look for job titles by keyword. The third technique is the "Code Search" in which you search for vacancies by occupational code, DOT code, military code, or job number.

This Web site also contains links to the job banks of every state's Job Service offices, also called State Employment Services. If the URL for a state Job Service's job database listed in this chapter has changed, you should be able to find the new one at this site. Choose "Links to State Employment Service Web Sites."

You can also gain access to over 160 placement agencies by selecting "Links to Private Placement Agencies."

America's Job Bank also allows you to search through the **Occupational Outlook Handbook** which reports on long–term employment prospects in the 250 occupations that account for seven out of eight jobs in the U.S. The *OOH*, as it is affectionately called, includes information about each occupation such as usual work activities, earnings, and education and training requirements. The *Occupational Outlook Handbook* is also available in book form and is published in the early summer of even–numbered years ($18.95; available from the Job Search Resource Catalog at the end of this book).

The job database and job–matching services furnished by Job Service offices amount to a free employment service for professionals, technical, labor, trades, and office support workers. However, habitually–employed individuals rarely take advantage of these services. Perhaps they are turned off by the generic moniker for these offices: the "unemployment office." The savvy job seeker will not let misconceptions steer him away from a state's Job Service office no matter how high in the academic or non–profit hierarchy he wishes to work. These offices, or at least their job database which you can access yourself on the Internet, are a very effective source of job openings.

Please, no photocopying

Automated Labor Exchange. *ALEX* as its admirers call it, enables even the most challenged techno–bozo among us to easily access *America's Job Bank* or a state's own job database from computers located in public places around the state. Pioneered by the states of Virginia, Maryland, and a handful of others, each *ALEX* terminal is usually housed in a kiosk located at a shopping center, library, community college, or convenience store. Many use touch screens without a keyboard to make it simple to find listings of job vacancies that meet your criteria. You can print out the result of your search. This chapter will tell you which states operate *ALEX* kiosks and the types of places where you can find them. To get specific locations of *ALEX* kiosks, you should contact your closest state Job Service office.

Regional job–listing periodicals. Regional job–listing periodicals that cover several states can be excellent sources of local jobs. Several of these that are very specialized were described in earlier chapters of this book. This chapter identifies a few that are broader in scope. We suspect there may be more of these out there. If you come upon any that are not included in this chapter, could you please be so kind as to use the *Reader Feedback Form* to tell us about them so we can obtain a sample copy and include them in the next free *Update Sheet* to this book? You could also email them to us when you visit our Web site at URL: **http://job findersonline.com** to check the latest *Update Sheet* for this book and see the new job resources that are linked to our site.

Chapter newsletters and job services. The newsletters produced by the state or local chapters of many professional and trade associations often carry job advertisements. A chapter may also run a job–matching service or job hotline. Many run Web sites with jobs advertisements, a directory of individual members or companies, and/or a resume bank. You will need to contact the local organization to get details. Some of the state listings in this chapter of the *Non–Profits and Education Job Finder* include state and municipal directories that feature contact information for local and state sections of professional associations. For other states, you should contact the national headquarters of the appropriate professional or trade organization to obtain the address of the chapter president you wish to contact.

To find contact information on these national organizations, take a gander at the latest edition of the **National and Trade and Professional Associations of the U.S.** (Columbia Books, Suite 330, 1212 New York Ave., NW, Washington, DC 20005; phone: 202/898–0662; $80), which provides details on over 7,500 national trade and professional associations, many of which have state chapters. Even more on point is the companion volume, **State and Regional Associations** (Columbia Books, Suite 330, 1212 New York Ave., NW, Washington, DC 20005; phone: 202/898–0662; $65), which

By–pass the State of Confusion: Read chapters 1 and 2 first

Resources for deciding where to live and work

If you're not really sure where, geographically speaking, you want to work, you can learn a lot about different cities by obtaining the latest *Location* Report (Location Guides, P.O. Box 58506, Salt Lake City, UT 84158; phones: 800/846-6310, 801/645-7252; $27.95 plus $3/shipping, 228 pages, published every April and November; see the coupons near the end of this book for a $5 discount). You'll be presented with statistics on over 800 cities and all 50 states; local contacts such as newspapers, public libraries, and chambers of commerce; local post-secondary schools; and state publications like business directories and local magazines.

The same publisher also publishes 200 *Location Guides* ($9.95 plus $3/shipping, published annually; see the coupons near the end of this book for a $3 discount), each for a different U.S. city. Each *Location Guide* includes a directory of major local employers and company headquarters; local contacts, chambers of commerce, extension services, libraries, and local governments; cost of living trends for the area; crime data; employment and salary trends; state licensing practices for different professions; health, retail, risks (flooding, earthquake, tornado, nuclear power plants, etc.), schools, weather, state agencies and contacts, environmental information, recreation, parks, forests, state departments of vital records, and more.

The monthly magazine *Blue Chip Job Growth Update* produced by the Bank One Economic Outlook Center (College of Business, Arizona State University, Station 4406, Tempe, AZ 85287-4406; phone: 602/965-5543; $79/annual subscription) offers timely data by state on nonagricultural job growth or loss in the construction, manufacturing, trade, and service industries. It also reports total nonagricultural job growth or loss during the past year for metropolitan areas in each state.

Two online sites complement these printed relocation resources with a vast array of information about cities and suburbs throughout the U.S. Visit *CityLink* at Internet URL: http://usacitylink.com/ and select "Visit a City." Then choose a state and then a city. For each city, you'll be linked to relocation resources for finding housing plus moving and storage services. You'll get more than the usual tourist information — demographic data including test scores for school districts, crime rates, housing costs, income — as well as information on colleges, public schools, libraries, and community services. The links to online sources of information about each city are quite broad in scope.

CityNet offers more colorful bells and whistles as it links you to sites with information on U.S. and foreign cities from its Internet URL at: http://www.city.net/. You can select from a list of "top cities" or search for a city by name. For each city, you will be linked to relocation information, city guides, colleges, yellow pages, and interactive maps that can find any address in the metropolitan area. There is very little overlap between the two sites.

Please, no photocopying

City and state job-finding tools

reports on 7,300 major professional associations that operate on a state or regional level. This is a excellent and *affordable* source for identifying state and local professional organizations that might offer local job services.

If your library does not have that extremely useful book, chances are good that it may have the superb ***Encyclopedia of Associations: Regional, State, and Local Organizations*** (Gale Research, Inc., 835 Penobscot Bldg., Detroit, MI 48226; phone: 800/877–4253; $530/five–volume set, $125 for each regional volume individually, 6,000 pages total, published annually). This directory describes over 100,000 non–profit organizations with multi–state, state, city, or local scope and interest, including professional associations for just about every non–profit and education occupation. It's also available on the Internet for a fee. Call 800/877–4253 ext. 1882 for details. It's a good source for finding state and local professional organizations that might furnish local job services.

Local newspapers. In a handful of states, the classified section of local newspapers is one of the best sources for jobs with non–profits and educational institutions. Because more than half the nation's newspapers have gone online, you can access their job listings even if you don't live within the cities they serve. If you don't know the URL for a newspaper's Web site, use one of the search engines described in Chapter 2 to find it.

Over 24 major newspapers have joined together to offer their job classifieds at a single Web site, ***CareerPath.com*** (CareerPath.com, Times Mirror Square, Los Angeles, CA 90053). Go to URL: **http://www.career path.com/** and select "Jobs" where you can search by keyword. You can specify which newspapers you want to include in your search and can choose between the ads that appeared in the current week's papers or the previous Sunday. The operator claims to have over 150,000 ads for current job openings in its database — mostly for private sector positions. This site also offers links to each participating newspaper's home page.

Local job ad periodicals. Local employment periodicals are springing up across the country. These tabloids, which are usually available free at bookstores and newspaper bins, contain nothing but job ads and a few stories about the job search. While most of the jobs advertised in them are for private sector positions, they usually have some positions with non–profits advertised as well. Education jobs are rarely advertised in these periodicals. A small number of these periodicals are included in this chapter. If you know of a local job–listing publication that includes non–profit positions that is not included in this chapter, please tell us about it so we can add it to our *Update Sheet* and share your find with other job seekers. Please use the *Reader Feedback Form* at the end of this book or send us an email from our Web site to fill us in on it so we can obtain a sample copy and include it in the next *Update Sheet* for this book.

By–pass the State of Confusion: Read chapters 1 and 2 first

State associations of non-profit organizations. We've been able to identify associations of non-profit organizations for most states and include all job publications and services they operate, as well as any relevant directories they publish. Even if an association doesn't offer any direct job sources, it may still serve as an informal clearinghouse for job opportunities. You can't lose by contacting the association in the states where you're seeking work and asking if they can give you any hints for finding a job with a non-profit in that state.

The Internet. This chapter includes Internet job sources for nearly every state in the Union. However, like everything else on the 'Net, these sites with job-finding resources can change frequently. Two excellent Web sites can keep you up-to-date.

A Guide to Job Resources by US Region maintained by the Office of Career Services at the College of William and Mary will keep you current. Go to Internet URL: **http://www.wm.edu/csrv/ career/stualum/jregion .html#top**. Part I of this site is national in scope; it links you to Web sites that list jobs from throughout the U.S. But Part II connects you to Web sites and local newspapers that focus on an individual state or metropolitan area. Part III offers links to short-term jobs such as fieldwork, internships, summer jobs, and post-graduate options. This is a great place to keep on top of local job sources as new ones blossom and established ones mature.

The resourceful job seeker will also use *The Riley Guide: Employment Opportunities and Job Resources on the Internet* to supplement the online job services listed in this chapter for each state. Go to URL: **http:// www.jobtrak.com/jobguide** and select "Resources for Jobs in Each State of the U.S." Click on the state that interests you and you'll see a list of Web sites, gopher sites, user newsgroups, and mailing lists within a state that may focus on specific cities or professions within that state. As explained in Chapter 2, there's a whole lot more information available at this site that will help your job search.

Employment agencies, recruiters, outplacement.
While you should always be cautious with employment agencies, the legitimate ones can sometimes place you in a job. Executive recruiters and outplacement firms are even more effective. But be cautioned that fewer than 200 recruitment firms work with non-profits and educational institutions.

Several of the directories listed in this chapter include contact information on employment agencies and recruiters, executive recruiters, executive search firms, outplacement services, referral services, career consultants, and resume preparation services that serve a metropolitan area. Each book proffers advice on how to choose these agencies and services. For each agency, you'll be given its address, phone number, contact person, and the

Please, no photocopying

Alabama

occupations in which it specializes. The best lists of recruiters that work with non-profits and educational organizations appear in several directories of executive recruiters described in Chapter 3 under "Directories."

Foundations and grants. To help you locate grant funds, as well as foundations within your state for which you might wish to work, this chapter describes directories of foundations for most of the 50 states. We included only fairly recent directories for which we could verify publication information and their contents. We left out directories that are now out-of-print. As always, most foundations do not award grants to individuals. However, we do note when a directory includes some foundations that issue grants to individuals.

Now that you've actually read the introduction to this chapter and learned about the plethora of job-quest tools available for the different types of job searches — demonstrating that you are an increasingly astute job seeker — go to the section for each state that interests you. You should also check the Index because a number of job sources that focus on one or two professions in just one state are listed in other chapters of this book and are referenced in the Index. Look in the Index under the name of the state as well as under the occupation that interests you to find these additional job sources.

Job and grant sources by state

Alabama

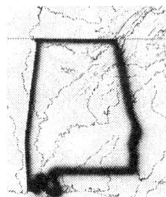

AlaWeb! enables you to search for job vacancies by keyword. Go to Internet URL: **http://alaweb.asc.edu/** and pick "Employment & State Jobs" and then choose "Job Bank and Alabama Department of Industrial Relations." Next select "Alabama State Employment" and then "Search for Jobs in Alabama."

ALEX kiosks are located in several shopping malls in Birmingham and Montgomery.

To locate any of the state's 41 **Job Service Offices**, contact the Employment Services Division (Department of Industrial Relations, 649 Monroe St., Montgomery, AL 36131; director's phone: 334/242-8003). You can also access these locations on the Internet at URL: **http://www.asc.edu/archives/adahindx.html** and selecting "Agencies, State Directory" or at the *AlaWeb!* site at URL: **http://alaweb.asc.edu/** and choosing "State Government" and then selecting "State Agencies." You'll find links to the home pages of state agencies where you'll find the Job Service offices.

By-pass the State of Confusion: Read chapters 1 and 2 first

Foundations and grants

Alabama Foundation Directory (Birmingham Public Library, Government Documents Department, 2100 Park Pl., Birmingham, AL 35203; phone: 205/226–3600) $28/prepaid only, 104 pages, 1996. Reports on over 500 foundations: areas of interest, officers.

A Guide to Funders in Central Appalachia and the Tennessee Valley (Appalachia Community Fund, Suite 206, 517 Union Ave., Knoxville, TN 37902; phone: 423/523–5783) $27, 300+ pages, January 1994. Among the 399 funders reported on are those that give grants in northern Alabama. Includes everything you need to seek funding: contact name, types of grants, grant application process, average grant size, plus how to write a grant proposal, funders from outside the region that make grants in the region, religious funding sources, and Japanese corporations with grant-making programs.

Alaska

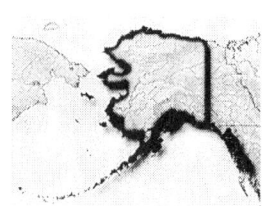

Membership List (Association of Nonprofit Corporations, c/o Nancy K. Scheetz–Frymiller, President, P.O. Box 100956, Anchorage, AK 99510; phone: 907/274–1880) $75/non–profit nonmember, $25/member, database updated continuously. You'll get the addresses and phone numbers for the 450 non–profits that belong to this organization.

Find **Job Service Offices** by contacting the Alaska Employment Service (Department of Labor, Suite 208, 111 W. Eighth St., P.O. Box 25509, Juneau, AK 99802-5509; phone: 907/465-4531). You can also get the latest list of these offices on the Internet at URL: **http://www.state.ak.us/local/akpages/LABOR/home.htm**. Select "Job Seekers' Resource Page" and then select "Department of Labor Offices." Finally, choose "Alaska Employment Services Offices" to get the list with addresses and phone numbers.

Job Hotlines. Several of the Alaska Employment Service Offices offer a daily recorded job hotline message which includes the following information about non–profit and education positions as well as private sector and government job openings:

Anchorage: Professional, technical, and clerical positions: 907/269–4740; crafts and trades: 907/269–4730; part–time: 907/269–4735; youth: 907/269–4750.

Eagle River (907/694–6999): titles of rush and hard–to–fill jobs

Fairbanks (907/451–2875): titles and salary of all job openings, descriptions of some jobs

Please, no photocopying

Homer (907/235–7200): titles of all job vacancies

Juneau (907/790–4571): titles of new job openings

Kenai (907/283–4606): qualifications of all job openings, no salary information

Kodiak (907/486–6838): titles and salary of all job vacancies, descriptions of some positions

MatSu (907/376–8860): titles and salary of new job openings, titles only for previously listed positions

Seward (907/224–5274): titles of all job vacancies

Pacific Northwest Grantmakers Forum Member Directory (Pacific Northwest Grantmakers Forum, Suite 214, 1305 Fourth Ave, Seattle, WA 98101; phone: 206/624–9899) $39.74/out–of–state residents, $43/Washington state residents, 186 pages, published in March of even–numbered years. Among the nearly 100 or so grantmakers described in this directory are a handful from Alaska. Included in each listing are contact name's address and phone, application procedures, range of grant amounts awarded, and types of projects funded.

Arizona

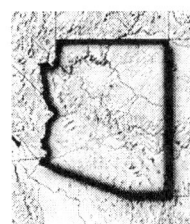

Rocky Mountain Employment Newsletter (Suite 309–BO, 10 Town Plaza, Durango, CO 81301; phone: 970/247–9550) 18 issues/year, $21/three–month subscription to one edition, $26/any two editions, $31/three editions, $36/four editions. Two and one–month subscriptions also available. Published in four editions: Arizona–New Mexico, Colorado–Wyoming, Idaho–Montana, and Washington–Oregon. Combined, the four editions include over 400 job openings, some in non–profits. The positions tend to orient toward the outdoors, with quite a few in natural resources, environment, and wildlife.

Arizona Careers Online, free. Go to Internet URL: **http://www.amsquare.com/america/arizona.html** and select "Candidate Services" for instructions on how to participate in the resume database at this site. You can submit your resume at this site. For a latest list of job hotlines in the state, select "Arizona Job Hotlines."

To locate **Job Service Offices**, contact the Employment and Rehabilitation Services Division (Department of Economic Security, P.O. Box 6123–010A, Phoenix, AZ 85005; director's phone: 602/542–5678).

By–pass the State of Confusion: Read chapters 1 and 2 first

Foundations and grants

Arizona Foundation Directory 1995 (Junior League of Phoenix, P.O. Box 10377, Phoenix, AZ 85064; phone: 602/234–3388) $15, 74 pages. Profiles more than 100 foundations that have awarded at least $500 in grants. Descriptions include contact persons, sample grants, number of grants and dollar amounts.

Arkansas

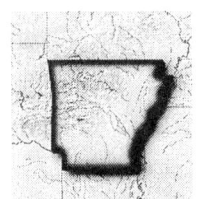

Grant Seekers Horizon (Nonprofit Resources, Inc., Suite 403, 500 Broadway, Little Rock, AR 72201–3342; phone: 501/374–8515) ten issues/year, $75/nonmembers, free/members. Occasional job listings.

Arkansas Employment Security Department Job-Matching Service (Employment Security Department, Capitol Mall, Little Rock, AR 72201; director's phone: 501/682–2121; available at any of the 30 local Employment Security Department offices) free. A job seeker completes the service's resume form and is then matched with jobs. The service contacts matched applicants to arrange job interviews with employers. Applications are kept active for 60 days.

For information on the location of the 30 **Job Service Offices** (known in Arkansas as local Employment Security Department offices), contact the Employment Security Department, (Room 506, ESD Building, P.O. Box 2981, Little Rock, AR 72203; phone: 501/682–2121). Each office has *ALEX*. You can also get this list of Job Service Offices at Internet URL: **http://www.state.ar.us/** and selecting "Index" and then "Telephone Directory — State Agencies and Services."

California

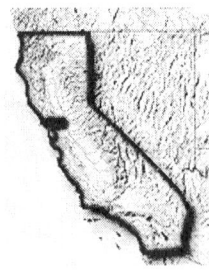

Opportunity NOCs (The Management Center, Suite 800, 870 Market St., San Francisco, CA 94102; phone: 415/362–9735, ext. 107) weekly, $24/three–month subscription, $48/six months, $67/annual, non–profit organizations: $45/annual subscription. From 70 to 150 positions with non–profits in the Bay Area and Sacramento are described in every issue.

Opportunity NOCs (Center for Nonprofit Management in Southern California, Suite 1100, 315 W. 9th St., Los Angeles, CA 90015; phone: 213/623–7080) biweekly, individuals:

California

$16/three-month subscription, $46/annual; non-profit organizations: $20/annual subscription. Each issue is filled with 50 or more vacancies in all aspects of non-profits in southern California, mostly the Los Angeles area.

JobSmart (Bay Area Library and Information System) free. On the Internet go to URL: **http://www.jobsmart.org/** and behold its wealth of job resources, mostly focused on northern California. Try not to be overwhelmed. To find job openings in northern California, select "Job ads" and then choose "Northern California Job Banks." You'll find links to scores of job banks that list jobs of all types as well as a link to a site where bulletin board services with job ads are listed. By the time you read this, this site may also serve southern California as well as the northern half of the state.

There's still more here. You can get the phone numbers for over 500 job hotlines, some for non-profits and schools of all types, by selecting "Job Hotlines." Next you select the area code for the city in which you want the job hotlines. Finally, you select the occupational area and you'll have the job hotline numbers on your screen.

And there's more.... You can find links to salary surveys conducted in the Bay area by selecting "Salary Info" and then "Salary Surveys" and selecting "Bay Area Surveys" under "General Salary Surveys."

24-Hour Recorded Job Lines for the San Francisco Bay Area offers the job hotline numbers of numerous school districts, colleges, and research institutions as well as links to their Internet Web sites. Go to URL: **http://wwww.webcom.com/~rmd/bay_area/joblines.html** where you'll find the job lines grouped by county.

The Advocate (Public Interest Clearinghouse, 100 McAllister St., San Francisco, CA 94102-4978; phone: 415/255-1714) eight issues/year, $75/annual subscription, $50 if also subscribing to *PiES Job Alert!* described under "Job ads" in the "Legal services" chapter. Describes several dozen jobs, largely in California, of interest to law students such as internships, clerkships, and work-study positions with legal services and non-profits.

The CAN Alert (California Association of Nonprofits, Suite 705, 315 West 9th St., Los Angeles, CA 90015; phones: 213/347-2070, 800/776-4226 for California residents only) bimonthly, free/members only. Lists occasional job ads.

CAN Nonprofit List of Agencies (California Association of Nonprofits, Suite 705, 315 West 9th St., Los Angeles, CA 90015; phones: 213/347-2070, 800/776-4226 for California residents only) continuously updated computer database, call for rates. You can request a list of some 2,000 CAN members and of more than 10,000 non-profits throughout the state, and obtain specialized lists for non-profits by city and zip code address.

By-pass the State of Confusion: Read chapters 1 and 2 first

Travels with Farley reprinted by permission of Phil Frank. Copyright 1988. All rights reserved.

Non–Profit Directory of Santa Clara County (The Nonprofit Development Center, Suite 212, 1922 The Alameda, San Jose, CA 95126; phone: 408/248–9505) free at Internet URL: **http://www.npdc.org**. Includes addresses, phone numbers, contact names, and board members for 2,300 non–profit organizations in Santa Clara and Monterey counties.

Directory of Bay Area Public Interest Organizations (Public Interest Clearinghouse, 100 McAllister St., San Francisco, CA 94102–4978; phone: 415/255–1714) $27, 168 pages, 1991. Features 600 organizations working for social change in the nine–county San Francisco Bay Area. Indexed by subject and county. Includes a chapter on finding paid public interest jobs in the Bay Area that tells you about over 40 local job resources including local periodicals with job ads and job services. Most recent edition published in 1991.

Public Interest, Private Practice: A Directory of Progressive Private Law Firms in Northern California (Public Interest Clearinghouse, 100 McAllister St., San Francisco, CA 94102–4978; phone: 415/255–1714) $11, 20 pages, 1993, new edition expected by June 1997, same price. Lists over 200 for–profit law firms that devote a substantial portion of their legal work to the public interest.

How to Get a Job in Southern California (Surrey Books; available from the Job Search Resources Catalog at the end of this book) $16.95, 452 pages, 1997. Although mostly filled with private sector employers, this easy–to–use book tells you whom to contact for job vacancies at a moderate number of non–profit employers in southern California in social services, foundations, and education. Even more importantly, it gives you details on the local chapters of professional and trade associations you may wish to join for networking purposes or which may publish a periodical with jobs ads or operate a local job service. Some local chapters may be large enough to hire staff. It also includes information on local job hotlines, Internet Web sites of many local employers, and local trade magazines plus career consultants.

How to Get a Job in the San Francisco Bay Area (Surrey Books; available from the Job Search Resources Catalog at the end of this book) $16.95, 390 pages, 1996. Although mostly filled with private sector employers, this

Please, no photocopying

easy-to-use book tells you whom to contact for job vacancies at a moderate number of non-profit employers in the metropolitan area in social services, foundations, and education. Even more importantly, it gives you details on the local chapters of professional and trade associations you may wish to join for networking purposes or which may publish a periodical with jobs ads or operate a local job service. Some local chapters may be large enough to hire staff. It also includes information on local job hotlines, Internet Web sites of many local employers, and local trade magazines plus career consultants.

Wage & Benefit Survey for Northern California (The Management Center, Suite 800, 870 Market St., San Francisco, CA 94102; phone: 415/362-9735) call for prices, annual. This is a comprehensive report of current salaries and benefits paid by non-profit organizations in northern California.

Wage & Benefit Survey of Southern California Nonprofit Organizations (Center for Nonprofit Management in Southern California, Suite 1100, 315 W. 9th St., Los Angeles, CA 90015; phone: 213/623-7080) $250, 160 pages, annual in April. This is a comprehensive report of current salaries and benefits paid by non-profit organizations in southern California, by position, organization, budget, education requirements, location, gender, and field of service.

To locate **Job Service Offices**, contact the Employment Development Department (P.O. Box 826880, MIC 62, Sacramento, CA 94280-0001; phone: 916/653-0707). You can also locate these offices on the Internet at two locations: URL: **http://www.ca.gov/** and selecting "Hello, May We Help You?" and then picking "Agency Index;" and at URL: **http://wwwedd.cahwnet.gov/** and clicking on "Job Service" and then choosing "List of EDO JobService Locations."

Foundations and grants

Guide to California Foundations (Northern California Grantmakers, Suite 742, 116 New Montgomery St., San Francisco, CA 94105; phone: 415/777-5761) $31.33, 700 pages, July 1996. Includes descriptions of 1,110 foundations that annually award grants that total at least $40,000. Each entry includes a contact name, the foundation's purpose and fields of grantmaking, range of awards, giving patterns, officers and directors, and application procedures.

San Diego County Foundation Directory (San Diego Community Foundation, Suite 500, 1420 Kettner Blvd., San Diego, CA 92101; phone: 619/239-8815) $25, 270 pages, 1994 (new directory available in autumn of 1997). Reports on application procedures, range of grants, type of support, contact person, and directors for 252 foundations.

By-pass the State of Confusion: Read chapters 1 and 2 first

Foundation Directory Santa Clara and Monterey Counties (The Nonprofit Development Center, Suite 212, 1922 The Alameda, San Jose, CA 95126; phone: 408/248–9505) $29.95 plus $3/shipping, 86 pages, also available free at Internet URL: **http://www.npdc.org**, published each spring. Provides contact person and phone number, application guidelines, preferred program areas, and more for 75 to 100 foundations.

Corporate Contributions Guide to Santa Clara County (The Nonprofit Development Center, Suite 212, 1922 The Alameda, San Jose, CA 95126; phone: 408/248–9505) $39.95 plus $3/shipping, 97 pages, also available free at Internet URL: **http://www.npdc.org**, published each spring. Provides contact person and phone number, application guidelines, preferred program areas, and more.

Colorado

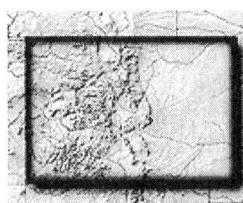

CANPO Newsletter (Colorado Association of Nonprofit Organizations, Suite 1060, 225 E. 16th Ave., Denver, CO 80203–1614; phone: 303/832–5710) bimonthly, nonmembers/call for annual subscription rate, free/members. Five to six job ads appear under "Job Board" along with a "Situations Wanted" section.

Rocky Mountain Employment Newsletter (Suite 309–BO, 10 Town Plaza, Durango, CO 81301; phone: 970/247–9550) 18 issues/year, $21/three–month subscription to one edition, $26/any two editions, $31/three editions, $36/four editions. Two and one–month subscriptions also available. Published in four editions: Colorado–Wyoming, Arizona–New Mexico, Idaho–Montana, and Washington–Oregon. Combined, the four editions include over 400 job openings, some in non–profits. The positions tend to orient toward the outdoors, with quite a few in natural resources, environment, and wildlife.

Colorado Directory of Nonprofits (Colorado Association of Nonprofit Organizations, Suite 1060, 225 E. 16th Ave., Denver, CO 80203–1614; phone: 303/832–5710) $15/nonmembers, $10/members, last edition 1993. Lists executive directors, addresses, phone numbers, budget range, geographic area served, statement of purpose, and number of employees and volunteers for 1,500 501(c)(3)s.

Job Book (Colorado Association of Nonprofit Organizations, Suite 1060, 225 E. 16th Ave., Denver, CO 80203–1614; phone: 303/832–5710) free. CANPO maintains this informal resource at its office. Feel free to walk in and scan this looseleaf book for 30 to 40 job opening announcements.

Colorado's Job Bank is located on the Internet at URL: **http://www.co.jobsearch.org/** where you can enter the job database by choosing "Search for Work in Colorado." This site includes a list of job hotlines.

Please, no photocopying

Touch Colorado kiosks are linked into *America's Job Bank*. Kiosks are located at many community colleges, libraries, municipal buildings as well as at the local Job Service Offices.

To locate **Job Service Offices,** contact the Department of Labor and Employment (Tower 2, Suite 400, 1515 Arapahoe St., Denver, CO 80202; phone: 303/620–4701).

Foundations and grants

Colorado Foundation Directory (Junior League of Denver, 6300 E. Yale Ave., Denver, CO 80222–7184; phone: 303/692–0270) $15, 142 pages, issued in March of even–numbered years. Offers details on over 200 foundations: purpose statement, field of interest, sample grants, etc.

Connecticut

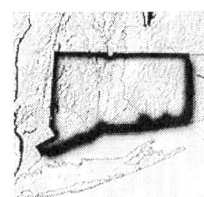

Opportunity NOCs New England (Executive Service Corp., 211 Congress St., Boston, MA 02110; phone: 617/357–0849) biweekly, $12/three–month subscription/individuals only, $45/annual subscription/individuals, $30/annual/non–profits. About 40 job vacancies for all levels of work in non–profits appear in the typical issue. Job ads are posted on the Internet a week after they appear in the periodical. Go to URL: **http://www.opnocs.org**.

Connecticut's Job Bank is located at Internet URL: **http://www.ctdol.state.ct.us/**. To access the job database, select "Employment Services" and then choose "Search for Work." Select "Connecticut Works" to see the directory of the state's Job Service Offices.

To locate the state **Job Service Offices** (called Job Centers in Connecticut) in Ansonia, Bridgeport, Bristol, Danbury, Danielson, Enfield, Hamden, Hartford, Manchester, Meriden, Middletown, New Britain, New London, Norwich, Stamford, Torrington, Waterbury, and Willimantic, see the state government section (the blue pages) of the local white pages telephone directory or contact the Connecticut Department of Labor (200 Folly Brook Blvd., Wethersfield, CT 06109; phone: 860/566–5104) for a list of Job Center Offices. Kiosks that are hooked into the *America's Talent Bank* system are located at state Job Service Offices, colleges, and some companies that are undergoing downsizing.

By–pass the State of Confusion: Read chapters 1 and 2 first

Foundations and grants

Job Listing Service (The Foundation Center, 79 Fifth Ave., Eighth floor, New York, NY 10003; phone: 212/620-4230) free, walk-in service only. Positions with non-profit entities in Connecticut and elsewhere are listed here. These job vacancies can be viewed *only* in person. They are *not* published.

Delaware

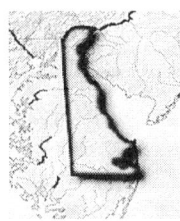

Opportunity NOCs (The Nonprofit Management Development Center, LaSalle University, 1900 W. Olney, Philadelphia, PA 19141-1199; phone: 215/951-1701) monthly, $10/three-month subscription, $30/annual subscription; non-profit organizations: $12/annual subscription. Around 40 positions with non-profits in Delaware, southern New Jersey, and Pennsylvania are described in every issue.

DANA Monthly (Delaware Association of Nonprofit Agencies, Suite 102, 100 W. 10th St., Wilmington, DE 19801; phone: 302/777-5500) monthly, free/members only. A few ads for positions with non-profits are advertised in this newsletter.

Mailing List (Delaware Association of Nonprofit Agencies, Suite 102, 100 W. 10th St., Wilmington, DE 19801; phone: 302/777-5500) $50. This is a computer-generated mailing list of addresses on labels for more than 1,500 non-profits, so it is about as up-to-date as possible.

Wage and Benefits Survey of Delaware Nonprofits (Delaware Association of Nonprofit Agencies, Suite 102, 100 W. 10th St., Wilmington, DE 19801; phone: 302/777-5500) $30/nonmembers, $15/members, 40 pages, annual. Survey includes wages and benefits by administrative position and clerical support up to directors, by size of budget of agency, and by rate of increase.

To locate the state's five **Job Service Offices** in Dover, Newark, Georgetown, and Wilmington, contact First Step Employment and Training (Delaware Department of Labor, The Hudson State Service Center, 501 Ogletown Rd., Newark, DE 19711; phone: 302/368-6825). You can also get their addresses and phones on the Internet at URL: **http://www.state.de.us/** and choosing "Government."

Foundations and grants

Directory of Delaware Grantmakers (Delaware Community Foundation, P.O. Box 1636, Wilmington, DE 19899; phone: 302/571–8004) $28, 109 pages, 1994. Describes hundreds of foundations, charitable trusts, and other donors; purpose statement, officers, type of recipient, analysis of grants.

District of Columbia

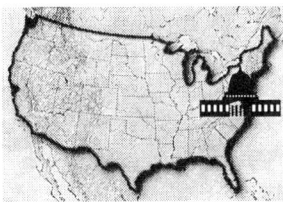

Community Jobs: The Regional Newsletter D.C. Area (ACCESS: Networking in the Public Interest, Suite 838, 1001 Connecticut Ave., Washington, DC 20036; phone: 202/785–4233) semi-monthly, $25/three–month subscription, $39/six–months, $69/annual; but if you also subscribe to the national edition of *Community Jobs*, you can get *Community Jobs/D.C.* for just additional $5/three months, $10/six months, $20/year; see the description of *Community Jobs* in Chapter 3 under "Job ads." Includes advertisements for positions with a broad range of non–profits in the Washington, D.C. metropolitan area. The vast majority of these job announcements do not appear in the national edition of *Community Jobs*.

The Nonprofit Agenda (Washington Council of Agencies, Suite 925, 1001 Connecticut Ave., NW, Washington, DC 20036; phone: 202/457–0540) bimonthly, free/members only and non–profit agencies. A handful of job ads appear under "Classified." They also keep on file a list of updated job announcements.

Opportunities in Public Affairs (Brubach Publishing Company, P.O. Box 34949, Bethesda, MD 20827; phone: 301/571–0102) $29/two–month subscription, $49/four months, $69/six months, $129/annual, $8.95/single issue. You'll find announcements of over 300 positions with non–profits; private companies in government affairs, public relations, broadcasting, and publishing; and local, state, and federal government agencies. In addition to job announcements, this periodical also reports on unadvertised jobs its editors have uncovered. Most job openings are in the District of Columbia area.

The Washington Job Source (MetCom, Inc.; available from the Job Search Resources Catalog at the end of this book; $16.95, 475 pages, 1997. Among the 2,100 potential employers listed are a good number of non–profit organizations and professional associations that hire staff as well as federal agencies, Congressional offices, and corporations. You get the name, address, and phone number of the person to contact about job vacancies

By–pass the State of Confusion: Read chapters 1 and 2 first

as well as a description of the agency and the number of employees. Focuses on employers that offer entry level positions, middle-management opportunities, and internships. Includes employment agencies and executive recruiters.

1997 Internships (Peterson's Guides; for your convenience this book is available from the Job Search Resources Catalog at the end of this book) $24.95. With a new edition each October, this 535-page book describes several hundred internship opportunities in and around the District of Columbia, mostly with the federal government, but also a good many in the non-profit sector.

Internships and Job Opportunities in New York City and Washington, DC (Graduate Group, P.O. Box 370351, West Hartford, CT 06137; phone: 860/233-2330) $27.50, published annually. Describes internship and job opportunities in a wide variety of fields.

Washington 96 (Columbia Books, Suite 330, 1212 New York Ave., NW, Washington, DC 20005; phone: 202/898-0662) $85, published annually each June. Nearly 1,200 pages of 4,000 addresses, phone numbers, and information on non-profit associations, companies, and government agencies in the D.C. area. Includes chapters on national associations, labor unions, law firms, medicine and health, foundations and philanthropy, science and policy research, education, religion, cultural institutions, clubs, and community affairs.

The Capitol Source: The Who's Who, What, Where in Washington (National Journal, Inc., 1501 M St., NW, Washington, DC 20005; phones: 800/424-2921, 202/739-8467) $24.95. Published in April and October, this directory includes names, addresses, and phone numbers for the District of Columbia. Also included are corporations, interest groups, think tanks, labor unions, real estate, financial institutions, trade and professional organizations, law firms, political consultants, advertising and public relations firms, private clubs, and the media. All entries are also available on computer diskette.

ALEX system terminals are available at the District's three **Job Service Offices**, which are called Employment Service Centers. The main office is at 500 C St., NW, Washington, DC 20001; phone: 202/724-7100. The Petworthy Employment Service Center is at 4120 Kansas Ave., NW, Washington, DC 2004; phone: 202/576-7474. The Northwest Employment Service Center is at 25 K St., NE, Washington, DC 20002; phone: 202/724-2316.

Foundations and grants

Guide to Greater Washington D.C. Grantmakers (The Foundation Center, 79 Fifth Ave., New York, NY 10003; phones: 800/424-9836, 212/620-4230) $65, 233 pages, July 1996. Published in conjunction with the Washington Regional Association of Grant Makers, this resource reports details on 946

Please, no photocopying

independent, corporate, and public grantmakers based in D.C., Maryland, and Virginia. The volume features descriptions of 1,800 recently awarded grants. Each entry includes contact person, areas of interest, application guidelines, financial and grant data, and more.

Florida

Newsletter of the Florida Association of Nonprofit Organizations (FANO, Suite 206, 7480 Fairway Dr., Miami Lakes, FL 33014; phones: 305/557-1764, 800/362-3266 for Florida residents) bimonthly, free. Eight to 30 job ads for all positions in the non-profit sector appear in the typical issue.

FANO Salary Survey (Florida Association of Nonprofit Organizations, Suite 206, 7480 Fairway Dr., Miami Lakes, FL 33014; phone: 305/557-1764, 800/362-3266 for Florida residents) annual, contact for price. This survey covers wages and benefits by size of non-profit agency budget.

You can find faculty, administration, and support positions at all state universities in the state at Internet URL: **http://www.fsu.edu/Jobs.html**. This site also offers information on salary ranges. There are also links to other Internet sites with academic positions.

Workforce Florida allows you to search for job vacancies by county, region, or statewide at Internet URL: **http://www.jbw.fdles.state.fl.us/** and choosing "Job Listings" which gets you to "Workforce Florida's Private Sector Job Search Facility." You can also locate state Job Service Offices by selecting "Jobs and Benefits" and then "Jobs and Benefits Offices."

Miami Job Source (MetCom, Inc.; available from Planning/Communications catalog at the end of this book) $15.95, 276 pages, 1997. Gives you the number of employees and the name, address, and phone number of the hiring contact for non-profits, health care institutions, and educational institutions, plus federal, state, and local government agencies and companies in the Miami area. Includes job hotlines, employment agencies, recruiters, and Internet Web pages. Includes information on more than 5,000 contacts. The entries focus on employers that offer middle management, entry level, and internship positions. Also included is a directory of Florida Job Service Offices.

To locate **Job Service Offices**, contact the Department of Labor and Employment Security (2012 Capital Cr., SE, Tallahassee, FL 32399-2154; phone: 904/488-4398).

By-pass the State of Confusion: Read chapters 1 and 2 first

Foundations and grants

The Complete Guide to Florida Foundations (John L. Adams & Co., Suite 1560, 9350 S. Dixie Hwy., Miami, FL 33156; phone: 305/670–2203) $90 plus $4 shipping, 450 pages, published each January. Details more than 1,500 foundations: officers, total grants, range of grants, funding priorities, and geographic preferences.

A Guide to Florida State Programs (Florida Funding Publications, Suite 1560, 9350 S. Dixie Hwy., Miami, FL 33156; phone: 305/670–2203) $80, published early each autumn. Describes state-funded grant programs by state government department: contact persons and phone numbers, program description, eligibility, deadlines, fund availability, matching requirements, and more.

Georgia

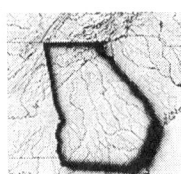

Opportunity NOCs (Nonprofit Resource Center, Suite 220, 50 Hurt Plaza, Atlanta, GA 30303; phone: 404/688–4845) semimonthly, $15/three-month subscription, $30/six months, $45/annual. Ads for 30 or more vacancies primarily in the Atlanta area appear every issue.

Wage and Benefits Survey for Georgia Nonprofits (Nonprofit Resource Center, Suite 220, 50 Hurt Plaza, Atlanta, GA 30303; phone: 404/688–4845) contact for price, November 1996. This is a comprehensive report on compensation with non-profit organizations in Georgia.

How to Get a Job in Atlanta (Surrey Books; available from the Job Search Resources Catalog at the end of this book) $16.95, 412 pages, 1997. Although filled mostly with private sector employers, this easy-to-use book tells you whom to contact for job vacancies at a moderate number of non-profit employers in the metropolitan area in social services, foundations, and education. Even more importantly, it gives you details on the local chapters of professional and trade associations you may wish to join for networking purposes or which may publish a periodical with jobs ads or operate a local job service. Some local chapters may be large enough to hire staff. It also includes information on local job hotlines, Internet Web sites of many local employers, and local trade magazines plus career consultants.

Georgia Career Resources is located at Internet URL: **http://www.careers.org/reg/crusa-ga.htm**. Here you will find links to a number of local job databases, home pages of potential employers, and other career resources including a newsgroup with hundreds of jobs in Georgia posted, albeit mostly in the computer and high technology industries, at the Internet address: **news:atl.jobs**. As of this writing, the state does not operate an

Internet-based job listing service. However, check the state's home page at URL: **http://www.state.ga.us/** to see if one has been recently established.

Job Information Service (Georgia Department of Labor, 148 International Blvd., NE, Atlanta, GA 30303; phone: 404/656–3017). Descriptions of non–profit sector vacancies throughout the state, and nation, are available on a computerized statewide database which can be viewed at any of the department's 54 **Job Service Offices** throughout the state. Contact the department for a list of these offices or check the local phone book.

Foundations and grants

Georgia Giving: The Directory of the State's Foundations (Capital Consortium, Suite 312, 2700 Wycliff Rd., Raleigh, NC 27607; phone: 919/783–9199) $55, 920 pages, 1995. Profiles over 836 foundations: trustee, limitations, application procedures, sample grants. Also available on a DOS–formatted 3.5–inch floppy disk.

A Guide to Funders in Central Appalachia and the Tennessee Valley (Appalachia Community Fund, Suite 206, 517 Union Ave., Knoxville, TN 37902; phone: 423/523–5783) $27, 300+ pages, January 1994. Among the 399 funders reported on are those that give grants in northern Georgia. Includes everything you need to seek funding: contact name, types of grants, grant application process, average grant size, plus how to write a grant proposal, funders from outside the region that make grants in the region, religious funding sources, and Japanese corporations with grant-making programs.

Hawaii

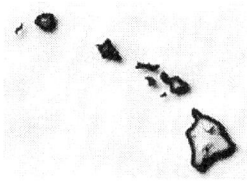

The Honolulu Advertiser (P.O. Box 3350, Honolulu, HI 96813; phone: 808/952–5011) published weekly on Sunday. Write for subscription prices.

Star–Bulletin (P.O. Box 3350, Honolulu, HI 96813; phone: 808/952–5011) published Monday through Sunday. Write for subscription prices.

The state participates in *America's Job Bank* through Internet URL: **http://www.aloha.net/~edpso/**. Just choose "America's Job Bank" to access this nationwide job database. There are also links to other job banks here. To get a directory of state Job Service Offices, select "One–Stop Centers for Workforce Assistance."

Kiosks connected to *America's Job Bank* are located in shopping malls and community colleges as well as at the state's Job Service Offices.

By-pass the State of Confusion: Read chapters 1 and 2 first

For information on **Job Service Offices**, contact the Workforce Development Division of the Department of Labor and Industrial Relations, 830 Punchbowl St., Honolulu, HI 96813; phone: 808/586–8812).

Foundations and grants

Directory of Charitable Trusts and Foundations for Hawaii's Non–Profit Organizations (Helping Hands Hawaii, Suite 430, 680 Iwilei Rd., Honolulu, HI 96817; phone: 808/536–7234) $25 plus $2/shipping, 144 pages, 1996. Describes over 80 foundations and charitable trusts.

Idaho

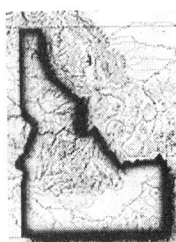

Rocky Mountain Employment Newsletter (Suite 309–BO, 10 Town Plaza, Durango, CO 81301; phone: 970/247–9550) 18 issues/year, $21/three–month subscription to one edition, $26/any two editions, $31/three editions, $36/four editions. Two and one–month subscriptions also available. Published in four editions: Idaho–Montana, Colorado–Wyoming, Arizona–New Mexico, and Washington–Oregon. Combined, the four editions include over 400 job openings, some with non–profits. The positions tend to orient toward the outdoors, with quite a few in natural resources, environment, and wildlife.

Nonprofit Computerized Label Service (Northwest Regional Facilitators, 525 East Mission Avenue, Spokane, WA 99202–1824; phone: 509/484–6733) 10¢ per name. Includes names and addresses for some 600 non–profit organizations in the states of Idaho and Montana.

Idaho Works offers a database of jobs in the state at Internet URL: **http://www.doe.state.id.us/** and selecting "Job Search." Next pick "Self–Directed Job Search" and choose the occupation and region within the state that interest you. You can get a directory of state Job Service Offices by picking "General Information" and then clicking on "Department of Labor Directory."

Kiosks connected to the state's job database are located in shopping centers, public libraries, very large companies, and the state's Job Service Offices.

For the addresses and phones of **Job Service Offices**, contact the Department of Employment (317 Main St., Boise, ID 83735; phone: 208/334–6010).

Foundations and grants

Directory of Idaho Foundations (Caldwell Public Library, 1010 Dearborn St., Caldwell, ID 83605–4195; phone: 208/459–3242) $15, 106 pages, published in every odd–numbered year. Covers 123 foundations. Includes range of grants, sample grants, application information.

Illinois

Monthly Memo to Members (Illinois Association of Nonprofit Organizations, Suite 3000, 8 S. Michigan Ave., Chicago, IL 60603; phone: 708/386–9385) monthly, free/members, $30/annual nonmember subscription. The "Nonprofit Job Line" column includes announcements of 10 to 30 openings with non–profit entities, particularly upper–level positions. Also includes notices of available grants under "Grant Information."

Directory of Internships in Illinois Non–Profit Organizations (Illinois Association of Nonprofit Organizations, Suite 3000, 8 S. Michigan Ave., Chicago, IL 60603; phone: 708/386–9385) $25, 1994. Features detailed descriptions of 80 or more internships, largely in the Chicago area.

Illinois Nonprofit Directory (Council of Illinois Nonprofit Organizations has disbanded.) The last one produced is available for viewing at the Donors Forum of Chicago (Suite 740, 208 S. LaSalle St., Chicago, IL 60604; phone: 312/578–0090). It describes over 1,700 leading non–profits in Illinois. Identifies department heads, including personnel directors.

Illinois Nonprofit Salary and Benefit Survey (Council of Illinois Nonprofit Organizations has disbanded.) Available for viewing at Donors Forum of Chicago (Suite 740, 208 S. LaSalle St., Chicago, IL 60604; phone: 312/578–0090). Gives information on salaries and benefits for 66 job functions and nine different responsibility levels with non–profit organizations that have annual revenues up to $10 million.

How Do We Compare? (Council of Illinois Nonprofit Organizations has disbanded.) The last edition of this was published in November 1994 and is available for viewing at the Donors Forum of Chicago (Suite 740, 208 S. LaSalle St., Chicago, IL 60604; phone: 312/578–0090). Compares salary and fringe benefits paid by non–profits to those paid by the private sector.

How to Get a Job in Chicago (Surrey Books; available from the Job Search Resources Catalog at the end of this book) $16.95, 378 pages, 1997. Although filled mostly with 1,800 private sector employers, this easy–to–use book tells you whom to contact for job vacancies at a moderate number of non–profit employers in the metropolitan area in social services, foundations, and education. Even more importantly, it gives you details on the

By–pass the State of Confusion: Read chapters 1 and 2 first

local chapters of professional and trade associations you may wish to join for networking purposes or which may publish a periodical with jobs ads or operate a local job service. Some local chapters may be large enough to hire staff. It also includes information on local job hotlines, Internet Web sites of many local employers, and local trade magazines plus career consultants.

Illinois Department of Employment Security Home Page features a state database of job openings. Go to Internet URL: **http://il.jobsearch.org/** and choose "Job Services" where you can pick between conducting a self-directed job search where you can seek openings by location and occupation, or search for openings by occupational code.

Illinois Department of Employment Security Offices (1300 S. Ninth St., Springfield, IL 62705; phone: 217/785-5069; 401 S. State St., Chicago, IL 60605; 312/793-3500). Eighty-four of these **Job Service Offices**, now dubbed Illinois Employment and Training Centers, across the state offer computer-based job searches. For a list of Job Service offices, contact one of these offices, see the state government section of your local white pages telephone directory, or on the Internet at URL: **http://il.jobsearch.org/** select "Local and Regional Office Listing."

Foundations and grants

Corporate Foundations in Illinois – A Directory (c/o Ellen Dick, 838 Fair Oaks, Oak Park, IL 60302; phone: 708/386-9385) $35/mail orders only, 1997. Reports details on over 125 corporate foundations (including Japanese foundations) and gift-matching programs: contact person, fields of interest, program and geographic limitations, application deadlines, grant amounts, officers and directors, and in-kind services contact person.

Illinois Foundation Directory (Foundation Data Center, 401 Kenmar Cr., Minnetonka, MN 55305; phone: 612/542-8582) $675, $255/annual update service (includes three updates a year, effectively giving you a new edition each quarter). Reports details on 1,930 Illinois foundations: contact person, officers and directors, territory and interest areas covered, list of grant recipients and amounts.

The Directory of Illinois Foundations (Donors Forum of Chicago, Suite 735, 208 S. LaSalle St., Chicago, IL 60604; phone: 312/578-0175) $75, 350 pages, published each August. Presents details on over 350 Illinois foundations and trusts with assets of at least $100,000 and total grants of $50,000 or more each year: contact person, geographic limits, contact and application procedures, deadlines, total grants, grant range, officers, and directors. Includes selected information on another 1,300 corporate, independent, and community foundations plus detailed tables on the assets and grants of the 100 largest Illinois foundations.

Please, no photocopying

Members and Forum Partners Directory (Donors Forum of Chicago, Suite 735, 208 S. LaSalle St., Chicago, IL 60604; phone: 312/578–0175) $40, 100 pages, issued each February. Offers information on over 150 Donors Forum member foundations and corporate giving programs: names and phone numbers of contact persons and professional staff, total grants, availability of grant guidelines, and principle funding areas. Includes information on over 700 non–profit organizations, donor affinity groups, and regional associations of grantmakers.

Report on Capital/Endowment Fund Campaigns in the Greater Chicago Area (Donors Forum of Chicago, Suite 735, 208 S. LaSalle St., Chicago, IL 60604; phone: 312/578–0175) $30, published each summer. Reports on over 100 Illinois non–profit organizations conducting capital and endowment fund campaigns.

Indiana

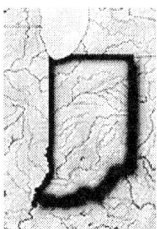

Indiana Department of Workforce Development Home Page features several job databases at Internet URL: **http://www.dwd.state.in.us**/. To search for jobs just in Indiana, pick "ALEX – Automated Labor Exchange." To search for jobs nationally using America's Job Bank, select "Job Banks." You can locate a directory of the state's Job Service Offices by choosing "One Stop Career"and then "Indiana's Directory of One Stop Locations."

The state operates about 15 *ALEX* kiosks located in shopping malls, libraries, and municipal buildings in addition to those at Workforce Development offices.

Indiana Department of Workforce Development (10 N. Senate Ave., Indianapolis, IN 46204; phones: 800/437–9136, 317/232–6702) has personnel who specialize in matching applicants with jobs through the statewide automated **Job Service** Matching System. This service is available only by an in–person visit to a IDWD office. Write for a list of the 25 offices or consult the state government section in local telephone directories. All these services are free.

Foundations and grants

Directory of Indiana Donors (Indiana Donors Alliance, Suite 700, 22 E. Washington St., Indianapolis, IN 46204–3529; phone: 317/630–5200) $51/nonmembers, $41/members, 500 pages, 1997. (Available on CD–ROM, call for rates.) Profiles 1,585 active grantmaking foundations, charitable trusts, corporate giving programs, and scholarship programs: contact person, range of grants, eligibility for grants, geographic and program preferences, limitations, and application information.

Iowa

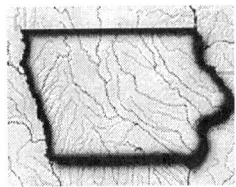

Iowa Jobs is located on the Internet at URL: **http://www.state.ia.us/jobs/applying.htm**. Simply click on "Iowa Jobs" where you will then get to choose between "IA Full Time" and "IA Part Time" job databases to search. You can also obtain a directory of state **Job Service Offices** by choosing "Workforce Center Offices."

PC Job Search (Iowa Workforce Development (1000 E. Grand, Des Moines, IA 50319; phone: 515/281–5365) free to schools, libraries, and other organizations that will offer access to this software at no charge. This software allows you to download the job vacancies in the state's job database to a personal computer on a daily basis.

The state operates a number of *ALEX* kiosks in shopping malls and grocery stores.

To locate **Job Service Offices**, contact Iowa Workforce Development (1000 E. Grand, Des Moines, IA 50319; phone: 515/281–5365).

Kansas

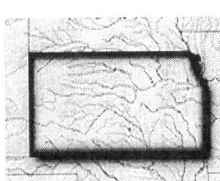

Job Opportunities: Business, Industry, Government (Career Services, Emporia State University, Campus Box 4014, Emporia, KS 66801–5407; phone: 316/343–5407) weekly March through August, semiweekly the rest of the year, $42/six–month subscription, $76/annual subscription. Despite its title, many of the 80 or so jobs listed here are with non–profits and educational institutions, most of which are located within the state.

Kansas Job Bank appears on the Internet at URL: **http://www.tyrell.net/~kdhr/**. Select "Job Bank" where you will have four choices: "Register as a Job Seeker" (your registration is confidential); "Search Job Listings" by keyword, county, region, or date posted; "Resume Service" that places your electronic resume in the state's resume database for one year (you are notified by email of jobs that fit your experience and education); and "JobMatch Service" where you specify the county in which you'd like to work, type of job, and full–time or part–time. You are notified by email when jobs that match your criteria are entered into the state's job database.

Please, no photocopying

Kentucky

To find **Job Service Offices**, contact the Employment and Training Division of the Department of Human Resources (401 SW Topeka Blvd., Topeka, KS 66603; phone: 913/296–7474).

Foundations and grants

The Directory of Kansas Foundations (Topeka Public Library Foundation Center Collection, 1515 SW. 10th St., Topeka, KS 66604; phone: 913/233–2040) $55, 254 pages, published in autumn of odd–numbered years. Reports on over 300 trusts and foundations: application information, limitations, types of support and sample grants, funding priority areas, and board members.

Kentucky

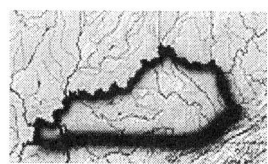

Kentucky's Job Bank resides on the Internet at URL: **http://ky.jobsearch.org/**. You can conduct a self–directed job search or search by keyword.

The state operates *ALEX* computer terminals at each of the 28 **Job Service Offices**. To locate these offices, contact the Field Services Division, Department for Employment Services (Suite 2W, 275 E. Main St., Frankfort, KY 40621; phones: 800/562–6397, 502/564–7456).

Foundations and grants

The Kentucky Foundation Directory (MR & Company, P.O. Box 9223, Cincinnati, OH 45209; phone: 513/871–9436) $50 plus 3 percent sales tax for Ohio residents, 100 pages, 1997. Reports on 178 Kentucky foundations and charitable trusts: areas of interest, officers and trustees, application procedures, sample grants, financial data.

A Guide to Funders in Central Appalachia and the Tennessee Valley (Appalachia Community Fund, Suite 206, 517 Union Ave., Knoxville, TN 37902; phone: 423/523–5783) $27, 300+ pages, January 1994. Among the 399 funders reported on are those that give grants in eastern Kentucky. Includes everything you need to seek funding: contact name, types of grants, grant application process, average grant size, plus how to write a grant proposal, funders from outside the region that make grants in the region, religious funding sources, and Japanese corporations with grant-making programs.

By–pass the State of Confusion: Read chapters 1 and 2 first

Louisiana

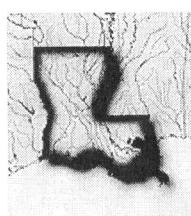

Louisiana Department of Labor Home Page on the Internet at URL: **http://www.ldol.state.la.us/** offers a statewide job database. Select "INFO Louisiana" and then "Job Listings," "Department of Labor Job Listings," and finally "Louisiana" or "National" or "Search." To get a directory of Job Service Offices, select "INFO Louisiana" and then "Department of Labor Job Listings," and finally "Office Locations."

For information on the location of **Job Service Offices**, contact the Department of Labor (1001 N. 23rd Street, Baton Rouge, LA 70804; phone: 504/342–3111).

Foundations and grants

Foundations and Funding Sources of Louisiana (Resource Review LLC, P.O. Box 12603, Lake Charles, LA 70612–2603; phone: 318/855–3466) $53 plus $2.50 shipping, 171 pages, 1994. Profiles 266 Louisiana foundations and 27 out-of-state foundations that target Louisiana; gives contact names, funding interests, sample list of grants awarded, and geographic focus.

Maine

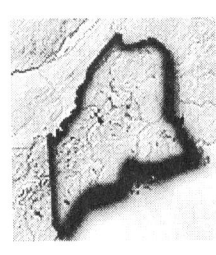

Opportunity NOCs New England (Executive Service Corp., 211 Congress St., Boston, MA 02110; phone: 617/357–0849) biweekly, $12/three–month subscription/individuals only, $45/annual subscription/individuals, $30/annual/non–profits. About 40 job vacancies for all levels of work in non-profits appear in the typical issue. Job ads are posted on the Internet a week after they appear in the periodical. Go to URL: **http://www.opnocs.org**.

Maine Sunday Telegram and ***Portland Press Herald*** (P.O. Box 1460. Portland, ME 04104; phone: 207/780–9000) are the best sources of job openings for non-profit sector positions throughout the state.

Department of Labor Home Page on the Internet at URL: **http://www.state.me.us.labor/jsd/jobserv.htm** offers a job database. Select "Search Maine Jobs" which will enable you to conduct a self-directed job search or search by occupational codes.

Please, no photocopying

To locate **Job Service Offices**, contact the Department of Labor, State House Station #54, Augusta, ME 04333; director's phone: 207/624–6390).

Foundations and grants

Directory of Maine Foundations (University of Southern Maine, Maine Grants Information Center, USM Library, P.O. Box 9301, Portland, ME 04104; phone: 207/780–5029) $15 prepaid, 48 pages, 1996. Reports on giving activities of about 200 Maine foundations, charitable trusts, and corporate giving programs: contact person, sample grants, amounts awarded.

Maryland

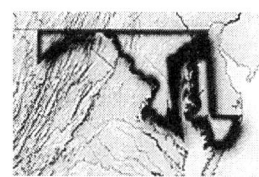

Community Jobs: The Regional Newsletter D.C. Area (ACCESS: Networking in the Public Interest, Suite 838, 1001 Connecticut Ave., Washington, DC 20036; phone: 202/785–4233) semimonthly, $25/three–month subscription, $39/six–month subscription, $69/annual subscription; but if you also subscribe to the national edition of *Community Jobs,* you can get *Community Jobs/D.C.* for an additional $5/three months, $10/six months, $20/year; see the description of *Community Jobs* in Chapter 3 under "Job ads." Includes advertisements for positions with a broad range of non–profits in the Washington, D.C. metropolitan area. The vast majority of these job announcements do not appear in the national edition of *Community Jobs.*

Opportunities in Public Affairs (Brubach Publishing Company, P.O. Box 34949, Bethesda, MD 20827; phone: 301/571–0102) biweekly, $29/two–month subscription, $49/four months, $69/six months, $129/annual, $8.95/single issue. You'll find announcements of over 300 positions with non–profits; local, state, and federal government agencies; and private companies in government affairs, public relations, broadcasting, and publishing. In addition to job announcements, this periodical also reports on unadvertised jobs its editors have uncovered. Most job openings are in the District of Columbia metropolitan area.

Maryland's Job Bank is located on the Internet at URL: **http://md.job search.org/**. First select "Search for Work in Maryland" or "Menu Search" that will give you lists of occupations and locations by which to search. You can also search by keyword. If you pick "Code Search," you can search for vacancies by occupational, DOT, military code, or job numbers. A directory of the state's Job Service Offices is also available at this site.

Baltimore Job Source (MetCom, Inc.; available from the Job Search Resources Catalog at the end of this book) $15.95, 305 pages, 1997. Gives you the number of employees and the name, address, and phone number of the hiring contact for non-profits, health care institutions, and educational institutions, plus federal, state, and local government agencies and companies in the Baltimore and Annapolis areas. Includes job hotlines, employment agencies, recruiters, and Internet Web pages. Includes information on more than 5,000 contacts. The entries focus on employers that offer middle management, entry level, and internship positions. Also included is a directory of Maryland **Job Service Offices**.

The Washington Job Source (MetCom, Inc.; available from the Job Search Resources Catalog at the end of this book; $16.95, 475 pages, 1997. Among the 2,100 potential employers listed are a good number of non-profit organizations and professional associations that hire staff as well as federal agencies, Congressional offices, and corporations. You get the name, address, and phone number of the person to contact about job vacancies as well as a description of the agency and the number of employees. Focuses on employers that offer entry level positions, middle-management opportunities, and internships. Includes employment agencies and executive recruiters.

Washington 96 (Columbia Books, Suite 330, 1212 New York Ave., NW, Washington, DC 20005; phone: 202/898–0662) $85, published every June. Nearly 1,200 pages of 4,000 addresses, phone numbers, and information on non-profit associations, companies, and government agencies in the D.C. area, including suburban Maryland. Includes chapters on national associations, labor unions, law firms, medicine and health, foundations and philanthropy, science and policy research, education, religion, cultural institutions, clubs, and community affairs.

Baltimore/Annapolis (Columbia Books, Suite 330, 1212 New York Ave., NW, Washington, DC 20005; phone: 202/898–0662) $60, published in odd-numbered years. Here are nearly 600 pages of addresses, phone numbers, and information on 2,000 non-profit organizations and private sector businesses and companies in these two parts of Maryland. Included are chapters on the media, business, national associations, labor unions, law firms, medicine and health, foundations and philanthropy, science and policy research, education, religion, cultural institutions, clubs, and community affairs.

MANPO Membership Directory (Maryland Association of Nonprofit Organizations, 22 Light St., Baltimore, MD 21202–1075; phone: 410/727–6367) free/members only, annual each January. Lists over 800 member groups.

Job-Matching Service (Office of Employment Services and Training, Department of Labor, Licensing and Regulation, 1100 N. Eutaw St., Baltimore, MD 21201; director's phone: 410/767–2173) free. Matches your skills to job vacancies. Available at Job Service Offices throughout the state.

Maryland was among the first states to use *ALEX*, the *A*utomated *L*abor *EX*change computer service that enables job seekers to look up job vacancies in Maryland and nationwide, themselves. *ALEX* terminals are available

Please, no photocopying

at Job Service Offices and in shopping malls, libraries, and schools. Note that many of the *ALEX* terminals in Maryland give you access only to jobs within the state and are not part of the national hookup.

To pinpoint **Job Service Offices**, contact the Office of Employment Services and Training (Department of Labor, Licensing and Regulation and Placement Administration, Room 209, 1100 N. Eutaw St., Baltimore, MD 21201; director's phone: 410/767–2173).

Foundations and grants

Annual Index of Foundation Reports and Appendix (Maryland Attorney General, 200 St. Paul Pl. Baltimore, MD 21202; phone: 410/576–6491) $95, issued each January. Reports on over 500 foundations that have filed with the state's Attorney General: foundation managers, contact person, application process, contributions, and more.

Guide to Greater Washington D.C. Grantmakers (The Foundation Center, 79 Fifth Ave., New York, NY 10003; phones: 800/424–9836, 212/620–4230) $65, 233 pages, July 1996. Reports details on over 945 independent, corporate, and public grantmakers based in D.C., Maryland, and Virginia. The volume features descriptions of 1,800 recently awarded grants.

Massachusetts

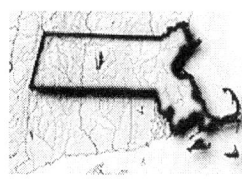

Opportunity NOCs New England (Executive Service Corp., 211 Congress St., Boston, MA 02110; phone: 617/357–0849) biweekly, $12/three–month subscription/individuals, $45/annual subscription/individuals, $30/annual/non–profits. About 40 job vacancies for all levels of work in non–profits appear in the typical issue. Job ads are posted on the Internet a week after they appear in the periodical. Go to URL: **http://www .opnocs.org**.

Boston Globe (Community News Dealer Company, 61st Ave., Waltham, MA 02254; phone: 617/446–1818). You can also access the last two weeks of job ads from the *Boston Globe* on the Internet at URL: **http://www.boston.com** by selecting the "Jobs" button and then "Job Search." You can specify the job category or location. You can also use the internship resume and job databases where over 50 internships are listed. As of this writing this is a painfully slow web site due to excessively complicated graphics.

By–pass the State of Confusion: Read chapters 1 and 2 first

Foundations and grants

Massachusetts Grantmakers (Associated Grantmakers of Massachusetts, 294 Washington St., Suite 840, Boston, MA 02108; phone: 617/426–2606) $50, 350 pages, 1997. Describes over 450 foundations and corporate grant makers: contact person, whether support is given to non–profit organizations and/or individuals, program emphasis and grantmaking philosophy, geographic focus, and application procedures. This book is essentially the same as the state's Attorney General's ***Directory of Foundations in Massachusetts*** (Massachusetts Attorney General, State House, Boston, MA; phone: 617/426–2606).

Michigan

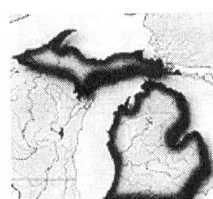

Job Service is located on the Internet at URL: **http://www.mesc.com/**. Select "Looking for a Job?" and then "MESC's Michigan Job Bank" where you can search by job title, location, or a text string. You can locate Job Service Offices by clicking on "Find the Closest Job Service Office."

To find **Job Service Offices**, contact the Employment Security Commission (7310 Woodward Ave., Detroit, MI 48202; phones: 800/638–3994, 313/876–5022).

Foundations and grants

The Michigan Foundation Directory (Michigan League for Human Services, Suite 401, 300 N. Washington Sq., Lansing, MI 48933; phone: 517/487–5436) $35/nonmembers plus $2/shipping, prepaid only, $30/members of Michigan League for Human Services or Council of Michigan Foundation, 290 pages, published in even–numbered years with a free supplement sent in odd–numbered years. Covers over 1,144 foundations granting at least $25,000 yearly, 377 foundations awarding over $50,000 a year in grants, and 79 corporate giving programs: contact person, purpose and activities, geographic priorities, grant ranges, officers and trustees. Includes analysis of grantmaking patterns and a guide to proposal writing.

Minnesota

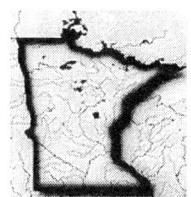

Minnesota Educator's Placement Service (P.O. Box 526, Stillwater, MN 55082; phone: 612/430-2005) bi-weekly; call or write for prices. This vacancy list features scores of positions in Minnesota for teachers, administrators, and educators at all levels of education.

Minnesota Nonprofit Directory (Minnesota Council of Nonprofits, Suite 250, 2700 University Ave., West, St. Paul, MN 55114; phone: 612/642-1904) $45/nonmembers, $27/members; everyone add 6.5 percent sales tax plus $2.50/shipping, 295 pages, published in the last quarter of even-numbered years. For each of over 3,000 Minnesota non-profits, you'll get the executive director's name, number of employees, a program description, revenue sources, expenses, and assets. Indexed by activity area and geography. Mailing labels are also available.

Minnesota Nonprofit Survey: Factors in Executive Director Compensation (Minnesota Council of Nonprofits, Suite 250, 2700 University Ave., West, St. Paul, MN 55114; phone: 612/642-1904) $7 plus 6.5 percent sales tax and $2/shipping, 20 pages. Activity area, location, budget size, structure, and gender are all reported to be elements affecting the salary received by executive directors of non-profits in Minnesota.

Human Services Survey of the Twin Cities (James M. Beaton, PAIRS Inc., P.O. Box 4335, Industrial Station, St. Paul, MN 55104-4335; phone: 612/690-2644) $300, 133 pages, published each April. Reports on salaries for over 125 different job categories with over 140 human services agencies in the St. Paul-Minneapolis area.

Human Services Benefits Survey of the Twin Cities (James M. Beaton, PAIRS Inc., P.O. Box 4335, Industrial Station, St. Paul, MN 55104-4335; phone: 612/690-2644) $300, 57 pages, every three years, last published 1996. Reports on benefits paid to employees in 14 major areas based on a survey of more than 140 human services agencies in the St. Paul-Minneapolis area.

Minnesota Department of Economic Security Home Page on the Internet at URL: **http://mn.jobsearch.org/** includes 12,000 job vacancies in its job database which is updated every weekday. Select "MN Job Bank" to access the job database. Choose "Local Offices" to get a directory of state Job Service Offices."

Minnesota Job Seeker's Sourcebook (Resource Publishing Group; available from the Job Search Resources catalog at the end of this book) $21.95, 288 pages, annual. This thorough directory includes addresses and phone numbers for all Job Service Offices and Workforce Centers in the state as well as job hotlines for specific companies, resume databases and job-match-

By-pass the State of Confusion: Read chapters 1 and 2 first

ing services, local professional associations (for networking purposes and possible local job services), employment agencies and recruiters, and much more. Most of the job sources for Minnesota described immediately above come from this book. I'll break my rule of not endorsing specific job sources in this instance. If you need to buy just one book to help you find a job in Minnesota, get the *Minnesota Job Seeker's Sourcebook.*

For information on the location of **Job Service Offices**, called Job Service Centers, get the *Minnesota Job Seeker's Sourcebook* (described above) or contact J.S./R.I. Operations (Department of Economic Security, 390 N. Robert St., St. Paul, MN 55101; phone: 612/296–3644).

Foundations and grants

Minnesota Foundation Directory (Foundation Data Center, 401 Kenmar Cr., Minnetonka, MN 55343; phone: 612/542–8582) $450, $475/annual update service which includes three updates a year, effectively giving you a new edition each quarter. Reports details on over 875 Minnesota foundations: contact person, officers and directors, territory and interest areas covered, list of grant recipients and amounts.

Guide to Minnesota Foundations and Corporate Giving Programs (Minnesota Council on Foundations, Suite 800, 706 Second Ave. South, Minneapolis, MN 55402; phone: 612/338–1989) $50 plus $3 shipping, 330 pages, issued in odd–numbered years. Describes over 720 grantmakers: program interests, range of grants, sample grants, officers, and directors. Also lists foundations that do not accept applications.

Minnesota Grants Directory (Minnesota Council of Nonprofits, Suite 250, 2700 University Ave., West, St. Paul, MN 55114; phone: 612/642–1904) $25 plus 6.5 percent sales tax and $2.50/shipping, 82 pages, published every June. Provides information on 250 Minnesota foundations, corporate and religious giving programs, and government grants for non–profits: contact person, deadlines, availability of funds, staff, trustees, and more.

Mississippi

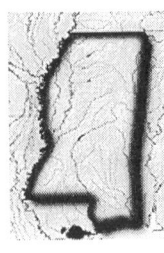

Mississippi 501 News (Mississippi Center for Nonprofits, Suite B, 612 North State St., Jackson, MS 39202; phone: 601/968–0061) quarterly, free. Occasional job listings.

The state has *ALEX* terminals at its Job Service Offices and many state institutions of higher education. As of this writing, there is no Internet–based job database operated by the state. Be sure, however, to check the state's home page at URL: **www.state.ms.us/** in case one has been recently established.

For a list of **Job Service Offices**, contact the Mississippi State Employment Service (1520 W. Capitol St., Jackson, MS 39203; phone: 601/354–8711) for a copy of the *Directory of Employment Service Offices*.

Foundations and grants

A Guide to Funders in Central Appalachia and the Tennessee Valley (Appalachia Community Fund, Suite 206, 517 Union Ave., Knoxville, TN 37902; phone: 423/523–5783) $27, 300+ pages, January 1994. Among the 399 funders reported on are those that give grants in Mississippi. Includes everything you need to seek funding: contact name, types of grants, grant application process, average grant size, plus how to write a grant proposal, funders from outside the region that make grants in the region, religious funding sources, and Japanese corporations with grantmaking programs.

Foundations and Funding Sources of Mississippi (Resource Review LLC, P.O. Box 12603, Lake Charles, LA 70612–2603; phone: 318/855–3466) $37 plus $2.50 shipping, 138 pages, 1995. Profiles 144 Mississippi foundations and 45 out–of–state foundations that target Mississippi. Also included in each profile are contact names, funding interests, sample list of grants awarded, and geographic focus.

Missouri

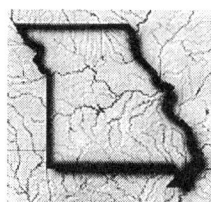

The St. Louis Directory (The Business Factory) free. Go to the Internet at URL: **http://directory.st–louis.mo.us/** where you can find profiles of more than 70 non–profit organizations plus educational institutions in the St. Louis area. Some of the profiles include job listings or links to home pages where you may find job openings.

Missouri Wage Surveys and ***Employment Projections*** (Department of Labor and Industrial Relations, Research and Analysis Section, P.O. Box 59, Jefferson City, MO 65104; phone: 573/751–3591) free. The wage survey is published on an ad hoc basis. The employment projections report is published annually.

Missouri Works offers a state job bank at Internet URL: **http://www.works.state.mo.us/mw2a.htm**. Select "Missouri Job Openings" where you will find job vacancies posted by occupation and region. You can get a directory of state Job Service Offices by choosing "DOLIR," then "Division of Employment Security," and then "Job Service Local Offices."

To locate **Job Service Offices**, contact the Division of Employment Security (Labor and Industrial Relations Department, 421 E. Dunklin, Box 59, Jefferson City, MO 65104; director's phone: 573/751–3215).

By–pass the State of Confusion: Read chapters 1 and 2 first

Foundations and grants

The Directory of Missouri Foundations (Swift Associates, 8122 Edinburgh Dr., St. Louis, MO 63105; phone: 314/725–6834) $40 plus $3.50/shipping, Missouri residents add $2.30 sales tax, 150 pages, published in January of even–numbered years. Reports on over 1,000 foundations that make grants to organizations or individuals: contact person, funding priorities, grant amounts, assets, total contributions, and trustees.

Directory of Missouri Grantmakers (The Foundation Center, 79 Fifth Ave., New York, NY 10003; phones: 800/424–9836, 212/620–4230) $75, 159 pages, June 1995. Reports details on over 800 independent, corporate, community, and local family foundations based in Missouri.

The Directory of Greater Kansas City Foundations (Clearinghouse for Midcontinent Foundations, P.O. Box 22680, Kansas City, MO 64113; phone: 816/235–1176) $58, 200 pages, annual in February. Features detailed profiles on nearly 500 foundations and trusts in the eight–county greater Kansas City metropolitan area: contact person, officers and directors, recipient information, range of grants, limitations, purpose, and more. Available for $90 in a quarterly–updated electronic version on a DOS or Windows™–formatted 3.5–inch floppy disk

Montana

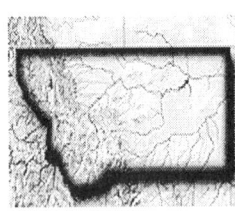

Rocky Mountain Employment Newsletter (Suite 309–BO, 10 Town Plaza, Durango, CO 81301; phone: 970/247–9550) 18 issues/year, $21/three–month subscription to one edition, $26/any two editions, $31/three editions, $36/four editions. Two and one–month subscriptions also available. Published in four editions: Montanta–Idaho, Colorado–Wyoming, Arizona–New Mexico, and Washington–Oregon. Combined, the four editions include over 400 job openings, some in non–profits. The positions tend to orient toward the outdoors, with quite a few in natural resources, environment, and wildlife.

Nonprofit Computerized Label Service (Northwest Regional Facilitators, 525 East Mission Ave., Spokane, WA 99202–1824; phone: 509/484–6733) 10¢ per name. Includes names and addresses for some 600 non–profit organizations in the states of Idaho and Montana.

Montana Job Source is located on the Internet at URL: **http://jsd_server.dli.mt.gov/**. To access the job database, select "Internet Self–Directed Job Search" and then choose from specific categories of jobs. Listings are updated daily. To get a directory of state Job Service Offices, pick "Montana Job Service Offices."

Please, no photocopying

ALEX kiosks are located at a number of post offices, libraries, grocery stores, and shopping malls as well as the state's Job Service Offices.

Directory of Job Service Offices (Job Service Division, Department of Labor and Industry, P.O. Box 1728, Helena, MT 59624; phone: 406/444–4100) free. Lists detailed information on the state's 23 **Job Service Offices.**

Foundations and grants

The Montana Foundation Directory (Montana State University–Billings, Grants Center, 1500 N. 30th, Billings, MT 59101–0298; phone: 406/657–2040) $10, 200 pages, annual in May. Reports on some 180 foundations in Montana and about 20 out-of-state foundations that serve Montana: contact person, application procedures, areas of interest, and geographic preferences.

Nebraska

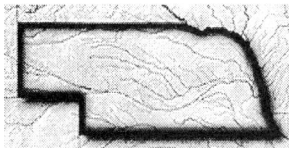

Nebraska Job Source resides on the Internet at URL: **http://www.lincnet.com/lincnet/pages/njs/njsmain.htm**. As of this writing there is no job database. You should check this site for any recent additions.

ALEX kiosks are located at a number of government offices, libraries, grocery stores, gas stations, and shopping malls as well as the state's Job Service Offices.

Job seekers can access *America's Job Bank* at Job Service Offices.

To locate **Job Service Offices**, contact the Job Service Division (Department of Labor, 550 S. 16th St., Lincoln, NE 68509; phone: 402/471–9828).

Foundations and grants

Nebraska Foundation Directory (Junior League of Omaha, 608 N. 108th Ct., Omaha, NE 68154; phone: 402/493–8818) $20, 42 pages, last published in December 1995. Reports on over 200 foundations: officers, statement of purpose.

By–pass the State of Confusion: Read chapters 1 and 2 first

Nevada

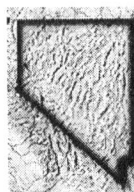

To obtain a list of **Job Service Offices**, contact the Employment Security Department (500 E. Third St., Carson City, NV 89713; phone: 702/687–4630).

Foundations and grants

Nevada Foundation Directory (Las Vegas–Clark County Library District, Attn: Reference, 1401 E. Flamingo Rd., Las Vegas, NV 89119; phone: 702/733–7810) $17, 1994. Profiles foundations, state funding, and block grants in Nevada and those that fund projects in Nevada: contact person, field of interest, sample grants.

New Hampshire

Opportunity NOCs New England (Executive Service Corp., 211 Congress St., Boston, MA 02110; phone: 617/357–0849) biweekly, $12/three–month subscription/individuals only, $45/annual subscription/individuals, $30/annual/non–profits. About 40 job vacancies for all levels of work in non–profits appear in the typical issue. Job ads are posted on the Internet a week after they appear in the periodical. Go to URL: **http://www.opnocs.org**.

Local job openings with educational institutions and non–profits are advertised in local newspapers and ***The New Hampshire Sunday News*** (P.O. Box 9555, Manchester, NH 03108; phone: 603/668–4321), ***Maine Sunday Telegram*** (P.O. Box 1460, Portland, ME 04104; phone: 207/775–5811), and ***Boston Globe*** (Community News Dealer Company, 61st Ave., Waltham, MA 02254; phone: 617/446–1818). You can also access the last two weeks of job ads from the *Boston Globe* on the Internet at URL: **http://www.boston.com** by selecting the "Jobs" button and then "Job Search." You can specify the job category or location. You can also use the internship resume and job databases where over 50 internships are listed. As of this writing this is a painfully slow web site due to excessively complicated graphics.

New Hampshire Works currently offers a job bulletin board service at the Internet address: **telnet://nhworks.state.nh.us/**. For information on how to use it, go on the Internet to URL: **http://www.nhworks.state.nh.us/**. You can also access a directory of the state's Job Service Offices here by selecting "Local Offices."

To locate the state's 12 **Job Service Offices**, contact the Bureau of Employment Services (Department of Employment Security, 32 S. Main St., Concord, NH 03301; phone: 603/224–3311).

Foundations and grants

Directory of Charitable Funds in New Hampshire (Department of Justice, Division of Charitable Trusts, 33 Capitol St., Concord, NH 03301; phone: 603/271–3591) $5, 84 pages, 1995. Describes over 240 foundations: purpose statement, officers, and assets.

Northern New England Nonprofits Membership Directory (Granite State Association of Nonprofits, 125 Airport Rd., Concord, NH 03301; phone: 603/225–0900) $15/nonmembers, free/members, 50 pages, 1995. List of 300 members: addresses, phone numbers, mission statements, and more.

New Jersey

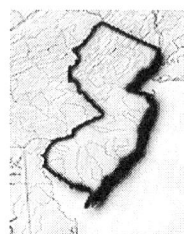

Opportunity NOCs (The Nonprofit Management Development Center, LaSalle University, 1900 W. Olney, Philadelphia, PA 19141–1199; phone: 215/951–1701) monthly, $10/three–month subscription, $30/annual subscription; non–profit organizations: $12/annual subscription. Around 40 positions with non–profits in Delaware, southern New Jersey, and Pennsylvania are described in every issue.

Community Jobs: The Regional Newsletter N.Y./N.J. (ACCESS: Networking in the Public Interest, Suite 838, 1001 Connecticut Ave., Washington, DC 20036; phone: 202/785–4233) semimonthly, $25/three–month subscription, $49/six–month subscription, $89/annual subscription; but if you also subscribe to the national edition of *Community Jobs,* you can get *Community Jobs/N.Y./N.J.* for just additional $5/three months, $10/six months, $20/year; see the description of *Community Jobs* in Chapter 3 under "Job ads." Includes advertisements for positions with a broad range of non–profits in the New York and New Jersey metropolitan area. The vast majority of these job announcements do not appear in the national edition of *Community Jobs.*

Dialogue (Center for Nonprofit Corporations, 15 Roszel Rd., Princeton, NJ 08540; phone: 609/951–0800) eight issues/year, $225/nonmember annual subscription, free/members. Two or three job ads appear under "Classifieds."

By–pass the State of Confusion: Read chapters 1 and 2 first

CNC Salary Survey (Center for Nonprofit Corporations, 15 Roszel Rd., Princeton, NJ 08540; phone: 609/951–0800) contact for price, 24 pages, 1996. Lists positions by budget, staff size, gender, geographic location, and benefits.

Workforce New Jersey Public Information Network features both job and resume databases at Internet URL: **http://nj.jobsearch.org/** and at URL: **http://www.wnjpin.state.nj.us/**. Select "Jobs" to access New Jersey Job Search as well as links to local newspapers and other job sites. You can conduct a self–directed job search and seek positions by keyword, or search by occupational, DOT, or military code. Choose "List a Resume"to electronically place your resume into *America's Talent Bank* where employers from throughout the country can access it.

To find out about non–profit job opportunities check *ALEX* computer terminals located at public libraries, county colleges, shopping malls, and at all the state's Job Service Offices.

Job Service Offices (Division of Workforce New Jersey, Department of Labor, John Fitch Plaza, CN 055, Labor Building 4th Floor, Trenton, NJ 08625; phone: 609/984–2244). Request this list of the 24 full–service **Job Service Offices** and 13 satellite offices.

Foundations and grants

Job Listing Service (The Foundation Center, 79 Fifth Ave., Eighth floor, New York, NY 10003; phone: 212/620–4230) free, walk–in service only. Positions with non–profit entities in New Jersey and elsewhere are listed here. These job vacancies can be viewed *only* in person. They are *not* published.

The Mitchell Guide to Foundations and Their Managers: New Jersey (The Mitchell Guide, 430 Federal City Rd., NJ 08502; phone: 609/737–7224) $85/prepaid, includes UPS shipping, 600 pages, issued in March of even–numbered years. Provides information on 400+ foundations: foundation managers, restrictions and program priorities, sample grants. Most of these are small family–run foundations, and thus not good for seeking out jobs but worthwhile for contacts and grant information.

New Jersey Notes (The Mitchell Guide, 430 Federal City Rd., NJ 08502; phone: 609/737–7224) bimonthly, $35/annual subscription. Supplements *The Mitchell Guide to Foundations, Corporations, and Their Managers: New Jersey* described immediately above, with information about new foundations and grant programs, and changes in existing foundation funding programs. Most of these are small family–run foundations, and thus not good for seeking out jobs but worthwhile for contacts and grant information.

New Mexico

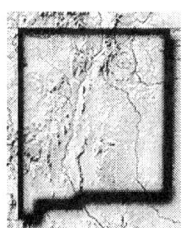

Rocky Mountain Employment Newsletter (Suite 309–BO, 10 Town Plaza, Durango, CO 81301; phone: 970/247–9550) 18 issues/year, $21/three–month subscription to one edition, $26/any two editions, $31/three editions, $36/four editions. Two and one–month subscriptions also available. Published in four editions: New Mexico–Arizona, Colorado–Wyoming, Idaho–Montana, and Washington–Oregon. Combined, the four editions include over 400 job openings, some in non–profits. The positions tend to orient toward the outdoors, with quite a few in natural resources, environment, and wildlife.

Albuquerque Journal (7777 Jefferson, NE, Albuquerque, NM 87109; phone: 505/823–4400; $39/six–month Sunday mail subscription). The Sunday edition is the best source of ads for jobs in three–fourths of the state. For the southern and southeast portions of the state, see the Sunday *El Paso Times* (300 N. Campbell, El Paso, TX 79901; phone: 915/546–6260; $8.75/one month mail subscription, $26.25/three months; $52/50/six months, $105/annual). For jobs in the extreme southern section, beginning with Clovis and going south, the Sunday editions of the local newspapers from nearby Texas are the best sources.

To locate **Job Service Offices**, contact the Department of Labor (401 Broadway, NE, Albuquerque, NM 87102; phone: 505/841–8520). A directory of these offices can be found on the Internet at URL: **http://wwww.state.nm.us/dol** and then selecting "How to Reach Use" and then "Workforce Development Centers."

New York

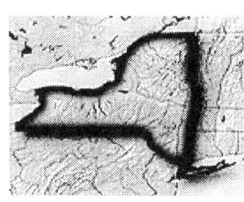

Community Jobs: The Regional Newsletter N.Y./N.J. (ACCESS: Networking in the Public Interest, Suite 838, 1001 Connecticut Ave., Washington, DC 20036; phone: 202/785–4233) semimonthly, $25/three–month subscription, $49/six–month subscription, $89/annual subscription; but if you also subscribe to the national edition of *Community Jobs*, you can get *Community Jobs/N.Y./N.J.* for just additional $5/three months, $10/six months, $20/year; see the description of *Community Jobs* in Chapter 3 under "Job ads." Includes advertisements for positions with a broad range of non–profits in the New York and New Jersey metropolitan area. The vast majority of these job announcements do not appear in the national edition of *Community Jobs*.

By–pass the State of Confusion: Read chapters 1 and 2 first

Job Listing Service (The Foundation Center, 79 Fifth Ave., Eighth floor, New York, NY 10003; phone: 212/620–4230) free, walk–in service only. Positions with non–profit entities in New York and elsewhere are listed here. These job vacancies can be viewed *only* in person. They are *not* published.

The Village Voice (VV Publishing, 36 Cooper Sq., New York, NY 10003; phone: 800/857–2997) weekly on Wednesday, $53/annual subscription (U.S.), $87/foreign; $2.25/single issue at bookstores and newsstands. The "Classifieds" section has several hundred ads for jobs primarily in the New York metropolitan area, including a good number of positions in the entertainment industry, the arts, and some with non–profits.

New York City Nonprofits Mailing List (Community Studies of New York, Attn: Rita Manning, Suite #5, 350 E. 78th St., New York, NY 10021; phone: 718/263–0103) 20¢ per name/general public, 10¢ per name/non–profits, $60 minimum charge, available printed, as self–adhesive mailing labels (three across), or on 3.5–inch MS–DOS disks in dBase or ASCII text. Contains names, addresses, and telephone numbers of approximately 13,000+ non–profit organizations. Data is sorted by 21 categories, among them: geographic location, number of employees, tax status, site or parent organization, activities, social services, health/mental health, arts and culture, schools, auxiliary services, religion, foundation, trade association, housing, and other. Be sure to specify the geographic areas you want, size of the non–profit organizations, and number of employees. If ordering the information on disk, specify the data format.

The Source Book 1995–96: Social and Health Services in the Greater New York Area (Oryx Press, Suite 700, 4041 N. Central, Phoenix, AZ 85012–3397; phone: 800/279–6799) $60.50, 1,200 pages, 1995. Produced by the United Way of New York City and the City of New York, this directory describes hospitals, social service organizations, libraries, and about 2,000 other non–profit public and private agencies in the New York City metropolitan area.

Greater Capital Region Human Services Directory (Council of Community Services, Suite 1, 200 Henry Johnson Blvd., Albany, NY 12210; phone: 518/434–9194) $17 plus $3/shipping, 170 pages, published every February. Includes descriptions of about 1,500 non–profit human service agencies and 600 private care providers located in Warren, Washington, Saratoga, Fulton, Montgomery, Schenectady, Albany, Schoharie, Rensselaer, Green, and Columbia counties.

How to Get a Job in New York City and the Metropolitan Area (Surrey Books; available from the Job Search Resources Catalog at the end of this book) $16.95, 360 pages, 1996. Although filled mostly with private sector employers, this easy–to–use book tells you whom to contact for job vacancies at a moderate number of non–profit employers in the metropolitan area in social services, foundations, and education. A large number of non–profit organizations have their national headquarters in New York and its environs. Even more importantly, this book gives you details on the local chapters of professional and trade associations you may wish to join for networking purposes or which may publish a periodical with jobs ads or operate a local job service. A good many local chapters may be large enough to hire staff. It also includes information on local job hotlines, Internet Web sites of many local employers, and local trade magazines plus career consultants.

Internships and Job Opportunities in New York City and Washington, DC (Graduate Group, P.O. Box 370351, West Hartford, CT 06137; phone: 860/233–2330) $27.50, published annually. Describes internship and job opportunities in a wide variety of fields.

New York State Department of Labor Home Page includes two useful job databases at Internet URL: **http://www.labor.state.ny.us/**. Select "Looking for a Job?" and then click on "New York's Job Search and Employment Information." This is the only site we know of that also includes apprenticeships. Choose "Interested in Finding Out About Apprenticeships?" You'll find a list of openings for apprentices in the trades for the entire state. By picking "Directories" on the home page, you'll access the directory of state Job Service Offices.

To find **Job Service Offices**, tagged Community Service Centers in New York, contact the Department of Labor (Room 590, State Campus Building #12, Albany, NY 12240; phone: 518/457–3584).

Foundations and grants

New York State Foundations: A Comprehensive Directory (The Foundation Center, 79 Fifth Ave., New York, NY 10003; phones: 800/424–9836, 212/620–4230) $180, 1,095 pages, published in May of odd–numbered years. Reports details on over 5,500 independent, corporate, and community foundations based in New York State. Also includes information on over 900 grantmakers from outside the state that fund non–profits within New York State.

Guide to Grantmakers in the Rochester Area: 1995–1997 (Rochester Grantmakers Forum, 55 St. Paul St., Rochester, NY 14604; phone: 716/232–2380) $58, individuals add 8 percent sales tax, 324 pages, published in the summer of odd–numbered years. Includes over 150 sources of funding, lists of sample grants, common application and report form, and types of support index.

The Mitchell Guide to Foundations, Corporations, and Their Managers: Central New York, including Binghamton, Corning, Elmira, Geneva, Ithaca, Oswego, Syracuse, Utica (Rowland L. Mitchell, Jr., P.O. Box 172,

Scarsdale, NY 10583; phone: 914/723-7770) $40/includes shipping, 1997. Provides information on over 90 foundations: managers, sample grants financial data.

The Mitchell Guide to Foundations, Corporations, and Their Managers: Long Island, including Nassau and Suffolk Counties (Rowland L. Mitchell, Jr., P.O. Box 172, Scarsdale, NY 10583; phone: 914/723-7770) $40/includes shipping, 1997. Provides information on over 180 foundations: managers, sample grants financial data.

The Mitchell Guide to Foundations, Corporations, and Their Managers: Upper Hudson Valley, including Capital Area, Glens Falls, Newburgh, Plattsburgh, Poughkeepsie, Schenectady (Rowland L. Mitchell, Jr., P.O. Box 172, Scarsdale, NY 10583; phone: 914/723-7770) $40/includes shipping, 1997. Provides information on over 60 foundations: managers, sample grants financial data.

The Mitchell Guide to Foundations, Corporations, and Their Managers: Westchester, including Putnam, Rockland and Orange Counties (Rowland L. Mitchell, Jr., P.O. Box 172, Scarsdale, NY 10583; phone: 914/723-7770) $40/includes shipping, 1996. Provides information on over 215 foundations: managers, sample grants financial data.

The Mitchell Guide to Foundations, Corporations, and Their Managers: Western New York, including Buffalo, Jamestown, Niagra Falls, Rochester (Rowland L. Mitchell, Jr., P.O. Box 172, Scarsdale, NY 10583; phone: 914/723-7770) $40/includes shipping, 1997. Provides information on over 130 foundations: managers, sample grants financial data.

North Carolina

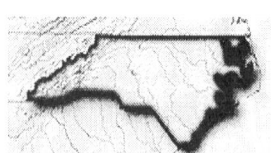

Philanthropy Journal of North Carolina (Suite 805, Five W. Hargett St., Raleigh, NC 27601; phone: 919/899-3742) monthly, $60/annual subscription. The "Job Opportunities" section contains ads for about five to 20 positions, mostly for senior-level jobs with non-profit organizations and universities; lots of fundraising positions. For job listings on the Internet, go to URL: **http://philanthropy-journal.org** and select "Nonprofit Jobs," where you will find about 20 detailed vacancy listings for nonprofit positions in North Carolina. Be sure to check out the extensive links by selecting "Meta-Index for Nonprofit Organizations," which the *New York Times* said is "a good starting point to explore philanthropy on the Internet." To find job listings, however, you'll need to do a lot of searching.

Please, no photocopying

Membership Directory of the North Carolina Center for Nonprofits (North Carolina Center for Nonprofits, Suite 506, 4601 Six Forks Rd., Raleigh, NC 27609–5210; phone: 919/571–0811) contact for price, 100 pages, 1997. You'll get a brief description of 1,080 non–profit agencies that includes name, address, phone, and contact name.

ESC Online offers a job database with over 20,000 job vacancies in North Carolina at Internet URL: **http://www.esc.state.nc.us/**. Select "Search for Job Openings" and then choose "Internet JIS." To see a directory of local Job Service Offices, pick "Local Office Directory" on the home page.

To locate **Job Service Offices**, contact the Employment Security Commission (P.O. Box 25903, Raleigh, NC 27611; phone: 919/733–7522).

Foundations and grants

North Carolina Giving: The Directory of the State's Foundations (Capital Consortium, Suite 312, 2700 Wycliff Rd., Raleigh, NC 27607; phone: 919/783–9199) $162, 1,092 pages, 1996. Profiles over 865 foundations: trustee, limitations, application procedures, sample grants. Also available on a DOS–formatted 3.5–inch floppy disk.

North Carolina Corporate Giving (Capital Consortium, Suite 312, 2700 Wycliff Rd., Raleigh, NC 27607; phone: 919/783–9199) $113, 300 pages, 1995. Profiles 278 corporations' philanthropic programs: direct giving, giving through foundations, in–kind gifts, and matching gifts. Includes contact names, addresses, and phone numbers.

A Guide to Funders in Central Appalachia and the Tennessee Valley (Appalachia Community Fund, Suite 206, 517 Union Ave., Knoxville, TN 37902; phone: 423/523–5783) $27, 300+ pages, January 1994. Among the 399 funders reported on are those that give grants in western North Carolina. Includes everything you need to seek funding: contact name, types of grants, grant application process, average grant size, plus how to write a grant proposal, funders from outside the region that make grants in the region, religious funding sources, and Japanese corporations with grantmaking programs.

North Dakota

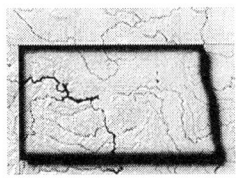

Job Placement offers a job database that is updated daily at Internet URL: **http://www.state.nd.us/jsnd/lmi.htl**. Just select "North Dakota Job Listings" and then pick "North Dakota Job Opportunities" to access the job database which you can search by keyword, occupational code, DOT code, or military code.

By–pass the State of Confusion: Read chapters 1 and 2 first

Job Service North Dakota (1000 E. Divide Ave., P.O. Box 5507, Bismarck, ND 58506; phone: 701/328-2836). Announcements for jobs can be viewed at any of the state's 20 local **Job Service Offices**. Ask for the brochure entitled *Your Step-by-Step Guide to Using Job Service.* You can also get the addresses of the Job Service Offices at Internet URL: **http://www.state.nd.us/jsnd/contacts.htm**.

Ohio

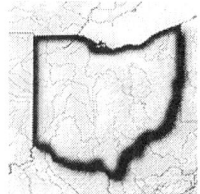

Opportunity NOCs (Ohio Association of Nonprofit Organizations, P.O. Box 164353, Columbus, OH 43216-4353; phone: 614/224-1336) biweekly, contact for subscription rates after September 1, 1997. This periodical is expected to start publishing by early fall 1997. For its first three months it will cover northeastern Ohio. After that it may cover the entire state. You can expect about 40 job vacancies for all levels of work in non-profits to appear in the typical issue.

Ohio Bureau of Employment Services Home Page allows you to browse job listings within regions at Internet URL: **http://www.state.oh.us.obes/** by picking "Main Menu" and then "Ohio Job Net." To see a directory of state Job Service Offices, click on "Office List."

To obtain a list of the state's 60 **Job Service Offices**, contact the Communications Division of the Bureau of Employment Services) 145 S. Front St., P.O. Box 1618, Columbus, OH 43216; phone: 614/466-3859). Ask for the *Customer's Guide to Services* brochure.

Foundations and grants

Charitable Foundations Directory of Ohio (Office of the Attorney General, Charitable Foundations Section, 4th Floor, 101 E. Town St., Columbus, OH 43215-5148) $7.50 (includes postage), March 1997. Reports on some 2,600 charitable organizations that make grants: contact person, restrictions, purpose, number of grants awarded.

The Cincinnati Area Foundation Directory (MR & Company, P.O. Box 9223, Cincinnati, OH 45209; phone: 513/871-9436) $50 plus 3 percent sales tax for Ohio residents, 90 pages, February 1996. Describes over 220 foundations and charitable trusts: areas of interest, officers and trustees, application procedures, sample grants, financial data.

The Cleveland Foundation Directory (MR & Company, P.O. Box 9223, Cincinnati, OH 45209; phone: 513/871–9436) $50 plus 3 percent sales tax for Ohio residents, 1997. Reports on about 280 Cuyahoga County foundations and charitable trusts: areas of interest, officers and trustees, application procedures, sample grants, financial data.

Oklahoma

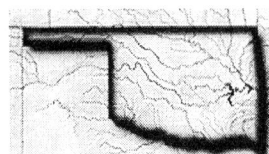

Oklahoma's Job Net gives you access to a job database at Internet URL: **http://www.oesc.state.ok.us/jobnet/default.htm**. Select "Job Search by Occupation" or "Job Search by Keyword." To see a directory of state Job Service Offices, pick "OESC Home Page" and then "Local Office Directory."

To pinpoint **Job Service Offices**, contact the Employment Security Commission (2401 N. Lincoln Blvd., Oklahoma City, OK 73152; phone: 405/557–0200).

Foundations and grants

The Directory of Oklahoma Foundations (Foundation Research Project, P.O. Box 1146, Oklahoma City, OK 73101; phone: 405/235–5603) $25/prepaid, $30/billed, 146 pages. 1995. Profiles more than 100 Oklahoma foundations: contact person, application procedures, restrictions, funding emphasis, financial data.

Oregon

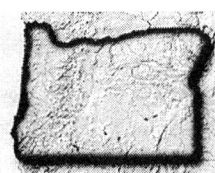

Rocky Mountain Employment Newsletter (Suite 309–BO, 10 Town Plaza, Durango, CO 81301; phone: 970/247–9550) 18 issues/year, $21/three–month subscription to one edition, $26/any two editions, $31/three editions, $36/four editions. Two and one-month subscriptions also available. Published in four editions: Oregon–Washington, Colorado–Wyoming, Arizona–New Mexico, and Idaho–Montana. Combined, the four editions include over 400 job openings, some with non–profits. The positions tend to orient toward the outdoors, with quite a few in natural resources, environment, and wildlife.

Oregon Employment Department Home Page is at Internet URL: **http://www.emp.state.or.us/**. Select "Oregon Online" and then "Commerce" to access the job database. Alternatively, you can pick "Jobs" and then "Job Listings." The state operates touch–screen kiosks connected to this

By–pass the State of Confusion: Read chapters 1 and 2 first

job database at 157 shopping centers, libraries, colleges, supermarkets, and even fast food restaurants ("I'll have a Big Mac and job to go, please."). For a directory of these sites, choose "Jobs" and then click on "Touch Screen Locations." For a list of state Job Service Offices, select "Jobs" and then pick "Employment Office Locations."

How to Get a Job in Seattle/Portland (Surrey Books; available from the Job Search Resouces Catalog at the end of this book) $16.95, 486 pages, 1996. Although filled mostly with private sector employers, this easy-to-use book tells you whom to contact for job vacancies at a moderate number of non-profit employers in the Portland metropolitan area in social services, foundations, and education. Perhaps more importantly, it gives you details on the local chapters of professional and trade associations you may wish to join for networking purposes or which may publish a periodical with jobs ads or operate a local job service. Some local chapters may be large enough to hire staff. It also includes information on local job hotlines, Internet Web sites of many local employers, and local trade magazines plus career consultants.

Field Office Directory (Oregon Division, 875 Union St., NE, Salem, OR 97301; phones: 503/378-3211, 800/237-3710 within Oregon only). Contact these folks for this list of 46 local **Job Service Offices** at which listings of job vacancies are available.

Foundations and grants

The Guide to Oregon Foundations (Information and Referral, P.O. Box 637, Portland, OR 97207; phone: 503/226-3099, ask for Claudia Moorad) $33, 185 pages, published in spring of odd-numbered years. Reports on general purpose foundations, special purpose foundations, and national or regional foundations with an active interest in Oregon: contact person, purpose statement, financial data, officers, and sample grants.

Pacific Northwest Grantmakers Forum Member Directory (Pacific Northwest Grantmakers Forum, Suite 214, 1305 Fourth Ave, Seattle, WA 98101; phone: 206/624-9899) $39.74/out-of-state residents, $43/Washington state residents, 186 pages, published in March of even-numbered years. Among the nearly 100 or so grantmakers described in this directory are many from Oregon and Alaska. Included in each listing are contact name's address and phone, application procedures, range of grant amounts awarded, and types of projects funded.

Please, no photocopying

Pennsylvania

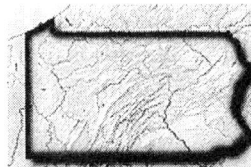

Opportunity NOCs (The Nonprofit Management Development Center, LaSalle University, 1900 W. Olney, Philadelphia, PA 19141–1199; phone: 215/951–1701) monthly, $10/three–month subscription, $30/annual subscription; non–profit organizations: $12/annual subscription. Around 40 positions with non–profits in Pennsylvania, southern New Jersey, and Delaware are described in every issue.

In Pittsburgh (In Pittsburgh Publishing, 2000 E. Carson St., Pittsburgh, PA 15203; phone: 412/488–1212) free at selected bookstores and other public places, $35/six–month mail subscription, $60/annual. The "Classifieds" section includes about 30 ads for jobs of all sorts including a fair number of positions in the arts.

Pittsburgh Job Source (MetCom, Inc.; available from the Job Search Resources Catalog at the end of this book) $15.95, 276 pages, 1997. Gives you the number of employees and the name, address, and phone number of the hiring contact for non–profits, health care institutions, and educational institutions, plus federal, state, and local government agencies and companies in the Pittsburgh area. Includes job hotlines, employment agencies, recruiters, and Internet Web pages. Includes information on more than 5,000 contacts. The entries focus on employers that offer middle management, entry level, and internship positions. Also included is a directory of Pennsylvania Job Service Offices.

Job Listing Service (The Foundation Center, 79 Fifth Ave., Eighth floor, New York, NY 10003; phone: 212/620–4230) free, walk–in service only. Positions with non–profit entities in Pennsylvania and elsewhere are listed here. These job vacancies can be viewed *only* in person. They are *not* published.

Mailing List (Pennsylvania Association of Nonprofit Organizations, 132 State St., Harrisburg, PA 17101; phone: 215/956–2335) $40.25, continuously updated. The mailing list totals more than 200 members.

The state has placed *ALEX* kiosks in ten shopping malls and municipal buildings, in addition to all Job Service Offices.

Obtain locations of **Job Service Offices** from the Bureau of Employment Services and Training (Department of Labor and Industry, 12th Floor, Seventh and Forster Streets, Harrisburg, PA 17121; phone: 717/787–3354).

By–pass the State of Confusion: Read chapters 1 and 2 first

Foundations and grants

Directory of Pennsylvania Foundations (Triadvocates Press, P.O. Box 336, Springfield, PA 19064; phone: 610/544–6927) $68.50, 464 pages, 1995. Provides summary data of name, address, and status on over 1,900 foundations; plus full profiles on over 1,400 foundations: application guidelines, directors and trustees, major interests.

Rhode Island

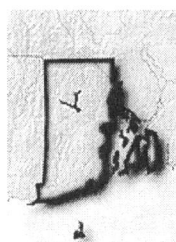

Opportunity NOCs New England (Executive Service Corp., 211 Congress St., Boston, MA 02110; phone: 617/357–0849) biweekly, $12/three–month subscription/individuals only, $45/annual subscription/individuals, $30/annual/non–profits. About 40 job vacancies for all levels of work in non–profits appear in the typical issue. Job ads are posted on the Internet a week after they appear in the periodical. Go to URL: **http://www.opnocs.org**.

Rhode Island Department of Employment and Training Home Page includes a job database at Internet URL: **http://www.det.state.ri.us/**. Select "Rhode Island Job Bank" or "Heard It Through the Grapevine" to access the job database where you can conduct a self–directed job search or seek vacancies by occupational, DOT, or military code. To discover the locations of local Job Service Offices, select "Directory of Local Offices."

At the Warwick Mall, in Warwick, RI, the Department of Employment and Training maintains a "Video Wall" where it posts job vacancies, the location and phone number of state Job Service Offices, and other information about finding jobs in the state.

Find the nine **Job Service Offices**, by contacting the Department of Employment and Training (101 Friendship St., Providence, RI 02903; phone: 401/277–3722) or see your telephone directory.

South Carolina

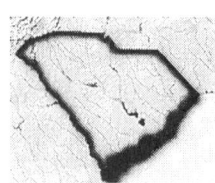

South Carolina Security Commission Home Page does not yet include a job database. But it probably will in the near future — so be sure to check it out yourself at Internet URL: **http://scjob .sces.org/**. To get a directory of state Job Service Offices, select "Offices."

To locate the state's 38 **Job Service Offices**, contact the Employment Security Commission (1550 Gadsden St., Columbia, SC 29202; phone: 803/737–2400).

Please, no photocopying

Foundations and grants

South Carolina Foundation Directory (South Carolina State Library, Attn: Foundation Directory, P.O. Box 11469, Columbia, SC 29211; phone: 803/734–8666) call for price, 390 pages, 1997. Around 300 foundations are described: areas of interest, range of grants, geographic limitations, principal officer.

South Dakota

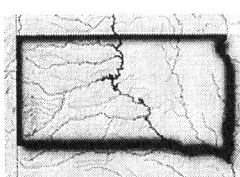

South Dakota Department of Labor Home Page is located on the Internet at URL: **http://www.state.sd.us/state/executive/dol/dol.htm**. Select "South Dakota's Job Search Page" to conduct a self–directed job search or to search by occupational, DOT, or military code. Choose "16 Field Offices" to get the addresses and phone numbers for the state's Job Service Offices.

The state has placed a number of *ALEX* kiosks in grocery stores.

Job openings in the non–profit sector can be found by contacting a local **Job Service Office**. You can obtain a list of these offices by contacting the South Dakota Department of Labor (P.O. Box 4730, Aberdeen, SD 57402–4730; phones: 800/592–1882, 605/622–2302). The offices are computerized, so you can obtain up–to–the–minute information on job openings in South Dakota and nationally.

Foundations and grants

The South Dakota Grant Directory (South Dakota State Library, 800 Governors Dr., Pierre, SD 57501; phone: 605/773–3131) $7, 1995. Over 300 grantmaking institutions are profiled: eligibility requirements, purpose statements, application procedures.

Tennessee

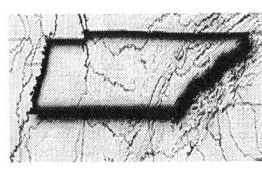

Directory of Community Services (Council of Community Services, 2012 21st Ave., South, Nashville, TN 37212; phone: 615/385–2221) $25/two–volume set plus $4/shipping, volume available individually for $13 each plus $2/shipping each. The 400–page Volume One covers over 460 agencies in Davidson County where Nashville rests. Over 520 agencies located in 21

By–pass the State of Confusion: Read chapters 1 and 2 first

surrounding counties are described in the 412-page Volume Two. Each agency description includes a contact person, area served, services offered, and clientele.

Salary Survey (Council of Community Services, 2012 21st Ave., South, Nashville, TN 37212; phone: 615/385-2221) $21.95, 20 pages, annual. Covers all levels of positions with non-profits throughout Tennessee.

Tennessee: America at Its Best is the home page of the state's Department of Employment Security, located at Internet URL: **http://www.state.tn .us/employsecurity/**. Pick "Job Search" and then "Job Search in Tennessee" to conduct a self-directed job search or to search by occupational, DOT, or military code. To find the local state Job Service Offices, select "Job Search" and then "Local Offices."

To obtain a list of **Job Service Offices**, contact the Department of Employment Security (500 James Robertson Parkway, 12th Floor, Davy Crockett Tower, Nashville, TN 37245-0001; phone: 615/741-4171).

Foundations and grants

Grantseekers Guide to Tennessee Funders (Center for Nonprofit Management, 250 Venture Cr., Nashville, TN 37228; phone: 615/780-2448) $99, plus $4.50 shipping, 392 pages, July 1995. Profiles over 150 corporate givers.

A Guide to Funders in Central Appalachia and the Tennessee Valley (Appalachia Community Fund, Suite 206, 517 Union Ave., Knoxville, TN 37902; phone: 423/523-5783) $27, 300+ pages, January 1994. Among the 399 funders described are ones that award grants in Tennessee. Includes everything you need to seek funding: contact name, types of grants, grant application process, average grant size, plus how to write a grant proposal, funders from outside the region that make grants in the region, religious funding sources, and Japanese corporations with grantmaking programs.

Texas

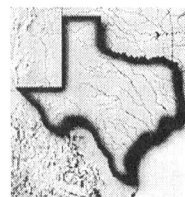

Opportunity NOCs (Center for Nonprofit Management, 2900 Live Oak St., Dallas, TX 75204; phone: 214/826-3470) semimonthly, $15/three-month subscription, $45/annual; non-profit organizations: $45/annual subscription. Ads for 45 or more vacancies throughout the state appear every issue. You can advertise your availability under "Positions Wanted."

Please, no photocopying

JOBTRAC BBS – The Dallas Jobs Network (6856 Arboreal Dr., Dallas, TX 75231; modem phone only: 214/349–0527) free. Set your modem at 8–N–1 and connect at up to 14,400 baud. This bulletin board service includes job databases with hundreds of job opportunities within Texas (mostly in the Dallas/Fort Worth area) in all fields: non–profits, education, human services, government, secretarial, technical, sales, accounting, computers, administration, engineering, medical, temporary services, contract work, bookkeeping, clerical, bench work, processing, blue collar, and anything professional. In many cases you can download job descriptions that interest you. You can also send your resume by modem directly to many of the employers in these databases. It also includes resume databases. Allow some time when you dial up *JobTrac* since *JobTrac* contains a very extensive collection of job database files for positions throughout the country as well as Texas.

Texas Workforce Commission Home Page, located on the Internet at URL: **http://www.twc.state.tx/twc.html**, provides instructions on how to download the files that constitute *TWC Job Express*, the state's database of job openings. Updated each weekday morning, this database must be downloaded or viewed on the TWC Direct BBS, a bulletin board service at 512/475–4893 (8 bits, 1 stop bit, no parity, full duplex, set terminal to emulate VT–100 or VT–102, turn off line wrap). You can get full instructions on the home page by selecting "TWC Job Express." To see a directory of state Job Service Offices, pick "Office Directories."

The state maintains a number of ***InfoTexas*** kiosks at shopping centers, libraries, and groceries. Each touch–screen kiosk allows you to search "Job Express" for non–profit jobs in Texas and to use *ALEX* to search for jobs throughout the country.

The Texas Workforce Commission operates a statewide, computer–assisted job matching system at its 100 **Job Service Offices**. Request a list of these offices from the TWC State Office (101 E. 15th St., Austin, TX 78778–0001; phone: 512/463–2222) or see the state government section of the local telephone directory.

Foundations and grants

Directory of Texas Foundations (Nonprofit Resource Center, P.O. Box 15070, San Antonio, TX 78212–8270; phone: 210/227–4333.) $120, 300 pages, annual in January. Describes 1,689 foundations and charitable groups: contact person, application procedures, emphasis, restrictions, grant range, trustees.

Directory of Dallas Foundations (Dallas Public Library, Grants Information Service, 1515 Young St., Dallas, TX 75201; phone: 214/670–1484) call for price and availability, 500+ pages, 1997. Reports on hundreds of private foundations: contact person, interests, officers, number of grants awarded.

By–pass the State of Confusion: Read chapters 1 and 2 first

Directory of Tarrant County Grant Makers (Funding Information Center, Texas Christian University, TCU Box 298410, Fort Worth, TX 76129; phone: 817/921–7664) $60 plus $3.50/shipping, published each October of even–numbered years. Reports on more than 140 foundations and other grant makers: types of support, fields of interest, trustees.

Utah

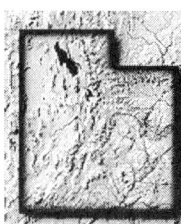

Utah Nonprofits Association Membership List (UNA, 183 W. 1700 South, Salt Lake City, UT 84115; phone: 801/485–9146) available free on the Internet. Go to URL: **http://www.nonprofit.utah.org/una**, and select "Current Membership List," which provides organization name, key contact, phone, and address. You can find more contacts by clicking on "Utah Nonprofit Links," which gives you the home pages of nonprofit organizations throughout the state.

Utah Job Service operates a state job database on the Internet at URL: **http:udesb.state.ut.us/**. Pick "Job Bank" to see job vacancies. Select "Talent Bank" to submit your electronic resume to *America's Talent Bank*. To see the directory of Job Service Office locations, click on "Help" in the graphical rendering of an office on the home page.

The state has placed a good number of kiosks at airports, stores, museums, and shopping centers where you can access the state's job database and *America's Job Bank*. These locations are listed in the *Access Utah!* brochure available from the Utah Job Service described below.

Job listings are available by in–person application at the Utah Job Service (720 South 200 East, Salt Lake City, UT 84111 (phone: 801/536–7000), or 5735 S. Redwood Rd., Salt Lake City, UT 84107; phone: 801/269–4700), and 22 other Job Service Offices.

To locate all of Utah's **Job Service Offices**, contact the Utah Department of Employment Security (140 East 300 South, P.O. Box 45249, Salt Lake City, UT 84145–0249; phone: 801/536–7400).

Vermont

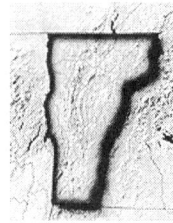

Opportunity NOCs New England (Executive Service Corp., 211 Congress St., Boston, MA 02110; phone: 617/357–0849) biweekly, $12/three–month subscription/individuals only, $45/annual subscription/individuals, $30/annual/non–profits. About 40 job vacancies for all levels of work in non–profits appear in the typical issue. Job ads are posted on the Internet a week after they appear in the periodical. Go to URL: **http://www.opnocs.org**.

Vermont Department of Employment and Training Home Page is located on the Internet at URL: **http://www.cit.state.vt.us/det/dethp.htm**. Click on "Full Time Jobs" or "Part Time Jobs." You can apply electronically. You can also place your resume in the *Vermont Talent Bank* electronically at this site. Resumes are kept on file for six months. To see a list of state Job Service Offices, click on "One–Stop Career Centers and District Offices."

To locate **Job Service Offices**, called Career Resource Centers, contact the Department of Employment and Training (P.O. Box 488, Montpelier, VT 05601–0488; phone: 802/828–4000).

Vermont Career Resource Centers (Vermont Department of Employment and Training, P.O. Box 308, Montpelier, VT 0308; phone: 802/828–4000) free. Provides job matching services. Resumes are kept on file up to three years.

Vermont Jobs Line (Vermont Department of Employment and Training, Office of Policy and Information, P.O. Box 488, Montpelier, VT 05601; phone: 802/828–4153) free. From within Vermont, call 800/464–4473; from outside the state dial 802/828–3939. This 24–hour job hotline can be called with a touch–tone or rotary telephone. The only difference is that rotary users must clearly enunciate their choices (eliminating Mick Jagger from ever using this system). You must pronounce the number 0 as "zero," and say each digit separately such as "one two" for the number 12.

First you get to select one of the 12 regions within the state. Then you get to select if you want to hear the job listings placed only during the last 24 hours, or all the job listings. Finally, you select which of nine general occupation categories for which you want to hear job information. At any time you can press "1" to skip to the next job listing or the asterisk to hear a job listing again (you don't get either of these options if you use a rotary phone). When you find a job that is right for you, be sure to write down its job order number which is given at the end of its description. Then call or visit any Employment and Training office to discuss the job and get full details on how to apply. The department offers a brochure on how to use this service — it's yours for the asking.

DET Board (Vermont Department of Employment and Training, Labor Market Information, P.O. Box 488, Montpelier, VT 05601; phone: 802/828–4153) free, updated daily. Anyone with a personal computer and modem can access this 24–hour a day electronic bulletin board which features job opening bulletins that are a condensed version of the job openings available at local Job Service Offices. If you find a job opening in your occupation, you should contact the local Job Service office for more information and procedures on how to contact the employer. The job title, a brief description, wage, town, and job order number are shown. Within

By–pass the State of Confusion: Read chapters 1 and 2 first

Vermont, have your modem dial up 800/924–4443. From out of state, dial 802/828–4108 or 802/828–4322. Set your modem to run at 14,400 bps and set your communication parameters at 8–N–1; full duplex. At the new user sign on, type "new" as your USER–ID. To see job openings, choose "J" to learn how to use the system. You can download information. The department has a short brochure that explains how to use the system. Ask for the *DET Board PC Access to Labor Market Information* brochure. If you have questions about the system, call Michael Griffen at 802/828–4153 (voice).

Virginia

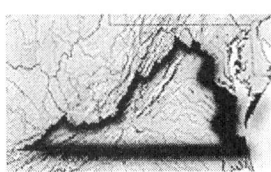

Community Jobs: The Regional Newsletter D.C. Area (ACCESS: Networking in the Public Interest, Suite 838, 1001 Connecticut Ave., Washington, DC 20036; phone: 202/785–4233) semimonthly, $25/three–month subscription, $39/six–month subscription, $69/annual subscription; but if you also subscribe to the national edition of *Community Jobs,* you can get *Community Jobs/D.C.* for just an additional $5/three months, $10/six months, $20/year; see the description of *Community Jobs* in Chapter 3 under "Job ads." Includes advertisements for positions with a broad range of non–profits in the Washington, D.C. metropolitan area. The vast majority of these job announcements do not appear in the national edition of *Community Jobs*.

Opportunities in Public Affairs (Brubach Publishing Company, P.O. Box 34949, Bethesda, MD 20827; phone: 301/571–0102) $29/two–month subscription, $49/four months, $69/six months, $129/annual, $8.95/single issue. You'll find announcements of over 300 positions with non–profits; private companies in government affairs, public relations, broadcasting, and publishing; and local, state, and federal government agencies. In addition to job announcements, this periodical also reports on unadvertised jobs its editors have uncovered. Most job openings are in the District of Columbia area.

The Washington Job Source (MetCom, Inc.; available from the Job Search Resources Catalog at the end of this book; $16.95, 475 pages, 1997. Among the 2,100 potential employers listed are a good number of non–profit organizations and professional associations that hire staff as well as federal agencies, Congressional offices, and corporations. You get the name, address, and phone number of the person to contact about job vacancies as well as a description of the agency and the number of employees. Focuses on employers that offer entry level positions, middle–management opportunities, and internships. Includes employment agencies and executive recruiters.

Please, no photocopying

Virginia

Washington 96 (Columbia Books, Suite 330, 1212 New York Ave., NW, Washington, DC 20005; phone: 202/898-0662) $85, published annually each June. Nearly 1,200 pages of 4,000 addresses, phone numbers, and information on non-profit associations, companies, and government agencies in the D.C. area, including suburban Virginia. Includes chapters on national associations, labor unions, law firms, medicine and health, foundations and philanthropy, science and policy research, education, religion, cultural institutions, clubs, and community affairs.

Virginia Employment Commission Home Page is located at Internet URL: **http://va.jobsearch.org/**. Choose "Job Seeker Services" to access the state's database and conduct a self-directed job search, search by keywords, or search by occupational, DOT, or military code. Select "VEC Local Offices" to see a directory of the state's Job Service Offices.

Virginia was one of the first states to use *ALEX*, which enables job seekers to look up themselves job vacancies in Virginia and nationwide. *ALEX* terminals are available at Job Service offices and in shopping malls, drivers license exam stations, libraries, schools, and some temporary employment agencies.

Locate a local State Employment Service Office (Job Service) through a local telephone directory's state government section or obtain a list of the 39 local **Job Service Offices** from the Virginia Employment Commission (703 E. Main St., Richmond, VA 23219; phone: 804/786-7097).

Foundations and grants

Virginia Giving: The Directory of the State's Foundations (Capital Consortium, Suite 312, 2700 Wycliff Rd., Raleigh, NC 27607; phone: 919/783-9199) $77, 1,054 pages, 1994. Profiles over 846 foundations: trustee, limitations, application procedures, sample grants. Also available on a DOS-formatted 3.5-inch floppy disk.

Virginia Corporate Giving (Capital Consortium, Suite 312, 2700 Wycliff Rd., Raleigh, NC 27607; phone: 919/783-9199) $118, 300 pages, 1997. Profiles 270 corporations' philanthropic programs: direct giving, giving through foundations, in-kind gifts, and matching gifts. Includes contact names, addresses, and phone numbers. Also available on a 3.5-inch floppy disks for use in Windows™.

A Guide to Funders in Central Appalachia and the Tennessee Valley (Appalachia Community Fund, Suite 206, 517 Union Ave., Knoxville, TN 37902; phone: 423/523-5783) $27, 300+ pages, January 1994. Among the 399 funders reported on are those that give grants in southeastern Virginia. Includes everything you need to seek funding: contact name, types of grants, grant application process, average grant size, plus how to write a

By-pass the State of Confusion: Read chapters 1 and 2 first

grant proposal, funders from outside the region that make grants in the region, religious funding sources, and Japanese corporations with grant-making programs.

Guide to Greater Washington D.C. Grantmakers (The Foundation Center, 79 Fifth Ave., New York, NY 10003; phones: 800/424–9836, 212/620–4230) $65, 233 pages, July 1996. Reports details on over 945 independent, corporate, and public grantmakers based in D.C., Maryland, and Virginia. The volume features descriptions of 1,800 recently awarded grants.

Washington

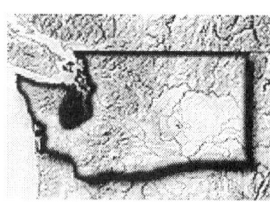

Job Bulletin #2: Business, Industry, and the Public Sector (University of Washington, Center for Career Services, Box 352190, Seattle, WA 98195–2190; phone: 206/254–0194) weekly, $40/three–month subscription. Sixty to 70 announcements of job vacancies appear in the typical issue. Only about 10 percent of the jobs are for positions in the non–profit sector.

Northwest Nonprofit (Northwest Regional Facilitators, 525 East Mission Avenue, Spokane, WA 99202–1824; phone: 509/484–6733) bimonthly, $40. Occasional notices of job openings under "Events and Announcements."

Nonprofit Computerized Label Service (Northwest Regional Facilitators, 525 East Mission Avenue, Spokane, WA 99202–1824; phone: 509/484–6733) 10¢ per name. Includes names and addresses for some 2,000 non–profit organizations in the state of Washington.

Rocky Mountain Employment Newsletter (Suite 309–BO, 10 Town Plaza, Durango, CO 81301; phone: 970/247–9550) 18 issues/year, $21/three–month subscription to one edition, $26/any two editions, $31/three editions, $36/four editions. Two and one–month subscriptions also available. Published in four editions: Washington–Oregon, Colorado–Wyoming, Arizona–New Mexico, and Idaho–Montana. Combined, the four editions include over 400 job openings, some in non–profits. The positions tend to orient toward the outdoors, with quite a few in natural resources, environment, and wildlife.

How to Find a Good Job in Seattle (Barrett Street Productions; available from the Job Search Resouces Catalog at the end of this book) $21.95, 440 pages, published each February. Author Linda Carlson presents details on virtually every conceivable job resource for Seattle and the Puget Sound area. Get the name, address, and phone of the human resources manager for hundreds of non–profit agencies, plus the name, address, and phone for hundreds of *local* professional organizations you can use for networking purposes or to see if they offer any job services. Also included are 24–hour job hotlines for scores of local schools and non–profit agencies,

Washington

eight local job bulletins, directories, local periodicals with job ads, and great advice on transportation and child care, evaluating job offers, and a directory of alumni and civic organizations you can use for networking purposes. I'm going to make an exception to my rule of neutrality to suggest that if you obtained one book to help you get a job with a non-profit or in education in the Puget Sound area, this is the one to get.

How to Get a Job in Seattle/Portland (Surrey Books; available from the Job Search Resouces Catalog at the end of this book) $16.95, 486 pages, 1996. Although filled mostly with private sector employers, this easy-to-use book tells you whom to contact for job vacancies at a moderate number of non-profit employers in the metropolitan area in social services, foundations, and education. Even more importantly, it gives you details on the local chapters of professional and trade associations you may wish to join for networking purposes or which may publish a periodical with jobs ads or operate a local job service. Some local chapters may be large enough to hire staff. It also includes information on local job hotlines, Internet Web sites of many local employers, and local trade magazines plus career consultants.

The Right Connection is the state's main Internet source of job vacancies. Located at URL: **http://www.wa.gov/employ.html**, this site includes both job and resume databases. Select "Welcome to Work" which will take you to the "Washington Online Reemployment Kiosk" whose own URL is: **http://www.wa.gov/esd/employment.html**. Here you can choose "Work Announcement Database" to search for jobs or pick "JobNet" to search the same database of jobs listed with the state's Job Service Centers. Browse this "Reemployment Kiosk" site to find links to a plethora of additional job sources including local newspapers and usenet newsgroups. You can also participate in the state's resume database by selecting "Post a Resume." You will be contacted by email when a job matches your criteria.

Washington Employment Web (Tolt River Services, 32810 NE 40th Cr., Carnation, WA 98014; email: GWATTIER@aol.com) free. Located on the Internet at URL: **http://members.aol.com/gwattier/washjob.htm**, this delightful and thorough site includes 250 links to the home pages of private employers, public employers, the help wanted sections of local newspapers, and job databases for Washington state.

ALEX kiosks are located at supermarkets, college campuses, shopping centers, court houses, department stores, and supermarkets.

To locate **Job Service Offices**, contact Employment and Training Division (Employment Security Department, 605 Woodland Square Loop, Lacey, WA 98504; phone: 360/438–4610). These addresses are also available on the Internet at URL: **http://dial.wa.gov/**. Select the "Search by Department" button and look for the Employment Security Department. Once you find it, you'll need to browse the listings until you come upon the local offices where you'll find their addresses and phone numbers.

By-pass the State of Confusion: Read chapters 1 and 2 first

The state also offers biennial **Area Wage Surveys** that supply occupational wage and salary rates for clerical, managerial, professional, technical, and general occupations: average wage rates with high and low ranges, average hours worked, and occupational descriptions for each of the state's 39 counties. Each survey costs only $1 (add $2.50 shipping and handling for your entire order; Washington state residents must add 8 percent sales tax). Send your check or money order to: Washington State Employment Security Department, Labor Market and Economic Analysis – Publications, P.O. Box 9046, Olympia, WA 98507–9046 (phones: 800/215–1617, 360/438–4800).

You can also see these wage surveys on the Internet at *Washington's Online Reemployment Kiosk* at Internet URL: **http://www.wa.gov/esd/employment.html.** You'll have to weave your way to the surveys by first selecting "Washington State Labor Market Information," then "Exploring the Labor Market," "By Kind of Information," "Occupational Wage Surveys," and finally selecting the county for which you want data.

Foundations and grants

Charitable Trust Directory (Secretary of State, Charitable Trust Division, P.O. Box 40234, Olympia, WA 98504–0234; phone: 206/753–0863, ext. 4) $20, 490 pages, published each January. Reports on over 1,000 charitable organizations and trusts: purpose statement, sample grants, financial data, and officers.

Pacific Northwest Grantmakers Forum Member Directory (Pacific Northwest Grantmakers Forum, Suite 214, 1305 Fourth Ave, Seattle, WA 98101; phone: 206/624–9899) $39.74/out–of–state residents, $43/Washington state residents, 186 pages, published in March of even–numbered years. Among the nearly 100 or so grantmakers described in this directory are a number from Washington State. Included in each listing are contact name's address and phone, application procedures, range of grant amounts awarded, and types of projects funded.

West Virginia

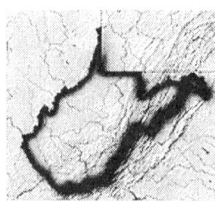

West Virginia's Job Bank is located at Internet URL: **http://wv.jobsearch.org/**. Select "Search for Work in West Virginia" to access the database and conduct a self–directed job search, search by keyword, or search by occupational code, DOT code, or military code. To get the addresses of the state's Job Service Offices, choose "Local Office Directory."

Please, no photocopying

The state has placed touch–screen *ALEX* kiosks in public locations throughout the state.

To locate **Job Service Offices**, contact the Bureau of Employment Programs (112 California Ave., Charleston, WV 25305–0112; phone: 304/558–2660).

Foundations and grants

West Virginia Foundation Directory (Kanawha County Public Library, Administrative Office, 123 Capitol St., Charleston, WV 25301; phone: 304/343–4646) $22.50, 66 pages, 1995. Profiles over 100 foundations: contact person, areas of interest, restrictions, application procedures, trustees.

A Guide to Funders in Central Appalachia and the Tennessee Valley (Appalachia Community Fund, Suite 206, 517 Union Ave., Knoxville, TN 37902; phone: 423/523–5783) $27, over 300 pages, January 1994. Among the 399 funders reported on are those that give grants in West Virginia. Includes everything you need to seek funding: contact name, types of grants, grant application process, average grant size, plus how to write a grant proposal, funders from outside the region that make grants in the region, religious funding sources, and Japanese corporations with grant-making programs.

Wisconsin

The Nonprofits Center of Milwaukee, Inc. (750 N. 18th Street, Milwaukee, WI 53233; phone: 414/344–3933) This extremely informal job service will send job descriptions out by request if you contact them by phone, or a list of more extensive job descriptions can be viewed on their job board at the agency's headquarters.

Wisconsin Job Net is located on the Internet at URL: http://www.dwd.state.wi.us/jobnet/. Pick "Search the Wisconsin Job Service Database." At this point you can also get a list of the state's Job Service Offices by selecting "Click here."

To locate **Job Service Offices**, contact the Job Service Division (Department of Industry, Labor, and Human Relations, P.O. Box 7903, Madison, WI 53707; phone: 608/242–4900).

By–pass the State of Confusion: Read chapters 1 and 2 first

Foundations and grants

Foundations in Wisconsin: A Directory (Marquette University Memorial Library, 1415 W. Wisconsin Ave., Milwaukee, WI 53233; phone: 414/288–1515) $52.80, 237 pages, published each August of even–numbered years thereafter. Profiles over 790 grantmaking foundations: officers and directors, grant range, purpose and interests, sample grants. An electronic version on floppy disk is available for $158; buy the disk and get the printcopy free.

Wyoming

Rocky Mountain Employment Newsletter (Suite 309–BO, 10 Town Plaza, Durango, CO 81301; phone: 970/247–9550) 18 issues/year, $21/three–month subscription to one edition, $26/any two editions, $31/three editions, $36/four editions. Two and one–month subscriptions also available. Published in four editions: Wyoming–Colorado, Arizona–New Mexico, Idaho–Montana, and Washington–Oregon. Combined, the four editions include over 400 job openings, some in non–profits. The positions tend to orient toward the outdoors, with quite a few in natural resources, environment, and wildlife.

Wyoming Employment Resources is located on the Internet at URL: **http://wyjobs.state.wy.us/**. For full–time jobs, pick "Wyoming Job Bank Search Engine." For part–time jobs, select "Wyoming Air National Guard." There are also links to other job search sites including *The Job Web*. To see a list of the state's Job Service Offices, select "Wyoming Employment Resources Offices."

The state maintains a system of *ALEX* kiosks at shopping malls, municipal buildings, libraries, grocery stores, and universities in addition to the ones at each Job Service Center.

To get the addresses of the 16 local **Job Service Offices** in Wyoming, contact the Employment Resources Division (Department of Employment, P.O. Box 2760, Casper, WY 82602; phone: 307/235–3200).

Foundations and grants

Wyoming Foundations Directory (Laramie County Community College, 1400 E. College Dr., Cheyenne, WY 82007; phone: 307/778–1205) $4 plus $1.25/third class postage or $3/first class postage, 1995. Gives details on over 230 public and private foundations: includes names of contact persons and statements of purpose.

Please, no photocopying

Index

As explained in Chapter 1 — the chapter that told you how to get the most out of this book, which, naturally nobody wants to read — this Index supplements the Table of Contents to help you find job sources for specialties that are not located where you would intuitively expect to find them. Look up the occupation you want in this Index. This will get you to the section of the chapters where there are job sources for this profession.

Be sure to check all sections of that chapter for job sources for this chosen profession. For example, the index entry may send you to the "Job ads" part of a chapter. Be sure to also look under the other headings ("Job services," "Directories," and "Salary surveys") because you will probably find additional job sources for that occupation under these other headings.

A

Accountants: 127, 175
Activity professionals: 247
Actors: 75
Administrators
  Mental Health: 245
African American culture
  Librarians: 191
  Museums: 191
Agents: 74
Agriculture
  Engineers: 58
Agronomists: 57
Alumni career services: 35
Animals: 60
  Animal rights: 34
Animators: 65
Anthropologists: 103 – 104, 111, 217, 238 – 240
  Education: 101
Antiques
  Dealers: 68
  Shows: 68
Apprentices
  New York: 297
Aquariums: 60, 191, 220

317

Arboretum: 130 – 132, 191
Archaeologists: 238, 240
  Education: 103
Architects: 175
  Education: 104
Archivists: 193, 206
Art: 191
  Art fairs: 68
  Computer: 66
  Dealers: 68 – 69
  Fairs: 68
  Galleries: 68 – 69, 191 – 192
  Museums: 192
  Therapy: 168
Artists
  Visual: 77
Arts
  Administrative: 74 – 75
  Contests: 135
  Education: 70, 110
  Fundraisers: 79
  Grants: 141
Association management: 33
  District of Columbia: 78
Athletics
  Coaches: 201
  College: 202
  Grants: 141
Attorneys
  Federal jobs: 179
  Religion: 208
  Universities and colleges: 93
Audiologists: 168, 244

B

Battlefields: 199
Benefits analysts: 128
Biologists: 121
Biotechnology: 232
Blind individuals
  Job Recorded Bulletin: 42
  Using the Internet: 20
Blood banks: 145 – 146
Blue collar: 256
Botanical gardens: 130 – 132
  California: 63

Broadcasting
  Religion: 208, 211
Business officers
  Universities and colleges: 92
Business schools
  Education: 106, 111

C

California
  Environment: 125
  Theater: 73, 76
  Volunteering: 47
Campgrounds: 199
Camps: 200 – 201
  Geosciences: 220
  Summer: 98, 201
  Youth work: 244
Canadian jobs: 98, 102, 110 – 111,
  113, 167, 249
Career counselors: 91
Career fairs
  Education: 89
Caretakers: 120
Cartographers
  Internships: 120
Cartoonists: 65
Chemists
  Education: 235
Child welfare
  Grants: 252
Civil liberties: 34
Classicists
  Education: 103, 112
Clerical: 217, 256
Co–op opportunities: 36
Coaches: 102, 202
  Education: 87, 202
Coaching: 169, 202
  College: 199, 202 – 203
  High school: 202
Coders: 207
College
  Athletics: 102, 202
  Business officers: 92
  Also see Education
  Junior colleges: 116

To sort it out, read chapters 1 and 2 first

Personnel: 91
Physical plant management: 115
Compensation analysts: 128
Compensation professionals: 80, 82
Computer science
Grants: 221
Programming: 83
Computers
Grants: 142
Conservators: 207
Construction: 173, 178
Constructors: 177 – 178
Cooks: 217
Cost estimators: 229
Counselors
Pastoral: 245
Crafts: 68, 174
Credit unions: 127 – 129
Criminal justice: 216
Criminologists: 104, 113, 217, 239
Education: 104
Cruise lines
Entertainers: 76
Curators: 68, 190 – 191

D

Dance: 65
Education: 70, 110
Deafness: 243
Design
Surface and Textile: 66
Developers: 175
Developmental disabilities: 245
Dietitians: 147, 149
Direct care workers
Mental Health: 245, 252
Disabilities
Jobs for people with disabilities: 45
Training: 246
District of Columbia
Association management: 78
Legal services: 181
Dormitory directors: 93

E

Earth sciences: 123, 219 – 220
Education: 220
Economic development
Internships: 174
Economists: 173
Education: 44, 191
Academic advisors: 201
Accountants: 128
Administration: 100, 221
Administrators: 85, 87, 90 – 92, 99, 104 – 106
Admissions counselors: 91
Agricultural engineers: 58
Agriculture: 61
Agronomy: 61
Allied health: 150 – 151
Anthropologists: 101, 103, 111, 238, 240
Archivists: 239
Art: 65
Arts: 73
Astronomers: 236
Astrophysicists: 236
Broadcasting: 77, 184 – 185, 187
Canada: 100, 102, 108 – 111, 113
Christian: 110, 212
Coaches: 201 – 202
Communications: 183, 189
Computers: 83 – 84, 214
Construction trades: 174
Constructors: 173
Continuing education: 101
Criminal justice: 104, 216 – 217
Culinary arts: 114
Deaf or hard of hearing: 243 – 244
Dentists: 154
Dermatologists: 149
Economists: 173
Engineers: 228
Environmental: 124
Ethnic studies: 101
Faculty exchange programs: 107
Film studies: 77, 185
Florida: 273
Geographic information systems: 176

See the first page of this Index for instructions

Grants: 136, 141
Health care: 150
Hebrew day schools: 98
Higher education: 33
Historians: 193, 239
History: 207
Horticultural science: 131 – 132
Hotel management: 114
Immunology: 148
Information systems: 84
Journalism: 184
Junior colleges: 116
Law: 179
Law schools: 109, 182
Lecturers: 135
Librarians: 193
Mathematics: 220, 235
Medical: 151, 156, 160
Medical schools: 146, 151
Minnesota: 287
Music: 113
Neuroscience: 146
North Carolina: 298
Nursing schools: 109, 163
Nutrition: 147
Obstetrics: 148
Optics: 231
People with disabilities: 101
Pharmaceutical: 163
Physical education: 169
Physicians: 155
Physicists: 235
Physics: 214, 235 – 236
Plant health: 57
Plant pathologists: 59
Political scientists: 105, 239
Psychology: 105, 165
Research administrators: 214
School districts: 36
Science: 220
Social workers: 101
Sociologists: 101
Sports medicine: 148
Summer schools: 98, 201
Teachers of people with hearing impairments: 244
Teachers of people with visual impairments: 158
Technology: 220
Texas: 307
The arts: 65
Theater training: 76
Therapists: 245
Tourism industry: 114
Travel industry: 114
Urban affairs: 174
Urban planning: 171
Veterinary: 61
Veterinary science: 61
Visiting professors: 135
Vocational: 110
Wastewater: 121
Engineers: 40, 67, 112, 121
   Chemical: 227 – 228, 230, 233
   Civil: 219, 232
   Cost: 229, 232, 234
   Education: 103, 112, 231 – 233, 235
   Environmental: 120, 123, 229
   Foreign jobs: 232
   Grants: 141
   Materials: 229
   Universities and colleges: 92
   Also see the *Professional's Job Finder*
Entertainment: 66
   New York: 296
   Theme parks: 76
Environment: 34, 119, 263, 268, 276, 290, 295, 301, 312, 316
   California: 125
   Engineers: 229
   Internships: 119 – 120
   Summer jobs: 125
Environmental health: 148
Estimators: 174
Ethnic studies
   Education: 101
Executive search firms: 48
Expositions: 69

F

Facilities officers
   Universities and colleges: 92, 94
Fairs: 69
Family and consumer sciences
   Education: 105

To sort it out, read chapters 1 and 2 first

Index

Farming
  Agricultural engineers: 58
Federal jobs: 284
Festivals: 69
Fieldwork: 260
Film: 65, 74, 77
  Editors: 77
Financial: 127
Financial aid
  Administrators: 91, 93
Fish hatcheries: 120
Food
  Engineers: 58
Foreign jobs: 43
  Chemists: 219
  Education: 102, 110
  Engineers: 219, 232
  Foundations: 139
  Grants: 139
  Internships: 52
  Legal services: 180
  Museums: 191
  Research: 218
  Scientists: 219
  Special libraries: 196
Forestry
  Education: 106, 114
Foundations: 34
  Finding on Internet: 84, 142
Fundraisers: 79, 82, 204
  Human services: 248
  North Carolina: 298

G

Geneticists
  Plants: 59
Geographers: 173
  Education: 103
Geographic information systems: 173, 176
Geologists: 219 – 220
  Education: 103, 219
Geometric modelers: 214
Geoscience
  Museums: 220
GIS
  See Geographic information systems
Government affairs lobbyists: 81
Government jobs
  See the *Government Job Finder*
Grants
  Academic libraries: 114
  Addiction prevention: 167
  Addiction research: 167
  Alcohol abuse: 251
  Animal welfare: 62 – 63
  Anthropology: 136
  Aquariums: 63
  Architecture: 66
  Arts: 66
  Arts and cultural: 66, 69
  Athletics: 141
  Biomedical: 150
  Botanical gardens: 63
  Canada: 126
  Career guidance: 141
  Censorship issues: 188
  Child welfare: 251
  Colleges and universities: 114
  Community development: 177
  Computer science: 84, 221
  Computers: 84, 142
  Conservation: 125
  Construction: 142
  Continuing education: 90
  Court administration: 217
  Crime prevention: 217
  Crisis intervention: 167
  Dentists: 153
  Dependency programs: 152
  Design: 66
  Disabilities: 143, 152, 248, 252
  Disease prevention: 153
  Documentaries: 188
  Drop-out prevention: 99
  Drug abuse: 251
  Education: 98, 143
  Elementary education: 98 – 99
  Elementary school: 96
  Emergency shelters: 141
  Engineering and technology: 84
  Environment: 125 – 126
  Equipment: 142
  Finding on Internet: 84, 142
  General operating: 142

See the first page of this Index for instructions

Group homes: 167, 252
Health care: 142, 150 – 152
Health care education: 152
Health care research: 152
High technology: 84, 142
Historic preservation: 69
Historical societies: 69
Homeless: 177, 251
Homeless housing: 177
Housing: 177
Human services: 248
Immigrants: 141
Individuals: 134, 286, 290
International affairs: 178
International peace and security: 178
International studies: 240
Law: 240, 251 – 252
Law enforcement agencies: 217
Leadership development: 178
Legal services: 125
Libraries: 196
Literacy programs: 90
Media: 66, 69, 84, 188
Medical research: 153, 251 – 252
Mental health research: 167
Minority groups: 141
Museums: 69
Music: 69
Nursing homes: 153
Offender rehabilitation: 217
Online database: 138
Performing arts: 69
Physical fitness: 200
Planetariums: 221
Pollution abatement: 125
Poverty studies: 240
Prevention of abuse: 217
Prevention of exploitation: 217
Prevention of neglect: 217
Public administration: 178
Public health: 153
Public policy: 178
Publishing: 188
Rape prevention: 141
Recreation: 200
Religion: 212
Reproductive health care: 153
Research: 125, 215, 252
Residential treatment centers: 167
Science libraries: 221
Science museums: 221
Scientific associations: 221
Secondary education: 96, 98 – 99
Senior citizen studies and research: 251
Senior citizens: 248
Social research: 141
Social science: 240
Social services: 142, 152, 177, 212, 248, 251
Sports: 200
Student organizations: 114
Student services: 114
Teacher training: 99
The arts: 65, 69
Urban development: 177
Visual arts: 69
Women and girls: 141
Women's studies: 240
Writers: 172
Zoos: 63
Graphic artists: 186
Graphic designers: 66
Group homes: 243

H

Halfway houses
   Grants: 251
Headhunters: 48
Health care: 34, 36, 40
   Academic medicine: 146
   College health centers: 145
   Fundraisers: 79, 205
   Grants: 139, 141 – 142, 150
   Medical records: 147
   Medical transcription: 147
   New York: 296
   Philanthropy: 205
   Records: 207
   Also see the *Professional's Job Finder*
Hearing impairments: 243, 250
Historians: 68, 193, 207, 239 – 240
   Art: 64
   Education: 103
Historic preservation: 172

To sort it out, read chapters 1 and 2 first

Index

Historic sites: 199
HMOs: 251
Holography: 231 – 232
Home care: 148, 154, 246, 251 – 253
Home economists
    Education: 105
Home health management: 154
Horticulture: 131
    Therapy: 170
Hospices: 147 – 149, 153, 246, 250 – 251, 253
Hotel management
    Education: 114
Housing: 172, 175
    Affordable: 175
    Management agents: 175
Human resources
    Universities and colleges: 94
Human rights: 34
Humanities
    Grants: 139, 141
    Internships: 141

I

Illustrators: 66
Indexers: 186
Inspection firms: 215
Internet
    Finding foundations: 84, 142
Internships: 35 – 36, 39, 52, 120, 122, 125, 135, 174, 219, 260
    Actuaries: 235
    Animal shelters: 60
    Archaeologists: 240
    Art: 64
    Broadcasting: 184, 209
    Chicago area: 277
    District of Columbia: 272, 284
    Economic development: 174
    Education: 96
    Environment: 52, 120, 122 – 123
    Florida: 273
    Foreign: 52
    Health care: 149
    Historians: 240
    Horticulture: 130
    Humanities: 141
    Legal services: 181
    Maryland: 272, 284
    Massachusetts: 285
    Mathematics: 235
    Media: 186
    Military: 140
    Minorities: 140
    Museums: 190
    New York: 297
    Parks and recreation: 198
    Pennsylvania: 303
    People with disabilities: 140
    Physicists: 237
    Science museums: 190
    Virginia: 310
    Women: 141
    Youth workers: 244
Interpreters: 191 – 192, 244

J

Job hotlines
    Individual employers: 45
Journalists: 187

L

Labor: 39
Labor unions: 56
Laboratories
    Independent: 215
Laborers: 217
Lasers: 231 – 232
Learning disabilities
    Education: 87
Legal services
    California: 180
    District of Columbia: 181
    Public interest: 180
Lenders
    Housing: 175
Librarians: 68, 101, 193
    Education: 101, 103, 112, 186, 194, 197

See the first page of this Index for instructions

Also see the *Government Job Finder*
Libraries
  Grants: 221
  New York: 296
Lifeguards: 198, 201
Lobbyists: 55, 81
Long term care: 246 – 247
  Activity directors: 247
  Senior citizens: 247, 250

M

Managed care: 251
Management: 100
Market analysts: 214
Marketing: 189
  Research: 189
Mathematicians: 220
  Education: 103
Mathematics
  Grants: 142
Mechanics
  Education: 106
Media: 65
  Education: 101, 186, 194
  Religion: 210 – 211
Medicine
  Education: 104, 221
  Experimental: 145
Meeting planners: 81
Memorials: 199
Mental Health
  Direct care workers: 245, 252
Meta–lists
  Internet job resources: 32
Metallurgists: 229
Models: 74 – 75
Monuments: 199
Multimedia: 65
Museums: 191, 220
  Art: 64, 69, 192
  California: 63
  History: 240
Music
  Classical: 70, 72
  Education: 70, 91, 102, 110
  Religion: 209 – 210

N

Natural resources: 119 – 120
Nature centers: 198 – 199
New York
  Theater: 76
Newsgroups: 36
  For specific cities: 36
  For specific occupations: 36
  For specific states: 36
Newspapers: 186
Nurses: 217
Nursing homes: 153 – 154, 253
Nutrition
  Education: 102

O

Occupational therapists: 245
Office support: 39
Online media: 184
Opera: 70
  Management: 71
Optics: 231 – 232
Oregon
  Education: 86
Organizers: 171 – 172
  Youth work: 244

P

Painters: 64
Parks: 198
  Urban: 199
Part–time
  Wyoming: 316
Pennsylvania
  Theater: 74 – 75, 77
Pesticides: 59
Pharmacists: 217
Philanthropy
  Religion: 212
Photographers: 64 – 65, 75

To sort it out, read chapters 1 and 2 first

Index

Physical education: 169, 202
Physical therapists
    Geriatrics: 168
    Hand therapy: 168
    Home health care: 168
    Industrial rehabilitation: 168
    Long-term Care: 168
    Orthopedics: 168
Physicians
    Criminal justice: 216
Physicists
    Education: 235
    Health: 121
Physics
    Education: 104
Placement agencies: 256
Planetariums: 191, 220, 236
    Grants: 221
Planners: 171, 175
    Camps: 201
    Environmental: 123
    Health care: 150
    Meeting: 81
Poets: 65
Political science
    Grants: 240
Political scientists: 105, 239
Politics: 34
Psychiatrists
    Community: 245
Psychologists: 165, 217, 243
Psychology
    Education: 105
Public interest
    California: 266
    Law: 179

R

Reading
    Education: 87
    Recreation: 198
    Special: 199
Recruiters: 256
    Executive: 48
Rehabilitation: 253
    Education: 106, 169

    Management: 246
REITS: 129
Religion
    Broadcasting: 188 – 189, 211
    Education: 104, 209
    Grants: 262, 275, 281, 289, 299, 306, 312, 315
    Media: 189
    Philanthropy: 205
    Social services: 246
Religious
    Fundraisers: 79
Research
    Administrators: 92
    Biotechnology: 232
    Computers: 83 – 84, 214
    Criminal justice: 216
    Dental: 154
    Education: 102, 111
    Environment: 121
    Horticultural science: 131
    Medical: 145, 150 – 151, 155
    Optics: 231 – 232
    Physicists: 235
    Physics: 104
    Plant pathologists: 59
    Political scientists: 105, 239
    Science: 104, 221
    Social science: 240
Research administrators: 94
Residents
    Physicians: 159
Respiratory therapists: 148

S

Safety: 216
    Universities and colleges: 94
Sanitarians: 148
School districts
    Searchable database: 36
School principals: 91
School superintendents: 90
Science
    Crop and soil: 57
    Education: 87 – 88, 103 – 104, 221
    Grants: 136, 141

See the first page of this Index for instructions

Mathematicians: 220
Museums: 190
Sculptors: 64, 67
Search firms: 48
Seasonal jobs
   Parks and recreation: 198
Secretaries: 79
   Legal secretaries: 180
   Texas: 307
Sign language interpreting: 243
Social services: 34
   New York: 296
   Private agencies: 247
   Religion: 246
Social workers: 165, 216, 242 – 243
   Education: 101, 105, 107
   hospitals: 153
   Religion: 208
Sociologists: 104, 217, 239
   Education: 101
Special recreation
   See Recreation
Speech pathologists: 170, 216, 245
Speech therapists: 168 – 170
Sports
   College: 203
   Education: 87, 102, 202
Sports Medicine: 168
Statisticians
   Education: 103
Submit to exhibitions
   Visual arts: 77
Summer jobs: 260
   Camps: 200
   Environment: 125
   Expeditions: 200
   Recreation: 200
   Theater: 76

T

Teachers: 88
   See Education
Technical: 39
Technical writers: 214
Technicians
   Research: 215

Technology: 220
Television: 74
Temporary work
   Environment: 122
Theater: 73
   Administrative: 74 – 75
   Boston: 75
   Education: 70, 110
   Regional: 76
   San Francisco: 73
   Summer jobs: 76
   Training: 76
Theme parks
   Entertainers: 76
Therapists
   Art: 168
   Outdoor: 201, 247
   Physical: 168
Therapy
   Adventure–based: 249
   Children and family: 243
   Experiential: 249
   Family: 245
   Horticultural: 170
   Physical: 158
   Rehabilitation: 246
Tourism industry
   Education: 114
Toxicologists: 148
Trades: 39, 217, 256
Trails: 199
Training
   Environment: 126
   Experiential: 249
Translators: 186
Travel industry
   Education: 114

U

Unions: 56
Urban studies
   Grants: 240

To sort it out, read chapters 1 and 2 first

V

Veterinarians: 61, 144
Veterinary technicians: 61
Victim assistance: 249
Videographers: 65
Visiting nurse associations: 251
Visual artists: 77
Visual arts: 77
Visual impairments
    Using the Internet: 20
Volunteering: 46 – 47

W

Washington
    Education: 86
Wildlife refuges: 199
Writers
    Freelance: 186

Y

Youth workers: 243, 252
Youths
    Troubled: 201, 247

Z

Zoos: 60, 191, 220
    California: 63
    Grants: 63

See the first page of this Index for instructions

Budget-stretching discount coupons

Instructions for using these budget-stretching discount coupons

To make the job search a little easier on your bank account, several publishers of key job sources described in the *Non-Profits and Education Job Finder* are graciously offering our readers discounts on their publications, discounts unavailable anywhere else.

To use a coupon, simply photocopy the coupon you want to use. ***Only photocopies will be accepted***. Do *not* cut out the page. Send the photocopy of the coupon with a letter to the address shown on the coupon. In your letter, state your name and address and specify which subscription and publication you would like. Be sure to include a check or money order for the proper amount.

 These coupons can be used for new subscriptions only.

 Prices can change. If a price has changed when you mail your coupon and payment, the discount applies to the new price in effect at that time.

Save $3 to $19 on your new subscription to:
Social Service Jobs

For a description of this periodical, see page 243.

One year, currently $118, you pay just $99
Six months, currently $62, you pay just $52
Three months, currently $42, you pay just $39

 Send a photocopy of this coupon, your letter, and your check to:
Social Service Jobs, Dept. NPJF,
10 Angelica Dr., Framingham, MA 01701

This offer expires on July 1, 2000.

Save $10 on your new subscription to:
ArtSEARCH

For a description of this periodical, see page 73.

Currently $54/individuals, $75/institutions, you pay only $44/individuals, $65/institutions.

Send a photocopy of this coupon, your letter, and your check to:
ArtSEARCH, Theatre Communications Group, Dept. NPJF,
355 Lexington Ave., New York, NY 10017

This offer expires on July 1, 2000.

Add a free issue to your new subscription to:
Environmental Opportunities

For a description of this periodical, see page 120.
This coupon entitles new subscribers to an additional month on their six-month ($26) or one-year ($47) subscription (a $4.50 value).

Send a photocopy of this coupon, your letter, and your check to:
Environmental Opportunities, Dept. NPJF,
P.O. Box 4379, Arcata, CA 95518

This offer expires on July 1, 2000.

Save $5 to $10 on your new subscription to:

Community Jobs: The National Employment Newspaper for the Non-Profit Sector
Community Jobs: New Jersey/New York
Community Jobs: Washington, DC

For a description of these periodicals, see page 39.

Currently a six month subscription to any of these editions costs $39/each; you pay only $34/each.
Currently an annual subscription to any of these editions costs $69/each; you pay only $59/each.

Send a photocopy of this coupon, your letter, and your check to:

ACCESS, Dept. NPJF, Suite 838,
1001 Connecticut Ave., NW, Washington, DC 20036

This offer expires on July 1, 2000.

Only photocopies of coupons will be accepted

Add one to four free issues to your new subscription to:
ASAE Career Opps
For details on this periodical, including subscription rates, see page 78.
Meeting and Hospitality Opportunities Report
For details on this periodical, including subscription rates, see page 79.
Public Relations Career Opportunities
For details on this periodical, including subscription rates, see page 184.

For each of these periodicals, this coupon entitles you to an extra four free issues on an annual subscription, two extra free issues on a six-month subscription, and one additional free issue on a three-month subscription.

Send a photocopy of this coupon, your letter, and your check(s) payable to the newsletter(s) you are ordering, to:
[title of the newsletter you are ordering], Dept. NPJF, Suite 1190, 1575 I St., NW, Washington, DC 20005
This offer expires on July 1, 2000.

Save $5 on your new subscription(s) to:
Rocky Mountain Employment Newsletter

For a description of this periodical, see page 263.

The length of each subscription is three months.
Any one edition, currently $21, you pay only $16
Any two editions, currently $26, you pay only $21
Any three editions, currently $31, you pay only $26
All four editions, currently $36, you pay only $31

Be sure to specify the edition(s) you want.

Send a photocopy of this coupon, your letter, and your check to:
Intermountain Publishing & Referral Service, Dept. NPJF,
Suite 309, 10 Town Plaza, Durango, CO 81301
This offer expires on July 1, 2000.

Save $5 to $10 on your new subscription to:
National Ad Search

For a description of this periodical, see page 86.

Six weeks, currently $40, you pay only $35
Three months, currently $75, you pay only $70
Six months, currently $145, you pay only $135
One year, currently $235, you pay only $225

Send a photocopy of this coupon, your letter, and your check to:
National Ad Search, Dept. NPJF, P.O. Box 2083, Milwaukee, WI 53201

This offer expires on July 1, 2000.

See page 328 for instructions on using these coupons

Save 17 to 30 percent on your purchase of the
Location Report
Location Guide (specify U.S. city or cities)

For descriptions of these reports, see page 258.

Save $5 on the purchase of one copy of the *Location Report* currently $27.95, you pay only $22.95 plus $3/shipping.
Save $3 on the purchase of each *Location Guide* (specify one U.S. city per *Guide*) currently $9.95/each, you pay only $6.95/each plus $3/shipping.

Send a photocopy of this coupon, your letter, and your check to:

Location Guides, Dept. NPJF, P.O. Box 58506,
Salt Lake City, UT 84158

This offer expires on July 1, 2000.

Save 10 percent on your new subscription(s) to:

PR Marcom Jobs East
PR Marcom Jobs Mid-America
PR Marcom Jobs Southern California
PR Marcom Jobs Northern California and Pacific Northwest
The Source

For descriptions of these periodicals
see page 185 and the pages that follow it.

For each of the four *PR Marcom Jobs...* (specify fax or mail) periodicals:
Four-month subscription, currently $59, you pay $53.10
Six-month subscription, currently $69, you pay only $62.10
One-year subscription, currently $99, you pay only $89.10
The Source, currently $29, you pay only $26.10

Send a photocopy of this coupon, your letter, and your check to:

Rachel P.R. Services, ATTN: J. Brett–Elspas, Dept. NPJF, Suite 200C,
1650 Pacific Coast Highway, Redondo Beach, CA 92077

This offer expires on July 1, 2000.

Only photocopies of coupons will be accepted

Job search resources catalog

This is the "catalog at the end of the book" that is noted several times in the preceding pages. Contact us to receive a free copy of *Job Quest,* our annual catalog of 400 career books, videos, and software programs. Also be sure to check our Internet site where our full catalog and the free *Update Sheet* for the *Non–Profits and Education Job Finder* appear. If we move, you can always find our new real world address by visiting our Web site at URL: **http://jobfindersonline.com**.

The following career resources, many of which are mentioned in previous chapters, are available directly from Planning/Communications. Photocopy and complete the following form, or list the titles and the quantity of each, include postage (see the formula on page 337), and send your order with payment to:

PLANNING/COMMUNICATIONS
7215 Oak Avenue
River Forest, Illinois 60305–1935

To order, call toll–free: 888/366–5200 (orders only)
For information or inquiries, call: 708/366–5200
Weekdays: 9 a.m. to 6 p.m. Central Standard Time

Individuals and private companies must prepay; colleges, libraries and bookstores can use purchase orders ($50 minimum). We accept telephone and fax orders paid with VISA or MasterCard. Be sure to include your card number and expiration date in faxed or mail orders.

We will always send you the most recent edition of a book or software program. Call or write for resale prices on our *Job Finder* books and for special quantity discounts. *Please note that prices are subject to change without notice.*

Order Form

Title	Price	x #	= Total
Job Finders Series			
Non–Profits and Education Job Finder [paperback]	$16.95	x ____	= $_____
Non–Profits and Education Job Finder [hard cover]	$32.95	x ____	= $_____
Government Job Finder [paperback]	$16.95	x ____	= $_____
Government Job Finder [hard cover]	$32.95	x ____	= $_____
Professional's Job Finder [covers business world][paperbk.]	$18.95	x ____	= $_____
Professional's Job Finder [hard cover]	$36.95	x ____	= $_____

Job search resources catalog

International Job Finder [available Sept. 1997] [paperbk.]	$16.95	x ____	= $_____
International Job Finder [hard cover]	$32.95	x ____	= $_____

Internet Job Search Resources *(See Chapter 2)*

Internet Jobs Kit [**Save $11** off the $49.95 list price]	$38.95	x ____	= $_____
The Guide to Internet Job Searching	$12.95	x ____	= $_____
How to Get Your Dream Job Using the Web	$34.99	x ____	= $_____
Be Your Own Headhunter Online	$16.00	x ____	= $_____
Net Jobs: Use the Internet to Land Your Dream Job	$20.00	x ____	= $_____
Cyberhound's Guide to Internet Databases	$99.00	x ____	= $_____
Dial Up! Gale's Bulletin Board Locator	$49.00	x ____	= $_____
Electronic Job Search Revolution	$12.95	x ____	= $_____
Hook Up, Get Hired!	$12.95	x ____	= $_____

Job Hotlines *(See Chapter 3)*

The National Job Hotline Directory	$14.95	x ____	= $_____

Careers With Non-Profits and in Education

Non-Profits and Education Job Finder [paperback]	$16.95	x ____	= $_____
Jobs and Careers with Nonprofit Organizations	$15.95	x ____	= $_____
Good Works: A Guide to Careers in Social Change	$24.00	x ____	= $_____
Making a Living While Making a Difference	$10.95	x ____	= $_____
100 Jobs in Social Change	$14.95	x ____	= $_____
100 Jobs in the Environment	$14.95	x ____	= $_____
Careers in Environment	$13.95	x ____	= $_____
Job Opportunities in Health Care	$21.95	x ____	= $_____
Jobs in Arts and Media Management	$21.95	x ____	= $_____
Cyberhound's Guide to Associations and Nonprofit Org.	$79.00	x ____	= $_____
How to Get a Job in Education	$15.95	x ____	= $_____
Alternative Careers for Lawyers	$15.00	x ____	= $_____
Great Jobs for Sociology Majors	$11.95	x ____	= $_____
Great Jobs for Art Majors	$11.95	x ____	= $_____
Great Jobs for Liberal Arts Majors	$11.95	x ____	= $_____
Great Jobs for Psychology Majors	$11.95	x ____	= $_____

Government Careers

Government Job Finder [paperback]	$16.95	x ____	= $_____
Book of U.S. Government Jobs [book only]	$18.95	x ____	= $_____
Book of U.S. Government Jobs [book & Windows™ disk]	$34.95	x ____	= $_____
Book of U.S. Postal Exams	$18.95	x ____	= $_____
Civil Service Handbook	$10.95	x ____	= $_____
Complete Guide to Public Employment	$19.95	x ____	= $_____
Directory of Federal Jobs and Employers	$21.95	x ____	= $_____
Federal Applications That Get Results	$23.95	x ____	= $_____
Federal Jobs in Law Enforcement	$14.95	x ____	= $_____
Federal Jobs: The Ultimate Guide	$15.95	x ____	= $_____
Find a Federal Job Fast	$15.95	x ____	= $_____
Federal Personnel Guide	$ 9.95	x ____	= $_____
How to Find an Overseas Job with the U.S. Government	$28.95	x ____	= $_____
Police Officer	$13.95	x ____	= $_____

Feel free to photocopy this catalog
To order: 888/366-5200 weekdays, 9 a.m. to 6 p.m. CST

Post Office Jobs	$17.95	x ____	=	$_____
Quick & Easy Federal Jobs Kit [software: single user]	$49.95	x ____	=	$_____

Executive Recruiters, Employment Agencies, etc. *(See Chapter 3)*

Job Hunter's Yellow Pages	$19.95	x ____	=	$_____
Directory of Executive Recruiters	$44.95	x ____	=	$_____
Directory of Executive Recruiters, Corporate Edition	$149.00	x ____	=	$_____
Guide to Executive Recruiters	$24.95	x ____	=	$_____

City and State Job-Finding Resources *(See Chapter 30)*

Minnesota Job Seekers Sourcebook	$21.95	x ____	=	$_____
How to Find a Good Job in Seattle	$21.95	x ____	=	$_____
Baltimore Job Source	$15.95	x ____	=	$_____
Miami Job Source	$15.95	x ____	=	$_____
Pittsburgh Job Source	$15.95	x ____	=	$_____
Washington Job Source [District of Columbia]	$16.95	x ____	=	$_____
How to Get a Job in Atlanta	$16.95	x ____	=	$_____
How to Get a Job in Chicago	$16.95	x ____	=	$_____
How to Get a Job in New York	$16.95	x ____	=	$_____
How to Get a Job in San Francisco Bay Area	$16.95	x ____	=	$_____
How to Get a Job in Seattle/Portland	$16.95	x ____	=	$_____
How to Get a Job in Southern California	$16.95	x ____	=	$_____

Adams Media JobBank Series [features businesses; *very few* non-profits or schools]

Adams JobBank Software [Save 10%]	$53.95	x ____	=	$_____
Atlanta JobBank	$16.95	x ____	=	$_____
Austin-San Antonio JobBank	$16.95	x ____	=	$_____
Boston JobBank	$16.95	x ____	=	$_____
Carolina JobBank	$16.95	x ____	=	$_____
Chicago JobBank	$16.95	x ____	=	$_____
Cincinnati JobBank	$16.95	x ____	=	$_____
Cleveland JobBank	$16.95	x ____	=	$_____
Denver JobBank	$16.95	x ____	=	$_____
Dallas-Fort Worth JobBank	$16.95	x ____	=	$_____
Detroit JobBank	$16.95	x ____	=	$_____
Florida JobBank	$16.95	x ____	=	$_____
Houston JobBank	$16.95	x ____	=	$_____
Indianapolis JobBank	$16.95	x ____	=	$_____
Las Vegas JobBank	$16.95	x ____	=	$_____
Los Angeles JobBank	$16.95	x ____	=	$_____
Minneapolis-St. Paul JobBank	$16.95	x ____	=	$_____
Missouri JobBank [Price increases to $16.95 in March 1998]	$15.95	x ____	=	$_____
New Mexico JobBank	$16.95	x ____	=	$_____
Metro New York JobBank	$16.95	x ____	=	$_____
Northern New England JobBank	$16.95	x ____	=	$_____
Philadelphia JobBank	$16.95	x ____	=	$_____
Phoenix JobBank [Price increases to $16.95 in March 1998]	$15.95	x ____	=	$_____
Pittsburgh JobBank	$16.95	x ____	=	$_____
Portland, Oregon JobBank	$16.95	x ____	=	$_____

Feel free to photocopy this catalog
To order: 888/366-5200 weekdays, 9 a.m. to 6 p.m. CST

Job search resources catalog 335

San Francisco Bay Area JobBank	$16.95	x ____	= $____
Salt Lake City JobBank	$16.95	x ____	= $____
Seattle JobBank	$16.95	x ____	= $____
Tennessee JobBank [Price changes to $16.95 in March '98]	$15.95	x ____	= $____
Upper New York JobBank	$16.95	x ____	= $____
Virginia JobBank	$16.95	x ____	= $____
Metro Washington DC JobBank	$16.95	x ____	= $____
Wisconsin JobBank	$16.95	x ____	= $____

Internships *(See Chapter 3)*

America's Top Internships	$20.00	x ____	= $____
The Internship Bible	$25.00	x ____	= $____
Internships (Peterson's Guides)	$24.95	x ____	= $____
Internships: The Hot List for Job Hunters	$19.95	x ____	= $____
Summer Jobs for Students	$16.95	x ____	= $____
International Internships & Volunteer Programs	$18.95	x ____	= $____
Volunteer America	$89.95	x ____	= $____

International Careers

International Job Finder [available beginning Sept. 1997]	$16.95	x ____	= $____
How to Find an Overseas Job with the U.S. Government	$28.95	x ____	= $____
Almanac of International Jobs and Careers	$19.95	x ____	= $____
International Internships and Volunteer Programs	$18.95	x ____	= $____
Jobs Worldwide	$17.95	x ____	= $____
Guide to Careers in World Affairs	$14.95	x ____	= $____
Jobs for People Who Love Travel	$15.95	x ____	= $____

Key Career Resources

What Color is Your Parachute?	$16.95	x ____	= $____
Change Your Job, Change Your Life	$17.95	x ____	= $____
College Grad Job Hunter	$14.95	x ____	= $____
Vocational Careers Sourcebook	$79.00	x ____	= $____
Occupational Outlook Handbook	$18.95	x ____	= $____
Career Guide for Creative & Unconventional Careers	$11.95	x ____	= $____
Do What You Are: Discover the Perfect Career for You Through the Secrets of Personality Type	$16.95	x ____	= $____
Follow Your Career Star: A Career Quest Based on Inner Values	$15.00	x ____	= $____
Joyce Lain Kennedy's Career Book 3rd edition	$17.95	x ____	= $____
MTV's Now What!?	$12.00	x ____	= $____
Job Search: The Total System	$14.95	x ____	= $____
Job Discrimination: How to Fight, How to Win	$15.00	x ____	= $____
Minority Career Guide	$12.95	x ____	= $____
Colorblind Career	$16.95	x ____	= $____
How to Succeed in Business Without Being White	$25.00	x ____	= $____
Doing It for Ourselves: Success Stories of African American Women in Business	$12.00	x ____	= $____
Big Book of Opportunities for Women	$39.95	x ____	= $____
How to Raise a Family and a Career Under One Roof	$15.95	x ____	= $____
Every Woman's Essential Job Hunting & Resume Book	$10.95	x ____	= $____

Feel free to photocopy this catalog
To order: 888/366-5200 weekdays, 9 a.m. to 6 p.m. CST

If You Can Raise Kids, You Can Get a Good Job	$17.50	x ____	= $_____
Resumes for Re–Entry: A Handbook for Women	$10.95	x ____	= $_____
Job Strategies for People with Disabilities	$14.95	x ____	= $_____
Successful Job Search Strategies for the Disabled	$14.95	x ____	= $_____
Career Success for People with Physical Disabilities	$16.95	x ____	= $_____
College & Career Success for Students with Learning Disabilities	$14.95	x ____	= $_____
So What If I'm 50?	$12.95	x ____	= $_____
Resumes for the Over 50 Job Hunter	$15.95	x ____	= $_____

Resumes and cover letters *(See Chapter 2)*

WinWay Resume for Windows Software [Save 25%]	$52.46	x ____	= $_____
Electronic Resumes	$19.95	x ____	= $_____
Electronic Resume Revolution, 2nd edition	$12.95	x ____	= $_____
Adams Resumes & Cover Letters Software [Save 10%]	$35.95	x ____	= $_____
Best Resumes for Educational Professionals	$14.95	x ____	= $_____
Dynamite Resumes	$14.95	x ____	= $_____
High Impact Resumes & Letters	$14.95	x ____	= $_____
Portfolio Power	$14.95	x ____	= $_____
Resume Catalog: 200 Damn Good Examples	$15.95	x ____	= $_____
Resumes for Dummies	$12.99	x ____	= $_____
Wow! Resumes for Creative Careers	$10.95	x ____	= $_____
Cover Letters for Dummies	$12.99	x ____	= $_____
Dynamite Cover Letters	$14.95	x ____	= $_____
201 Killer Cover Letters	$16.95	x ____	= $_____

Interviewing

Interview for Success	$15.95	x ____	= $_____
Common Mistakes People Make in Interviews {video}	$79.95	x ____	= $_____
Complete Q & A Job Interview Book	$14.95	x ____	= $_____
Dynamite Answers to Interview Questions	$11.95	x ____	= $_____
A Funny Thing Happened at the Interview	$12.95	x ____	= $_____
Information Interviewing	$10.95	x ____	= $_____
Job Interviewing for Students	$11.95	x ____	= $_____
Job Interviews for Dummies	$12.99	x ____	= $_____
NBEW's Interviewing, 2nd edition	$11.95	x ____	= $_____
101 Dynamite Questions to Ask at Your Job Interview	$13.95	x ____	= $_____
Power Interviews	$14.95	x ____	= $_____
Smart Woman's Guide to Interviewing and Salary Negotiation	$12.99	x ____	= $_____

Networking

Dynamite Networking for Dynamite Jobs	$15.95	x ____	= $_____
NBEW's Networking	$10.95	x ____	= $_____

Salaries *(See Chapter 3)*

American Almanac of Jobs and Salaries	$20.00	x ____	= $_____
Dynamite Salary Negotiations	$13.95	x ____	= $_____
Negotiating Your Salary	$11.95	x ____	= $_____
Perks and Parachutes: Negotiating Your Best Possible Employment Deal	$25.00	x ____	= $_____

Feel free to photocopy this catalog
To order: 888/366-5200 weekdays, 9 a.m. to 6 p.m. CST

Job search resources catalog

       Merchandise Subtotal: $_____

☛ **Add shipping:** $5.00 for the first item plus $1 for + **$ 5.00**
 each additional item; use next line to calculate:

☛ # of additional items: _____ x $1/each = + $_____

☛ **Illinois residents only:** Add 7.75% sales tax + $_____

☛ ***Overseas orders:** Add an <u>additional</u> $14 per book for airmail
 (if actual postage is less, we will refund the difference to you) + $_____
  *= Orders to U.S. possessions, military addresses, and to Canada
  do not require this additional overseas postage.

☛   **Total enclosed:** $_____

☐ Check here to receive Planning/Communications'
  free *Job Quest* catalog of 400 job-quest books and software

Ship to:

Please print clearly or type.

Name _____

Address _____

  _____
  For UPS delivery, please give full street address and apartment number.

City-State-Zip _____

Home phone number: _____/_____
                NPJF97

☐ **Enclosed is my check or money order for $_____ made out to:
Planning/Communications**

☐ **Please charge $_____ to my VISA or MasterCard**

Card number: _____

Expiration date: _____

Signature (if charging this order):

_____
Please sign your name exactly as it appears on your VISA or MasterCard.

***Feel free to photocopy this catalog
To order: 888/366-5200 weekdays, 9 a.m. to 6 p.m. CST***

Reader feedback form

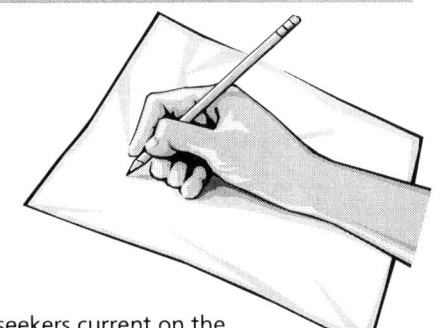

Help us keep you and your fellow job seekers current on the job resources described in the *Non-Profits and Education Job Finder*.

If you discover that the information about a job source in this book has changed — a new phone number, address, prices, title, etc. — or has been terminated, let us know as soon as possible so I can add them to the free *Update Sheet* and to our Internet home page noted in Chapter 1. If a typographical error slipped by our proofreaders, please let us know so we can correct it.

If you can't track down a job source because it has moved, tell us and we'll try to find it for you and put the new information in the *Update Sheet*. Be sure to include a self-addressed stamped envelope with your request.

And please let us know what we can do to make this book even more helpful. If nothing else, we are always open to suggestions.

If you run out of space, just attach another sheet. Please send your comments to me at Planning/Communications, 7215 Oak Avenue, River Forest, IL 60305. If we've moved, you can get our new real world address from our Web site at URL: **http://jobfindersonline.com**. Remember, you can simply photocopy this page.

Thanks for your help, feedback, and support.

Daniel Lauber

Include page number(s): _____

_____
_____
_____
_____
_____
_____

Purely optional: Clearly print your name, address, and evening phone number below in case we need to reach you for more information. **If you're asking us to find a job source you can't track down, please also include a self-addressed stamped envelope.**

About the author

Daniel Lauber, AICP, may be the only career author to write a successful amicus curiae brief for a case before the U.S. Supreme Court. As one of the nation's leading experts on fair housing law for group homes and halfway houses for people with disabilities, he wrote an amicus brief on behalf of the American Planning Association in support of a group home's legal position that prevailed in *City of Edmunds vs. Washington State Building Codes Council,* 115 S.Ct. 1776 (1995).

Dan has worked for the American Society of Planning Officials and served as a consultant to non-profits on writing grant applications and developing computer capabilities. He has been an adjunct professor at two colleges.

Dan worked for local and state government in Illinois as an award-winning city planner from 1972 through 1980. Since then he has served local and state governments as a planning consultant and, since 1985, as a land-use attorney.

In addition writing to this book, Dan is author of the **Government Job Finder, Non-Profits' Job Finder,* Professional's Job Finder, International Job Finder, Job Finder's Tool Kit** (software),* **Professional's Private Sector Job Finder,* The Compleat Guide to Finding Jobs in Government,* The Compleat Guide to Jobs in Planning and Public Administration,*** and **The Compleat Guide to Jobs in Planning.***

The *Non-Profits Job Finder* won a 1994 Pewter Award in *Publishing & Production Executive* magazine's "Gold Ink Awards" competition. The second edition of the *Government Job Finder* received a "Benjamin Franklin Award" for "Most Improved Redesign" from the Publishers Marketing Association in 1995.

Dan has appeared on ABC television's *Good Morning America* and CNBC-TV's *Steals and Deals* and *Today's Business,* as well as on over 100 radio stations throughout the country. He is also a frequently-requested speaker at job fairs, job clubs, and national conventions of professional associations.

At age 35 he was elected the youngest president ever of the 29,000-member American Planning Association while attending the Northwestern University School of Law full-time. In 1992 he was elected President of the American Institute of Certified Planners. He has chaired two American Bar Association subcommittees.

He received his Masters of Urban and Regional Planning in 1972 from the University of Illinois-Urbana, and B.A. in sociology from the University of Chicago in 1970. He received his J.D. from Northwestern University School of Law in 1985.

He has written dozens of articles on planning and law issues in professional publications and the popular press. He created the "Condo Watch" column for the *Chicago Sun-Times* in 1979. When not immersing himself in the preparation of this book, he spends most of his time as an attorney and expert witness in zoning cases on behalf of people with disabilities who wish to live in group homes.

* = *Out of print and superseded by the current Job Finder Series.*